KU-504-546

Leading managing caring:

understanding leadership and management in health and social care

Edited by

Sara MacKian and Joan Simons

LONDON AND NEW YORK

Published by

Routledge
2 Park Square
Milton Park
Abingdon OX14 4RN

in association with

The Open University
Walton Hall
Milton Keynes MK7 6AA

Simultaneously published in the USA and Canada by

Routledge
711 Third Avenue
New York, NY 10017

Routledge is an imprint of the Taylor & Francis Group, an informa business

First published 2013

Copyright © 2013 The Open University

All rights reserved. No part of this publication may be reproduced, stored in a retrieval system, transmitted or utilised in any form or by any means, electronic, mechanical, photocopying, recording or otherwise, without written permission from the publisher or a licence from the Copyright Licensing Agency Ltd. Details of such licences (for reprographic reproduction) may be obtained from the Copyright Licensing Agency Ltd, Saffron House, 6–10 Kirby Street, London EC1N 8TS (website www.cla.co.uk).

Edited and designed by The Open University.

Printed and bound in the United Kingdom by Bell & Bain Ltd, Glasgow.

This publication forms part of the Open University module K313 *Leadership and management in health and social care.* Details of this and other Open University modules can be obtained from the Student Registration and Enquiry Service, The Open University, PO Box 197, Milton Keynes MK7 6BJ, United Kingdom (tel. +44 (0)845 300 60 90; email general-enquiries@open.ac.uk).

www.open.ac.uk

British Library Cataloguing Publication Data:

A catalogue record for this book is available from the British Library.

Library of Congress Cataloging-in-Publication Data:

A catalog record for this book has been requested.

ISBN 978 0 4156 5851 5 (paperback)

ISBN 978 0 4156 5850 8 (hardback)

1.1

Contents

BMA LIBRARY
BRITISH MEDICAL ASSOCIATION

Contributors

Hilary Brown is professor of social care at Canterbury Christ Church University and a specialist in adult safeguarding issues and learning disability. She has contributed to policy development and practice, chairs a Safeguarding Adults Board in London, leads the serious case review panel for a large local authority and works in the NHS as a psychotherapist with people with learning disabilities.

Julie Charlesworth has over 20 years' experience of working in universities, researching and teaching social sciences, public policy and management. She is now a freelance consultant specialising in public and voluntary sector management.

Jeanette Copperman is a lecturer in social work at The Open University. She trained originally as a community social worker and practised in a variety of voluntary and statutory social work and health settings. Her research interests include social inclusion, social inequalities within mental health, women and violence, user involvement and activism and inter-professional practice. She has a particular interest in participatory research methods which involve service users.

Rod Earle is a lecturer in youth justice at The Open University with a background in youth justice and criminology. His research interests include gender, ethnicity and identity in prison, criminal records and social exclusion, and affective youth justice. He has a particular interest in ethnographic research methodologies.

Michelle Gander is the head of planning and resources for the Faculty of Health and Social Care at The Open University; a chartered manager and member of the Chartered Management Institute and has recently completed her MBA. She has experience of teaching students in various subjects and has carried out research in environmental engineering and gender and organisations.

Richard Hester is a senior lecturer at The Open University with an academic and practice background in the youth justice system and crime prevention. He has a particular interest in the social control of gypsies and travellers, engaging with young people through outdoor education and the impact of high modernity on crime and security. Richard was assistant director of The Rainer Foundation (1987–1996), a national children's charity, and a fellow of the Institute of Leadership and Management (2003–2006).

Rebecca Jones is a lecturer in health and social care at The Open University. Her research interests are in ageing, sexuality and especially sexuality in later life. She chairs the Centre for Ageing and Biographical Studies (CABS) at The Open University. Outside academia, she has worked in the voluntary sector for 20 years and managed volunteers and staff, working as both an employee and a trustee of a range of charitable organisations.

Chris Kubiak is a lecturer in the Faculty of Health and Social Care at The Open University. He has developed courses in areas such as youth justice, health and social care and practice-based learning for support workers. His research work has included studies of online learning communities, school-based learning networks, practice-based education and the work-based learning of support workers in health and social care.

Helen Lomax is a senior lecturer in the Faculty of Health and Social Care at The Open University. Her research interests include the role of policy, popular culture and professional discourses in shaping parenting and childhood experiences. Her methodological interests encompass the development of visual methods as a means of understanding health and social inequalities and contemporary childhoods.

Sara MacKian is a senior lecturer in health and wellbeing in The Open University's Faculty of Health and Social Care. Her research focuses on how individuals, communities and organisations interact around issues of illness, health and wellbeing. This has led to a range of studies exploring ME, parenting, sexuality, spirituality and civil participation in health systems development.

Leona McCalla is a lecturer in health, community and social care at the University of Gloucestershire, and has worked in a range of health and social care settings with a variety of service user groups, including adults who experience a learning disability, individuals with acquired head injuries, vulnerable older people and adults who experience mental health problems. She has a particular interest in inter-professional working and carer support.

Martin Robb is a senior lecturer in the Faculty of Health and Social Care at The Open University, where his research has focused mainly on issues related to masculinity and childcare, including studies of fathers and male childcare workers, as well as recent work exploring the role of gender identities in work with young men. Before joining the OU he worked in a number of community education projects with young people and adults.

Anita Rogers is an international human resource educator, researcher and organisational development specialist and the director of Edgework Consultancy. She has extensive experience in leading organisation and culture change, leadership development and institutionalising diversity.

Chris Russell trained as a lawyer but soon discovered he was really more interested in what was going on behind the case than the case itself. He consequently retrained as a social worker which he believes provides a window on to the mechanics of society. Chris is currently a social worker in adult services in Worcestershire and a part-time social work lecturer at the University of Gloucestershire.

Joan Simons is the assistant head of department in the Faculty of Health and Social Care at The Open University, and has a practice background in nursing and managing children's pain. Her research explores how nurses manage children's pain in practice as well as parental involvement in managing post-operative pain in their children. Joan also has research and practical expertise in management and leadership in health and social care, with a particular interest in the role of coaching.

Wayne Taylor is a lecturer in youth justice team at The Open University, having previously worked as a case manager, and training and development officer in youth offending and probation services in the Midlands. His research interests focus on sociology and criminology, including criminal justice policy, and children and young people, as well as wider issues of social policy, such as social exclusion and justice and the social construction of gender.

Liz Tilley is a lecturer in the Faculty of Health and Social Care at The Open University. Her research interests include learning disability policy and practice, and the role of advocacy and user-led organisations in health and social care. Liz is the current chair of the Social History of Learning Disability Research Group.

Jan Walmsley is visiting professor of leadership development and workforce planning at London's South Bank University. She has worked at The Open University and The Health Foundation and now runs her own consultancy specialising in advising health care organisations on workforce development, implementation of training and development linked to organisational goals.

Special thanks

This book serves as a textbook for the Open University module K313 *Leadership and management in health and social care*. Each module at The Open University is put together by a team of experts in their field, through a lengthy and fastidious process of production to ensure our students receive the best possible learning materials. The authors in this book consist of academics and practitioners with a range of backgrounds, including sociologists, geographers, management theorists, nurses, social workers and people with experience of working in youth justice. Thanks must go to each and every one of them. In addition to this collective knowledge, each chapter has gone through a rigorous process of reviewing with other experts in the field – both academics and practitioners. We would therefore also like to thank all of those reviewers for their critical and insightful comments which considerably strengthened the final output.

During the process of writing the book and the wider module materials we also consulted closely with six key leaders and managers across health and social care, selected for their varied roles, experience and expertise to bring up-to-date case study materials and ideas to the text. So thanks also go to them for their time and commitment to the project: Shirley Findlay, SACRO (Safeguarding Communities – Reducing Offending), Kilmarnock, Scotland; Sheraz Khan, a GP practice manager, White City London; Stephanie Last, a clinical nurse manager, Waddon Way Day Centre, Milton Keynes; Vivian McConvey, the chief executive of VOYPIC (Voice of Young People in Care), Belfast; Julie Player, a clinical ward manager, Royal United Hospital Bath; Anita Rogers, of Edgework Consultancy and former chair of Ceredigion and Mid Wales NHS Trust.

Final thanks go to Sarah O'Donoghue for keeping the project always on track despite the considerable challenges and time pressures thrown our way.

Chapter 1 Preparing to lead

Sara MacKian, Chris Russell and Leona McCalla

1.1 Introduction

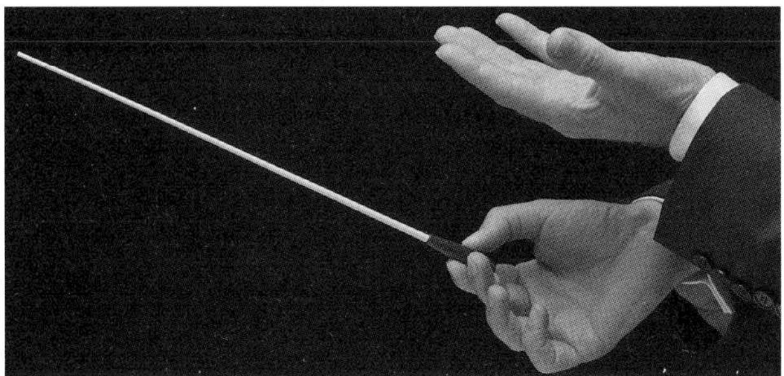

Figure 1.1 What do you need in order to lead?

> Management matters. Without it, nothing happens. From deciding on and buying the weekly grocery shop to designing, building and running the giant atom-smasher at Cern, nothing effective happens without budgeting, scheduling and implementation.
>
> (The King's Fund, 2011, p. 1)

> Your boss is talking about it, the Government says how important it is, the newspapers deplore the lack of it … leadership is needed 'at all levels' – in all situations.
>
> (Pedler et al., 2004, p. viii)

In these turbulent times, the health and social care sector is under increasing pressure to deliver more and more for less and less. Increasingly complex care needs mean that now, more than ever, the effective integration of health and social care services is essential. To ensure that the interface between health and social care does not become a battleground, it is important to appreciate the different rules and guidelines which underpin diverse practice and professional groups, and to make sure that all staff and service users are involved creatively in designing and leading change (Harvey et al., 2009).

Synergy: when two or more things function together to produce a result that is not independently obtainable. As the Greek philosopher Aristotle said: 'The whole is greater than the sum of its parts.' (Figure 1.1)

In this context, it is essential to ensure that the most effective managers and leaders are in place to guarantee efficiency and effectiveness, working in tune with their staff in a synergistic way. But what sort of managers? And what types of leaders? They will have to understand how people work, how relationships are formed or not, and how organisations shape people's ability to function. They will need to be able to manage staff, control budgets and mobilise a diverse range of people in responding to complex challenges.

Many books on leadership or management focus almost exclusively on the tools and personal qualities of successful managers and leaders, with little critical analysis of the organisational context they may be working in, let alone any broader acknowledgement of the political, economic or social climate. The assumption seems to be that if managers can only get themselves right then they will be free to lead unhindered, as if operating in a vacuum. However, the world is rarely that straightforward, even for the most effective of leaders or most diligent of managers. Other books therefore explore leadership and management as complex and distinct processes which require insight into theoretical understandings of what makes a good or effective leader or manager in their particular context. While many notable books do just this (for example, Bennis, 2009; Kotter, 1990; Northouse, 2009; Daft, 2010), they are predominantly written from a 'business' perspective and fail to address a health and social care workforce.

Other publications split health from social care, focus on the American experience, or fail to provide any practical tools to translate the wealth of theoretical insights into meaningful action. However, this book aims to acknowledge the wider contextual issues which impact on management and leadership in health and social care, and to facilitate an understanding of them which is realistic, yet empowering, for existing and aspiring managers or leaders.

Given the sheer complexity of the health and social care system, it is little wonder that leadership and management are so important. Even so, political and public opinion on the role of managers in health and social care is not universally sympathetic. Eighty-five per cent of the public support the idea of reducing the number of managers in the NHS (Ipsos MORI, 2009), and many believe that 'box ticking' and bureaucracy are given higher priority than caring for service users. However, such simplistic statements belie a complex picture and ignore the crucial point that when effective leadership and management are *lacking* in caring contexts, the results can be catastrophic:

> The Caleb Ness enquiry into the death of an 11-week-old baby in Edinburgh … catalogued difficulties with the lack of co-ordination between services; poor administrative systems; poor chairing of meetings; lack of proactive senior social worker involvement … Each of the areas outlined demonstrated the catastrophic impact when leadership and management was not carried out in an effective manner …
>
> (Watson, 2008, p. 323)

Hard-hitting cases such as the death of a baby highlight precisely why effective management and leadership are so essential in health and social care. It is not just a question of running an efficient business or making innovative cost savings – managers in this sector are dealing with life-and-death situations. Effective management, underpinned by strong leadership, can work towards preventing such catastrophes, and in this book we aim to provide the foundations for achieving this.

This chapter begins by asking three core questions.

- What is the difference between 'managing' and 'leading' and how do they complement each other?
- What are the foundations underpinning a caring approach to management and leadership?
- How can you begin to prepare for a management or leadership role in health and social care?

1.2 Leading, managing, caring in practice

Case study 1.1: Anwen

Anwen worked as a project manager for a group of wards in a district general hospital, with responsibility for overseeing the introduction of new efficiency measures. She was very proud of how dedicated the nurses were to implementing the changes, despite being overworked due to staff shortages.

Anwen met monthly with a business director from the Trust to report progress. She always felt frustrated in these meetings as she was worried the nurses were losing morale and she wanted recognition from the director for their hard work. But his remit was simply to collect the progress figures.

Increasingly, for many managers, there is pressure not just to achieve existing goals, but to go beyond those and think of better ways to get things done: to *lead change*. Hence, there is a blurring of the boundaries between management and leadership, and yet there are important distinctions that need to be acknowledged. Anwen's experience illustrates this. She made a breakthrough when she realised there were competing expectations of her in her role as 'project manager' and 'team leader'. The director was motivated not by how hard people were working but by the need to complete his monthly report. However, Anwen's team wanted recognition for hard work even when 'results' were not great. Having reflected on this, she realised it was up to *her* to provide that recognition and motivation as the director was motivated by other issues.

Was Anwen a leader or a manager? Was the director a leader or a manager?

Anwen was discovering that there were subtleties involved in applying her management and leadership skills. She clearly had a role to play in motivating and leading her team, but she also had to manage conflicting expectations. Managers such as Anwen often feel inadequately supported, and find dealing with pressures from above *and* below difficult to handle as a result (Jack and Donnellan, 2010).

Clearly, differentiating leadership and management is not easy (Larkin, 2008). Anwen, like many people in positions of responsibility, had to act as both leader and manager, but what does this mean, and is it realistic? Anwen's experience illustrates the complexity of trying to be an effective leader and an efficient manager at the same time. This is because some elements that might be associated with the two are very different (Figure 1.2).

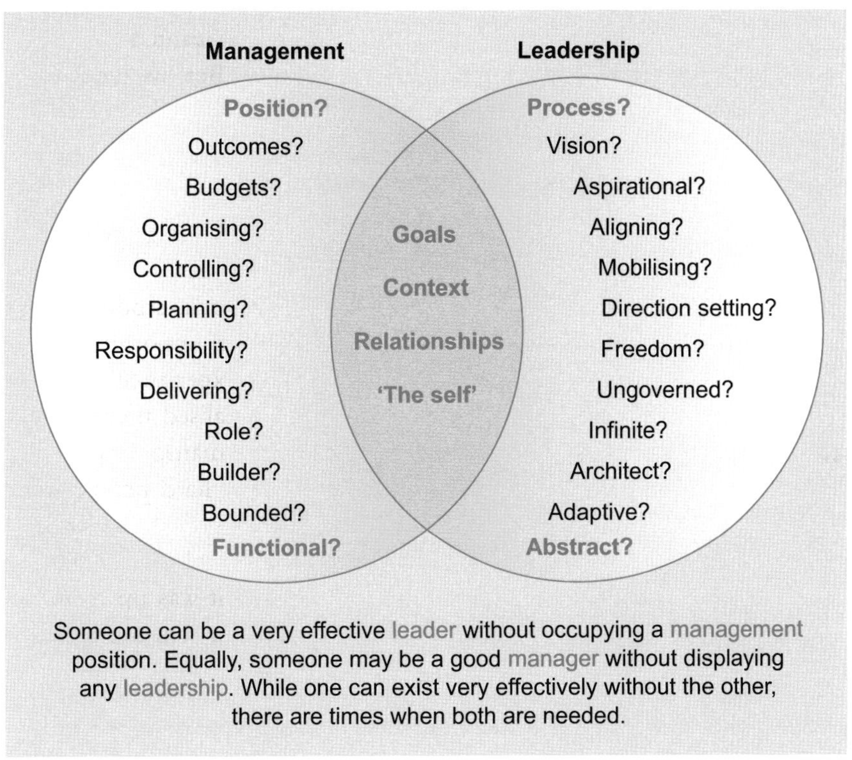

Figure 1.2 Thinking through the concepts of management and leadership

Both leadership and management are concerned with outcomes or goals – which may be the same or very different – but they involve taking different approaches to get there. A manager may have a set of job descriptions, organisational aims and even disciplinary procedures which can help to frame the way they achieve their goals. However, a leader may not necessarily wield such formal power, and may have to rely instead on their ability to motivate other people around a shared vision (Kotter, 1990). Larkin (2008) suggests management tends to focus on the outcomes first and 'pushes' people towards them, whereas leadership starts with the people as a means of achieving those outcomes and tries to 'pull' them in that direction. What differentiates leadership from management for Larkin, then, is the approach but, despite such differences, the two can work together very successfully (Kotter, 1990).

'A manager's job is to keep an existing machine running; a leader's job is to continually change the machine ...' (Robbins and Finley, 2004, p. 119). Do you agree with this statement?

Managers have to work within strictly imposed boundaries determined by budgets, forecasting and efficiency measures, while leaders often have the freedom to think beyond those potentially constraining factors with more creativity, inspiration and vision. So managers work towards consistency and order, whereas leaders inspire change and movement (Kotter, 1990). However, both play equally important and fundamental roles in any organisation, and such distinctions can come crashing down with the practicalities of everyday work. As Anwen's experience shows, a manager might have to be creative about making things happen in different ways for different people, and being an effective leader is something that can help here. She realised that complaining about her team's workload was ineffective; it was more important to motivate her staff and lead by example. Anwen, therefore, acted as a broker for her staff, ensuring senior management received the hard data on progress while also ensuring her staff received motivational support and recognition. She was both a manager who wanted to lead her team, and a leader who recognised the requirements of management. As Vicki Taylor says:

> If you are a manager, you show leadership when you assess effectively the capacity of your staff to fulfil the mandate of your organisation, and then provide the necessary direction, support, participation and autonomy to get things done.
>
> (Taylor, 2007, p. 32)

In her relationship with the director, Anwen had to focus on the goal of providing the data without getting frustrated by other concerns. Her example therefore shows that, in addition to being *goal aware* as a manager, an element of *self-awareness* is useful, as is a clear understanding of key *relationships* and attentiveness to wider organisational *context*. Figure 1.3 shows these four aspects of awareness as the key building blocks to support anyone in becoming a fully rounded and *caring* manager. Although there are important distinctions between managers and leaders, the building blocks of a **fully rounded caring manager** are the same as those for a **fully rounded caring leader**.

'Leadership and management differ from each other, not in what they want to achieve, but more in the means and approaches taken to get there' (Larkin, 2008, p. 24).

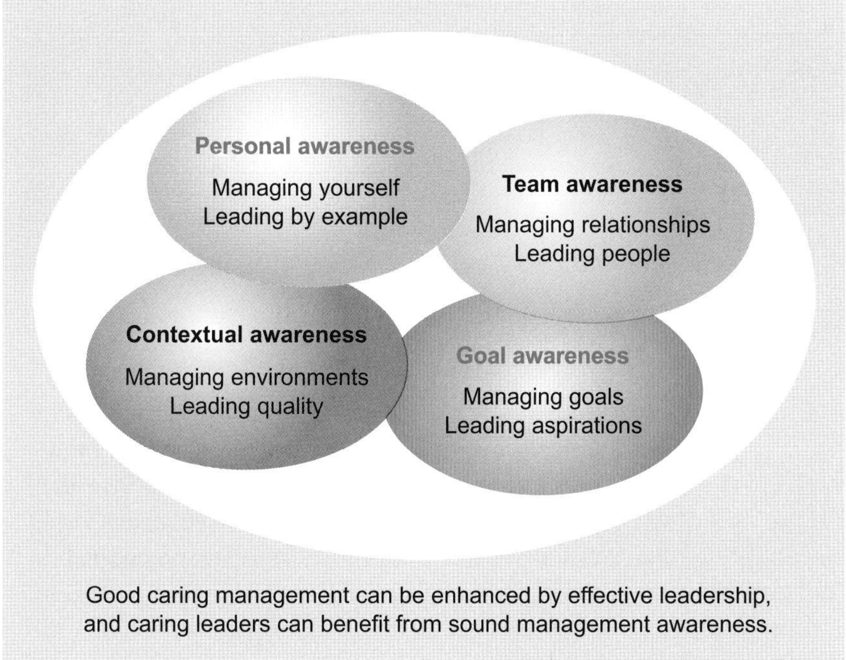

Figure 1.3 The four building blocks of a **fully rounded caring manager**

These four building blocks form a firm foundation to understanding and practising leadership and management in health and social care, and the chapters in this book all link to this core foundation. **Personal awareness** is perhaps the most obvious place to start, as only by understanding ourselves effectively can we hope to begin to understand our relationships with other people; so this building block is explored further later on in this chapter.

First, however, we look at how management and leadership have been conceptualised historically within service provision, and what that tells us about the role of managers and leaders in the sector today.

1.3 Leading, managing, caring in context

Figure 1.4 The changing face of care: (a) a workhouse in the 19th century; (b) a modern family consultation

> ... the parish authorities magnanimously and humanely resolved, that Oliver should be 'farmed', or, in other words, that he should be dispatched to a branch-workhouse some three miles off, where twenty or thirty other juvenile offenders against the poor-laws rolled about the floor all day, without the inconvenience of too much food or too much clothing, under the parental superintendence of an elderly female, who received the culprits at and for the consideration of sevenpence-halfpenny per small head per week.
>
> (Dickens, 1838, *Oliver Twist*, p. 5)

> Never underestimate. People even with complex needs can enjoy different experiences very, very much when you give them the opportunity to. Everybody is an individual ... we are dealing with individuals.
>
> (Last, 2012)

Anyone who works in health and social care is consistently expected to recognise, acknowledge and adhere to a *concept of care*; but how care is defined and managed has changed over time. It is helpful to think about a distinction between 'caring for' and 'caring about' (Clarke, 2001). The former focuses on task and activity and, however uncaring the 'elderly female' in *Oliver Twist*, there was some understanding that she was caring *for* these 'juvenile offenders'. Caring *about*, however, centres on feeling emotional concern, which comes through much more clearly in the second, present-day quotation, from Stephanie Last, care manager of a day centre for adults with profound and multiple disabilities. To some extent, formal care provision has to prioritise the mechanics of caring *for*. Yet today it is widely accepted that the caring manager should never lose sight of the need to care *about* as well: to care about service users and their families, the people they manage and the service they provide. This book, therefore, is about how to facilitate a *caring approach* to leading and managing in health and social care.

In 1942, William Beveridge first proposed the introduction of a comprehensive 'welfare state', incorporating a national social security system and health service free at the point of delivery. Since then, ideas about how the delivery of care should be managed have shifted and changed. High profile, often controversial, leaders – from William Beveridge and Aneurin Bevan (1952) through to a succession of contemporary government ministers – have been at the forefront of these changes. However, beneath them, everyday leaders and managers have been tasked with getting the job done. The evolving demands of the population have meant that what started out as a short-term plan, with limited funding, has changed into a complex public sector with unprecedented costs, requiring efficiencies at every level to enable it to be sustainable in the 21st century. Nevertheless, while patterns of service design, delivery and management may alter with changing circumstances – and it is impossible to do justice to the full history here – the everyday tribulations and triumphs of those who work in health and social care remain the same: managers are still tasked with providing the best outcomes for service users, and inspirational leaders are still working hard to motivate and enthuse staff.

Before Beveridge's vision, from the 19th to the early 20th century, the social and political consensus was that health and social care should be provided locally, often by charitable organisations, to individuals who were in most need and deserving of help. Although, as the quotation from *Oliver Twist* suggests, very few were considered truly 'deserving'! However, a new welfare settlement began to emerge after the first world war (1914–1918), when political demands for a 'land fit for heroes', combined with concerns over Britain losing its competitive edge, contributed to changing views about how health and social care should be organised and managed (Hughes and Lewis, 1998; Aaron et al., 2005). The result was an unprecedented level of state intervention in people's lives which signalled a more centralised approach to the management of services. The period of change which followed was populated by pioneering leaders who had a strong vision of what they wanted to achieve (Box 1.1).

Box 1.1: It is never easy being a pioneer

Figure 1.5(a) Dr George M'Gonigle (1889–1939): the 'Housewives' Champion'

In 1936, George M'Gonigle (Figure 1.5a), Medical Officer for Health in Stockton-on-Tees, North East England, published a groundbreaking study – *Poverty and Public Health* – which challenged the political orthodoxy of the time (M'Gonigle and Kirkby, 1936). This study showed that poverty, not ignorance, was the cause of morbidity and mortality among poor people. Known as the 'Housewives' Champion', M'Gonigle was a pioneer of public health advocacy in the 1930s and his findings remain relevant to society today although history has all but forgotten him (Bambra, 2011).

Figure 1.5(b) Lord William Beveridge (1879–1963): social welfare reformer

William Beveridge (Figure 1.5b) was a key architect of social welfare reform in Britain, with his vision of using state power to tackle the 'five giants' of want, disease, ignorance, squalor and idleness. Yet, in his autobiography, he said the British government was not immediately convinced to act on his vision (Beveridge, 1953). Despite the popularity of Beveridge's National Health Service today, his ideas were not universally embraced at the time (Jacobs, 1992).

In the *Report of the Committee on Local Authority and Allied Personal Social Services* (1968), Frederic Seebohm (1909–1990) had a revolutionary vision of unified social services departments that overhauled the way social work was managed. Recommending generic training for social workers, the idea was taken on wholeheartedly, although problems quickly emerged (Jones and Lowe, 2002).

As the vision of universal welfare provision began to be realised, some practitioners felt their autonomy being undermined, for example doctors who had previously managed their own services (Aaron et al., 2005). However, for others it seemed the system was increasingly being managed in a way which served professional and organisational needs more than the needs of service users themselves. Even apparently progressive changes proved to have problematic consequences, such as Frederic Seebohm's vision of unified social services departments providing a more coordinated approach to social care (Seebohm, 1968). His much applauded vision was to have generic social workers not divided by client group or discipline, but weaknesses quickly emerged and such non-specialised approaches have since been criticised for leading to 'chaotic ineffectiveness' (Marsland, 1980, p. 31). Meanwhile, technology and mechanisation were seen as symbols of a progressive state, and institutionalisation was promoted as the modern way to organise and manage care. New groups, such as pregnant women, saw their care routinely hospitalised for the first time in state-run hospitals, following a carefully planned and standardised model. However, critics suggested an unreflective administrative approach emerged which was insufficiently concerned with the needs – or rights – of the service user (Illich, 2010).

As hospital births became more common, childbirth was reconceptualised as an 'abnormal', pathological event that required clinical supervision. Criticism grew that the management requirements of hospitals and doctors were being put before what was actually needed by the women themselves.

However, a population which was increasing in size, living longer, and demanding ever more complex care solutions, was soon putting pressure on visions of universal provision and it became questionable whether this particular welfare settlement was sustainable. By the late 1970s, pay and conditions in state-run institutions were also being scrutinised with public-sector industrial action becoming commonplace. From 1979, successive Conservative governments advanced the idea that market values and individualism should underpin the management of health and social care services. In 1983, the Griffiths Report introduced a purchaser–provider split and a new level of administration and bureaucracy emerged associated with this internal market. At the same time, pressure from service user movements was growing and political recognition of the need to respond to this opened up a new area of concern for service managers.

The newly elected Labour government in 1997 remained committed to the principles of the market, adding a rhetoric of joined-up services, service user involvement and partnership. With the publication of *Modernising Government* in 1999, there was a strong call to leadership to drive cultural change and 'meet the needs of citizens, not the convenience of service providers' (Cabinet Office, 1999, paragraph 3.1). Managers were now tasked to deliver integrated, efficient services, personalised to the individual needs and demands of service users, and it was envisaged that, in doing so, they would need to learn from the latest ideas in management and leadership (HMSO, 1999).

The pursuit of integration and personal choice continued under the Conservative–Liberal Democrat Coalition government from 2010, thus demonstrating a cross-party commitment to reforming public services through marketisation and increased competition. More recently, with a continued drive for localism, there has also been a push for the decentralisation of power to the 'lowest appropriate level' (HM Government, 2011), with front-line staff managing and leading decision making (Kwarteng et al., 2011).

Devolution across the nations of the United Kingdom has, of course, also had a considerable impact on management practice at the local level.

Since the 1980s, therefore, successive governments in the UK have sought to introduce a more businesslike and locally driven approach to the management of care, which has led to a change in the way the role of managers is conceived and a change in the terminology used (see Chapter 14 for more on this). Martin and Learmonth (2012) suggest early managers in the welfare system were perceived as performing an 'administrative' function, maintaining the existing situation. By the 1980s, a language of 'management' dominated, reflecting a growing business approach. This was subsequently replaced in the 1990s by an assertion that management should be about 'leadership' at all levels.

Today, a narrative of both management and leadership is central to policy and provision in health and social care. It is characterised by a language of 'choice', 'quality', 'value for money' and 'efficiency'. Furthermore, with a growing emphasis on service users, their carers and local communities taking the lead in shaping local services, leadership is often expected to come from outside the formal organisational setting, adding another layer of complexity (see Chapter 13 for more on service user involvement). But what does this mean for people tasked with delivering care?

While public service values of universal provision continue to underpin some of the more recent developments (see, for example, Welsh Assembly Government, 2011), some critics are concerned that how we manage and deliver care has been reduced to a question of economic efficiencies. For managers, the challenge of deploying resources effectively within budget is becoming considerably harder, and concerns have been expressed that the marketisation of care risks re-igniting the ethos of 'the deserving and undeserving' (Aldgate and Dimmock, 2003).

Does an increasingly market-led system of care provision undermine the moral and ethical obligation to care?

As a manager, how would you combine a management focus on eligibility, performance and efficiencies with a personal vision to truly care about outcomes for service users?

Regardless of which political party is in charge and where, the role of management and leadership within health and social care will continue to evolve. It is important to be aware of this shifting environment because it shapes the context in which managers and leaders operate:

> Context is vital: what works here and now may not work in another place and at another time. There is no right way to lead: if you do get it right here and now there is no guarantee that this will work in the same way in another situation, or even in the same situation some time later.
>
> (Pedler et al., 2004, p. 6)

Nevertheless, even with such uncertainty and change, the basic building blocks of leading, managing and caring can form a firm foundation from which to start. At the heart of any manager's job or leader's vision should always be the goal of ensuring a good quality service (see Chapter 18), and a genuine commitment to approaching care in a caring manner (Taylor, 2007). A caring manager must also remember that leadership is not only about those high-profile, exciting, charismatic individuals who are seen as pivotal in making huge changes; it is also about everyday leadership:

> Leading people at work can be exciting, challenging and rewarding, but it often has to focus on the ordinary and less stimulating aspects of getting the job done well.
>
> (Larkin, 2008, p. 139)

This sort of leader is at the heart of a caring approach to management. Many of the services which are now taken for granted in our modern health and social care system would not be there without the excellent management and passionate leadership of ordinary people who saw better ways to care for people, and found opportunities to put them into practice (Taylor, 2007).

1.4 Leading by example: the importance of personal awareness

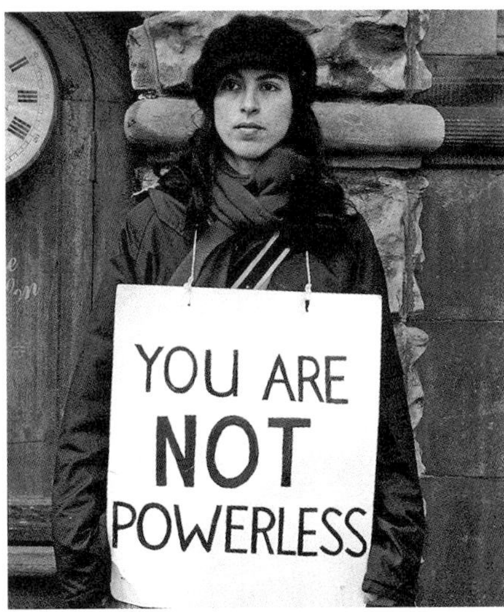

Figure 1.6 Discover your leadership potential

Today, it is increasingly clear that managers are being required to step up to the challenge of leadership. Anyone preparing for such a challenge can usefully start by looking at how they manage and lead themselves as this can have a huge impact on how they will go about managing and leading other people (Luthans et al., 2004; Pedler et al., 2004; Larkin, 2008).

Having self-confidence or belief in yourself as a manager is vital in health and social care. People's lives and livelihoods might depend on it. But can too much self-confidence be problematic?

Understanding self-confidence

How we think about ourselves can be a crucial factor in determining whether we maximise a management or leadership opportunity (Robbins and Finley, 2004). People with higher self-confidence work harder in approaching a task and feel less threatened by challenges (Hollenbeck and Hall, 2004). This does not mean a self-confident leader or manager does not feel fear – but it does mean they are aware of the potentially positive function of that fear in helping them focus on getting the task done.

While a lack of confidence undermines a person's ability to get things done, self-confidence can be increased, leading to significant performance improvements (Stajkovic and Luthans, 1998); and a self-*aware* person can increase their self-confidence. Hollenbeck and Hall

(2004) stress that self-confidence reflects our own *judgement* of ourselves, not necessarily our *actual ability*. As a judgement, it is open to change, and should be made honestly by weighing up ability, motivation and resources against the task at hand (Figure 1.7). This is where **personal awareness** is crucial. If someone is aware that they might undermine their own ability to get things done because they underrate their ability to achieve, they can make a conscious effort to change that mindset and boost their self-confidence.

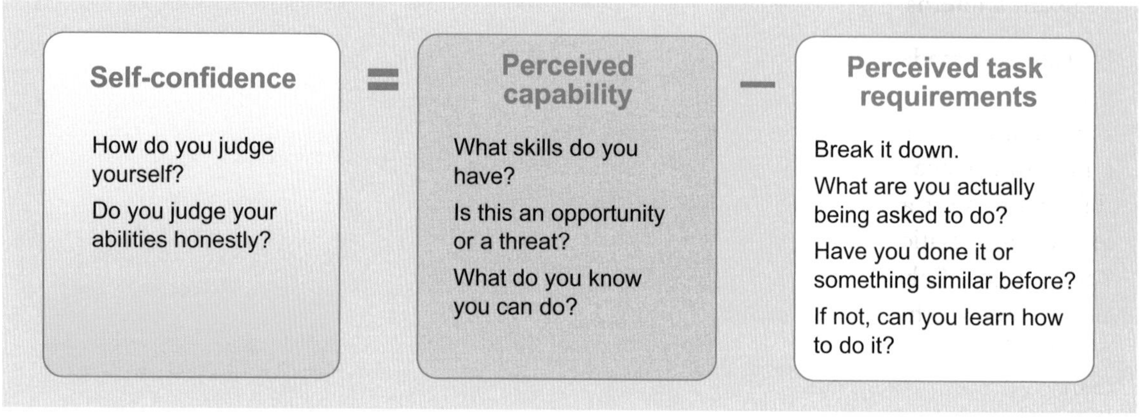

Figure 1.7 The 'self-confidence formula' (based on Hollenbeck and Hall, 2004)

A supportive manager should also be sensitive to opportunities for developing self-confidence in their staff through, for example, delegation, staff development, appraisal or coaching (see Chapters 9 and 10). However, this must always be done in a realistic and an empowering way because while self-confidence, hope and optimism might all be part of a 'positive psychological capital' which anybody can develop (Luthans et al., 2004), there are sometimes structural factors outside the control of individuals which might not be so easily overcome.

Case study 1.2: Rakesha

Rakesha was a team leader for a large, private, care home provider and was confident she could progress to become one of the company's registered care home managers. She had ten years' experience and had shown exceptional leadership qualities by designing successful projects building links between residents and the local community. Rakesha was aware that some team leaders she knew had been invited to an internal training programme to support their career development, and wondered why she hadn't been offered the opportunity.

She spoke to her line manager and he was extremely supportive but also totally honest. He said, although it would be denied officially, women, and especially black and minority ethnic (BME) women, had struggled in the organisation to progress to being registered managers and they were underrepresented on the company's internal training scheme.

Initially, this made Rakesha very angry and upset, and she decided it probably wasn't worth even trying. But her line manager reminded her of her initial confidence, and they decided to set up a plan to achieve her goal. He suggested it was important for Rakesha to start attending more high-profile meetings to gain greater organisational 'savviness' and to make herself more visible. Another goal Rakesha set herself was to run a lunchtime meeting about some of the projects she had initiated and to invite key players along. Her manager also said he knew of a BME-registered manager in another region, who might be interested in mentoring Rakesha.

Surely Rakesha's organisation had a legal and moral duty not to discriminate? Why should she have to personally overcome organisational failings? Even though legal duties and moral frameworks are in place, discrimination still happens. Chapters 16 and 19 explore further why Rakesha's manager might have felt the way he did.

Rakesha started with a high level of self-confidence but she still needed to put in place a realistic plan for reaching her end goal. Identifying personal goals is a useful tool to help manage your own career development, but it is not always easy to articulate what your goal is and how you might achieve it. Our **goal-setting tool** will help you here.

Rakesha and her manager worked to develop clear personal goals, but felt unable to tackle the organisational lack of awareness around the potential disadvantages that BME staff might experience. Therefore, despite the fact that self-confidence is a quality 'over which the person can have considerable control' (Hollenbeck and Hall, 2004, p. 258), there should always be a realistic understanding of the environment in which that individual is working. Understanding the diversity of a workforce is therefore a central part of any manager's role.

Setting goals demonstrates your belief that you can accomplish what you set out to do. What do your goals say about you?

The power of diversity

Rakesha had ambition and a plan. Yet in reality, even when women *do* reach management positions, they are less likely than men to reach the upper tiers (SSI/ADSS, 2002). Statistics on BME representation at senior level also demonstrate inequities. For example, while 9.4 per cent of the working-age population is BME, only 7.5 per cent of NHS executive directors are (DH, 2004). Also, little is known about wider patterns of leadership among women from BME backgrounds (Taylor, 2007). (See Boxes 1.2 and 1.3.)

Box 1.2: Enhancing Leadership Programme (ELP)

> BME staff are known to be under-represented at senior levels within the NHS. [ELP] was established with the overall aim of developing the leadership potential of BME staff … in order to begin tackling the issue of under-representation.
>
> (Tilley, 2005, p. 3)

ELP was implemented in a Strategic Health Authority (SHA) in England where BME staff constituted 30 per cent of the workforce, yet occupied a far lower percentage of senior management positions. BME managers are more likely than white managers to feel they have fewer opportunities to 'act up' and show their leadership potential (IDA/LRD, 2004). They also believe they miss out on career development opportunities, which are discussed through informal networks, and are not encouraged to pursue opportunities when they arise. The BME staff in this SHA were not accessing the same training and development opportunities as their non-BME colleagues; a key part of ELP was therefore enhancing personal belief and self-confidence. After the programme, over two-thirds of participants felt they had gained new leadership skills that were beneficial to their career (Tilley, 2005).

Box 1.3: Women in leadership and management

> The world of management is strongly dominated by men – and leadership is, or at least used to be, conventionally constructed mainly in masculine terms …
>
> (Kyriakidou, 2012, p. 4)

While evidence suggests that the leadership styles of women and men are not markedly different, stereotypical assumptions, such as 'women take care' and 'men take charge', continue to undermine career progression for women (Prime et al., 2009).

Qualities traditionally associated with leadership and management, such as assertiveness, are often perceived as more naturally 'male' (Watts, 2009). When male managers take on more 'feminine' characteristics, such as caring and cooperation, they are seen as going 'above and beyond' to engage with considerate leadership styles. When displayed by women leaders, such qualities are seen simply as 'what women do' (Loughlin et al., 2012). Even where there are mentoring arrangements, differences exist for men and women in terms of what they receive and the outcomes from it (Elliott et al., 2006).

So, even if it is not a reality, assumptions about the roles that men and women *should* play can have a profound effect on the roles they end up taking – or missing out on (Prime et al., 2009).

Stereotypical ideas about men being assertive, dominant and controlling, and women being submissive, caring and compassionate, can hold back women's progression in the workplace. What can a manager do to avoid this?

Increasing the workforce diversity is not only the right thing to do, it also reduces turnover rates and absenteeism among minority groups (Kandola and Fullerton, 2002). There are, therefore, clear benefits across an organisation, in addition to those experienced by individual staff, of enhancing management and leadership potential among all staff groups. Consequently, the aim of any manager should be to nurture and value *all* employees (Tilley, 2005). However, it appears from the evidence in Boxes 1.2 and 1.3 that both women and BME managers are expected to demonstrate *more* evidence of their abilities than their male white counterparts and this is often the result of unequal power relations.

In the previous case study, Rakesha did not have the power herself to overthrow long-standing inequalities in her workplace, but she could take steps to build her own personal power and increase her chances of promotion. Wong (2003) suggests feminist theorisations are helpful by understanding power as a relational, multidimensional web, with four key types of power emerging (Table 1.1).

Power can be 'negative, destructive or repressive' but, equally, it may be 'productive and generative' (Wong, 2003, p. 311).

Table 1.1 The 'web of power' (based on Wong, 2003, pp. 10–11)

Type of power	Description
Power-from-within	Personal power, the psychological power derived from self-confidence, self-esteem and self-respect
Power-to	The ability to take action, the power to participate and mobilise
Power-with	A collective force as people come together and cooperate to solve problems and achieve goals which they would be unable to realise alone
Power-over	A resisting force which can be negative when used to force someone to do something against their will, but also positive when used to overrule dominance and inequality

The idea that self-confidence is a powerful force in leadership and management is based on the idea that 'power-from-within' can be extremely effective. Rakesha worked on this principle when setting her goals. However, the suggestion that an individual can change their fortunes at work by developing their self-confidence must not be used to camouflage very real structural issues which remain beyond the control of individuals.

Management consultancy firms and life-coaching specialists may decree the solution lies within the individual but, for people in Rakesha's position, larger-scale organisational change may also be required. Research has shown other dominant cultural beliefs and practices can also impact on service management and care experiences, such as expectations around sexual orientation (Lee, 2007) or religion (Mir and Sheikh, 2010). Wong's framework of power can be used to understand the way different socio-cultural relationships – including gender, class, ethnicity, age and sexual orientation – result in unequal power relations.

You will encounter this 'web of power' throughout this book as an aid to understanding the dynamics at work in all aspects of management and leadership.

1.5 Book overview

Leadership and management present many challenges, but also many rewards (Larkin, 2008). This book acknowledges that there can be seemingly insurmountable organisational issues which any manager is likely to face, and that one of the biggest drivers for change within health and social care – the political system – is beyond the immediate day-to-day control of a single manager. Nevertheless, the authors of this book believe that knowledge of how organisations work and an understanding of some of the theoretical ideas about working relationships – coupled with an enhanced self-awareness – can create a more empowered manager or leader.

This book therefore encourages you to take a critical approach to the role of managers and leaders within the health and social care system. To help with this, it is divided into two core parts:

- Part 1 Leading, managing, caring in practice (Chapters 2–10)
- Part 2 Leading, managing, caring in context (Chapters 11–20).

Part 1 starts with the manager or leader as an individual and the personal relationships they experience as part of their everyday working life. Part 2 then moves on to locate those relationships in a broader context. Each part is prefaced by a brief introduction outlining the key topics that are covered.

Sound leadership also needs practical tools (Robinson, 2004) so, throughout the book, key 'tools' are introduced which we believe should be part of any effective manager's or leader's toolkit. You will be directed to them by an icon in the margin and you can find the tools at the end of the book.

While there are hundreds of potential tools available, ten core ones have been selected which:

- reinforce the principles of good management
- are widely applicable across health and social care settings
- can be used throughout a manager's or leader's career.

These tools are practical devices to aid creativity, problem solving and **personal awareness**. Used together, they can enhance personal growth, develop **goal awareness**, **team awareness** and **contextual awareness**, and support key principles in leading and managing change.

To further encourage your thoughtful engagement with the issues covered, regular reflection points and margin notes will prompt you to pause and think about alternative perspectives or consider challenging ideas. Key points at the end of each chapter will help you to summarise the main learning points before moving on.

At the same time as providing positive and practical tools to apply in the workplace, the authors of this book have not shied away from an honest evaluation of the dilemmas of management and leadership. Some managers can be overpowering, bullying and controlling, while others experience burn-out as the pressure of being in charge takes its toll. Front-line managers often find that meeting administrative demands distracts from engaging with staff around important care issues (Cathcart et al., 2010). Often, 'management' seems to ask too much of already overstretched workers, leading to unintended problems which undermine the service being provided. Being able to analyse the pros and cons of bureaucracy, paperwork, reviews and assessments – alongside the core task of caring – can help a manager to think about optimum ways to design and manage procedures in the workplace and inspire others in the process. All of these aspects are explored in this book, which asks the difficult questions about what leading and managing care really means.

1.6 Conclusion

> Throughout the ages, individuals who have been seen as leaders have created change, sometimes for the better and sometimes not.
>
> (Kotter, 1990, p. 4)

The way in which care and its management are conceptualised is constantly changing. It is all too easy for managers to feel they are the victims of policy decided by other people, far removed from their everyday caring practice. However, everyone has a choice about how they respond to external change, and effective leadership is about taking the initiative and being creative in response to wider events, rather than adopting a negative, fatalistic attitude. Even if you are far removed from major political influences and decision making, you can still make a significant difference for yourself, your colleagues and service users. This book will show that, at every level, management and leadership are not simply about job titles, but about what is *achieved* in those roles. Learning skills for effective management and inspirational leadership should not be seen as isolated activities but as woven into the fabric of daily work.

This opening chapter aimed to consider the relationship between leadership, management and care. Different generations and their policy makers have attempted to shape how care is provided in different ways, but there has always been a role for managers and leaders in ensuring the best outcomes for service users. This book provides insight, inspiration and practical tools for approaching any leadership and management role with enhanced confidence and awareness. For, whatever challenges are thrown its way, the system will always need self-assured managers and responsive leaders to facilitate the delivery of safe, good quality care.

Key points

- Throughout the history of health and social care, leadership and management have played an important role in both high-profile changes *and* the day-to-day challenges of understanding, defining and providing care.
- Health and social care provision is a key site of political contestation, conceptualised and managed differently at different times by different people. This impacts on how managers and leaders choose to develop and change their practice.
- Management is often about ensuring the smooth running of the system; and leadership is often about inspiring people to do things differently. However, managers and leaders do not have to work against each other; they can work together, support each other, and are often required to be embodied in one person doing one job.
- Great leaders and effective managers need a firm belief in what they are doing and that they can make a difference. One of the core qualities of any individual who has to lead, guide, inspire or manage others is therefore self-confidence.
- Generic leadership characteristics and management skills are often presented context-free. However, the challenges faced by managers within health and social care are always context-specific. An effective leader or manager needs to ensure, therefore, that generic tools or ideas are applied with an awareness of the context in which they are working.
- The four basic building blocks of caring leadership and management are **personal awareness**, **team awareness**, **goal awareness** and **contextual awareness**.

References

Aaron, H.J., Schwartz, W.B. and Cox, M. (2005) *Can We Say No? The Challenge of Rationing Health Care*, Washington, DC, Brookings Institution Press.

Aldgate, J. and Dimmock, B. (2003) 'Managing to care', in Henderson, J. and Atkinson, D. (eds) *Managing Care in Context*, London, Routledge/The Open University, pp. 1–26 (K303 Set Book).

Bambra, C. (2011) 'Lessons from the past: celebrating the 75th anniversary of "Poverty and Public Health"', *Journal of Public Health*, 20 September, pp. 1–2.

Bennis, W. (2009) *On Becoming a Leader*, New York, Basic Books.

Bevan, A. (1952) *In Place of Fear*, London, Heinemann.

Beveridge, W.H. (1953) *Power and Influence: An autobiography*, London, Hodder and Stoughton.

Cabinet Office (1999) *Modernising Government*, London, HMSO.

Cathcart, E.B., Greenspan, M. and Quin, M. (2010) 'The making of a nurse manager', *Journal of Nursing Management*, vol. 18, pp. 440–7.

Clarke, A. (2001) *The Sociology of Healthcare*, Harlow, Pearson Education.

Daft, R.L. (2010) *The Leadership Experience* (5th edition), Mason, OH, Thomson South Western.

Department of Health (DH) (2004) *Survey to Monitor NHS Equalities and Education Targets 2004*, London, DH.

Dickens, C. (1838) *Oliver Twist* (Wordsworth Classics edition, 2000), Ware, Wordsworth Editions Limited.

Elliott, C., Leck, J., Orser, B. and Mossop, C. (2006) 'An exploration of gender and trust in mentoring relationships', *Journal of Diversity Management*, vol. 1, no. 1, pp. 1–12.

Griffiths, E.R. (1983) *NHS Management Inquiry Report* (The Griffiths Report), London, DHSS.

Harvey, S., Liddell, A. and McMahon, L. (2009) *Windmill 2009: NHS response to the financial storm*, London, The King's Fund.

Her Majesty's Government (2011) *Think Local, Act Personal*, London, The Stationery Office.

Her Majesty's Stationery Office (HMSO) (1999) *Modernising Government*, London, HMSO.

Hollenbeck, G.P. and Hall, D.T. (2004) 'Self-confidence and leader performance', *Organizational Dynamics*, vol. 33, no. 3, pp. 254–69.

Hughes, G. and Lewis, G. (1998) *Unsettling Welfare: the reconstruction of social policy*, London, Routledge.

Illich, I. (2010) *Limits to Medicine: Medical nemesis* (1st edition 1976), London, Marion Boyars Publishers Limited.

Improvement and Development Agency and Leadership Research and Development (IDA/LRD) (2004) *Prospects: Diversity and the career progression of managers in local government*, London, IDA.

Ipsos MORI (2009) 'Public Spending Index – November 2009' [Online]. Available at www.ipsos-mori.com/researchpublications/researcharchive/2518/Public-Spending-Index-November-2009.aspx (Accessed 3 December 2012).

Jack, G. and Donnellan, H. (2010) 'Recognising the person within the developing professional', *Social Work Education*, vol. 29, no. 3, pp. 305–18.

Jacobs, J. (ed.) (1992) *Beveridge 1942–1992: papers to mark the 50th anniversary of the Beveridge Report*, London, Whiting and Birch Books.

Jones, M. and Lowe, R. (2002) *From Beveridge to Blair: The first fifty years of Britain's Welfare State 1948–98*, Manchester, Manchester University Press.

Kandola, R. and Fullerton, J. (2002) *Diversity in Action: Managing the mosaic* (2nd edition), London, CIPD.

Kotter, J. (1990) *A Force for Change: How leadership differs from management*, New York, The Free Press.

Kwarteng, K., Patel, P., Rabb, D., Skidmore, C. and Truss, E. (2011) *After the Coalition*, London, Biteback Publishing.

Kyriakidou, O. (2012) Guest editorial: 'Gender, management and leadership', *Equality, Diversity and Inclusion*, vol. 31, no. 1, pp. 4–9.

Larkin, E. (2008) *Ready to Lead? Prepare to think and act like a successful leader*, Harlow, Pearson Education Limited.

Last, S. (2012) Interview for K313 module video, Milton Keynes, The Open University.

Lee, A. (2007) '"I can't ask that!" Promoting discussion of sexuality and effective health service interactions with older non-heterosexual men', in Clark, K., Maltby, T. and Kennett, P. (eds) *Social Policy Review 19*, Bristol, The Policy Press, pp. 127–50.

Loughlin, C., Arnold, K. and Bell Crawford, J. (2012) 'Lost opportunity: is transformational leadership accurately recognized and rewarded in all managers?', *Equality, Diversity and Inclusion*, vol. 31, no. 1, pp. 43–64.

Luthans, F., Luthans, K.W. and Luthans, B.C. (2004) 'Positive psychological capital: going beyond human and social capital', *Business Horizons*, vol. 47, no. 1, pp. 45–50.

M'Gonigle, G. and Kirkby, J. (1936) *Poverty and Public Health*, London, Victor Gollancz.

Marsland, D. (1980) 'Novelty, ideology and reorganisation: threats to the value of youth work', in Anderson, D. (ed.) *Ignorance of Social Intervention*, London, Croom Helm, pp. 21–43.

Martin, G.P. and Learmonth, M. (2012) 'A critical account of the rise and spread of "leadership"', *Social Science and Medicine*, vol. 74, no. 3, pp. 281–8.

Mir, G. and Sheikh, A. (2010) 'Fasting and prayer don't concern the doctors ... they don't even know what it is', *Ethnicity and Health*, vol. 15, no. 4, pp. 327–42.

Northouse, P. (2009) *Leadership Theory and Practice* (5th edition), London, Sage.

Pedler, M., Burgoyne, J. and Boydell, T. (2004) *A Manager's Guide to Leadership*, Maidenhead, McGraw-Hill Professional.

Prime, J.L., Carter, N.M. and Welbourne, T.M. (2009) 'Women "take care", men "take charge": managers' stereotypic perceptions of women and men leaders', *The Psychologist–Manager Journal*, vol. 12, pp. 25–49.

Robbins, H. and Finley, M. (2004) *The Accidental Leader*, San Francisco, Calif., Jossey-Bass.

Robinson, D. (2004) *Unconditional Leadership*, London, Community Links.

Seebohm, F. (1968) *Report of the Committee on Local Authority and Allied Personal Social Services*, London, HMSO.

Social Services Inspectorate and Association of Directors of Social Services (SSI/ADSS) (2002) *Women ... Rising? Achieving equality and diversity in leadership*, Bristol, SSI.

Stajkovic, A. and Luthans, F. (1998) 'Social cognitive theory and self-efficacy', *Organizational Dynamics*, vol. 26, no. 4, pp. 62–74.

Taylor, V. (2007) 'Leadership for service improvement: Part 3', *Nursing Management*, vol. 14, no. 1, pp. 28–32.

The King's Fund (2011) *The Future of Leadership and Management in the NHS*, London, The King's Fund.

Tilley, L. (2005) 'Evaluation of a leadership programme for BME staff in the NHS', unpublished research, London, North East London SHA.

Watson, J.E.R. (2008) '"The times they are a changing" – post qualifying training needs of social work managers', *Social Work Education*, vol. 27, no. 3, pp. 318–33.

Watts, J.H. (2009) 'Leaders of men: women "managing" in construction', *Work, Employment and Society*, vol. 23, no. 3, pp. 512–30.

Welsh Assembly Government (2011) *Sustainable Social Services for Wales: A framework for action*, Cardiff, WAG.

Wong, K.-F. (2003) 'Empowerment as a panacea for poverty – old wine in new bottles? Reflections on the World Bank's conception of power', *Progress in Development Studies*, vol. 3, no. 4, pp. 307–22.

Part 1

Part 1 Leading, managing, caring in practice

Sara MacKian and Joan Simons

Introduction

In Chapter 1 you saw just how fundamental leadership and management are to providing effective, good quality health and social care services. You saw how the two areas overlap, intertwine and sometimes diverge, but together form a natural partnership: leadership helps to set the vision, and management helps you to get there. Chapter 1 also introduced the four basic building blocks of a **fully rounded caring manager or leader – personal awareness, team awareness, goal awareness** and **contextual awareness** – and explored Wong's 'web of power', highlighting the power dynamics underpinning all relationships.

Building on this foundation, Part 1 moves on to explore in more detail what managing and leading mean *in practice*. What are the qualities of a good manager? How can a leader make a difference? And how can they work effectively in the complex and fluid landscape of a constantly changing health and social care sector? What are the personal qualities and social skills someone needs to survive in such a role? Part 1 encourages you to reflect on these questions, and on the skills and qualities required of effective managers. It also explores the implications of constant change within health and social care systems, and the demands this places on both individuals and teams.

Part 1 covers the following two areas.

Chapters 2–5 deal with **approaching leadership, management and care**. The focus is on the *individual* approach to care and what it means to be a leader or a manager in health and social care today. This begins with Chapters 2 and 3 exploring in more depth the understanding of management and leadership which underpin this book. Chapter 2 explores the important transition from practitioner to manager, what is expected of a manager, and what it means to take a 'proactive' approach to the role. Wayne Taylor suggests that, while any manager's role has certain demands and constraints placed on it, there is also considerable room for making choices and a proactive manager can work with these factors to achieve the best outcomes for both staff and service users.

Developing this theme, in Chapter 3 Joan Simons and Helen Lomax explore the growing importance of leadership at all levels in health and social care provision, and how vision has emerged as a core feature. They provide an overview of theoretical perspectives on leadership, giving an insight into its contested and evolving nature and its relationship to the shifting social, political and economic landscape. These two chapters, with their emphasis on *proactive management* and *visionary leadership*, form a springboard from which to explore the rest of this book.

Chapters 4 and 5 both concentrate on the often very stressful and changing nature of working in this sector. First, Liz Tilley and Rebecca Jones explore why change seems to lie in the very fabric of health and social care. They ask why it has so frequently failed to deliver on grand promises, but they also suggest how change can be a positive force to improve the quality of care that is provided. In Chapter 5, Wayne Taylor then explores the more personal dimensions of dealing with stress, anxiety and transitions in the workplace, and how managers can support individual staff and teams through these difficult periods.

Chapters 6–10 look at **managing relationships** and build on the previous chapters by exploring the complex human *relationships* which lie at the heart of any management or leadership role, and how to develop them effectively. In Chapter 6, Helen Lomax begins by unpicking the role of identity in the health and social care workplace, drawing on sociological and psychologically informed insight to develop a better understanding of the role of identity in managing both people and relationships.

Chapters 7 and 8, by Julie Charlesworth, move on to explore the complex dynamics at work in managing and leading teams and partnerships. The language of teams, teamwork and partnership is woven through health and social care practice, but often there is a lack of clarity about what a successful team looks like or how an effective partnership might be established and maintained. These two chapters explore why working together is seen as central to delivering high-quality services, in particular by looking at the role of power – and the manager's response to that – in collaborative settings.

Working with complex teams and managing a diverse range of individuals with a caring face places many demands on a manager, not only in terms of supporting teams to reach their set goals, but also in supporting each individual to realise their full potential. The final two chapters of Section 2 therefore explore how a manager can support individual development to ensure each member of their team can function effectively.

In Chapter 9, Chris Kubiak introduces a 'leading learning model' which involves balancing organisational, individual and team needs. He suggests that a caring approach to continuing professional development involves recognising the need for both formal and informal learning, and that this requires careful management of the process as well as strong leadership of the learning environment. In Chapter 10, Joan Simons builds on the idea of a supportive learning environment by exploring the growing role of coaching in health and social care management. While becoming a qualified coach may not be an aspiration for every manager, Simons shows how the ideas underpinning coaching can be used to develop a style or an approach to managing everyday situations in the workplace which can be particularly supportive of individual development needs.

Throughout Part 1, the authors draw on carefully selected case study examples to demonstrate how theoretical understanding can support attempts to work through complex situations *in practice*. As you progress through this first part of the book, take time to stop your flow of reading to think about the questions posed in the reflection points. You will also encounter a range of tools we have identified as being useful to managers and leaders. They will enable you to grow in confidence in your role and support you in dealing with the challenges inherent in working in health and social care. And do not forget to keep the four building blocks in mind, together with Wong's web of power, as you develop your understanding of what it means for *you personally* to be a manager or leader *in practice*.

Chapter 2 The proactive manager

Wayne Taylor

2.1 Introduction

Figure 2.1 'The reasonable man adapts himself to the world: the unreasonable one persists in trying to adapt the world to himself. Therefore all progress depends on the unreasonable man.'
(George Bernard Shaw, 1903)

> Leadership is not about who you are; it's about what you do … [it involves] the challenge of taking people and organisations to places they have never been before, of doing something that has never been done before, and of moving beyond the ordinary to the extraordinary.
>
> (Kouzes and Posner, 2012, p. 15)

Managing in health and social care has always been a challenge. In fact, as emphasised throughout this book, it is a *complex* challenge, often involving a complicated interplay between the concepts of management and leadership. This challenge was introduced in Chapter 1 and is explored in detail in the rest of this book, examining the various components of this challenge and giving you the tools to enable you to succeed, as you develop your effectiveness as a manager and leader of other people. In this chapter, we focus on the *attitude* with which you should approach the management/leadership challenge to get the most out of your role for yourself, your colleagues and the organisation, as well as for the people who use your services.

Your attitude to problems will probably determine whether they are resolved and solutions are found or whether they continue as 'problems'. There is wide agreement that a positive attitude is more likely to lead to success than a negative one; in particular, because a positive attitude is often based on a belief that progress can be achieved and the world *can be changed*, thereby making it a *better* place. There is also strong evidence to suggest that a positive attitude can be contagious, generating positivity in other people. This inspirational nature of positivity also means that managers who display it tend to gain and maintain popularity among their peers and co-workers.

George Bernard Shaw (1856–1950), Irish author, co-founder of the London School of Economics and Nobel Prize winner, gave his prize money 'to the poor writers of Sweden, thus telling the prize-giving committee in effect that charity should begin at home' (Harris, 2008, p. 287). Was he an 'unreasonable man'?

So what does a positive attitude consist of, and how does it influence our relationships with the world? For Shaw (Figure 2.1), it was about being unreasonable – in the sense of being unwilling to accept the world as it is when there are problems or difficulties in that world. Instead, he urged everyone to do more in developing their sense of personal agency and in *proactively* seeking to change the world for the better; in other words, to avoid complacency.

The aim of this chapter is to explore what it means to be a 'proactive' manager in health and social care. To do this, it draws on an early definition of the proactive individual that fits very well with Shaw's 'unreasonable' man, as:

> [O]ne who is relatively unconstrained by situational forces, and who effects environmental change. [...] Proactive people scan for opportunities, show initiative, take action, and persevere until they reach closure by bringing about change. They are pathfinders ... who change their organization's mission or find and solve problems. They take it upon themselves to have an impact on the world around them.
>
> (Bateman and Crant, 1993, p. 105)

The strength of this definition is that it captures the two core features of proactivity: 'an *anticipatory element*, involving acting in advance of a future situation, such as "acting in anticipation of future problems, needs, or changes"' and an emphasis on '*taking control* and causing change [by] "controlling a situation … rather than waiting to respond to it after it happens"' (Parker and Collins, 2010, p. 634, emphasis added). For Crant (2000) this correspondence reflects the fact that proactive behaviour is inherently radical in challenging the status quo and in taking a personal initiative in improving current circumstances or creating new ones.

As will be discussed, there is a distinction in the literature – and in practice – between proactivity at the individual level, at the team level, and at the organisation level (although the boundaries may be blurred). Hence, this chapter looks at what managers can do to develop their own proactive methods and skills as well as what they might do to promote a proactive ethos within their team and the wider organisation. The chapter, then, is about *managing*: exploring how newly appointed managers can *proactively* manage the different demands made on them; how they can be clear about the objectives of their organisation and their role in achieving these (while adopting a critically informed approach to matters of work design and staffing); how they can manage themselves in unpredictable environments; and how they can use their **personal awareness** and emotional intelligence in problem solving and decision making. At the same time, this chapter is also about proactive *leadership*: examining how managers can inspire by example; how they can use the skills and ideas in this book to build cohesive and effective teams; and how they might begin to develop a style of leadership that actively challenges and changes the disabling features of the physical and social environment at work.

This chapter addresses the following core questions.

- How can you manage the transition from practice to management in health and social care?
- What does it mean to be a proactive manager?
- What are the strengths and weaknesses of a proactive approach to teamwork?
- How is proactive behaviour related to leadership and organisational change?

2.2 From practitioner to manager

Figure 2.2 Becoming a manager means learning new skills and juggling competing demands

Welcome to the manager's world! If you are new to the role, you have entered an exciting and highly challenging terrain of multiple (often contradictory) demands (Figure 2.2), constant change and – as the contributors in Box 2.1 show – forceful critics!

Box 2.1: What do you think of your manager?

Evidence from Community Care (2008) suggests that managers are often seen in a negative light:

> 'Many excellent footballers go into team management and fail disastrously, much to the fans' disgust. I'm afraid it would appear to be the same for practitioners.'
>
> 'To be fair there are good and bad examples of any kind of worker in every job in the world, however I must say that I am appalled by how many examples of bad management I have seen in social care.'

> 'My last manager was an absolute waste of space. His entire focus was on keeping senior management happy.'

For people managing health and social care services for the first time, there is often some anxiety and concern about the transition from being a practitioner to being a manager (Reynolds, 2003). Knowing the commonalities and distinctions between these two roles can assist in easing this transition. In fact, managers with knowledge and experience of practice have a wealth of expertise they can draw on. This should provide a solid foundation for acquiring and developing management and leadership skills. For example, making and maintaining relationships with service users and colleagues, carrying out assessments, planning appropriate responses, evaluating interventions in terms of risk and potential for harm, and developing arrangements for joint working are all skills that can be useful to the new manager. Significantly, many of these skills involve working with people, which gives them an immediate connection with much managerial work.

'Sometimes you have to play the part of a manager before you feel as if you really *are* a manager' (Reynolds, 2003, p. 16).

Given these similarities, why do new managers sometimes attract the kind of practitioner comments cited in Box 2.1? Good practice and good management both involve working with people to achieve tasks. The core difference – and the factor most likely to result in negative assessments of performance if mishandled – is that the manager's focus is on managing the practice of other people. Hence, like the footballer-turned-manager, to be successful, the practitioner-turned-manager needs to focus less on the detail of the individual game and more on the wider objectives of the team and the club. At the same time, the manager must also maintain a strategic view in terms of the primary task of the organisation (without attracting the criticism that they are only concerned with the imperatives of senior management!).

But what about situations where the problems seem more intractable? Consider the experience of Christie Watson, a practising nurse, in Box 2.2, where she reflects on the financial constraints arising from the economic crisis of 2008.

Box 2.2: Time to care?

I've worked as a nurse for the last 18 years ... I am proud to be a nurse, and to work for the NHS. ...

In my area of work – ... paediatric intensive care – standards of nursing are consistently excellent. I've only worked a few shifts on care-of-the-elderly wards, but enough to see some major differences. But why is nursing so different in different areas of the hospital?

In my experience the nurses are trained in the same way, and go into the profession for the same single reason: in order to care for people. But there is a major difference. In children's intensive care there is one nurse to one patient, and a team of support nurses: an education nurse, a consultant nurse, a project management nurse, a bereavement nurse specialist, as well as a nurse designated to cover breaks, and one nurse to manage the shift. Some days are busy, even with all those people, but on the majority of days there is time to care; there is time to be a nurse.

On the few occasions that I've worked on a care-of-the-elderly ward I have not had that time. There was usually a fairly newly qualified staff nurse in charge, and a health care assistant. And 32 beds. It was impossible. We worked a 13-hour day with no time for breaks. ... People were left in wet or soiled beds while we prioritised patients who had suddenly deteriorated. There was no chance to think about dignity or nutrition – things that nurses value so highly. It was heartbreaking. I felt so sorry for our patients. The standard of care we were able to give was terrible. These elderly patients deserved the very best of nursing, but it was a miracle that they were simply alive at the end of the shift.

We were forced to make some terrible choices, and to have to make such decisions on a day-to-day basis is beyond my capabilities. I've experienced how awful it feels to see a loved one suffer due to poor nursing care. The nurses I worked with wanted to care – there were simply not enough of them to be able to do the job properly. I have so much admiration for the

> nurses who work in those areas and manage to give good – even adequate – care with such inadequate levels of staffing.
>
> (Watson, 2012)

In what ways are both practitioners and managers contributing to the problems highlighted by Christie Watson?

As a manager in health and social care, you manage the practice of other people and have a professional responsibility to ensure that practice standards are maintained, practitioner skills and knowledge are kept up to date, and practitioners are supported through very complex and personally demanding practice roles (Rosen, 2000). Yet, as Watson shows, these objectives may be more difficult to achieve in underfunded areas of health and social care. This is increasingly likely as a consequence of forced reductions in local authority spending and the increasing costs of service provision. This is represented in the 'graph of doom' (Figure 2.3), which predicts that the rising costs of social care, combined with cuts in public spending, could overwhelm all other council services by 2020 (Local Government Association, 2012).

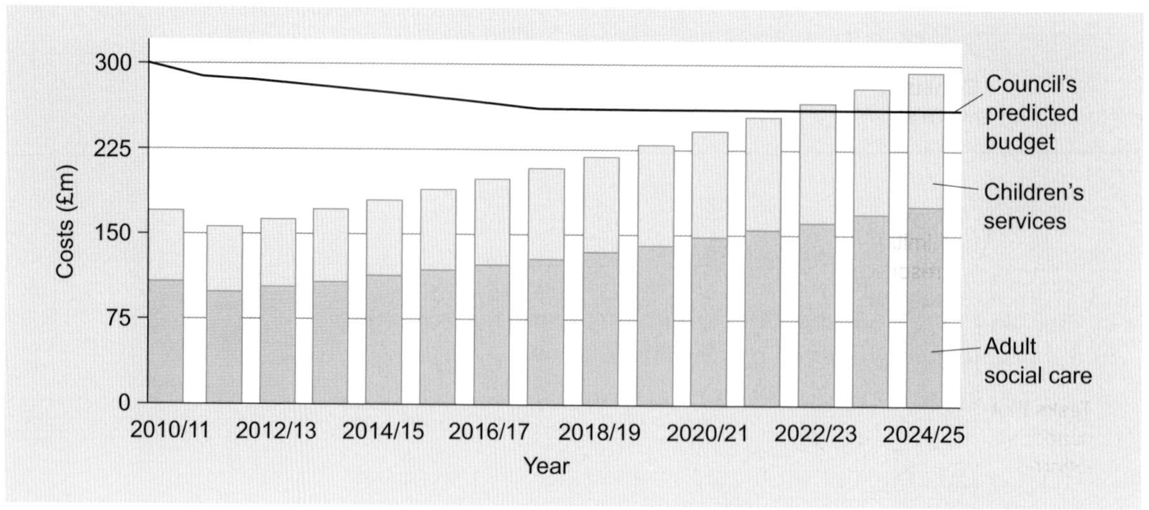

Figure 2.3 Barnet Council's 'graph of doom', showing the predicted combined effects of spending reductions and increasing service costs for 2010–2025 (LGA, 2012)

'Management remains caught between two opposing imperatives: attempts at regulating employees too tightly runs the risk of endangering the employees' creativity and commitment to management goals, while empowering employees runs the risk of reducing management control' (Geary and Dobbins, 2001, p. 5).

According to classical management theory (Fayol, 1949, cited in Fells, 2000), effective management involves concentrating on five key elements.

1 *Planning:* examining the future and devising a course of action.
2 *Organising:* making clear lines of authority and responsibilities.
3 *Coordinating:* timing and sequencing activities to ensure movement towards the end goal.
4 *Commanding:* providing direction and motivation to employees to put the plan into action.
5 *Controlling:* monitoring progress and making the necessary adjustments.

However, more contemporary ideas have tended to reject the very controlled and controlling aspects of Fayol's model, which often fails to fit with the more nuanced understandings of management and leadership in favour today (this is discussed further in Chapter 3). For example, a more positive way of looking at the tension between what is possible and what is not is to think of it in terms of demands, constraints and choices (Figure 2.4).

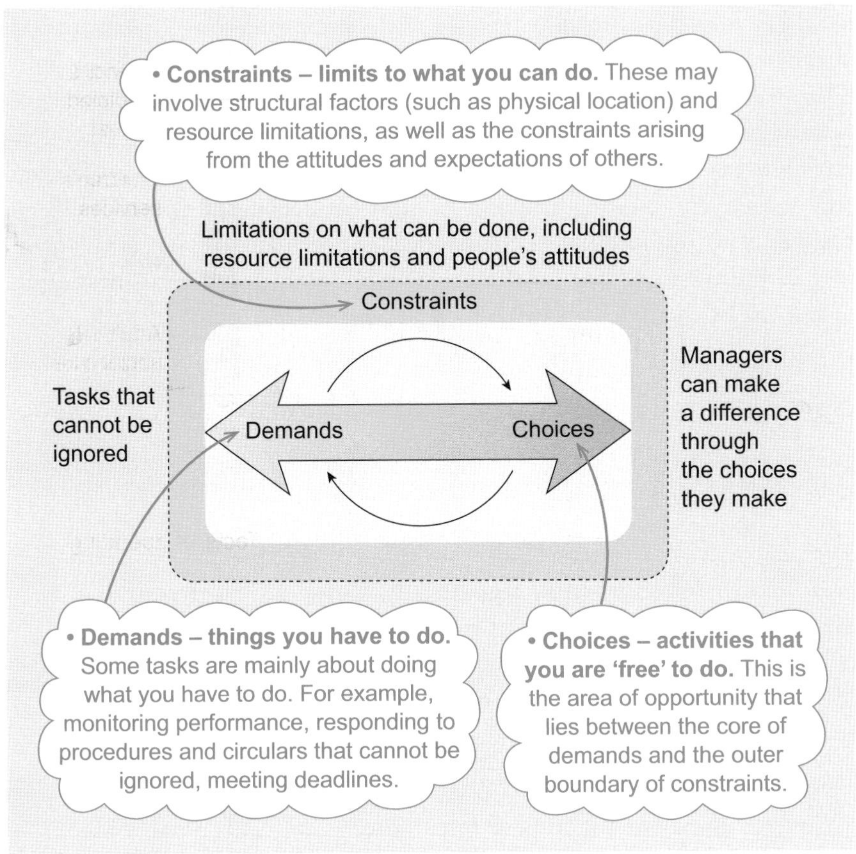

Figure 2.4 Demands, constraints and choices (based on Stewart, 1991, pp. 14–16)

Stewart (1991) suggests that many managers either do not recognise they have choices, have a restricted view of the choices open to them, or may actively restrict these choices through their own (in)actions. This is partly because it can be difficult to think strategically about work if you have no experience of adopting this perspective. Note that the outer boundary of 'constraints' is represented as a broken line. This indicates that even the constraints can change: they may shift over time, or the boundary may be redrawn by a forward-thinking, proactive manager. For Stewart, the key question managers should ask themselves is 'What should I be doing?'

Being proactive involves taking the initiative that is aligned with your personal values and taking responsibility for your choices and their consequences.

Stewart's model is especially informative in a discussion of management and leadership because, while it does not underestimate the restrictions imposed by demands and constraints, it emphasises the *choices* that remain open to managers. Of course, professions will vary in the degree to which they can offer flexibility to their employees and – particularly in times of financial restraint or political disfavour – the fraught relationship between demands and constraints can significantly reduce what choices are available. Nevertheless, the message – that effectiveness lies in the proactive and creative exercise of choice (Fuller and Marler, 2009; Gong et al., 2012) and the seizing of opportunities – fits well with the ideas of agency and empowerment (Wong, 2003) as well as the four building blocks of the **fully rounded caring manager** promoted in this book (see the next section).

It is here that the literature around proactivity can be useful in extending choices in both management and leadership.

2.3 Characteristics of a proactive manager

The centrality of a proactive attitude to achieving positive results has been known for some time. Significantly, Covey (2004) described it as the first and most important of his seven habits for managerial effectiveness, while 'being forward looking' has consistently been cited over the last 40 years (Kouzes and Posner, 2012) as one of the four attributes practitioners most value in their managers (the other three being that they are honest, competent and inspiring).

Chapter 1 discussed the inquiry into the case of Caleb Ness, where several failings – including a 'lack of proactive senior social worker involvement' – led to tragic consequences. In fact, the importance of being proactive in health and social care has been a key aspect of the political vision for these services since the turn of the century (Neate, 2000). A lack of proactivity is generally viewed with concern because the absence of vigilance is often accompanied by a reactive 'fire-fighting' approach to potential problems. Conversely, the advantages of a proactive approach have been identified in a wide range of individual behaviours, including: adjusting to new job conditions; using your initiative; expressing your 'voice' (including whistleblowing); selling critical issues to leaders; advocating for service improvement; taking charge and bringing about change; self-initiated role expansion (or 'job crafting'); problem solving; and network building (Bierhoff and Muller, 2005; Belschak and Den Hartog, 2010; Parker and Collins, 2010). It is clear, therefore, why managers in health and social care should be proactive, but what characteristics are needed to take a proactive stance?

The majority of research into proactive behaviour has focused on the individual and on distilling the individual characteristics associated with being proactive. As already noted, the proactive personality has been defined as a disposition towards taking action to influence your environment and bring about change. This disposition has been linked to a range of proactive behaviours such as problem solving, innovation, entrepreneurship and career initiative. It has also been associated with strong consequential or future-focused reasoning and an active orientation towards learning. However, do not be despondent if you feel you currently lack a proactive personality, as the evidence suggests it can be developed (Frese et al., 2007).

Parker and colleagues (2006) investigated both personality and work environment as antecedents of proactive behaviour that might be subject to cognitive–motivational interventions. Focusing on problem solving and idea implementation as key proactive behaviours, the authors found that several factors were critical in facilitating and motivating proactivity at work (see Box 2.3).

Box 2.3: Facilitating proactivity at work

Role breadth self-efficacy

Individuals who feel capable of performing particular tasks tend to carry them out more effectively, persist at them, cope more effectively with change, choose more difficult goals, and adopt more efficient task strategies. Because it raises an individual's feelings of control and perceived likelihood of success, self-efficacy is seen as crucial to proactive behaviours such as using initiative and taking charge, as well as for related behaviours such as expressing dissent and voice.

Control appraisal

This refers to the individual's expectations that they will have control over situations and particularly that they have an impact on work outcomes. Frese and Fay (2001) argued that an individual with this type of orientation will have a strong sense of responsibility, will not give up easily, will search for opportunities to act, should have high hopes for success, and will actively search for information.

Change orientation

Motivation is also important in dealing with the negative consequences of proactive behaviour, such as having an active orientation towards change and a positive approach to errors. Most significantly, this orientation is about taking responsibility for the work environment.

Flexible role orientation

Proactive individuals define their roles broadly and, as such, feel ownership of organisational goals and problems beyond their immediate technical responsibilities.

(Based on Parker et al., 2006, pp. 638–9)

What is especially interesting about the study by Parker and colleagues and other research (Grant and Ashford, 2008; Parker and Collins, 2010) is the suggestion that there is a higher-order structure in which behaviours are grouped in terms of their impact at different *levels* of the organisation. This is significant because it suggests that being proactive is important at the individual level, the team level and the organisation level; and that the three complement one another (see Box 2.4).

Box 2.4: The proactive context

The individual

At this level, the proactive use of practical techniques, such as seeking feedback, career planning and 'job crafting' (Oldham and Hackman, 2010), can enhance the performance of the individual, if this is combined with a reflective awareness of both personal and organisational goals.

The team

Individual proactive work behaviour (taking charge, expressing voice, being innovative, emphasising problem prevention, etc.) is also important for team performance. Here the proactive manager can improve motivation by offering an example to others and by developing their emotional intelligence in their interaction with their team.

The organisation

An awareness of the organisation's fit with the wider external environment is also crucial for managers concerned to influence organisational strategy. Here proactive strategic behaviours, such as 'scanning' and 'issue selling', can be useful, while a strong sense of **contextual awareness** is also important in terms of setting individual and team goals.

From a management perspective, this overlapping of proactive behaviours at individual, team and organisation levels also suggests the different actions a manager might take. For example, impacting on the internal environment through modelling individual proactive work behaviours, supporting the proactive behaviour of others, and considering priorities at the strategic level (Neale and Griffin, 2006; see the case study below).

Case study 2.1: Chris

Chris was a newly appointed Senior Probation Officer with considerable practice experience who took over a team with which he was already familiar. He knew the job well 'from the ground', having worked as a probation officer for 15 years. He also had a good 'bird's-eye view' of the organisation from his involvement in training and auditing and as an active member of the union. He was well informed about practice and keen to support his team in performing well. But he also knew the workload issues they faced. Basically, the Probation Service was facing a crisis of excessive demand and, unable to control this, his team were being swamped by cases they had neither the time nor the resources to deal with. This left them demoralised and unable to do anything other than react to the latest crisis.

Chris understood how that felt. He knew that the idea of 'making a difference' had always been one of his own key motivations. The problem was that there were simply too many low-risk cases clogging up the system. This had been proved by researchers and recognised by senior management and Chris was aware that some form of prioritisation based on risk was inevitable. It was just a matter of time.

Adopting a proactive approach, Chris called his first meeting with the team, explained his thinking and discussed his plans. He then announced that he would be reducing everyone's caseload by prioritising resources on higher-risk cases, while merely monitoring those assessed as posing no risk to others. Where this involved a departure from the national standards of the Probation Service, he was prepared to countersign each case file confirming this. He had even had a stamp saying 'AUTHORISED DEPARTURE FROM NATIONAL STANDARDS' made for this very purpose!

'When uncertainty is high, work-roles cannot be formalized precisely; they must emerge dynamically in response to changing conditions and demands. Proficient compliance with specifications is not sufficient; nor is it enough just to adapt and respond to these dynamic changes. Individuals need to take charge of situations, anticipate problems before they arise, and initiate change in the work system and work-roles' (Williams et al., 2010, p. 302).

This case study is based on the author's personal experience. It is a good example of how proactivity is integral to both caring management and effective leadership. This can be seen by considering the case study in the light of the four building blocks of the **fully rounded caring manager**. Chris displayed a strong sense of **personal awareness**, reflecting on his own practice experience to manage – and lead – by example. He was also acutely aware of his **team** and that the organisational **goals** they were struggling with were unrealistic and unattainable. Drawing on an equally strong **contextual awareness**, he was able to intervene proactively, to alter the goals in a manner that he knew complied with the wider 'vision' of the organisation. Hence, Chris took charge, displayed individual initiative, and engaged in problem prevention. He used strategic scanning to anticipate organisational responses and take the lead with these, and in management meetings he used the team's strong performance in high-risk cases to 'sell' his approach. His proactive approach was successful and the model was replicated across the organisation.

2.4 Becoming a proactive manager

Figure 2.5 Proactivity needs to be nurtured, both in yourself and in other people

Case study 2.2: Wendy

Wendy was a newly qualified manager of a supported housing scheme for older people with mental health problems. She had considerable experience working in this field – with specific expertise in dementia care – but she was fully aware that being the manager was a whole new ball-game! Surveying her new environment, she used the four building blocks of the **fully rounded caring manager** to take stock of her situation. She saw low staff morale in the team, which meant people were losing their self-confidence and forgetting their overall goal; as a result, there was inadequate service provision and poor patient satisfaction. This was manifested in a variety of ways: evidence of social isolation and low mood in the residents, communication difficulties, and challenging behaviour. Clearly, neither the residents nor the team members were happy.

Wendy asked herself what she could do to put the situation right.

How might a strong sense of personal awareness help you to practise more proactively?

It was suggested in the Introduction that being proactive is about attitude. Wendy was clearly demonstrating a proactive attitude in her new environment: an environment which reflected similar problems to those portrayed by Christie Watson in Box 2.2. At the same time, however, it is neither desirable nor possible for one individual to take on everything, and processes can also be devised to encourage a proactive approach in others. Wendy's reflections led her to the conclusion that her colleagues, on the whole, appeared to lack a proactive attitude. Actively practising individual proactive behaviours will help in developing *your own* skills as well as enabling you to encourage *others* to develop *theirs* (Figure 2.5). This is what Wendy felt was needed in her workplace.

So what are the attributes and skills associated with a proactive manager? Well, it seems that personal characteristics such as confidence, hope and optimism operate as the positive psychological capital that can

boost proactive behaviour. In terms of skills, **personal awareness** appears to provide a strong impetus for proactivity at an individual level. Some people, like Wendy, appear to be naturally self-aware, and have a reflective understanding of themselves and how this influences their performance as a manager. Others have considered this issue less, but there are ways to help develop **personal awareness**. The **personal awareness tool** does precisely this. Even if you do demonstrate a good level of self-awareness, working with this tool can help to clarify self-perception and enhance your overall effectiveness.

Personal awareness is fundamental to proactivity at the individual level; however, encouraging proactivity at the team level also requires emotional intelligence to improve relationships and inspire other people.

Emotional intelligence

Being emotionally intelligent involves being able to actively identify, understand, process and influence your own emotions and those of other people, to guide feeling, thinking and subsequent behaviours and interactions. Clearly, therefore, an individual with emotional intelligence has many of the skills necessary to both manage and lead proactively because they can inspire others and bring with them a particular vision (Chapter 3 has more on leadership and vision). Goleman et al. (2002) classify these skills into the four areas described in Box 2.5.

Box 2.5: Proactive skills

Self-awareness

This means having a deep understanding of your emotions as well as your strengths and weaknesses. It means being honest with yourself. Self-aware leaders understand their values, goals and dreams, as well as having a propensity for self-reflection. Developing skills of self-reflection can help a leader to be measured in their responses rather than react impulsively. For example, Wendy showed she was self-aware by reflecting on her lack of experience as a manager, despite her considerable practice experience.

Self-management

This involves the ability of a leader to manage their emotions through self-control. A manager who has self-control stays calm and clear-headed during a crisis, and has the ability to remain calm when confronted with a challenging situation. For example, Chris demonstrated self-management by calmly taking control of the impending workload crisis.

Social awareness

This involves a leader having empathy for others, which means listening attentively and grasping other people's perspectives, allowing them to communicate their feelings. By doing so, leaders can foster an emotional climate so that staff who work with service users will keep the relationship on the right track. Socially aware leaders monitor the satisfaction levels of patients or service users, to ensure they receive the care they need. For example, Wendy's scanning of the environment demonstrated her social awareness of the low mood of the staff and residents and an understanding of why some of the challenging behaviour was occurring.

Relationship management

This involves a leader engaging staff around a shared vision to achieve their goals. This can be done by inspiring staff, as well as by being persuasive and engaging in gaining commitment from them. Such leaders also work to develop their staff, as well as acting as change agents when required, and in the face of conflict they use their ability to see different perspectives to work towards conflict resolution. For example, Chris's proactive approach really helped to ease relationships when pressure and the potential for tension were high.

Do you think an organisation can have emotional intelligence?

Parker (2008) suggests that a consensus is developing among researchers that managing and understanding other people's emotions is a crucial aspect of leadership. It has been suggested that high levels of emotional intelligence within organisations are likely to enhance the transformational style of leadership that is required to create and maintain a positive working environment (see Chapter 3 for more on transformational leadership). You can see how this happened in the continuing case study of Wendy.

Case study 2.3: Wendy (continued)

Wendy began to operate proactively when she decided that something *could* be done. High levels of self-confidence and **personal awareness** meant that she could present the team with a positive attitude. She identified three goals: to proactively address current (and potential) management problems; to improve staff morale; and to enhance the wellbeing of residents. She introduced weekly staff meetings to discuss these goals and adopted an 'open door' policy for staff concerns.

The results were impressive: morale increased quickly when staff and residents responded to her approach and began to believe that something *could* be done. Better still, Wendy soon found other people behaving in an increasingly proactive way, enthused by her vision.

Wendy's experience suggests that proactivity can be generated through communicating positivity and vision. For people with proactive personalities this is strengthened by being in a proactive team. So the proactive manager benefits not only from being self-aware but also by drawing on their emotional intelligence to develop proactive relationships across the team:

> [T]eam proactivity is collective in emphasis: it is about the way the team behaves as a group, that is, as an interdependent and goal-directed combination of individuals … As such, proactive team performance is not the same as the sum of individual team member proactive performances, such as multiple individual team members acting proactively to contribute to individual or team goals … Individuals within a team might behave proactively, such as by introducing new methods, but unless this effort is coordinated, the team itself might not be proactive.
>
> (Williams et al., 2010, p. 302)

'Commitment' refers to the emotional bond between individuals and broader groups such as teams, professions, unions and organisations. Who and what do you feel committed to and how does this enhance your proactive potential?

2.5 The proactive leader

> Because there is so much pressure on all levels of management to meet budgets, eligibility criteria and targets there is little space left for creativity and making a difference.
>
> (Social worker, quoted in Community Care, 2008)

Reflecting on the challenge in the quotation in the Introduction, Kouzes and Posner (2012) identified the five practices of 'exemplary leadership' as being able to:

1 Model the way.

2 Inspire a shared vision.

3 Challenge the process.

4 Enable others to act.

5 Encourage the heart.

By now, you can probably see how each of these practices is enhanced by adopting a proactive approach. In fact, leadership has been identified as one potentially important contextual influence on proactivity (Crant, 2000); although this appears to depend on the type of leadership. Strauss et al. (2009) considered the links between leadership and proactive behaviour and noted a positive association with transformational leadership, where 'leaders influence followers' values, attitudes and emotions and motivate followers beyond expectation' (p. 280) by focusing on change and improvement (Chapter 3 develops this in more detail). Strauss and colleagues draw on the wider literature to make several interesting distinctions that can clarify thinking about proactive leadership. For instance, they distinguish between proficient and proactive behaviour, describing the latter as actively going beyond the core tasks of getting the job done, to developing self-initiated goals

Proficiency is what you need to do to *keep* your job. Proactivity is what you need to do to *transform* your job.

which develop that job further. You can see how this happened in the continuing case study of Wendy.

Case study 2.4: Wendy (continued)

Doing her best to be honest, appear competent and be inspirational, Wendy presented a vision to her team based on establishing a proactive process at the heart of practice.

Drawing on her prior experience in a similar setting, she introduced a version of the Enriched Opportunities Programme (EOP). At the centre of this process there is a 'locksmith' – a role involving the practitioner in proactively working with individuals to unlock their potential for wellbeing. A central feature of the programme is the training offered to both the 'locksmith' and the wider staff, meaning proactive development across the team.

The emphasis on individual casework was attractive to Wendy's team and began to lead to improved staff–patient relationships. The response to her initiative was overwhelmingly positive, indicating that people were keen to learn the skills of proactivity if they could see it would help them make a difference.

The EOP was developed to help ensure people with mental health problems could continue to enjoy a good quality of life. Based on a structured, systematic and proactive approach, it demonstrates positive impacts on both service users and staff (Brooker et al., 2009).

Strauss et al. (2009) stress work-based commitment and role breadth self-efficacy (discussed earlier) as key motivational factors impacting on employees' proactive behaviour. They suggest that creating an environment where employees thrive can encourage them to take on new roles and associate themselves more closely with the goals of the organisation. It appears that the EOP model adopted by Wendy is an approach that encourages both. Evidence of the impact of the programme includes a significant decrease in hospital visits, a greater take-up of community-based services, a sustained reduction in feelings of depression, and an increase in feelings of wellbeing among residents (Brooker et al., 2009, 2011).

The example of Wendy using the EOP indicates that it is possible to make a difference – at a variety of levels – when you practise proactively as a manager. This is true even (or maybe especially) when the policy context is difficult. Like Wendy herself, staff internalised the Enriched Opportunities approach, behaving proactively themselves, and later distributing these skills by example to others.

Of course, there are limits to what a proactive approach can achieve when resources are limited and even Wendy will have to remain proactive in managing and leading her team through an extended period of severe financial constraint.

You will discover more about leadership in Chapter 3, at which point you might like to reflect back on this chapter's discussion of proactive behaviour when you consider transformational leadership and the place of vision in bringing together the individual and the team to achieve a collective goal:

> Communicating an appealing vision has long been considered a powerful factor in transformational leadership … an inspirational image of a desirable future could motivate employees to engage in proactive behaviours to help make this future become reality.
>
> (Strauss et al., 2009, p. 289)

2.6 Conclusion

This chapter began by reflecting on the radical nature of the proactive personality – someone who is keen to challenge the status quo and show personal initiative in improving current circumstances or creating new ones. The kind of person who changes the world!

The extent to which health and social care bodies can respond to radical demands from practitioners and managers – as you saw in the examples and case studies here – may vary from sector to sector. Sometimes, as in the case of the Enriched Opportunities Programme, there is scope to make a difference. At other times, however, the demands and constraints under which practitioners work – such as those described by Christie – are so severe that it appears any choice is severely restricted. Sometimes the problems are simply too intractable. In such circumstances, the proactive employee is likely to be one of the first to campaign against the strategic direction in which the organisation is moving – expressing their voice internally and, in the case of whistleblowing, externally – and thereby becoming Shaw's 'unreasonable man' or woman!

However, in less extreme circumstances as well, proactive behaviour has been highly effective in enhancing practice at the individual, team and organisation level by generating innovative solutions to work-based problems and by adopting a caring approach to managing and leading others. Here, the self-aware and emotionally intelligent manager can make a positive contribution by proactively considering issues of job design, and the extent to which work is allocated, to generate organisational commitment and maximise each individual's self-efficacy.

There are examples throughout this book which illustrate the value of ethically driven, proactive vision, and how these support and are supported by **personal**, **team**, **goal** and **contextual awareness**. Here you have also been introduced to the importance of vision and transformational leadership. The progressive nature of proactive behaviour seems confirmed by its close association with inspirational forms of leadership, where the proactive leader can enthuse other people with a vision of a better future. This important relationship between leadership and vision is discussed in the next chapter.

Key points

- Being proactive involves acting in anticipation of future problems and taking control and *causing* change, rather than waiting to *respond* after it happens.
- A new manager can build on the skills they developed as a practitioner but must combine these with a focus on managing others and being proactive in adopting organisational goals. Good **personal awareness** and emotional intelligence are key skills required for this.
- A proactive approach to managing and leading can resolve the tensions between 'control' and 'empowerment' and is consistent with a caring style of management.
- In dynamic and uncertain environments, employees who show initiative, think ahead and shape new opportunities also encourage a more adaptive and creative culture within their organisations. Individuals who feel a strong attachment to their organisation are more likely to suggest and implement initiatives to improve it.
- Managers play an important role in developing employees' proactive behaviours by ensuring role breadth self-efficacy and providing a collective vision. Therefore, transformational leadership plays an important part in modelling and developing proactivity at the individual, team and organisation level.

References

Bateman, T.S. and Crant, J.M. (1993) 'The proactive component of organizational behavior: a measure and correlates', *Journal of Organizational Behavior*, vol. 14, pp. 103–18.

Belschak, F.D. and Den Hartog, D.N. (2010) 'Pro-self, pro-social, and pro-organizational foci of proactive behaviour: differential antecedents and consequences', *Journal of Occupational and Organizational Psychology*, vol. 83, no. 2, pp. 475–98.

Bierhoff, H.W. and Muller, G.F. (2005) 'Leadership, mood, atmosphere, and cooperative support in project groups', *Journal of Managerial Psychology*, vol. 20, no. 6, pp. 483–97.

Brooker, D., Argyle, E., Clancy, D. and Scally, A. (2009) *The Enriched Opportunities Programme: A cluster randomised controlled trial of a new approach to living with dementia and other mental health issues in ExtraCare housing schemes and villages*, Bradford, Bradford Dementia Group.

Brooker, D., Argyle, E., Scally, A. and Clancy, D. (2011) 'The Enriched Opportunities Programme for people with dementia: a cluster-randomised controlled trial in 10 ExtraCare housing schemes', *Aging & Mental Health*, vol. 15, no. 8, pp. 1008–17.

Community Care (2008) What do you think of your manager? [Online]. Available at http://www.communitycare.co.uk/articles/14/03/2008/107603/the-greatest-management-clips-of-all-time-how-does-your-manager-compare.htm (Accessed 17 January 2013).

Covey, S. (2004) *The 7 Habits of Highly Effective People: Powerful lessons in personal change* (2nd edition), London, Simon and Schuster.

Crant, J.M. (2000) 'Proactive behavior in organizations', *Journal of Management*, vol. 26, no. 3, pp. 435–62.

Fayol, H. (1949) *General and Industrial Management* (translated by Constance Starrs), London, Sir Isaac Pitman & Sons Ltd.

Fells, M.J. (2000) 'Fayol stands the test of time', *Journal of Management History (Archive)*, vol. 6, no. 8, pp. 345–60.

Frese, M. and Fay, D. (2001) 'Personal initiative: an active performance concept for work in the 21st century', *Research in Organizational Behavior*, vol. 23, pp. 133–87.

Frese, M., Garst, H. and Fay, D. (2007) 'Making things happen: reciprocal relationships between work characteristics and personal initiative in a four-wave longitudinal structural equation model', *Journal of Applied Psychology*, vol. 92, pp. 1084–102.

Fuller, B. and Marler, L.E. (2009) 'Change driven by nature: a meta-analytic review of the proactive personality literature', *Journal of Vocational Behaviour*, vol. 75, no. 3, pp. 329–45.

Geary, J.F. and Dobbins, A. (2001) 'Teamworking: a new dynamic in the pursuit of management control', *Human Resource Management Journal*, vol. 11, no. 1, pp. 3–23.

Goleman, D., Boyatzis, R. and McKee, A. (2002) *The New Leaders*, London, Sphere.

Gong, Y., Cheung S.-Y., Wang, M. and Huang, J.-C. (2012) 'Unfolding the proactive process for creativity: integration of the employee proactivity, information exchange, and psychological safety perspectives', *Journal of Management*, vol. 38, no. 5, pp. 1611–33.

Grant, A.M. and Ashford, S.J. (2008) 'The dynamics of proactivity at work: lessons from feedback-seeking and organizational citizenship behaviour research', *Research in Organizational Behavior*, vol. 28, pp. 3–34.

Harris, F. (2008) *George Bernard Shaw*, Ware, Hertfordshire, Wordsworth Editions Limited.

Kouzes, J.M. and Posner, B.Z. (2012) *The Leadership Challenge: How to make extraordinary things happen in organizations* (5th edition), New York, Jossey-Bass.

Local Government Association (LGA) (2012) *Funding Outlook for Councils from 2010/11 to 2019/20*, London, LGA.

Neale, M. and Griffin, M.A. (2006) 'A model of self-held work roles and role transitions', *Human Performance*, no. 19, pp. 23–41.

Neate, P. (2000) 'Interview with John Hutton', *Community Care*, 9 November, p. 11.

Oldham, G.R. and Hackman, J.R. (2010) 'Not what it was and not what it will be: the future of job design research', *Journal of Organizational Behaviour*, vol. 31, pp. 463–79.

Parker, P. (2008) 'Emotional intelligence and leadership skills among NHS managers: an empirical investigation', *The International Journal of Clinical Leadership*, vol. 16, pp. 137–42.

Parker, S.K. and Collins, C.G. (2010) 'Taking stock: integrating and differentiating multiple proactive behaviors', *Journal of Management*, vol. 36, pp. 633–62.

Parker, S.K., Williams, H.M. and Turner, N. (2006) 'Modeling the antecedents of proactive behavior at work', *Journal of Applied Psychology*, vol. 91, no. 3, pp. 636–52.

Reynolds, J. (2003) 'Becoming a manager: acting or reacting?', in Seden, J. and Reynolds, J. (eds) *Managing Care in Practice*, London, Routledge/The Open University, pp. 3–32 (K303 Set Book).

Rosen, G. (ed.) (2000) *Integrity, the Organisation and the First-Line Manager*, Discussion Papers, London, National Institute for Social Work.

Shaw, G.B. (1903) 'Maxims for revolutionists', *Man and Superman* [Online], www.quotationspage.com/quote/2097.html (Accessed 17 January 2013).

Stewart, R. (1991) *Managing Today and Tomorrow*, Basingstoke, Macmillan.

Strauss, K., Griffin, M.A. and Rafferty, A.E. (2009) 'Proactivity directed toward the team and organization: the role of leadership, commitment and role-breadth self-efficacy', *British Journal of Management*, vol. 20, no. 3, pp. 279–91.

Watson, C. (2012) 'NHS reforms must give nurses time to care', *The Guardian*, 9 January. [Online]. Available at www.guardian.co.uk/commentisfree/2012/jan/09/nhs-reforms-nurses-times-care (Accessed 4 June 2013).

Williams, H.M., Parker, S.K. and Turner, N. (2010) 'Proactively performing teams: the role of work design, transformational leadership, and team composition', *Journal of Occupational and Organizational Psychology*, vol. 83, pp. 301–24.

Wong, K.-F. (2003) 'Empowerment as a panacea for poverty – old wine in new bottles? Reflections on the World Bank's conception of power', *Progress in Developmental Studies*, vol. 3, no. 4, pp. 307–22.

Chapter 3 Leadership and vision

Joan Simons and Helen Lomax

3.1 Introduction

Figure 3.1 'A leader is one who knows the way, goes the way and shows the way' (Maxwell, 2007, quoted in Dempsey and Forst, 2007, p. 72)

Leadership is increasingly defined within theory and policy as an activity which is central to *all staff* at *all levels*, and one which is increasingly allied to the modernisation and transformation of health and social care services. For Max Landsberg (2002), the essence of leadership is the ability to create vision, inspiration and momentum in a group of people. This chapter therefore builds on the discussion about contemporary management in Chapter 2, by exploring the relationships between leadership and vision and what they mean for managers, aspiring managers and practitioners in health and social care.

The imperative to transform and improve services reflects recent developments in leadership theory. There is a growing belief that the potential for leadership can be developed in a range of people and distributed throughout organisations, thereby fostering collaborative and integrative working to inform and contribute to an overall organisational vision (Ferlie and Shortell, 2001). This is mirrored in health and social care strategy in which the importance of identifying, nurturing and promoting talent and leadership at all levels is increasingly prioritised (Botting, 2011).

This chapter reviews historical and current leadership theories and explores the challenges in applying them to health and social care. It addresses the following core questions.

- How is leadership defined?
- What influence does vision have in effective leadership?
- What are the different leadership theories relevant to working in health and social care?
- How can leaders adapt their leadership style to meet the needs of different situations?

3.2 Defining leadership

Figure 3.2 What is leadership?

This section addresses the question what is leadership (Figure 3.2). Hartley and Allison (2003) explore the role of leadership in the context of the modernisation and improvement of health and social care services. In defining leadership, they distinguish between three different aspects: the person, the position, and the processes. Research has often focused on the characteristics, behaviours, skills and styles of leaders as people and the role of individuals in shaping events and circumstances. However, Hartley and Allison's 'three Ps' stress the importance of wider **contextual awareness** as well (one of the basic building blocks of caring leadership and management). Rogers and Reynolds (2003) added a fourth P – *purpose* – a reminder that **goal awareness** is also essential.

The attributes of *person*, *position*, *process* and *purpose* are useful when thinking critically about how leadership models operate in practice, including the limitations of single category explanations. They also encourage more critical thinking and dispel notions of leadership based on the characteristics or personality traits of the individual; for example, the idea that someone is a 'born leader' (Rogers and Reynolds, 2003). Similarly, a singular emphasis on 'position' ignores the influence that those without formal office may exert while overemphasising the authority of high office (which does not in itself guarantee leadership). Rather, in order to understand how leadership models operate in practice, it is more useful to think about the ways in which the characteristics of the 'person' and 'position' intersect with the 'process' (collaborative work with individuals, groups and organisations) and the contribution of the underlying strategic values, vision and objective ('purpose') (Table 3.1).

Table 3.1 The 'four Ps' of leadership

Leadership aspect	**Focus**
Person (character)	The character, behaviour, skill and interpersonal style (e.g. charismatic, controlling, supportive, aloof)
Position (role)	The office held (e.g. chief executive, senior manager, no formal position)
Process (how)	How leaders work with individuals, groups and organisations to find solutions to problems
Purpose (vision)	The contribution of the underlying strategic values, vision and objective

The four Ps help in understanding leadership as a set of processes which occur between and across individuals, groups and organisations. The role of the leader in relation to these processes is not to have exceptional capacity to provide solutions to problems. Instead, it is to work with other people 'to find workable ways of dealing with issues for which there may be no known or set solutions' (Hartley and Allison, 2003, p. 298). Case study 3.1 gives you an opportunity to consider these different aspects from the perspective of a social worker.

Case study 3.1: A manager who demonstrated the four Ps of leadership

Sheila articulated what we were there for. She put the clients first. She allocated work openly, allowing team members to work to their strengths. Sheila was nice and polite but firm, with a transparent strategy that had a client focus. She led from the inside, not from on high. She was part of the team, but there was never any doubt that she had the authority of a manager and she wasn't frightened to use her authority.

Her manner was pleasant and she treated people with respect. Good practice has much to do with respect for the client group and the knock-on effect for workers. Sheila was a good communicator, positively or negatively, and always dealt with people straight, not behind their backs. She gave good feedback.

Sheila had personal authority that came from her behaviour as well as her professional expertise. She also had the authority of her position. She demonstrated many characteristics that enabled her to build trust and commitment in her staff. She modelled integrity, respect and care.

(Based on Rogers and Reynolds, 2003, pp. 58–9)

The description of Sheila infuses the different aspects of leadership with a sense of a particular style of doing things that is rooted in the values of health and social care services. Sheila the *person* is described as nice, polite, a good communicator, reliable, while at the same time being firm and always dealing with people 'straight'. These characteristics underpinned Sheila's role or *position*. She is described as having personal authority that came from her behaviour as well as her professional expertise and the authority of her role. In relation to the last two Ps – *process* and *purpose* – Sheila clearly worked effectively with her staff to find solutions to problems.

The 'four Ps' provide a comprehensive way of thinking about leadership in action, and they reflect the four building blocks of a **fully rounded, caring manager** which were introduced in Chapter 1 as the foundation to effective leadership and management in health and social care. However, in the past, leadership has not always been understood in such a holistic context. The next section provides a backdrop to the current view of leadership by exploring the historical development of leadership theory.

3.3 A historical perspective of leadership theories

The trait approach developed by Stogdill between 1949 and 1970 was one of the earliest and most influential attempts to develop a theory of leadership (Stogdill, 1974). This approach to theorising leadership is often called the 'great man theory' as it focused on describing the innate qualities of a 'great man' who was a great leader. This approach suggested that the following traits are essential to be a great leader and, furthermore, that the person is born with them (Northouse, 2010, pp. 20–1):

- intelligence
- self-confidence
- integrity
- sociability
- determination.

It is not surprising that such a theory held sway in the first half of the 20th century as there are many examples of great men who did possess such traits. One was the Indian nationalist leader Mahatma Gandhi, who was seen as an inspirational leader (Figure 3.3).

Figure 3.3 Mahatma Gandhi (1869–1948): one of the 'great men'

These 'great men' theories developed from the study of the lives of prominent people (invariably men) throughout history. Common traits were identified, many of which might still be used to describe contemporary leaders in popular ideas about what makes a good leader; for example, judgement, decisiveness, adaptability, alertness, confidence and integrity (Marquis and Huston, 2009).

Although it is still commonly accepted that the traits listed above are important requisites of successful leadership, it has been acknowledged that a person does not have to be born with these traits to be a leader, as they are skills that can be learned or acquired. In the case study above, Sheila clearly exemplifies many of the traits of a great leader; however, these are only one dimension of the leadership skills which enable her to lead effectively. She is also adaptable and creative in her approach to a constantly shifting health and social care landscape. In other words, as Sheila's leadership style exemplifies, a model of leadership based on traits alone fails to take account of the leader's situation and the need to be adaptable as a leader.

In response to trait theory, Katz (1955) developed an alternative leadership approach, focusing on skills which could be taught, as opposed to traits which were considered innate and fixed in an individual. By taking this approach, another era in leadership theory emerged, opening up the possibility that leaders could be developed. Katz (1955) suggested that skills are what leaders can accomplish whereas traits are what leaders are. The skills approach led to studies of skills for leadership, and the development of programmes of study which allowed students of leadership to engage in developing the necessary skills of leadership, such as persuasion, communication, decision making, teamworking, planning, vision and strategy.

Both trait and skill theories of leadership have their limitations because they do not include how the leader acts, or how they engage in leadership in practice with others. In the 1980s, several American studies explored different styles of leadership and how leaders act (Blake and Mouton, 1985). The main focus of this approach suggested that leaders engage in two primary behaviours: task behaviours and relationship behaviours. Blake and Mouton suggested, therefore, that there are two extremes of leadership concern: concern for results and concern for people. The leader who is concerned mainly with results cares little about people and operates in fear of something going wrong. In health and social care, such a leader would be focused on meeting targets, at the expense of their staff or service users. The other extreme of leadership concern is concern for people, where the leader cares little about results and operates entirely from a desire to be popular and approved of. In health and social care, such a leadership style would be ineffective, as a balanced approach to leadership, focusing on both results and people, is fundamental to the successful operation of any team.

Think about a leader you admire. Do they focus on people, results, or a mixture of both?

Clearly, a successful leader who manages to focus on people as well as results needs to wield a degree of power to influence both. Another perspective on leadership behaviour is, therefore, to look at the power that a leader might exert over their followers in a team. Three styles of behaviour can be plotted on a continuum, according to the type of power a leader might exert (Figure 3.4).

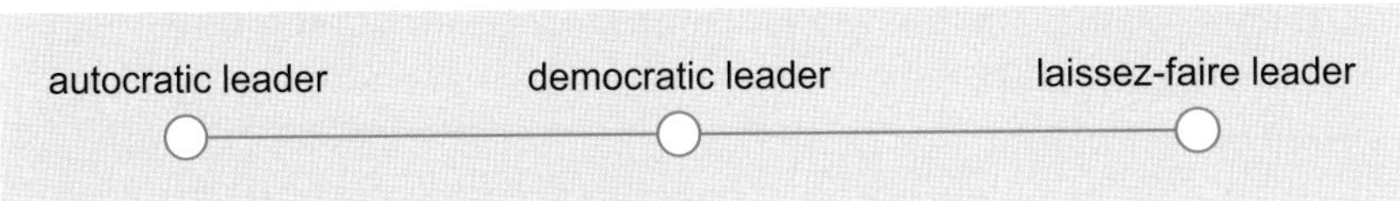

Figure 3.4 Styles of leadership behaviour

The autocratic leader exercises ultimate power in decision making and controls the rewards and punishments for the followers in conforming to their decisions. This type of leader is dictatorial and all-powerful. The democratic leader encourages all members of the team to interact and to contribute to the decision-making process. This leadership style shares the power between the leader and their followers. Sheila, in the earlier case study, is an example of a democratic leader. The laissez-faire leader deliberately decides to pass the focus of power to the followers. However, it is important to note that this style is distinct from 'non-leadership' when the leader refuses to make any decisions (Barr and Dowding, 2008).

Recalling Wong's web of power in Chapter 1 (which comprises power-from-within, power-to, power-over and power-with), what types of power are in evidence for these three behaviour styles?

You can see from this brief overview of three historical approaches to leadership theory (trait, skill and style of behaviour) that the focus of leadership theories has evolved from an approach focused on a clearly identifiable leader born with innate abilities, to one who can be developed with appropriate skills and training, depending on the needs of the organisation.

As any leader needs to be able to influence other people, they will benefit from an understanding of the way power operates around them. They may be laissez-faire and prefer others to develop their own power-from-within, or they may be autocratic and prefer to have power over others. Above all, an awareness of the different traits, skills and styles of leadership is important for anyone interested in developing their own capacity to lead (Table 3.2).

Table 3.2 Summary of leadership traits, skills and style or behaviour

Leadership traits (What you have as an individual)	Intelligence Self-confidence Integrity Sociability Determination
Leadership skills (What you can learn to become an effective leader)	Vision/strategy Communication Persuasion Adaptability Teamwork Decision making Planning
Leadership style or behaviour (How you operate as a leader)	Results focused Person focused Autocratic Democratic Laissez-faire

What are the similarities between the leadership traits identified in Table 3.2 and the traits expected of a professional working in health and social care?

As well as being aware of the different styles of leadership, the rapidly changing context of health and social care means that leaders must anticipate and be responsive to new policies and initiatives that impact on how they work. In doing so, they need to approach leadership as a collective endeavour to which all members of a team can contribute in order to achieve the organisation's vision.

3.4 Leadership and the place of vision

Figure 3.5 What does 'vision' look like?

Leadership is fundamentally about handling constant change, creating a vision (Figure 3.5), and engaging individuals in dealing with ever-changing situations while working towards that vision (Alban-Metcalfe and Alimo-Metcalfe, 2009). Most of the literature on vision suggests that it is a component of leadership that motivates people to higher levels of effort and performance. However, the vision of an organisation needs to be communicated to all levels of the workforce in order for this to happen. And there lies the challenge of having a vision that can apply throughout an organisation. Visions of exemplary transformational leaders are often highly inspirational, optimistic and future-oriented.

Conger and Kanungo (1998, p. 147) suggest that vision involves idealised goals, established by the leaders, representing a perspective shared by followers. Alongside this definition should be added a view of the future, so that the vision provides the *direction* to be followed. Most organisations have a 'vision statement'; the role of the leader is to motivate their team to align themselves with the vision statement and clearly articulate how they will achieve the vision.

So what does a vision do? The purpose of a vision is to clarify a set of ideals, and/or articulate a sense of purpose. However, many organisations work without aligning themselves to a vision, or they may have a formal vision statement that is not well communicated to their staff. Visionary leadership can positively affect motivation and wellbeing, leading to a sense of fulfilment, and a reduction in job-related stress, and creating a strong sense of team effectiveness (Strange and Mumford, 2005). But, as with any leadership tool, a vision will only be effective if it is done right, and the likelihood of success of a vision statement depends on the vision containing several characteristics:

- brevity
- clarity
- abstract and challenging
- states the organisation's purpose
- future focused
- sets a desirable goal
- matches the organisation's success measures.

(Kirkpatrick, 2008)

With an effective vision, everyone knows what they are doing and why they are doing it. Working in health and social care, a unit that is working towards a well-defined and well-communicated vision will create safer practice environments for, and enhance the quality of, care for service users (see Box 3.1).

Box 3.1: Examples of vision statements

> That all children with brain injuries, multiple disabilities and complex health needs have the opportunity to live the best life possible.
>
> (The Children's Trust, 2012)

> Our vision is an ambulance service for people in Scotland which is delivering the best patient care whenever and wherever it is needed.
>
> (Scottish Ambulance Service, 2012)

Looking at these two vision statements, although they are just over 20 words long, they are clear, challenging and focused on their organisation's future ideal state. The challenge for each service, if it wants to be successful in meeting its vision, is to put in place the necessary leadership to motivate staff.

The Work Foundation (2010, cited in NSASC, 2011) suggests that outstanding leaders focus on aligning people emotionally to a vision and aligning the needs of 'now' with a vision of the future. Adair's functional model of leadership embraces the mobilisation of vision as a central focus.

Adair's model of action-centred leadership

John Adair developed a model of leadership based on three overlapping circles, to represent what he suggests are three distinctive, but interrelated, areas involved in every leadership situation. As Box 3.2 shows, these carefully delineate the needs of individuals from those of the group and task. While, as Figure 3.6 illustrates, these may converge in different ways, they may also be quite separate and, indeed, may conflict. A successful leader will be skilled at identifying what these needs are and where they converge or conflict.

Box 3.2: A model of leadership based on needs

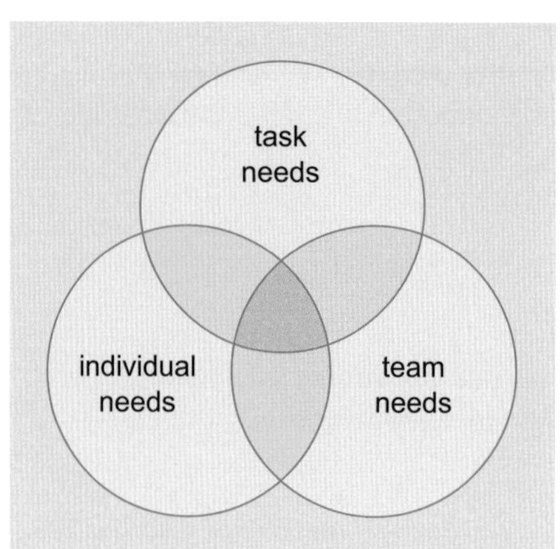

Figure 3.6 Adair's model of leadership (based on Adair, 2002, p. 76)

Task needs The difference between a team and a random group of people is that a team has a common purpose, goal or objective. If a work team does not achieve the required result or a meaningful result, it will become frustrated. Organisations have a core task: to provide a service, to make a profit, or even to survive. Achieving objectives is a major criterion of success for a leader.

Team needs In order to achieve these objectives, the team needs to be held together. Each person needs to be working in a coordinated fashion in the same direction. Effective teamwork will ensure that the contribution of the team is greater than the sum of its parts. Conflict within the team must be used effectively: disagreements can be productive and lead to new ideas, or they can be unproductive, creating tension and a lack of cooperation (see Chapter 7 for more on managing teams).

Individual needs Within working teams, individuals also have their own set of needs. They need to know what their responsibilities are and how well they are performing. They need an opportunity to demonstrate their potential and take on responsibility, and they need to receive recognition for good work (Adair, 2002, 2007).

How does Adair's model of leadership fit with the four building blocks of the fully rounded manager: personal awareness, team awareness, goal awareness and contextual awareness?

The next case study describes the journey of a nurse as she developed her leadership skills over time in a way which reflected a growing awareness of Adair's three areas.

Case study 3.2: Maz's leadership journey

Looking back now, I cringe at how ill prepared I was for my first role as leader in charge of a children's ward. As a student nurse, I had been taught an entirely task-oriented approach to 'get the job done'. As a newly qualified and inexperienced nurse, I applied the same sort of practices – it did not make me popular.

I had no appreciation of the needs of the individual or that we should have been working towards a common goal as a team. One member of staff, who wasn't happy with how I had allocated the responsibilities on a night shift, told me I was like Hitler! I left that job believing I didn't have what it takes to be an effective leader.

Many years later, I became the subject lead for a team of 18 lecturers. I struggled with not being able to say just how I felt if something was wrong. I needed to develop my emotional intelligence. However, by getting to know my new team and their individual preferences for how they liked to work, I realised that there are many ways of achieving a goal and my way might not be the best way. It was more important to harness my team's motivation in working towards a common goal and achieving the department's vision.

See Chapter 2 for more about emotional intelligence.

By letting my team know that I trusted and respected them as individuals, we were able to work together towards a common goal.

Clearly, over time, Maz developed her leadership role with some success. What gradually evolved through an eagerness to 'get it right' was an alignment with Adair's three distinct areas involved in a leadership situation.

According to Adair's model, the leader's role is to be aware of, and to manage, the tensions between the various needs as a result of the frequent conflicts between them. This demands a 'functional' approach to leadership that requires the leader to define the task, plan, evaluate, motivate, organise, and set an example. If, for instance, the leader of a unit, ward or nursing home concentrates all their efforts on the task of maximising the numbers of people admitted to it, while neglecting the training, encouragement and motivation of the staff members, there may well be short-term gains. However, over time, team members are likely to lose motivation and make less effort than they are capable of, which will, in turn, have a negative impact on outcomes.

Similarly, if a leader concentrates only on creating a team spirit and neglects the needs of specific individuals and the overall objective that the team needs to achieve, then maximum performance (as measured by intended outcomes) is unlikely. For example, certain individuals may feel that their personal contribution to the overall success of the team is not being acknowledged. If you have ever experienced some of these issues in your workplace, you may have been left with the feeling that a balance has not been achieved between the task, the team and the individual worker.

Looking back to the case studies above, can you identify a leader you know who has a leadership style similar to either Sheila or Maz?

3.5 Leadership theories that influence practice today

You have probably realised as this chapter progresses that approaches to modelling and theorising leadership are numerous and varied. This section explores some of the dominant approaches today and reflects on how they relate to the four basic building blocks of a caring approach to management and leadership.

Transformational and transactional approaches to leadership

James MacGregor Burns first used the term 'transformational leadership' in 1978 in his book *Leadership*. Burns believed that transformational leadership was about the fulfilment of 'higher-order' needs and the creation of a cycle of rising aspirations, with both the leader and the people being led ultimately being literally 'transformed' as individuals in the process of achieving their vision. Transformational leadership was seen as creating a sense of justice, loyalty and trust.

'The result of transforming leadership is a relationship of mutual stimulation and elevation that converts followers into leaders and may convert leaders into moral agents' (Burns, 1978, p. 4).

Bass suggests that 'Charisma is a necessary ingredient of transformational leadership' (1985, p. 31), and many commentators see charismatic and transformational leadership as interchangeable (for example, Rafferty, 1993). However, Bass (1985) goes on to say charisma alone 'is not sufficient to account for the transformational process'. Bass and Avolio (1990) identify charisma, or 'idealised influence', as only one of four behavioural components of transformational leadership: charisma, intellectual stimulation, individualised consideration, and inspirational motivation. According to this view, 'charisma is a separate component and is defined in terms of both the leader's behaviour (such as articulating a mission) and the followers' reactions (such as trust in the leader's ability)' (Conger and Kanungo, 1998, p. 14).

Recalling the first case study in this chapter, which qualities of transformational leadership did Sheila display?

Transformational leadership is sometimes considered to be an 'ideal' of leadership that goes beyond a simple question of charisma. However, it is also important to understand the context in which the leader is operating. The idea of transactional leadership helps to develop this.

Transactional leadership

Bernard Bass developed the notion of transactional leadership between the 1960s and 1980s, based on the idea of a contract process between the leader and the group. Bass (1985) suggests that transactional leadership includes the following characteristics:

- rewards and incentives to influence motivation
- an ability of the leader to monitor and correct followers in order to work effectively
- an explicit promise of tangible benefits for followers
- an ideological appeal.

This approach particularly suited the National Health Service (NHS) at the time, when the drive for more efficiency was first being formally introduced. It was felt that leaders and groups found mutual satisfaction with these transactional relationships, 'knowing where they stood' (Barr and Dowding, 2008).

The idea was developed and Marquis and Huston (2009, p. 42) identified the following characteristics of a transactional leader:

- focuses on management tasks
- acts as a caretaker
- uses trade-offs to meet goals
- examines causes
- uses rewards.

This list may be more 'managerial' in style than the sort of creative leadership we might expect in health and social care today. While a culture of following the rules has been found to be effective, especially where planning, organising and budget management are essential, Barr and Dowding (2008) suggest that transactional leadership has limited value where creativity is needed to deal with today's more complex organisations. It would appear, therefore, that transactional and transformational leadership both have a place as, in some ways, they complement each other, in the same way as leadership and management complement each other.

Applied leadership

In response to the plethora of theories on leadership, and the increasing political prioritisation of leadership, many organisations have looked inwards in order to identify their best leaders and understand what makes them effective. The National Skills Academy for Social Care published *Outstanding Leadership in Social Care* in 2011, the first document of its kind to provide a framework of three key principles that they suggest underpin outstanding leadership.

1 Thinking and acting systematically on behalf of the organisation.
2 People are the route to performance.
3 Leaders achieve through their impact on others.

These three principles were developed from a study by The Work Foundation (2010, cited in NSASC, 2011), which found that the highest-performing leaders shared a style of leadership that engaged and enabled their people to achieve more than they thought possible. This style of leadership can be broken down into nine broad themes (see Box 3.3).

Box 3.3: Characteristics of high-performing leaders

Outstanding leaders:

1 Think systematically and act long term.
2 Bring meaning to life.
3 Apply the spirit, not the letter of the law.
4 Are self-aware and authentic to leadership first, their own needs second.
5 Understand that talk is work.
6 Give time and space to others.
7 Grow people through performance.
8 Put 'we' before 'me'.
9 Take deeper breaths and hold them longer.

How might the themes in Box 3.3 support a leader who is trying to motivate a team around a particular vision?

Relationships with other people are a key part of leadership (**team awareness**). However, it is equally important to understand the context or situation in which the leader leads (**contextual awareness**). The next section therefore explores situational leadership theory.

Situational leadership theory

> I expect them to provide leadership to their teams. I expect them to understand and feel personally accountable in their positions of seniority. I expect them to be able to really model themselves on how I want leadership to look but in their leadership style they would be giving out messages that are absolutely consistent with the ones that we are working on together so that there is a coherence through the organisation.
>
> (Social care leader, quoted in NSASC, 2011, p. 80)

For some time, it was assumed that leaders could be matched with one of the textbook leadership styles – and that each leader would always use the same style. Research since the 1970s challenged this view, recognising that many leaders' styles could not be so emphatically identified (Goleman, 2000). Rather than being located in convenient boxes or categories, many leadership styles are more likely to be positioned somewhere on a continuum between authoritarian and laissez-faire (Barr and Dowding, 2008). In Maz's case, the development of her leadership style could be seen to move from a dictatorial authoritarian style towards a more facilitative approach that was matched to the situation she was dealing with.

Effective leaders respond to each new challenge by adjusting their style according to the situation, recognising that greater attention needs to be paid to the context in which both leaders and followers operate. This was acknowledged in Hersey and Blanchard's theory of situational leadership (see Box 3.4). This was formulated in the 1960s and has continued to evolve in response to the shifting social, economic and political context in which leaders operate (Hersey et al., 2008). Another contributor to the development of situational theory, also known as contingency theory, is Fiedler (1967). He proposed that exploring the relationship between an individual's personal style and the conditions found in the workplace can predict an individual's performance.

Box 3.4: A theory of situational leadership

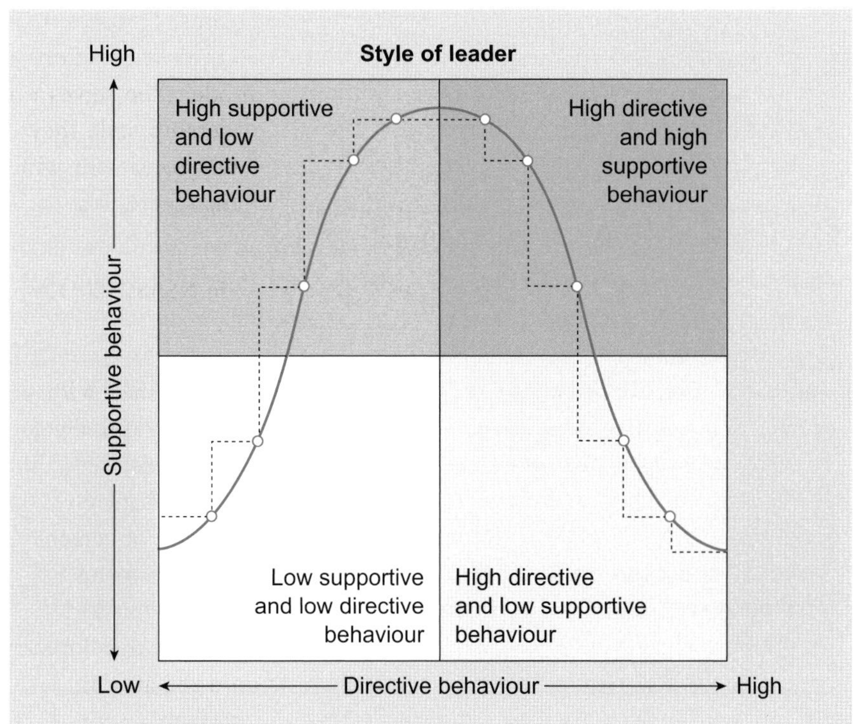

Figure 3.7 Situational leadership (Blanchard et al., 1986, p. 74)

A **high directive/low supportive** approach is appropriate for staff who have high commitment but low competence. This is a relationship that focuses on instruction.

A **high directive/high supportive** approach may be more effective with staff who have some competence but reduced motivation to accomplish the task. Leader behaviours include coaching, giving encouragement and asking for input. However, the final decision about what the aims and outcomes should be, and how to accomplish them, remains with the leader.

A **high supportive/low directive** approach is for staff who have competence but low commitment. This approach involves listening, praising, asking for input and giving feedback. Staff have control over day-to-day decisions, but the leader is available to help with problem solving.

> A **low supportive/low directive** approach is most effective with staff who have a high degree of commitment and competence. After agreeing what is to be done, the leader lessens involvement in planning and day-to-day details and even intervenes less with support.
>
> (Rogers and Reynolds, 2003, pp. 65–6)

In Figure 3.7, the leadership style changes from 'directing' to 'coaching' (see Chapter 10 for more on coaching), to 'supporting', and eventually 'delegating' as staff performance improves. This theory of situational leadership has considerable intuitive appeal, and has been used by numerous organisations, including major companies such as Xerox, IBM and Mobil Oil (Robbins and Judge, 2009). According to Manthey (1994), it is said to have revolutionised thinking about management behaviour, and has also been highly influential in health and social care.

Recall the case study of Maz's development of her leadership skills over time. Do you think she was a situational leader? Why?

The position of Hersey et al. (2008) is that leadership style is best assessed and used situationally. In other words, there is no single 'best style' for a leader. Rather, it depends on the environment in which it is being applied. Situational leadership theory reinforces the idea that leaders are responsible for fostering growth and development, both in themselves and in other people. This is exemplified in the following case of a social care manager.

Case study 3.3: A situational leader

> It's very hard for me, an email will come in or a phone call outlining something that's gone wrong, my immediate reaction is to immerse myself into it, to go and sort it out, a really action man approach.
>
> [It's] not my job, [it's] undermining for everybody in the chain who works for me and not the right thing to do so what I always do now is allow myself a period of reflection ... I talk

> to the senior people in the line and agree with them what they're going to do, whereas two years ago I imagine I would have *trodden all over them and sorted it out.*
>
> (Social care leader, quoted in NSASC, 2011, p. 71)

As this case shows, leaders need to have sufficient **self-awareness** to be able to decide when it is appropriate to 'back off' and enable others to 'step up' and take the lead. Situational leadership theory focuses on follower maturity – the ability and willingness of people to take responsibility for directing their own behaviour, in terms of both job maturity and psychological maturity. It is important to remember, therefore, that to have effective leadership there needs to be effective followership.

Followership is described as the relationship between leaders and followers, where each has different but equal roles, both geared towards a common purpose. Goleman et al. (2002) describe followers as the mirror image of leaders; however, there is an imbalance in the attention paid to followers and followership. Leadership theories often overlook the role of followers in advancing effective leadership. People with a high level of follower maturity have the knowledge, ability and experience to perform their job tasks without direction from others. They are self-motivated and willing to perform a task without the need for much encouragement from other people. Recognition by leaders of the role that followers play in working towards a common goal will enhance the likelihood of success.

What is your dominant leadership style? How easily do you adapt to different situations?

Given the complexity of leadership styles and thinking, Handy (1993) suggests that it is quite understandable if managers give up trying to identify a best fit and merely impose their habitual style on the task and their followers. However, he also suggests that an individual leader's ability to adapt is very largely governed by his or her relationship with the group, and that an effective leader needs to invest considerable energy in building the required relationship from the outset. Often this is about distributing leadership throughout a team or an organisation.

Distributed leadership

Figure 3.8 Leadership is not always about one person

An alternative way of thinking about leadership is to create an environment in which leadership is provided by many members of an organisation, rather than being vested in a few powerful individuals (Figure 3.8). The thinking behind such 'distributed' (or shared) leadership may be increasingly applicable in health and social care services which are becoming ever more complex to manage and lead. The delivery of care is shifting from teams working within hierarchical organisational structures towards multidisciplinary teams operating across practice boundaries. It is not surprising, therefore, that distributed leadership is now being promoted across both health and social care settings (see, for example, The King's Fund, 2011; National Skills Academy, 2011).

Could distributed leadership just be a clever way of getting people to do more for less?

In distributed leadership, the focus is on collegiality, joint action, sharing roles, opening up boundaries, fluidity, and harnessing all available expertise. In short, it involves letting go of the overall control associated with hierarchical management. Individuals at all organisational levels are encouraged to think of themselves as leaders, so that their individual skills and abilities are fully used and their talents are unlocked. What becomes important then is the collective leadership provided by both formal and informal leaders across an organisation (Day et al., 2004).

The complex processes involved in this form of leadership have implications for how organisations might be designed and managed. Both team and organisational performance are likely to suffer if different leaders cannot agree on what or how things should be done. Large organisations such as Social Services and the NHS are often criticised for their lack of communication between different sections or departments; considering how distributed leadership might be put in place could help here.

Trevor and Kilduff (2012, p. 150) suggest the focus should be on enabling coalitions, and that 'coexistence and collaboration within and across networks' are the charismatic qualities required in distributed leadership. They argue that, once more, charisma is integral to the development of leadership. However, rather than seeing charisma as a quality of the lucky few (the 'great men'), they suggest that charisma can be developed by leaders engaging closely with their teams, gaining advice from people, becoming experts, treating people with consideration, being available to give advice, and integrating with people at all levels. The implication is that leaders who focus on developing their emotional intelligence are in a good position to facilitate distributed leadership across their unit and, ultimately, across their organisation (see Chapter 2 for more on emotional intelligence).

What is the weakness in distributed leadership?

Box 3.5 describes an initiative by the NHS Leadership Academy (2011), focusing on the value of promoting distributed leadership.

Box 3.5: The Leadership Framework (NHS Leadership Academy, 2011)

With a greater demand for efficiency in public services, there is a real need to ensure that leaders are developed in a well-considered way that will equip them with the skills and ability to lead effectively. The NHS Leadership Academy framework (2011) provides a single overarching structure for the leadership development of staff across all disciplines, roles and functions, which can apply to staff at any stage of their career.

The framework was developed from the premise that acts of leadership can come from anyone in the organisation. It emphasises the responsibility of all staff in demonstrating appropriate behaviours, in seeking to contribute to the leadership process, and to develop and empower the leadership capacity of colleagues.

At the heart of the framework is the core vision of delivering a good quality service to users, carers and members of the public (Figure 3.9).

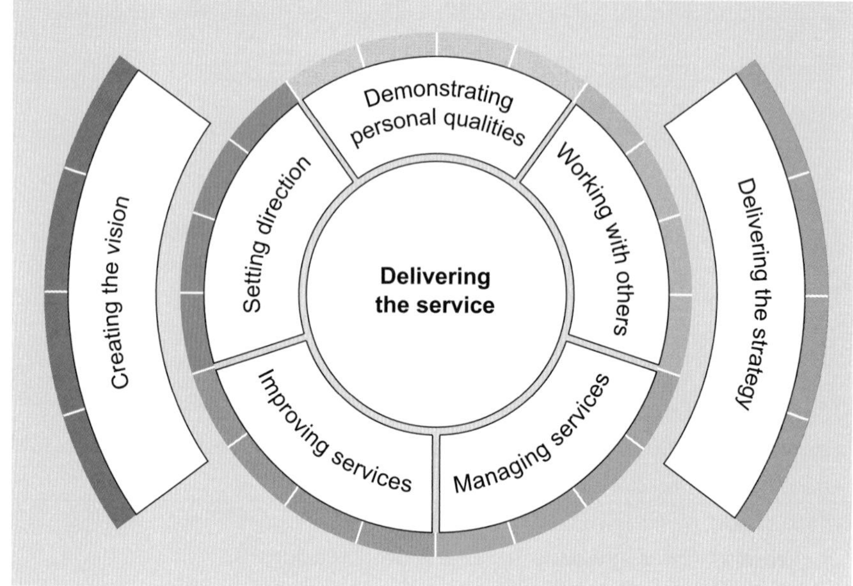

Figure 3.9 NHS Leadership Academy framework (2011)

The Leadership Framework outlines seven domains which are integral to improving quality and safety in any health and social care setting. There are five core domains (in the centre of Figure 3.9) in which all staff should be competent, and a further two domains (on the outer edges) which focus more on the role and contribution of those in senior positions or roles.

Earlier, this chapter explored Adair's action-centred leadership model, focusing on the task, the team and the individual. What similarities are there between Adair's model and the NHS Leadership Framework?

3.6 Conclusion

Enacting leadership with vision is about motivating and influencing people, and shaping and achieving outcomes. There is an array of leadership theories which can help to understand that process. However, theories are not right or wrong; their value lies in the extent to which they may be useful or effectively applied to a given situation. One thing this chapter cannot do is to tell you how to lead, as that depends on the situation you are in as a leader, as well as the goals and vision you are working towards in your organisation. But what is clear from this overview of key influential ideas about leadership is that, by working together across an organisation, leaders with a clear vision, who are aware of the needs of their team and the individuals within it, have the power to achieve greater efficiencies than working alone.

Once again, this reinforces the importance of the four basic building blocks of caring leadership and management. As a result of **personal**, **team**, **goal** and **contextual awareness**, leaders are more likely to meet their vision of providing quality care to service users and their families and carers.

This chapter has demonstrated that a leader in health and social care should be one who knows the way, goes the way and shows the way, as suggested in the opening quotation (Figure 3.1).

Key points

- Leadership as a set of processes occurs both among and between individuals, groups and organisations.
- Vision, when clearly articulated, is a core component of leadership that motivates people to higher levels of effort and performance.
- While it was once widely assumed that 'natural leaders' were born, research on leadership in action shows that leadership skills can be developed.
- Leadership is about handling constant change and adaptable leaders need to change their style to suit their situation.
- Distributed leadership has the potential to enhance the effectiveness of large, complex organisations.

References

Adair, J. (2002) *Effective Strategic Leadership*, London, Macmillan.

Adair, J. (2007) *Develop Your Leadership Skills*, London, Kogan Page.

Alban-Metcalfe, J. and Alimo-Metcalfe, B. (2009) 'Engaging leadership part one: competencies are like Brighton Pier', *International Journal of Leadership in Public Services*, vol. 5, no. 1, pp. 10–17.

Barr, J. and Dowding, L. (2008) *Leadership in Health Care*, London, Sage Publications.

Bass, B. (1985) *Leadership and Performance beyond Expectations*, New York, Free Press.

Bass, B.M. and Avolio, B.J. (1990) 'Developing transformational leadership: 1992 and beyond', *Journal of European Industrial Training*, vol. 14, no. 5, pp. 21–27.

Blake, R.R. and Mouton, J.S. (1985) *The Managerial Grid III*, Houston, Tex., Gulf.

Blanchard, K., Zigarmi, P. and Zigarmi, D. (1986) *Leadership and the One Minute Manager*, London, Collins.

Botting, L. (2011) 'Transformational change in action', *Nursing Management*, vol. 17, no. 9, pp. 14–19.

Burns, J.M. (1978) *Leadership*, New York, Harper and Row.

Conger, J.A. and Kanungo, R.N. (1998) *Charismatic Leadership in Organizations*, Thousand Oaks, Calif., Sage Publications.

Day, D.V., Gronn, P. and Salas, E. (2004) 'Leadership capacity in teams', *Leadership Quarterly*, vol. 15, no. 6, pp. 857–80.

Dempsey, J.S. and Forst, L.S. (2007) *An Introduction to Policing* (6th edition), New York, Cengage Learning.

Ferlie, E.B. and Shortell, S.M. (2001) 'Improving the quality of health care in the United Kingdom and the United States: a framework for change,' *The Milbank Quarterly*, vol. 79, no. 2, pp. 281–315.

Fiedler, F.E. (1967) *The Theory of Leadership Effectiveness*, New York, McGraw Hill.

Goleman, D. (2000) 'Leadership that gets results', *Harvard Business Review*, March–April, pp. 78–90.

Goleman, D., Boyatzis, R. and McKee, A. (2002) 'Primal leadership: the hidden driver in great performance', *Harvard Business Review on Breakthrough Leadership*, Boston, Mass., Harvard Business School Publishing Corporation, pp. 25–50.

Handy, C. (1993) *Understanding Organizations* (4th edition), London, Penguin.

Hartley, J.F. and Allison, M. (2003) 'The role of leadership in the modernization and improvement of public services', in Reynolds, J., Henderson, J., Seden, J., Charlesworth, J. and Bullman, A. (eds) *The Managing Care Reader*, Buckingham, Open University Press, pp. 296–305.

Hersey, P., Blanchard, K.H. and Johnson, D.E. (2008) *Management and Organizational Behavior: Leading human resources* (9th edition), Upper Saddle River, NJ, Pearson Education.

Katz, R.L. (1955) 'Skills of an effective administrator', *Harvard Business Review*, vol. 33, no. 1, pp. 33–42.

Kirkpatrick, S. (2008) 'How to build a better vision statement', *Academic Leadership Journal*, vol. 6, no. 4 [Online]. Available at www.academicleadership.org/262/how-to-build-a-better-vision-statement (Accessed 23 May 2012).

Landsberg, M. (2002) *The Tools of Leadership. Vision, Inspiration, Momentum*, London, Profile Books.

Manthey, M. (1994) *Leading an Empowered Organisation*, Minneapolis, Minn., Creative Nursing Management / Creative Healthcare Management.

Marquis, B. and Huston, C. (2009) *Leadership Roles and Management Functions in Nursing. Theory and Application* (6th edition), Philadelphia, Pa., Lippincott.

Maxwell, J.C. (2007) *The 21 Irrefutable Laws of Leadership* (2nd edition), Nashville, Tenn., Thomas Nelson.

National Skills Academy for Social Care (NSASC) (2011) *Outstanding Leadership in Social Care*, London, NSASC.

NHS Leadership Academy (2011) *Leadership Framework: A Summary*, London, NHS Institute for Innovation and Improvement.

Northouse, P.G. (2010) *Leadership: Theory and Practice* (5th edition), Thousand Oaks, Calif., Sage Publications.

Rafferty, A.M. (1993) *Leading questions: a discussion paper on the issues of nurse leadership*, London, King's Fund.

Robbins, S.P. and Judge, T.A. (2009) *Organizational Behaviour* (13th edition), Upper Saddle River, NJ, Prentice Hall.

Rogers, A. and Reynolds, J. (2003) 'Managing change', in Seden, J. and Reynolds, J. (eds) *Managing Care in Practice*, London, Routledge/The Open University, pp. 83–110 (K303 Set Book).

Scottish Ambulance Service (2012) 'Our vision' [Online]. Available at www.scottishambulance.com/TheService/vision.aspx (Accessed 19 April 2012).

Stogdill, R.M. (1974) *Handbook of Leadership: A survey of theory and research*, New York, Free Press.

Strange, J.M. and Mumford, M.D. (2005) 'The origins of vision: effects of reflection, models, and analysis', *The Leadership Quarterly*, vol. 16, no. 1, pp. 121–48.

The Children's Trust (2012) 'Our vision' [Online]. Available at www.thechildrenstrust.org.uk (Accessed 21 September 2012).

The King's Fund (2011) 'The future of leadership in the NHS' [Online]. Available at www.kingsfund.org.uk/publications/future-leadership-and-management-nhs (Accessed 15 June 2012).

Trevor, J. and Kilduff, M. (2012) 'Leadership fit for the information age', *Strategic HR Review*, vol. 11, no. 3, pp. 150–5.

Chapter 4 Managing change in health and social care

Liz Tilley and Rebecca L. Jones

4.1 Introduction

Figure 4.1 Are you all set for change?

In health and social care services, managing means managing change (Figure 4.1). In many ways, change is the very fabric of health and social care. Care provision is often required initially because of changes in people's lives which lead to a need for care and support services. Somewhat ironically, while the history of health and social care highlights the ongoing and recurring nature of change, people who use health and social care services report that their experience is too often one of continuity – of things not changing – and their experience is often poor (Beresford et al., 2011). This emphasises the importance of unpacking the concept of change: exploring why it has so frequently failed to deliver on the grand promises, and considering how it can be used to improve the quality of care that is provided.

Sometimes, the decision to change some aspect of a service comes from front-line managers, care workers or service users who are hoping to improve local practice. At other times, changes at the governmental or strategic planning level demand changes at the local level. In these cases, managers are reacting to decisions that are being made elsewhere and implementing someone else's change initiative. A delicate balance has to be struck in terms of responding to top-down decisions while managing the views of staff, who may be anxious or even resistant to the idea of change. Whatever the source of change, one of the most important aspects of managing it is, of course, to manage your relationships with staff and their relationships with one another; and to support colleagues through what can be an uncertain or a stressful process.

Visionary leadership and effective management go hand in hand when negotiating a successful change; and, indeed, the change process is an excellent example of when all four of the building blocks of the **fully rounded caring manager** (**personal awareness**, **team awareness**, **goal awareness** and **contextual awareness**) need to be in place. This chapter explores the possibilities for being proactive and reactive in relation to change (see Chapter 2 for more about the proactive manager). It focuses on knowledge, strategies and tools that will help you to plan and implement change, and to develop your capabilities to manage the unpredictable and unplanned aspects of change. Working with a change process aimed at an enhanced quality of service, and therefore quality of life for clients and workers, entails a range of competences, attitudes and skills that allow you and your colleagues to challenge assumptions, develop common understandings and exercise new behaviours.

This chapter addresses the following core questions.

- Why is change needed?
- Who and what can change?
- What are the complexities involved in managing change?
- How can change be led in practice?

4.2 The context of change in health and social care

The Royal Albert Hospital in Lancaster, in northern England, was a typical large Victorian institution for people with learning disabilities (Figure 4.2). In the 1980s and 1990s it was closed down (see Box 4.1).

Box 4.1: Changes in expectations

Figure 4.2 The former Royal Albert Hospital in Lancaster, northern England

> The world had passed it all by. They were institutions – literally. Nobody went in. The people that worked there had worked there for years ...The inspectors would go round, write a nice report ... This is when things had started to change, they had an inspection and it got a real slating did the Albert ... And of course the Albert hadn't changed, what had changed was people's perceptions, so what ten years ago was good was suddenly not very good at all. But the boss at the time made a very good point, 'What I want to know is for the last 25 inspections we've had, everything has been absolutely fantastic, and now everything's appalling. Why is it suddenly changed? Because the institution hasn't changed.' And the point he was making was valid. It wasn't the institution that had changed in any way whatsoever, what was happening was that

> people's expectations were different … And that was right and that's how change happens isn't it?
>
> (Bob Dewhirst, Royal Albert senior nursing lecturer, quoted in Ingham, 2011, pp. 115–16)

Bob Dewhirst says change happens because people's expectations change. Can you think of other examples in health and social care which illustrate this?

What if the resources needed to make a change are greater than the potential benefit? Is it sometimes better to just live with an imperfect system?

What this example shows so powerfully is that, while there is some continuity in the skills needed for health and social care, the structures, policies and ideologies within which those skills are practised are continually changing. Nigel Ingham's research also highlights the 'human face' of change, and the personal impact it has on staff and service users. While change is often focused on organisations, it is played out in practice through people, who experience and face the consequences of change.

Change certainly appears to be something of a constant in health and social care. When Peter Beresford and his colleagues carried out a research project between 2006 and 2008 on the implementation of personalisation policies in England, they acknowledged the depth and rapidity of change facing health and social care agencies. For example, within that two-year period, several leads in partner organisations left their posts, staff were made redundant and, in one local authority, a major restructuring of services occurred (Beresford et al., 2011). For harassed managers, changes introduced as a result of the changing political landscape can sometimes feel like a constraint on the smooth running of the organisation.

Why make a change?

Is it best to rip it up and start again?

If emerging evidence about change in health and social care suggests that its impact on the experiences of service users has been limited (Beresford et al., 2011), why do it? While the *implementation* of a change may be where some projects or policies fall down, there continue to be many reasons (moral, social, clinical, political, economic, technological) for introducing change. Sometimes change is called for in health and social care in the light of a serious crisis or service failing. As Beresford et al. (2011) argue, this can lead to an 'unhelpful cycle of change' (p. 362). They draw attention to child protection as a case in point. Despite active media interest and a major public inquiry after the death of 8-year-old Victoria Climbié in 2000, the cases of Peter Connelly (Baby P) and other young people since then demonstrate that high-level policy change has not transformed practice in every locality. Nevertheless, change continues to preoccupy the people involved in health and social care, including practitioners, managers, policy makers and service users and carers, precisely because people believe that things can be done better, in terms of either practice improvements at a local level, to make services more efficient, or in the pursuit of social justice.

Change also occurs because someone recognises, replicates and promotes an example of good practice (see, for example, Chapter 17 on the value of 'appreciative inquiry').

While the case for change may be strong, there is no blueprint or formula for making it work. However minor changes may seem, change is never a one-off event; nor does it follow an orderly sequence of stages. It is always a continuous and uncertain process which happens in a specific context (Pettigrew and Whipp, 1991). Understanding the context you work in and learning to manage your environment is an essential component of leading a successful change process, and one of the four building blocks of the **fully rounded caring manager**. Throughout this chapter you will be encouraged to consider **context** (alongside **personal**, **goal** and **team awareness**) in facilitating change.

4.3 Understanding the dimensions of change

Managers and workers often operate on several levels at the same time. From the perspective of a front-line manager, changes are often 'top-down' and imposed, such as the closure of the Royal Albert Hospital in Box 4.1. Some top-down changes have a legislative requirement, some changes come as guidance, and other changes are advocated as good practice; but they all have different implications. Changes can also be 'bottom-up', for instance introduced as a result of evaluation by service users, or suggested by front-line care workers, or because of the manager's own desire to raise standards of work in the team. The ideal solution is to find ways of harmonising imperatives from above with those arising from practice. But this is a complex task, as shown by the Standards We Expect project (Beresford et al., 2011) described in Box 4.2.

Box 4.2: The Standards We Expect project

This project was funded by the Joseph Rowntree Foundation, to support the implementation of greater choice and control for people who use health and social care services. The project was carried out in the context of a policy agenda that promoted more person-centred care (a top-down directive), but a growing awareness of the difficulties of achieving this in everyday practice.

The project's main aim was to achieve change in practice. It was led by Shaping Our Lives (a user-led organisation), but involved a wider consortium of academics, practitioners and other service users. Eight partner service-delivery organisations across health and social care were invited to participate and trial the new ways of working. These services were at various stages of implementing person-centred care.

The project's objectives were to:

1 Identify and develop ways of promoting person-centred systems, to empower both service users and staff.
2 Identify barriers in the eight local areas which may make this difficult.
3 Share knowledge and good practice across the eight sites.

(Based on Beresford et al., 2011, p. 399)

> Very early on, the project team recognised that they had to find ways to engage all stakeholders in the process of change. This included service users, staff, managers, senior leaders and commissioners, in order to explore both bottom-up and top-down perspectives on change. Interviews, meetings, seminars and workshops were held to get people's views and to facilitate an exchange of ideas. The project team worked with the eight sites (including day services, residential care units, primary care trusts and housing services) over a period of two years. They then evaluated what change – if any – they had supported.

What do you think were the advantages in the approach to change adopted in this project? What might some of the challenges have been?

The Standards We Expect project (Beresford et al., 2011) raises many important questions about what exactly constitutes change; why it is needed; and how to decide whether it has been achieved. As you will see throughout this chapter, scholars and practitioners have set out a wide range of models to understand, describe and support the process of managing change, each underpinned by a set of assumptions and a particular theoretical approach. Emerging from these models are specific tools that have become popular with managers across the private, public and voluntary sectors. Sometimes these models and tools can appear quite contradictory and, at times, you might wonder how you can possibly choose between them. But all of these models and tools have something to offer; and, as you become more familiar with them, you will begin to see the benefit of using a *combined* approach, whereby you assess which will be of greatest use to you, depending on the nature of the change that is required and your own particular context. It is about developing the skills and confidence to judge the strengths of the different approaches, as well as their limitations (Iles, 2006).

'There is no one right theory or approach to change management, rather there are multiple perspectives and lenses through which to view organisations and from which to develop ideas, actions and technologies for approaching change …' (Shacklady-Smith, 2006, p. 384).

To say that a lot has been written about organisational change and how to manage it is a slight understatement! There is no way in which all the ideas on this topic could be covered in one chapter. But one idea that has had a notable impact – in the fields of both practice and research – is that approaches to change can be divided broadly into 'planned change' processes and 'emergent change' processes.

Implementing 'planned' change

Classical scientific versions of change focused on change as a mechanistic event: a stable linear process that is rational and can be controlled as long as the 'change agents' plan effectively. According to planned change theorists, once a 'problem' has been diagnosed, a set of known steps can be taken to make the necessary change, with a clear end-state in sight. There is an assumption of 'plain sailing' with little interference from elsewhere. Probably the best known approach is the three-phase approach of the social psychologist Kurt Lewin (1958).

> This involves:
>
> - *unfreezing* the organisation from a presumed steady and stable state
> - *moving* towards new goals and [a] view of the future and
> - *refreezing* or stabilising the norms, values, behaviours and culture representing a desired end state.
>
> (Shacklady-Smith, 2006, p. 386)

Lewin's model has been very influential and continues to be used today. It provides a neat framework for thinking through the main elements of a change process and seems quite easy to use. Significantly, it positions the 'change agent' (for example, a manager) as being objective and able to stand outside the change process, observing, planning and tweaking it as necessary.

Consider briefly your own idea for a change project. Can you envisage how 'unfreezing–moving–refreezing' might help you pinpoint some issues you need to attend to?

Following on from Lewin, in 1996, John Kotter published his seminal work *Leading Change* in which he set out eight steps for leading change.

1 Create urgency, by getting key players to buy into the need for change.

2 Form a powerful coalition.

3 Create a vision for change.

4 Communicate your vision as much as possible.
5 Remove obstacles.
6 Create short-term wins.
7 Build on the change and don't declare victory too early.
8 Anchor the change in the organisational culture.

(Based on Kotter, 1996)

Kotter's eight steps represent a practical and systems-based approach to working carefully through the change process. It might be argued that these steps support the leadership element of change (particularly the focus on vision and communication), whereas Lewin's model is more focused on management (setting clear goals and targets and working out what processes are needed to get there). So both models have something useful to contribute to any change process. But it is also important to take a critical view of such frameworks and what they might actually mean in practice for someone tasked with delivering change. Consider the following two quotations.

> When you have change there'll always be casualties … That's life.
>
> (Gordon Greenshields, former Chief Executive of North West Regional Health Authority, quoted in Ingham, 2011, p. 268)

> I know that there were some casualties among the staff. Some staff I know found it difficult to become re-established after the Royal Albert closed, after their redundancy, because they were sort of older and felt they couldn't adjust to the new way of doing things as it were.
>
> (Senior manager, quoted in Ingham, 2011, p. 136)

Both of these are quotations from Ingham's research on the closure of the Royal Albert Hospital. The running down of it constituted a major change process: complex, expensive and sensitive. The directive to close was very much a top-down one (dictated by national policy), and was thus planned. This was a change that *had* to happen, but the challenge facing managers was to make the change as smooth as possible. Kotter's eight-step model might be seen as useful in this context. But the quotations touch on just how challenging a major change programme can actually be in practice. Both participants used the term 'casualties', indicating the almost military implications of change in some circumstances, and the trauma involved. The people at the top might view this as an inevitable removal of obstacles (Kotter's step 5), but the manager's words express the moral and ethical dilemmas that those tasked with implementing change often face. The uncertainty and loss involved in managing the change process is explored more fully in Section 4.5 of this chapter.

Returning to Lewin's model and Kotter's list, do you think it is more helpful to consider change in terms of organisations or individuals?

In practice, Lewin's model and Kotter's list are far more complex than they first appear, and working out precisely what is required at each stage is no mean feat. Indeed, a key criticism of this approach is that it presumes stability and order but people's experiences may feel much more like chaos. This is not to undermine or disregard the planned approach but, rather, it suggests the importance of paying close attention to the detail. While a planned approach to managing change might emphasise goal awareness – where you want to be after the change – it is important not to lose sight of the other important building blocks to effective management which can influence your chance of success in reaching that goal.

Directing 'emergent' change

While the general ideas underpinning planned change continue to influence and shape the way organisations work, over time this model has given way to theories of emergent change that emphasise the unpredictable nature of change as it unfolds. This understanding of the change process acknowledges the impact of internal and external factors which may not have been accounted for in a carefully planned process. Change here is viewed as an emergent process which is subject to disruption, breakdowns and breakthroughs, depending on the changing circumstances around it. This approach suggests that change should not be viewed as something which is managed by one person as a discrete event, but as something which every manager should constantly be tuned into.

Henry Mintzberg, the famous management strategist, coined the term 'emergent change'. He argued that managers need to spot patterns and trends and be prepared to take action, with or without a strategy or a plan (Hatch, 1997; Iles, 2006). If you think of change in this way, the role of the manager shifts from being the *planner* and *implementer* of deliberate change to a *harnesser* and *director* of more fluid change processes. Managers need to respond to issues that emerge, have the skills and resources to operate in uncertain conditions, and support their team through changes that are beyond their control. In a climate of major cuts to health and social care funding, managers are continuously reacting to external events, and having to reconcile these with internal tensions and conflicts. Managing an enforced reduction in staff capacity or funding cuts for essential service activities is one very clear example of how managers can be responding to a quickly changing service picture and having to work through complex changes with a diverse range of people, subject to, often conflicting, internal and external pressures. For instance, the growing number of people living with dementia is one example of where managers in health and social care are both responding to changes in the wider environment and planning strategies to meet local need (Figure 4.3).

Figure 4.3 Caring for people with dementia involves complex changes

Recalling the four buildings blocks of a fully rounded caring manager and what you read in Chapter 3, which qualities of leadership do you think are important to support managers to deal with emergent change?

There is a growing recognition in the literature of the role of strong leadership in helping organisations to avoid 'stuckness' (inertia or patchy implementation) and supporting progress in the change process (Smith and Berg, 1987). The empirical research by Higgs and Rowland (2010), which involved interviewing 33 leaders across the public, private and voluntary sectors, demonstrated that successful 'change stories' were influenced by leaders who were found to be:

- extremely self-aware, regularly seeking feedback, empathising with other people, and with an understanding of how to use their role in a change process (**personal awareness**)
- able to 'work in the moment', keeping the vision in mind, coping with emergent change, staying attentive and expectant, and available to work with what arises (**goal awareness**)

- mindful of the bigger picture, and almost demanding of the organisation around them to see and lead for everyone (**team awareness** and **contextual awareness**).

Higgs and Rowland concluded that, for change to be successful, leaders are needed who are aware of the systems underpinning their organisation that influence people's behaviours, but who also understand themselves, in terms of both the limits of their role and their power to influence. This seems to be an essential ingredient in managing emergent and unexpected change that gives little time for detailed planning and management of the change process.

According to the Greek philosopher Heraclitus (c. 535–475 BC), 'Change is the only constant'.

However, as more empirical research is done on how people in organisations actually talk about change, it has become apparent that an 'either/or' approach in terms of planned or emergent change is neither helpful nor a reflection of people's experiences of change (Ingham, 2011). In busy health and social care services, the chances are that most managers will – at some point in their careers – be responsible for both initiating change projects and responding to change initiatives that are imposed on them as a result of internal or external developments. To be a manager in health and social care you need to develop the skills to lead both planned and emergent change. The rest of this chapter introduces the knowledge and tools to support you in this process.

4.4 Implementing change

Despite a proliferation of ideas about why and how things *should* and *could* change, in reality, it is estimated that only one-third of change projects actually succeed (Nasim and Sushil, 2011). This is an extraordinary statistic. It raises many important questions that need to be addressed if managers are going to improve their chances of successfully implementing change. For example, do so many change projects fail because managers neglect to *plan* properly; perhaps managers are not quick enough to react to *emerging* changes in their organisation or the wider sector; perhaps efforts are not made to achieve sufficient 'buy-in' for the ideas by staff or other stakeholders; maybe managers are not drawing on change models or tools when they instigate a change process; perhaps they are drawing on them too rigidly and missing other important factors; or perhaps they lack the leadership skills to effectively support people through a period of change and fail to be proactive.

This brings us back to the importance of gaining insight into the factors that shape how change is experienced and managed in health and social care and exploring critically the models and tools that give us frameworks for approaching change (see Box 4.3).

Box 4.3: Change from within or change from without?

Some researchers suggest that major institutional change (such as encouraging a culture of independent living and person-centred care) requires an external 'jolt' that precipitates a shift in attitudes and behaviours, and 'change agents' who represent 'new blood' within an organisation (Barley and Tolbert, 1997; Hensmans, 2003; Reay and Hinings, 2005). According to 'institutional theory', as patterns of work and other activities become the 'norm', it is increasingly difficult for people inside the organisation to make a meaningful change (Zucker, 1987). Institutional theorists have argued that external forces are therefore required to 'shake things up'.

However, research suggests that sometimes major change is more successful when it is led by 'change agents' *within* the organisation, turning institutional theory completely on its head! This is what Reay and colleagues (2006) found in their empirical research project in a healthcare system in Alberta, Canada. The change process involved introducing a new work role – a nurse practitioner – who carried out specialised medical activities beyond the scope of a registered nurse. Despite initial resistance to the idea of this role from a range of stakeholders (including other nurses, doctors and managers), those championing its introduction finally achieved major success when the new role was formally recognised in legislation. The researchers argued that front-line managers had played a crucial role in the success of this initiative and, in many ways, were the 'unsung heroes'. They had engaged front-line workers and facilitated change at senior level.

Valerie Iles (2006) argues that managing a change requires managers to do the following if they are to have any chance of developing a successful strategic plan.

- Analyse your situation, using specific tools to do so.
- Identify key priorities and devise a plan of action to address them.
- Implement the plan.
- Monitor progress, again using tools that can help.
- Evaluate the outcomes.

Think about Iles's ideas as you read the case study below about a change initiative led by Joan Simons (who was then a senior nursing research fellow) and Louise MacDonald (a lead clinical nurse specialist in pain) (Simons and MacDonald, 2006).

Case study 4.1: Changing nursing practice to reduce children's pain

Joan and Louise knew that many nurses struggled to use validated pain assessment tools in their daily work, even though it was well proven that they helped reduce children's pain in healthcare settings. They wanted to change this, so they designed an action research project to implement validated pain assessment tools across ten wards of a hospital.

They began by meeting with senior ward managers and pain link nurses and surveying 100 nurses on their views of pain assessment tools. This suggested that nurses already believed that introducing pain assessment tools would improve pain management for children. The senior ward managers did not object to the plans, but neither did they express any interest in getting actively involved. Joan and Louise introduced teaching sessions on the wards and the Pain Control Service offered additional support to nurses in using pain assessment tools.

However, evaluations of using the tools after 6 and 12 months showed that, while nurses increasingly found them easier to use, some still felt that they represented more work. Twelve months after implementation, the majority of children who could have had a pain tool in use did not have one.

Although some progress had been made, Joan and Louise found themselves reflecting on why their change initiative had not been more successful. Crucial ingredients were in place: active involvement from key stakeholders; credible 'change' agents in the form of Joan and Louise; and face-to-face contact with practitioners to harness enthusiasm. But, in retrospect, they realised that what was missing was genuine organisational commitment to the change. While senior sisters did not object, they were not championing the use of these tools. This would have been a powerful motivator for the nurses.

Reflecting a few years later on what she could have done differently, Joan said:

> I realise now that we were too focused on the outcome we were hoping to achieve, i.e. getting nurses to use pain assessment tools, and not focused enough on the change process, and how challenging that was going to be. If I was doing this project again, I would build in time at the beginning of the process to gain robust organisational commitment before moving on to implementing the change.

Joan and Louise could have used the popular technique of force field analysis to assess the situation more fully. This would have made them think carefully about all the forces at work – those which were *supporting* the change as well as those which might be *blocking* it. Take a look at the **force field analysis tool** for more detail.

Looking at Iles's ideas, you can see that Joan and Louise drew on some of these recommendations, but not all of them. In retrospect, Joan acknowledged that they would have had greater success if they had drawn on tools to gain robust organisational commitment.

What do you think Joan and Louise could have done to secure this organisational commitment?

This case shows that analysing the issues and assessing the readiness for change is only the first step in managing a change process. Effective change requires that someone takes a lead, and some writers call this 'leading change' rather than 'leadership', to highlight the need to resolve not simply single issues but also a pattern of interwoven complexities (see, for instance, Pettigrew and Whipp, 1991). Whoever is leading change, or has a strong desire to see change happen, needs to think strategically about how to engage other people. Ideas are more likely to be adopted if they come from more than one person, hence the importance of involving others in discussion from the earliest stage and developing ideas together. People have their own ideas and are not just neutral receivers waiting for messages about what needs to be done. So, once you have started to involve others, expect the change process to take on a life of its own.

Using practical tools in the change process

Given the complexity of managing any change process, it is not surprising that several tools have been designed to help support change. For example, in the first stage, managers often do a PESTLE analysis to understand the 'big picture' (CIPD, 2010):

Political

Economic

Sociological

Technological

Legal

Environmental

PESTLE is, in effect, an audit of an organisation's surrounding influences, the results of which can be used to guide strategic decision making. This helps managers and leaders to think carefully about the context in which they work, and to pre-empt as many variables as possible that might impact on how change is implemented. A PESTLE analysis really helps to develop wide-ranging **contextual awareness** right from the start.

However, the information gathered from a PESTLE analysis is of greater use when drawn on for a **SWOT analysis** (Iles, 2006). The purpose of a SWOT analysis, which assesses Strengths, Weaknesses, Opportunities and Threats, is to move from *information* to *action*. Therefore, it provides a practical tool to inform the change process.

Focusing on both internal and external factors, a SWOT analysis supports managers to identify critical issues that must be addressed if they are to move their plan forward.

However, as Joan pointed out, the key issue for her project involved communicating with the relevant stakeholders. This involves engaging the right people, in the right way, at the right time. This is not always easy to do when you are a front-line manager. Perhaps you are new to the organisation; or maybe you have not had the necessary organisational 'exposure' to understand clearly who you need to be communicating with and how. In these circumstances, **stakeholder mapping** can be a highly practical and effective tool for identifying and communicating with your stakeholders. Indeed, this is a key facet of good management and leadership across a variety of activities, whether they involve major change or not.

4.5 Leading change and managing resistance

While people often talk about change in terms of 'organisational change', this chapter shows that managing change is more often than not about managing *people*. However, it goes beyond merely managing people. It requires managers to *lead* people through what might be an exciting, uncertain, anxious or even traumatic period. Tangible change can never really happen if managers cannot carry individuals and teams along with them.

'The consequences of change are quite different for those who feel in charge, with "their hands on the rug", from those "standing on the rug" as it is whipped away from under them' (Smale, 1998, p. 316, quoted in Beresford et al., 2011, p. 365).

But in practice, whether you are implementing a top-down directive for change or initiating your own change project, the people you work with are likely to have different levels of interest and commitment to making the change. Some may be keen to change their practice or may themselves have suggested the change; front-line staff may act as change agents as well as managers. Some may be passively uninterested (for example, the senior nurses in Joan and Louise's project). Others may actively resist the changes. This poses real challenges for managers. While stakeholder mapping and PESTLE or SWOT analysis can all support you in identifying who you need to influence, when and how, ultimately, a key role for managers is acknowledging and working through the emotional facets of change.

Change does not happen in a bubble; it takes place within the context of real working lives. Managers are often implementing changes that raise political complexities, ethical dilemmas, and sometimes genuine feelings of loss by staff and even service users. Consider the following quotation from a participant in Nigel Ingham's research on the closure of the Royal Albert Hospital (Box 4.1). Bernadette was involved in supporting people with learning disabilities to leave the institution, but she was acutely aware that the speed of change might lead residents to feel that their lives lived in the institution had somehow been cast as worthless.

> I thought they can't all leave this hospital and actually say, 'My life's wiped out … I've come out of this and people are saying to me, "You're in a rotten place and you've to go out into the community."' Because what it's actually saying is your life is negated. So I thought, 'Can't have this. We need to do something to give people histories here, to recognise it and say, "You have done this and you have done that."' Particularly the old ones who had been there quite a time.
>
> (Bernadette Hobson, Royal Albert voluntary services co-ordinator, quoted in Ingham, 2011, pp. 269–70)

Ingham's research highlighted that change processes are often positioned along ethical, and even ideological, lines. While there were strong financial drivers for the Royal Albert closure, senior leaders used persuasion and coercion based on a *moral* argument that institutionalisation was wrong and constrained people's freedom to live an ordinary life. This ethical framework was used to legitimise the closure, amid notable resistance from some members of staff. Interestingly, these 'resisters' also used moral arguments to make their point, arguing that closure created the potential for significant loss for service users who had lived in the institution all their lives, and among staff who had dedicated their careers to the Royal Albert (see Chapter 16 for more on the role of ethics and morals for managers in health and social care).

'Organisations which constantly reorganise themselves tend not to perform well' (David Nicholson, Chief Executive, NHS, Guardian Public Services Summit, 5 February 2009, quoted in Beresford et al., 2011, p. 353).

Although the closure of a big institution may appear removed from much of the everyday work of health and social care practice, Ingham's findings reflect a wider body of literature on change that is focused on the 'human' aspects of the process (Allcorn et al., 1996; Stein, 2001). It is well known that people in the health and social care sector frequently complain of 'change fatigue' – the apparent endless tidal wave of new initiatives. This can be difficult for staff to cope with, but it also creates particular challenges and tensions for managers (see Chapter 5 for more on managing and leading staff through stressful transitions). What we are beginning to understand more fully is that real change happens through interactions and social processes, i.e. it is relationship dependent. Therefore, a manager has a crucial role in *leading* staff and other stakeholders through the change process by communication and harnessing their collective power (Dopson et al., 2008).

Managing the psychological contract

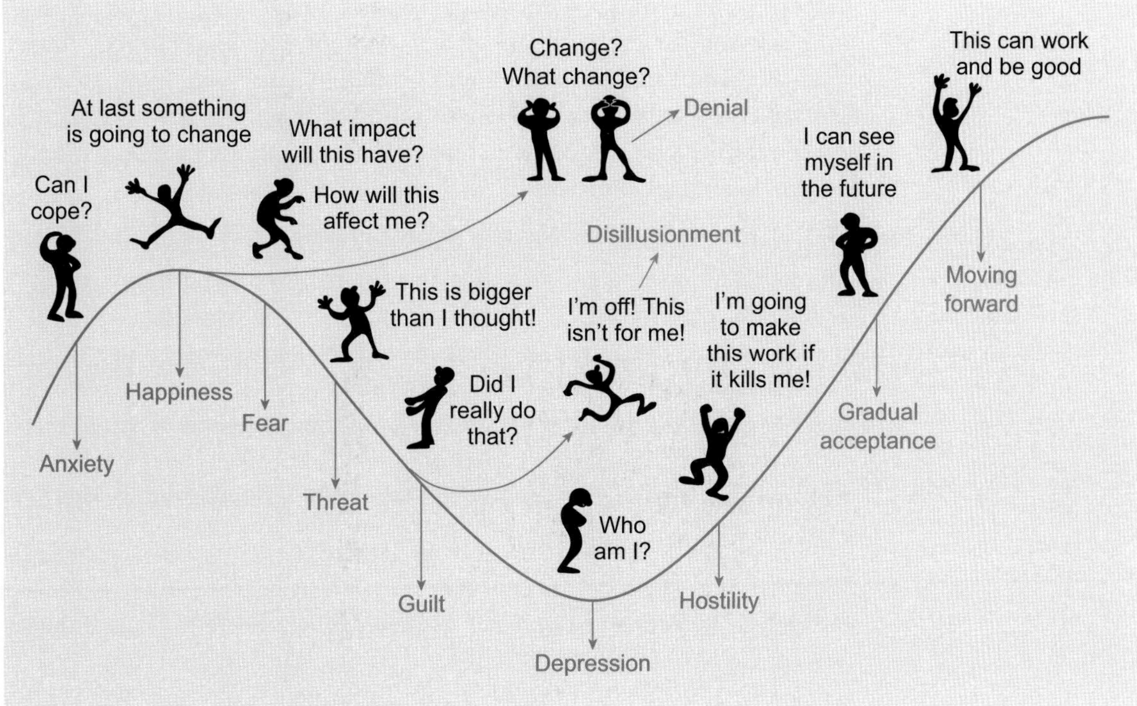

Figure 4.4 The change curve (EI4Change, 2012)

The way in which the 'psychological contract' plays a central role in how change is experienced in the workplace is now increasingly recognised. This idea can help in understanding better what change actually means for staff, which can help managers negotiate the process of change more sensitively and smoothly (Figure 4.4). The psychological contract (Morrison and Robinson, 1997) refers to the unwritten expectations that employees have of the organisation. It relates not only to factors such as pay and work but also to socio-emotional factors such as trust and loyalty. Thompson and Bunderson (2003) also argue that it involves an ideological element, something that captures the 'moral imagination'. This can be seen as particularly important in health and social care. People are often drawn to their work because they believe they can 'make a difference'; they are often highly committed to a cause.

Drawing on her research on the merger of three hospitals, Anita Rogers (2010) argues that staff viewed the organisation as breaching the psychological contract; they were angry and mystified by the speed and scale of the changes and were not convinced that the changes were driven by a desire to improve patient outcomes. As with the work of Ingham (2011), Rogers witnessed a sense of loss among employees, who were grieving for the past and who felt completely disconnected from what was happening around them. Her research showed that managers had failed to facilitate the change in terms of making sense and hope for the future. Instead, resistance turned into a loss of meaning. The change took place but, you might fairly ask, at what cost?

This does not mean that change inevitably breaches the psychological contract. Rather, it suggests that managers have a responsibility to understand the attachments their staff may have to particular contexts and ways of working, and to support staff to manage transitions in a focused and sensitive way. While the ultimate task of the manager may be to 'get the job done', it is necessary to support people through their concerns, anxieties, and even resistance, to ensure that change is achieved in a way that minimises the 'casualties' (see Chapter 5 for more on managing stress and transitions).

Managers must also be mindful that they are being continually observed and judged in periods of change. Articulating a version of change that is far removed from that expressed by staff can damage the change process – so managers must be in tune with people's experiences (Woodward and Hendry, 2004). This links clearly to the model of distributed leadership described in Chapter 3, and requires managers to actively encourage stakeholders to participate in the change process, even if this means supporting them through initial phases of resistance. In this way, managers can help to create communities of practice, where everyone is invited to take responsibility for the change in a way which promotes learning and excellence (rather than control) (Dopson et al., 2008), as you saw in the Canadian example in Box 4.3. This emphasises that implementing change is as much about leadership as it is about management.

4.6 Conclusion

While individuals have different attitudes to change – at one extreme, constantly seeking change and, at the other, avoiding it at all costs – change is a disruptive and often unpredictable occurrence for everyone. It rarely takes place in a straightforward fashion but is a meandering process with stops, starts and jolts in between. You may be halfway into a change initiative, but with new information and new learning gained, you may have to revisit your initial assessment and goals. Change requires attention to structural and procedural issues, and models, frameworks and tools can give guidance here; but it also requires attention to inevitable human concerns. However, despite the challenges, change represents real opportunities for managers to help improve health and social care services, which is why people keep on doing it!

This chapter touched on just some of the many models, frameworks and practical tools that can support front-line managers in planning their own change initiative, or responding to challenging and fast-moving changes from above. It highlighted the importance of **contextual**, **goal**, **team** and **personal awareness**, and showed that leadership and management are both required for successful change to happen. Above all else, this chapter argued that, while change takes place in the context of organisations, its true success depends firmly on *people*, and this is perhaps the greatest challenge and opportunity facing managers.

As a manager involved in change, maintaining openness, flexibility and tolerance of ambiguity can strengthen the possibilities of a successful outcome, as can strong leadership. Drawing on practical tools, combined with a realistic optimism and an emphasis on maintaining core values in providing care, can help managers to reframe the aims or effects of change.

Key points

- While change presents several challenges for managers in health and social care, it is often required to prompt an improvement in both services and people's lives.
- A number of tools can provide practical support to managers who are responding to top-down change or initiating their own change, but these should be drawn on with a critical approach and an awareness of the inherent complexities of change.

- While change takes place within organisations, it happens through people. Any manager implementing a change must understand who they need to influence, when and how. But they also need to be sensitive and prepared for the psychological disruption that change initiatives can present to staff.
- Successful change cannot be achieved through management or leadership alone. It requires the skills, competences and qualities of management and leadership working in tandem.

References

Allcorn, S., Baum, H.S., Diamond, M.A. and Stein, H.F. (1996) *The Human Cost of Management Failure: Organizational downsizing at a general hospital*, London, Quorum Books.

Barley, S.R. and Tolbert, P.S. (1997) 'Institutionalization and structuration: studying the links between action and institution', *Organization Studies*, vol. 18, pp. 93–117.

Beresford, P., Fleming, J., Glynn, M., Bewley, C., Croft, S., Branfield, F. and Postle, K. (2011) *Supporting People: Towards a person-centred approach*, Bristol, The Policy Press.

Chartered Institute of Personnel and Development (CIPD) (2010) *PESTLE Analysis Resource Summary* [Online]. Available at www.cipd.co.uk/hr-resources/factsheets/pestle-analysis.aspx (Accessed 21 November 2012).

Dopson, S., Fitzgerald, L. and Ferlie, E. (2008) 'Understanding change and innovation in healthcare settings: reconceptualizing the active role of context', *Journal of Change Management*, vol. 8, no. 3, pp. 213–31.

Emotional Intelligence 4 Change (2012) 'Lightbulb moments – building resilience with emotional intelligence' [Online]. Available at www.ei4change.com/reliance.htm (Accessed 27 November 2012).

Hatch, M.J. (1997) *Organization Theory: Modern, symbolic and postmodern perspectives*, Oxford, Oxford University Press.

Hensmans, M. (2003) 'Social movement organizations: a metaphor for strategic actors in institutional fields', *Organization Studies*, vol. 24, pp. 355–81.

Higgs, M. and Rowland, D. (2010) 'Emperors with clothes on: the role of self-awareness in developing effective change leadership', *Journal of Change Management*, vol. 10, no. 4, pp. 369–85.

Iles, V. (2006) *Really Managing Healthcare* (2nd edition), Maidenhead, Open University Press.

Ingham, N.W. (2011) *Organisational Change and Resistance: An oral history of the rundown of a long-stay institution for people with learning difficulties*, unpublished PhD thesis, Milton Keynes, The Open University.

Kotter, J.P. (1996) 'Leading change: why transformation efforts fail', reprinted in *Best of Harvard Business Review*, January 2007, Harvard Business School Press (Reprint R0701J).

Lewin, K. (1958) 'Group decisions and social change', in Swanson, G.E., Newcomb, T.M. and Hartley, E.L. (eds) *Readings on Social Psychology*, New York, Holt, Rhinehart and Winston.

Morrison, E.W. and Robinson, S.L. (1997) 'When employees feel betrayed: a model of how psychological contract violation develops', *Academy of Management Review*, vol. 22, pp. 226–58.

Nasim, S. and Sushil (2011) 'Revisiting organizational change: exploring the paradox of managing continuity and change', *Journal of Change Management*, vol. 11, no. 2, pp. 185–206.

Pettigrew, A. and Whipp, R. (1991) *Managing Change for Competitive Success*, Oxford, Blackwell.

Reay, T. and Hinings, C.R. (2005) 'The recomposition of an organizational field: health care in Alberta', *Organization Studies*, vol. 26, pp. 351–84.

Reay, T., Golden-Biddle, K. and Germann, K. (2006) 'Legitimising a new role: small wins and microprocesses of change', *Academy of Management Journal*, vol. 49, no. 5, pp. 977–98.

Rogers, A. (2010) 'Death by a thousand cuts: the psychological contract and organisational reconfiguration in health care', presentation at the British Academy of Management Conference, Sheffield, September.

Shacklady-Smith, A. (2006) 'Appreciating the challenge of change', in Walshe, K. and Smith, J. (eds) *Healthcare Management*, Maidenhead, Open University Press, pp. 381–98.

Simons, J. and MacDonald, L. (2006) 'Changing practice: implementing validated paediatric pain assessment tools', *Journal of Child Health Care*, vol. 10, no. 2, pp. 160–76.

Smale, G.G. (1998) *Mapping Change and Innovation*, London, National Institute for Social Work.

Smith, K. and Berg, D. (1987) 'A paradoxical conception of group dynamics', *Human Relations*, vol. 40, pp. 633–58.

Stein, H.F. (2001) 'Adapting to doom: the group psychology of an organization threatened with cultural extinction', *Political Psychology*, vol. 13, no. 1, pp. 113–43.

Thompson, J.A. and Bunderson, J.S. (2003) 'Violations of principle: ideological currency in the psychological contract',*Academy of Management Review*, vol. 28, pp. 571–86.

Woodward, S. and Hendry, C. (2004) 'Leading and coping with change', *Journal of Change Management*, vol. 4, no. 2, pp. 155–83.

Zucker, L.G. (1987) 'Normal change or risky business: institutional effects on the "hazard" of change in hospital organizations', *Journal of Management Studies*, vol. 24, pp. 671–700.

Chapter 5 Managing stress, loss and transition with a caring face

Wayne Taylor

5.1 Introduction

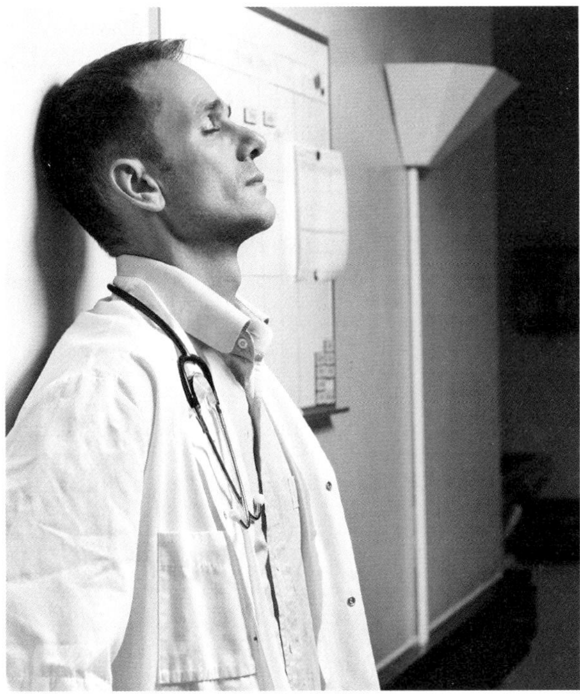

Figure 5.1 Working in health and social care can be extremely stressful, even at the best of times

In a book on the social determinants of health, the World Health Organization warns:

> As social beings, we need not only good material conditions but, from early childhood onwards, we need to feel valued and appreciated. We need friends, we need more sociable societies, we need to feel useful, and we need to exercise a significant degree of control over meaningful work.

> Without these we become more prone to depression, drug use, anxiety, hostility and feelings of hopelessness, which all rebound on physical health.
>
> (Wilkinson and Marmot, 2003)

Chapter 4 deals with managing change, and the intricacies of a manager's role in guiding and leading staff through periods of significant upheaval at work. However, even when not facing such major change, working within health and social care can be a stressful experience (Figure 5.1). On top of the daily strains of working with vulnerable people and complex care needs, individual staff members also deal with other trials and tribulations that are part of wider life experiences. So this chapter steps back from major organisational change to explore the more general and personal nature of work-based stress and wellbeing. Drawing on one unfolding case study, these issues are examined from the perspective of a manager who is concerned to follow the model of caring management and leadership advocated in this book.

We all face experiences of loss and transition in our lives. Some individuals do better – or show greater resilience – in coping than others, but everyone will struggle to cope at times. It has long been known that stressful circumstances – in which people experience worry, anxiety and/or an inability to cope – are damaging to health and may even lead to premature death (Wilkinson and Marmot, 2003). They are also likely to have an impact at work. At the time of writing (2012), stress was the biggest workplace hazard in the UK, affecting some 435,000 employees with a total of 9.8 million working days lost in 2008/09 (HSE, 2010). More worryingly still, there is some evidence to suggest that this is a rising trend, especially in areas of service provision such as education (Kinman, 2011) and health and social care. Here, limited (and often diminishing) resources result in continuing cuts in staffing levels and conditions at work. Such circumstances are likely to increase problems such as 'burn-out' (Bakker et al., 2008) and lead to poor morale and declining levels of motivation.

It is difficult to draw a clear line between stress arising from factors such as bereavement, loss and change and work-related stress caused by occupational culture and the wider contexts of politics and power because of the blurring caused by the porous nature of grief and emotional disturbance. In fact, this idea of blurring is a recurrent theme in this chapter. For example, open grief and obvious signs of anxiety necessitate a personal response that may infringe on some managers' perceptions of appropriate personal and professional relationships. Therefore, a key theme for this chapter is **personal awareness** – the first building block of the **fully rounded caring manager**.

The argument presented here is that the 'emotionally literate' manager (Goleman, 1995; Goleman et al., 2002) should care about work-based stress and the personal and interpersonal issues associated with it in a manner that Clarke (2001) suggests fulfils the moral and ethical obligation to care. This means going beyond the management function of caring for ourselves, the staff we supervise, and the users of the services we provide, to encompass the proactive leadership role of promoting wellbeing (Turner et al., 2002; Aked et al., 2008, 2010).

Someone who is emotionally literate understands both their own and other people's emotions. They have the ability to listen to and empathise with others, and can express emotions in a productive way.

The chapter begins by exploring what we understand about people's experiences of stress, loss and transition, and goes on to consider how these impact on the workplace. Drawing on both empirical evidence and theoretical models, it asks how the health and social care manager, committed to managing and leading 'with a caring face', might respond to these emotional disturbances as both a manager and a leader, maintaining their own wellbeing and promoting the wellbeing of other people.

The chapter concludes by returning to the warning by the World Health Organization cited above, to explore some of the wider themes of maintaining mental health and wellbeing in the frenetic world of health and social care.

More generally, this chapter explores the following three core questions.

- Why should a manager address issues of stress, loss and transition in the workplace?
- What are the key features of managing and leading 'with a caring face'?
- How can effective leadership help to deal with issues of stress, loss and anxiety?

5.2 Stress, anxiety and transition in the workplace

As suggested in the Introduction, working in health and social care is in itself stressful. Certain occupations seem to entail particularly high stress levels, for example practising medicine and nursing. Social care workers are also high on the list of people whose jobs make them prone to sickness and absenteeism because of stress.

Stress occurs when habitual psychological ways of coping with pressure fail or a physical illness develops as a result of psychological pressures. The cost of stress to individuals and their families is high, and so are the costs to society, as employees become sick or leave their jobs (Seden and Katz, 2003).

People working in health and social care may be particularly prone to 'compassion fatigue', a condition characterised by deep emotional and physical exhaustion and symptoms resembling depression and post-traumatic stress disorder (Figley, 2002; Adams et al., 2006).

Walsh (1987) suggests that the stresses experienced by social care professionals in their work make them particularly vulnerable to 'burn-out'. This is characterised by a state of physical, emotional and mental exhaustion, feelings of helplessness, and the development of negative attitudes towards self, work, life and other people (Walsh, 1987). Many people have some of these feelings, some of the time, but what characterises burn-out is its chronic and overwhelming nature. Walsh also suggests that the gap between the expectations workers may have of their roles and the realities of their work life may contribute to the stress they feel.

The first task of an effective manager in managing issues of work-related stress is to be open and honest – especially when resources are scarce. When the stress or anxiety is being caused by factors intrinsic to the workplace, the first concern should be to address these, where possible. In fact, there is a range of established organisational strategies for reducing stress, such as emphasising task and environmental redesign, flexibility, or participative management. A useful source here might be your union or professional association, which should be able to give you information on work-related stress in your sector, as well as details of campaigns, policy developments and other people you might contact.

Staff morale can be negatively affected by a manager who denies either organisational constraints or the impact of spending cuts. In conversation, practitioners often say that when managers minimise or ignore the demands and pressures on them, it contributes significantly to the levels of stress they experience (Seden and Katz, 2003), highlighting the unwitting role that managers can play in contributing to workplace stress.

At the same time, as Seden and Katz emphasise, a manager's daily work often brings them into contact with the emotions, feelings and reactions of staff – and service users – towards all kinds of life event. Personal events and life transitions in the private lives of the people we work with may exert as profound an influence on their performance and motivation at work as more tangible factors such as a decline in pay and/or conditions.

Becoming a manager can be a hugely stressful transition as you adapt to your new role in an organisation.

The concept of transition remains a powerful and persuasive concept in health and social care because it describes the impact of the changes and adjustments which happen to us all at various points in our lives. Experiences from being made redundant, retiring, changing partner or moving house, to bereavement and illness, are all key events that involve some form of emotional disturbance before the individual eventually returns to a new equilibrium. While transitions are part of most people's life experience, they deal with them differently, depending on how challenging it is for them, the amount of support available, and other stress factors in their life at the time. And this will affect how the transition is experienced. It is important for a manager to recognise this and to lead staff through transitions sensitively.

Transition has immediate relevance also for patients, service users and their carers, who may be facing transitions such as entering care, adjusting to a recent diagnosis, or facing the death of a loved one.

Bereavement, loss and grief

One of the biggest transitions everyone faces at some stage is the death of a loved one (Figure 5.2). The first part of the case study describes the effect on Dervla of her mother's death.

Case study 5.1: Dervla

The death of Dervla's mother hadn't been a shock; they had all seen it coming for months. Of course, it was a shock when she returned from the doctor's surgery and said she had cancer. The Macmillan nurses had been brilliant and were there to help them both face reality with courage. It wasn't the best six months of Dervla's life (her memory was all black and white, as if the colour had been washed out of the world) but her mother's faith had helped them both. It was also touching that the neighbours and everyone at the temple had been so supportive. It was nice to know that her mother would be missed by other people in the community. Although the death hadn't been a shock, the pain of her loss had been quite a shock to Dervla.

Figure 5.2 The epitaph of comedian Spike Milligan (1918–2002): (in Gaelic) 'I told you I was ill'

Grief is a natural response to any loss. Grief is felt when someone close to us dies, as in Dervla's case, but it can also be experienced in any separation from someone or something whose significance has an impact on our physical or emotional wellbeing. It is the emotional suffering you feel when something or someone you love is taken away. Any loss can cause grief, including the following:

- a relationship break-up
- loss of health

- losing a job
- loss of financial stability
- a miscarriage
- loss of social status
- death of a pet
- loss of a cherished dream
- a loved one's serious illness
- loss of a friendship
- loss of safety after a trauma
- children leaving home.

Usually, the more significant the loss, the more intense the grief. However, the intensity of the grief felt – and the ability to cope with this – depends on the person's level of resilience. Some people respond with intense emotions to relatively minor experiences of loss because their resilience is low.

5.3 Theories of loss and transition

Figure 5.3 Words associated with 'feeling loss'

The experience of loss can provoke a complexity of negative emotions (see Figure 5.3), impacting on the individual, those around them, and on society more generally. The theoretical material on understanding how we deal with loss and major transitions has developed over time and involves a variety of perspectives concerned with examining these different impacts. Generally, earlier theories concentrated on the individual, while more recent ones tend to focus as much on the social and cultural context as on the individual experiencing the loss (see Box 5.1).

Box 5.1: Research on loss

The three early major theories of loss are as follows.

John Bowlby (1969, 1973, 1980) was the first to argue that what he calls 'separation anxiety' is the price people pay for being attached to someone or something. Bowlby, and those who have adapted his ideas, present the force of attachment to the mother, other early care givers and significant people in our lives as a powerful and universal force. Since the early 1950s, Bowlby's theories about attachment have permeated studies and practice in care work, and have been critiqued, developed and refined to include attachment to culture and place. Bowlby's idea that attachment is a characteristic of human beings 'from cradle to grave' has been developed and attachment is viewed as a significant factor in adult life as well as in childhood.

Second, taking a more psychosocial approach, Colin Murray Parkes (1986) considered the social dimensions that explain losses and their psychological effects. He points out that people are generally good at adapting to change but suggests that some life events are more difficult, and so potentially more dangerous, than others. He identifies three distinguishing criteria for these most difficult changes, which he calls 'psychosocial transitions'. He argues that, as individuals, we all inhabit an 'assumptive world'; that is, a world that contains what we consider to be true based on our previous experiences. When new experiences challenge this truth, revising the assumptive world is not easy. Thoughts and behaviour can no longer be taken for granted. The familiar world becomes unfamiliar: we have to think before we act and this takes time and energy. We no longer have confidence in our assumptive world to keep us safe and the process of adaptation can be painful.

Third, Peter Marris (1986) offers a sociological explanation of loss, using three key concepts to explore the link between loss, transition and the way we experience the world.

- **The conservative impulse** – we all have an in-built bias towards predictability and resist change. The drive here is towards finding ways of feeling safe in our environment and of reducing uncertainty.
- **Structures of meaning** – similar to Parkes' idea of 'assumptive worlds', we all – if we are lucky – find attachment and meaning in our work environments. And struggle if we don't.
- **Grieving** – is the psychological process of adjustment to loss. It leaves us lost in previously familiar environments.

(Based on Seden and Katz, 2003, pp. 292–3)

Recall your own experiences of loss. Do any of these theoretical ideas help you to understand those experiences?

As understanding about experiences of loss and transition has grown, so has our ability to respond. Elisabeth Kübler-Ross (1970) pioneered methods in the support and counselling of personal trauma and grief associated with death and dying. Her ideas were used to dramatically improve the understanding and practice in hospice care, particularly through the application of her model of the five stages of grief (Table 5.1). Significantly, while her original focus was on death and bereavement, the 'grief cycle' model is useful for understanding our own and other people's emotional reaction to any personal trauma and change, irrespective of the cause.

Table 5.1 The five stages of grief (© Elisabeth Kübler-Ross, 1969)

Stage	Description
Denial	Denial is a conscious or unconscious refusal to accept facts, information, reality, etc., relating to the situation concerned. It's a defence mechanism and perfectly natural. Some people can become locked in this stage when dealing with a traumatic change that can be ignored. Death of course is not particularly easy to avoid or evade indefinitely.
Anger	Anger can manifest in different ways. People dealing with emotional upset can be angry with themselves, and/or with others, especially those close to them. Knowing this helps keep [them] detached and non-judgemental when experiencing the anger of someone who is very upset.
Bargaining	Traditionally the bargaining stage for people facing death can involve attempting to bargain with whatever God the person believes in. People facing less serious trauma can bargain or seek to negotiate a compromise. For example 'Can we still be friends?' when facing a break-up. Bargaining rarely provides a sustainable solution, especially if it's a matter of life or death.
Depression	Also referred to as preparatory grieving. In a way it's the dress rehearsal or the practice run for the 'aftermath' although this stage means different things depending on whom it involves. It's a sort of acceptance with emotional attachment. It's natural to feel sadness and regret, fear, uncertainty, etc. It shows that the person has at least begun to accept the reality.
Acceptance	Again this stage definitely varies according to the person's situation, although broadly it is an indication that there is some emotional detachment and objectivity. People dying can enter this stage a long time before the people they leave behind, who must necessarily pass through their own individual stages of dealing with the grief.

At which stage do you think Dervla was in this grief cycle?

The stages of the grief cycle can be thought of as a 'change model' for helping to understand and deal with the impact of trauma and emotional disturbance. It also reminds us that someone else's perspective – and their resilience in facing grief – may be different from our own, and they may experience each stage of grief differently. Managers are, therefore, required to deal with staff individually to meet their needs.

Quantifying stress

Despite this differential effect, researchers have attempted to quantify the emotional and/or the psychological impact of significant life events by devising scales to assess the emotional impact of a wide range of life events as experienced by the 'average' individual. One widely used example is a scale compiled by Holmes and Rahe (1967) which calculates the total score for a range of potentially difficult life events experienced in the same time period (Figure 5.4).

Can we – and should we – quantify human suffering?

Figure 5.4 Some like it hot?

Holmes and Rahe's stress scale (1967)

The complete scale covers more than 40 potentially stress-inducing items, including such events as the death of a spouse, divorce and imprisonment. Even positive stresses, such as getting married, going on holiday or Christmas, are included in the scale. Added together, the result is used to indicate susceptibility to stress. A score of less than 150 life change units suggests the individual has a 30 per cent chance of developing a stress-related illness. However, this rises to a 50 per cent chance when the score is between 150 and 299, and reaches 80 per cent when the score is over 300.

There are several versions of Holmes and Rahe's inventory which you can complete online.

Of course, it is difficult to quantify someone's response to such a diverse range of life events, and the scale has changed over time to reflect changing social expectations and cultural contexts. Nevertheless, it offers several useful insights into the ways in which we cope with transitions. Change, even when it is chosen and possibly positive, appears to contain the potential to be stressful. Significantly, it is worth noting that work-related events appear nine times as high-scoring stressful life events, including 'trouble with the boss', implying that, as a manager, you might be a 'stressful life event' for your staff.

How useful do you think standardised inventories, such as the Holmes and Rahe scale, are for a manager wanting to understand and support their staff?

5.4 Stress, health and wellbeing at work

Holmes and Rahe's scale is often used to assess the likelihood of someone being at risk because of high levels of stress. Any stress, which can lead to feelings of anxiety, insecurity, low self-esteem and lack of control, can have powerful effects on health. Such psychological risks accumulate during life and increase the chances of poor mental health and premature death (see Box 5.2). Long periods of anxiety and insecurity, and a lack of supportive friendships, are damaging in whichever period of life they arise. As a result, even if someone is not having to deal with a particular loss or transition, it is still important to be aware of all the factors which can cumulatively contribute to stress over time. A caring manager can try to put in place supportive systems to enhance wellbeing among all employees, at all times.

Box 5.2: Why do psychosocial factors affect physical health?

In emergencies, our hormones and nervous system prepare us to deal with an immediate physical threat by triggering the fight-or-flight response: raising the heart rate and increasing alertness. This diverts energy and resources away from both the cardiovascular and the immune system. For brief periods, this does not matter, but if people feel tense too often, or the tension goes on for a long time, they become vulnerable to a wide range of conditions including infections, diabetes, high blood pressure, heart attack, stroke, depression and aggression (Wilkinson and Marmot, 2003, pp. 12–13).

The next part of the case study concerns the effect on Dervla at work of her mother's death.

Case study 5.2: Dervla (continued)

At the time of the death of Dervla's mother, her manager, Angelique, felt that she had coped with her bereavement in a calm and emotionally mature manner. She admired her for it. But six months later, Angelique just didn't know what to make of Dervla. She used to be a manager's dream – always bubbly and bright, a keen team member, and always as sharp as a knife when it came to her caseload. But, these days, she seemed to be permanently sullen and irritable, uncharacteristically cynical in meetings and, as her last supervision made plain, at serious risk of losing her grip on her caseload. Angelique just didn't understand what was going on. She had always been close to Dervla but felt like they were drifting apart.

Dervla just didn't know what was going on. She had always loved work; the feeling that she was 'making a difference' helped her get out of bed in the morning. She used to find work cathartic and it had been a comfort to immerse herself in work during her mother's final months. But now she found that everything about work was just so exhausting. She began to fall behind not long after starting back and never seemed to have the energy to catch up again. Instead, more work came in and she began to feel overwhelmed. Normally, she would have gone to Angelique right away but she wasn't feeling normal. She didn't want to be seen as a failure at work as well!

Could Dervla be depressed as a result of her grief and the transition she has to make because of her loss?

High levels of stress can lead to burn-out, a sense of loss of control, disengagement from work and, ultimately, ill health. Dervla had experienced the trauma of losing her mother, and had also lost the sense of fulfilment from, and engagement with, work, which she used to enjoy. Employees who have a sense of energetic engagement in what they do find that, instead of experiencing work as stressful and demanding, they look on it as a positive challenge which enhances their wellbeing. According to Maslach and Leiter (1997), engagement is characterised by energy, involvement, and efficacy. They argue that, in the case of burn-out, energy turns into exhaustion, involvement into cynicism, and efficacy into ineffectiveness.

It seems important, therefore, that managers ensure staff can feel engaged at work, to enhance their overall wellbeing. Experiencing positive relationships, having some control over your life, and having a sense of purpose are all important attributes of wellbeing (Aked et al., 2010). A high level of wellbeing enhances health and our ability to cope with all aspects of life (MacKian, 2010). Perhaps not surprisingly, therefore, there has been much interest in the notion of wellbeing (Turner et al., 2002; Aked et al., 2008, 2010).

While it might seem obvious that an individual can do a lot to enhance their own wellbeing, such as taking time to relax, exercise or meditate, research suggests that enhancing wellbeing at the collective level, through connecting with other people, volunteering or taking on new responsibilities, can also enhance wellbeing, not only for the individual but also for the community involved (Aked et al., 2008).

5.5 Managing with a caring face

Figure 5.5 The workplace is not always stressful!

Case study 5.3: Dervla (continued)

Dervla was so ashamed. She had promised to present a review of recent literature on adoption law to the team. She'd had six months to do it. But she hadn't done it and now she was letting down Angelique. It wasn't that she didn't want to; rather, she never seemed to have the energy to sit down and start. She wasn't usually a procrastinator but her heart just was not in it. What did it matter anyway? The whole place just felt really negative these days; people didn't seem to look out for each other any more; everyone was so stressed trying to hold on to their jobs; Angelique was never around for them any more. Dervla just wanted to run away and hide.

In the case study, Angelique had become aware that Dervla was not coping, and arranged a meeting to discuss the situation. Angelique needed to ensure Dervla was on top of her workload, but realised she would have to handle the situation sensitively. In such situations, caring managers can draw on both management and leadership skills in developing a style of management that builds on their **personal awareness** and emotional intelligence, to support staff, acknowledging their humanity, and dealing sensitively with strong feelings.

This kind of approach can play an important part in retaining staff, keeping morale high, and enabling people to deal with the inevitable pressures of work in health and social care (Figure 5.5).

Case study 5.4: Angelique

Angelique recognised that Dervla was struggling with her workload and didn't seem to be as organised as she used to be. She wondered if Dervla might benefit from developing her time-management skills. She remembered she first began to use the technique when she had been studying and working. She had been amazed by the way it put her back in charge of her life at a time when she was under considerable stress. The great thing was that the idea of a work–life balance was built into planning and she thought this would help Dervla, but she wasn't sure how to broach the subject as Dervla was so prickly at the moment.

Angelique was drawing on her own experience to try to enhance Dervla's sense of control and wellbeing. Although she could not control the wider circumstances of Dervla's stress, she felt she could help Dervla develop her personal sense of control, or her 'power-from-within' (Wong, 2003; see Chapter 1).

Angelique had identified time management as an essential skill that helps to keep work under control, increase productivity and reduce stress. Poor time management leads to frustration, lack of motivation and poor self-esteem, and it can even undermine health and wellbeing. People working in health and social care often care for highly vulnerable people. Therefore, good time management is crucial to help ensure safety for yourself, the people you manage and the patients or service users. The **time management tool** will help you do this.

The build-up of stress in Dervla's life meant she was managing her time badly, resulting in more anxiety for her and potentially putting her clients at risk as well. In choosing to identify a practical tool that might support Dervla, Angelique was leading by example. Drawing on her own **personal awareness** of the benefits of good time management, she was confident that, together, they could improve the situation.

Case study 5.5: Dervla and Angelique

It definitely didn't happen in the way Dervla had anticipated. She had been dreading the supervision session and felt she was being persecuted by Angelique. As a result, she went into the meeting with a defensive strategy and an aggressive manner. However, something happened – something to do with the way Angelique was with her – that made her remember their friendship. Angelique had seemed so distant and out of reach recently, and yet here she was for her.

And that was when the floodgates opened. It all came out in sobbing gushes. Her husband's redundancy, her son's problems at school, her constant feeling of panic, and how isolated she felt at work when she used to love it. She told Angelique she felt totally inadequate when she had to go home at the end of the day to support her family and Angelique was always staying late, working weekends and never seemed to stop. Dervla didn't have the energy for that.

Clearly, there was more going on in Dervla's life than Angelique had realised. People have different thresholds for managing transition, depending on their previous experience and background. Marris (1986) suggests there are four sets of conditions that may help or hinder people to adjust when faced with loss or transition.

1 Childhood experiences of attachment affect our general world view and resilience in the face of loss.
2 Conflicting emotions or unresolved meaning can make the process harder.
3 The less opportunity to prepare for the loss or transition, the more traumatic the experience will be.
4 Events after the loss, or during the transition period, may support or frustrate the recovery process.

Dervla's transition after the death of her mother was being frustrated by other stressful factors in her life. Often, clumsily managed transitions become a crisis, and Dervla's situation could have precipitated a crisis in her work life as well. As you have also seen, people who feel engaged at work generally experience a greater sense of wellbeing and are therefore more able to cope with stress. While Dervla had personal problems she was facing *outside* work which were making her feel less able to cope *in* work, she also revealed to Angelique that something had changed *in the workplace* recently which undermined the comfort she used to feel there.

The meeting gave Angelique an opportunity to identify possible solutions to support Dervla through her ongoing stress and to prevent a crisis occurring. How effective do you think Angelique's solution of personal time management would be? What else might she have done as well?

5.6 Leading with a caring face?

Figure 5.6 What does your manager care about?

Can management lead with a caring face in the competitive market which is increasingly the context for health and social care? Everybody is under increasing pressure and even well-intentioned managers like Angelique can struggle to meet human needs as well as organisational needs (Figure 5.6).

Case study 5.6: Angelique (continued)

Angelique was desperate to manage Dervla in a caring way, but her lack of engagement with work was beginning to impact on the rest of the team and the targets they were working towards. Although Angelique wanted to support Dervla as an individual, as a manager, she also had to keep her eye on the wider team and she was under pressure to make efficiency savings. She had been working later and later, and couldn't remember the last time she had a weekend off. But she was in charge now and wasn't that how it was meant to be? Nobody else was going to do it!

For Dervla, her work life revolved around her own personal difficulties but, in her role as a manager, Angelique had to keep her eye on the team, their goals and the organisational context as well. However, it is questionable whether Angelique's approach is sustainable in the long run; as her stress levels increase, it will become increasingly clear to her that the life crises, losses, transitions and uncertainties that are part of other people's lives are also part of the manager's lot.

From your experience, can you think of a manager who seemed to be stressed? How did this manifest itself in the workplace? What impact did it have on you? What do you think could or should have been done to improve the situation?

As a manager and leader of others, Angelique could also have benefited from using the **personal awareness tool** reflectively; applying it to her own work–life balance and motivation, but recognising that other people will be different and hence have different needs and ways of coping.

An effective management response to work-based stress must involve **personal awareness** first and foremost. A manager can lead by example in managing their own wellbeing and encouraging this in others. Perhaps Angelique was focusing too much on helping Dervla develop *her* **personal awareness** that she was neglecting *her own* self-awareness. Dervla had suggested to Angelique that she had difficulty living up to her example, and this might have been undermining team morale for others as well. Managers must be aware of their own impact on the team, developing emotionally intelligent relationships with other people, and ensuring that relationships between team members promote rather than undermine collective wellbeing. As poor morale is also likely to impact on performance, a sensitive approach to individual and team wellbeing will also support **goal awareness**.

While all this might seem a tall order, research indicates that what is of most value, to most people and most often, is simply the commitment to be there, listening to the individual's concerns and providing emotional support (Kotter and Schlesinger, 2009). This suggests that emotional intelligence is integral to the wellbeing of the individual, the team, and the goals they aspire to.

The fourth building block of a **fully rounded caring manager – contextual awareness** – is also important here because it reiterates a key argument of this book. That is, in thinking about management and leadership, a focus on individual skills and personal qualities (while useful and, in the case of the issues discussed in this chapter, ethically necessary) only takes us so far. To go beyond this, it is necessary to engage in a critical analysis of these roles within the context of the organisation and with an understanding of the wider economic and political environment. This brings us back to the WHO report cited at the beginning of this chapter.

Loss, anxiety and the associated symptoms of stress are psychosocial problems that – alongside help and assistance to the individual – require social solutions. As the report goes on to argue, this necessitates a policy recognition that 'in schools, workplaces and other institutions, the quality of the social environment and material security are often as important to health as the physical environment' and 'institutions that can give people a sense of belonging, participating and being valued are likely to be healthier places than those where people feel excluded disregarded and used' (Wilkinson and Marmot, 2003, p. 13).

What else could Angelique have done? Was she addressing the individual at the expense of thinking about the wider context?

There is the danger that a manager dealing with individuals and their transition experiences, in their concern to support the very particular needs of that person, may either overlook or even try to downplay any wider structural or organisational issues that may be relevant. Talking to Dervla about her time-management skills and giving her a practical tool certainly looks like the actions of a caring and proactive manager; but what more might Angelique have done? Dervla's outburst focused on her personal emotions, feelings and problems, but having a meaningful role at work is one of the key contributors to overall wellbeing. So, if Dervla felt happier at work, it could have helped her to cope better with what was going on in her life.

Six months after a bereavement can be a key transition point as the individual tries to move towards the acceptance stage of Kübler-Ross's model. By then, colleagues very often have forgotten that there was a bereavement, as grief can be invisible, yet their bereaved colleague is still living with it daily. Angelique's recognition of her grief was probably well received, in making Dervla realise that she had good reason to feel unhappy and frustrated, and to not be coping as well as usual.

Chapter 4 shows how, when dealing with large-scale change, managers have to be sensitive to the psychological disruption that change initiatives can present to staff, and how an awareness of the organisational culture, and how that promotes or undermines change, is also important to support collective transition. But when the focus of transition is on one individual, there is the danger of overlooking wider organisational issues, which might, as in Dervla's experience, play a part in aggravating stress, at the expense of trying to fix the individual rather than the associated stress factors in the wider context.

What can a manager learn from this in terms of managing someone through a transition at work?

In the economic climate at the time of writing (2012), managers in health and social care are dealing with the complex fall-out from large-scale organisational changes due to austerity measures, alongside the inevitable individual casualties which result. The challenge for managers at such times is to support staff, both individually and collectively, when they might be facing uncertain personal futures as well as difficult organisational changes (Harvey et al., 2009).

5.7 Conclusion

Managing and understanding the impact of stress, loss and transitions is an important part of a manager's role. Losses of all kinds trigger a range of strong feelings and reactions, all of which are best acknowledged and managed openly in the workplace (Seden and Katz, 2003). Furthermore, most of the situations which bring people into contact with health and social care professionals and their managers involve elements of separation, transition and loss. So, a manager who is aware of different approaches to dealing with loss, stress and transitions is better placed to support people who use services, as well as those who provide them.

Effective management and leadership need to acknowledge the emotional impact of caring work on the people who do it. Managing a service can only be done well if account is taken of the consequences of stress and transition for everyone in the workplace, both employees and service users. The manager who 'leads by example', demonstrating an awareness that everyone is prone to stress, and likely to experience loss and other difficult transitions at some stage, is better placed to foster a work environment which supports individuals as needed. This can be a powerful (and therapeutic) model for others, enhancing the wellbeing of the whole organisation.

Key points

- Feelings of loss, anxiety, insecurity, low self-esteem, social isolation, and lack of control over work and home life, have powerful effects on people's health.
- While transitions are part of most people's life experience, factors such as the challenges to a person's assumptive world and structures of meaning, together with the amount of support available, will affect how the transition is experienced.
- Strategies for managing staff and service users who are experiencing loss, stress or transitions should reflect the recognised shift in emphasis from focusing on the individual to a greater awareness of the importance of the social and cultural context of health and social care.
- An appreciation of the stages of grief helps managers support their own and other people's emotional reaction to personal trauma and change, irrespective of the cause.

- Employees with a high level of wellbeing will feel more engaged, having a sense of energetic and effective connection with their work. Managers can lead by example and support staff wellbeing at the team or organisational level as well as at an individual level.
- Time management is an essential skill that can help individuals to keep their work under control, increase productivity and reduce stress. However, sometimes, addressing the culture of an organisation might be equally important in reducing stress in the workplace.

References

Adams, R.E., Boscarino, J.A. and Figley, C.R. (2006) 'Compassion fatigue and psychological distress among social workers: a validation study', *American Journal of Orthopsychiatry*, vol. 76, no. 1, pp. 103–8.

Aked, J., Marks, N., Cordon, C. and Thompson, S. (2008) *Five Ways to Wellbeing: the evidence*, London, New Economics Foundation.

Aked, J., Michaelson, J. and Steuer, N. (2010) *The Role of Local Government in Promoting Wellbeing*, London, Local Government Improvement and Development.

Bakker, A.B., Schaufeli, W.B., Leiter, M.P. and Taris, T.W. (2008) 'Work engagement: an emerging concept in occupational health psychology', *Work and Stress: An International Journal of Work, Health and Organisations*, vol. 22, no. 3, pp. 187–200.

Bowlby, J. (1969, 1973, 1980) *Attachment and Loss, Vols 1, 2 and 3*, London, Hogarth.

Clarke, A. (2001) *The Sociology of Healthcare*, Harlow, Pearson Education.

Elisabeth Kübler-Ross Foundation (1969) *Five stages of grief* [Table]. Available at http://www.ekrfoundation.org/five-stages-of-grief/ (Accessed 27 November 2012).

Figley, C.R. (2002) *Treating Compassion Fatigue*, New York, Brunner-Routledge.

Goleman, D. (1995) *Emotional Intelligence – Why it can matter more than IQ*, London, Bloomsbury.

Goleman, D., Boyatzis, R. and McKee, A. (2002) *The New Leaders*, London, Sphere.

Harvey, S., Liddell, A. and McMahon, L. (2009) *Windmill 2009: NHS response to the financial storm*, London, The King's Fund.

Health and Safety Executive (HSE) (2010) 'Self-reported work-related illness and workplace injuries in 2008/09', Results from the Labour Force Survey, London, HSE.

Holmes, T.H. and Rahe, R.H. (1967) 'The social readjustment rating scale', *Journal of Psychosomatic Research*, vol. 11, pp. 213–18.

Kinman, G. (2011) *The growing epidemic: Work-related stress in post-16 education*, London, UCU.

Kotter, J.P. and Schlesinger, L.A. (2009) 'Choosing strategies for change', in Price, D. (ed.) *Principles and Practice of Change*, London, Palgrave.

Kübler-Ross, E. (1970) *On Death and Dying*, London, Tavistock.

MacKian, S. (2010) 'Wellbeing', in Kitchen, R. and Thrift, N. (eds) *International Encyclopaedia of Human Geography*, Cambridge, Elsevier.

Marris, P. (1986) *Loss and Change*, London, Routledge and Kegan Paul.

Maslach, C. and Leiter, M.P. (1997) *The Truth about Burnout*, San Francisco, Calif., Jossey-Bass.

Parkes, C.M. (1986) *Bereavement: Studies of Grief in Adult Life*, London, Tavistock.

Seden, J. and Katz, J. (2003) 'Managing significant life events', in Seden, J. and Reynolds, J. (eds) *Managing Care in Practice*, London, Routledge/The Open University, pp. 277–301 (K303 Set Book).

Steiner, C. and Perry, P. (1997) *Achieving Emotional Literacy*, London, Bloomsbury.

Turner, N., Barling, J, and Zacharatos, A. (2002) 'Positive psychology at work', in Snyder, C. and Lopez, S. (eds) *The Handbook of Positive Psychology*, Oxford, Oxford University Press, pp. 715–30.

Walsh, J.A. (1987) 'Burnout and values in the social services profession', *Journal of Contemporary Social Work*, May, pp. 279–83.

Wilkinson, R. and Marmot, M. (eds) (2003) *The Social Determinants of Health: The solid facts* (2nd edition), Geneva, WHO.

Wong, K.-F. (2003) 'Empowerment as a panacea for poverty – old wine in new bottles? Reflections on the World Bank's conception of power', *Progress in Development Studies*, vol. 3, no. 4, pp. 307–22.

Chapter 6 Managing identities

Helen Lomax

6.1 Introduction

Figure 6.1 What makes workplace identities?

> Whether an organization, group, or person, each entity needs at least a preliminary answer to the question 'Who are we?' or 'Who am I?' …
>
> (Albert et al., 2000, p. 13)

Understanding workplace identity is of fundamental importance to leaders and managers in health and social care. Being attentive to people and their attachments and identifications is essential for managers and leaders seeking to achieve a working environment in which staff are supported to deliver high-quality care (The King's Fund, 2011).

This chapter draws on a range of theoretical approaches to consider how identities shape, and are shaped by, the health and social care workplace (Figure 6.1). Drawing on sociological and organisational theory, the chapter explores the ways in which workplace identities have been conceptualised; critically discusses the suggestion that traditional identities are becoming increasingly destabilised; and explores theoretical approaches which seek to understand contemporary workplace identity as being less fixed, more fluid and fragile. This chapter also discusses the challenges and uncertainties generated by new capitalism (Strangleman, 2012) and its consequences, in order to explore how leaders and managers can meet these challenges, and the ways in which they can adapt their leadership and management styles to work with staff to achieve quality services.

Using case studies, this chapter examines the following three core questions.

- What is workplace identity and why should it matter for leaders and managers in health and social care?
- Are workplace identities in flux and, if so, what are the consequences for leaders and managers?
- How can theoretical approaches to understanding identity support sound leadership and management in health and social care?

6.2 Identity matters

> Organizational scholars who study processes of employee identity but operating from a variety of otherwise disparate theoretical perspectives tend to agree on one thing: *an employee's level of 'identification' with workplace-related entities is a powerful concept in understanding their experiences and behavior at work.*
>
> (Jaros, 2009, our emphasis)

Organisational sociologists have long been interested in the ways in which workplace identities are formed. This attention has focused on the ways in which identities are shaped by socialisation and its relationship to the self. This includes the ways in which societal and organisational norms become translated into how individuals construct their identities, and the importance of group processes in maintaining different kinds of social identity. In medical sociology, this interest is articulated historically in the study of the occupational socialisation of professionals with seminal research exploring how professional identities are forged through the process of training and workplace cultures. For example, in a classic study of the occupational socialisation of nurses, Melia (1987) explored how trainee nurses learned to adopt work-based norms and values, mastering professional rhetoric and adapting their behaviour in order to 'pass' as nurses. Similarly, research by Hughes (1956) and Merton et al. (1957) explored how medical students learn the values which define and identify them as doctors through their socialisation at medical school.

These approaches draw on social identity theory (Tajfel and Turner, 1979; Dutton et al., 2010) which proposes that people's sense of self is profoundly shaped by their experiences and relationships with groups. Entry into a profession and the adoption of its norms and values confers a particular identity on an individual and offers the security of belonging and a sense of being part of a social group with a common history and a collective fate (Figure 6.2). Social identity theorists thus emphasise the important role that groups play in forming and structuring a person's sense of self, belonging, worth, purpose and potential (Haslam and van Dick, 2010) and can help to explain individuals' investments in particular professional and occupational identities which can offer important sources of status and power.

'Our sketch of professional socialization begins with the student arriving at the door of the institution as pristine and virginal as though untouched by Original Sin … [and] terminates with the day of graduation when, like the dolls in nurse–doctor play kits, young professionals move as equally substitutable units from the school assembly line … now fully garbed with the indisputable trappings of the professional' (Olesen and Whittaker, 1968, pp. 148, 149).

Figure 6.2 The making of 'the professional'

Can you recall your initial experiences of a new occupation? Did you 'fit' immediately or did you have to learn how to perform in that role?

In an important critique of social identity theory, Bucher and Strauss (1961) argued that the prominence given to occupational socialisation has resulted in an overemphasis on shared norms, values and role definitions as defining workplace behaviour, at the expense of acknowledging and understanding individual and intra-group differences and their consequences. Bucher and Strauss's critique is shared by Jaros (2009), who censures 'broad brush' approaches and their tendency to theorise particular 'types' of occupations as presumptively having the same identities, leading to an overemphasis on identity formation *within professions.* Moreover, as Olesen and Whittaker (1968) suggest in their humorous critique, a model based on social identification alone cannot account for the values that individuals bring to this process.

As the first case study explores, rather than being passively moulded by institutions, individuals make choices, 'talk back' to institutions, and bring their own values into play (Tew, 2006). However, the degree to which staff can do this in ways which enhance workplace practices is contingent on the skills of the manager and the style of leadership.

Case study 6.1: Workplace 'dis-identification'

Jasmine is a recently qualified social worker. She described her difficult experiences as a new member of a mental health team in a unit specialising in the treatment of eating disorders. Her dissonance centred on the treatment of young women with anorexia and, specifically, the management of ward rounds. While her training had led her to anticipate an inclusive patient-centred approach, these seemed to her to be highly staged encounters, almost exclusively focused on patients' weight gain (or its lack) and almost entirely a discussion among professionals. Patients themselves were rarely addressed.

The emphasis on weight (what one patient confided as 'fattening us up') and the objectification of patients during these encounters seemed antithetical to social models, reinforcing passivity and a child-like status for the young women. For Jasmine, too, there were serious challenges to her identity as a new member of staff and to the occupational identity she had imagined for herself, leading to strong feelings of antipathy and 'dis-identification' with her new role. Her discomfort was exacerbated when, on questioning this approach during a supervision session with her manager, Karen, she recalled being sharply told that 'This is the most efficient way of managing ward rounds; it's the way we have always managed it; there is no good reason to change it now.'

How might Jasmine's manager have managed this situation more effectively?

Karen's actions left Jasmine feeling that her opinions were of little value or, as she described, 'a small and insignificant cog in a very large wheel'. They also suggested a directive and coercive style of management through which Karen drew on her considerable status as Director of Services to exercise 'power-over' Jasmine to maintain the situation (Wong, 2003; Tew, 2006). Not only was this damaging to Jasmine's sense of identity, fostering a sense of uncertainty and a lack of confidence in her practice, it also indicates a low level of organisational emotional intelligence (see Chapter 2). As Lynch et al. (2011) suggest, poor organisational emotional literacy is associated with high levels of anxiety and a dearth of creative and innovative practice. Karen's actions also gave Jasmine very clear messages about the value the unit placed on dialogue and shared decision making, reinforcing organisational hierarchies and closing down opportunities for transforming services.

Jasmine's experience suggests that social identification is rarely a simple matter of conforming to social norms. Rather, people bring an assortment of social identifications (derived from gender, class and other forms of extraneous socialisation) which they draw on to actively shape a meaningful workplace identity. However, as Jasmine's experience suggests, the degree to which individuals can 'take action, participate and mobilise' (Wong, 2003) these in order to accomplish a meaningful workplace identity is contingent on the management culture and the degree of social leverage (social capital) that is available to individuals.

Social capital is the resource that we get from being embedded in mutually beneficial networks, relationships and communities.

'Power-with' – workplace identity as fluid and productive

> [W]orkplace identity is a nexus which links dynamics of power, control, resistance, gender, and skills.
>
> (Jaros, 2009)

'[T]he right look at the right time … These matters constitute the silent dialogue wherein are fused person, situation, and institution' (Olesen and Whittaker, 1968, p. 150).

In contrast to the functionalist approach suggested by Merton et al. (1957) and Hughes (1956), in which workers are conceptualised as passive recipients of culture, Bucher and Strauss (1961) proposed a dynamic model in which individuals are constituted by multiple identities and values, each of which is in constant evolution, conflict and change. To understand these processes, they suggested a focus on the mundane interactions that comprise the everyday experience of the workplace.

'Individuals form, transform, and modify how they define themselves and others in the context of work-based situations and activities' (Dutton et al., 2010, p. 265). Do you agree?

As the quotation from Olesen and Whittaker suggests, a focus on the minutiae of organisational culture is helpful for exploring the ways in which managers and staff shape workplace identities, including which workers have the social capital to 'remake' workplace identities and relationships (Billett and Pavlova, 2005). As you saw, in this regard Jasmine appeared to have little leverage. However, arguably, she could draw on her classed and gendered social capital (that is, her status as a degree-educated, 'cerebral' worker, which she has in common with her professional colleagues) in ways which are not available to all workers. As Lucas (2011) suggests, knowledge workers share a collective identity and intellectual capital (with managers and leaders) and, consequently, are in a better position to negotiate occupational and workplace identities. In contrast, workers who engage in the 'intimate messy contact' of work on bodies by (their own) bodies have less intellectual and social capital with which to negotiate their workplace and occupational identities. In many cases, these workers face an additional penalty as a result of their status as black and minority ethnic migrant workers (Dyer et al., 2008).

The status of particular occupational groups is important in the context of a rapidly changing health and social care sector and the reconstitution of work within it. Employees are less likely to remain in the same profession throughout their career; traditional 'male' jobs and specialisms have become (arguably) less gendered with men more likely to take on traditional 'caring' roles and women more likely to be employed in formerly 'male' specialities (McBride, 2011). Alongside what many people would see as positive changes have come challenges. Economic and political pressures have led to the reorganisation of services and the redefinition of terms of employment (McDowell, 2009), while the 'old certainties' of employment security and the erosion of traditional values of 'service', and its replacement with the language of the market, suggest less continuity for managers and staff alike.

Identities under threat

> A steady, durable and continuous, logically coherent and tightly-structured working career is … no longer a widely available option. Only in relatively rare cases can a permanent identity be defined, let alone secured, through the job performed.
>
> (Bauman, 1998, p. 27)

Bauman (1998) and other writers (for example, Beck, 2000; Felstead et al., 2009; Strangleman, 2012) suggest that global political and economic pressures are having a profound impact on the nature of employment. The threats to individual, collective and workplace identities are elaborated by the sociologist Richard Sennett (2008). He warns that people can no longer make sense of who they are through their work and, consequently, are denied opportunities to form meaningful work-based and positive self-identities. Sennett's argument gains currency from the notion that individuals obtain meaning from shared histories and psychological investments which are ruptured and damaged by change.

For people working in health and social care in the UK, the impact of recent reorganisations under the Health and Social Care Act 2012 may threaten a sense of collective identity as historical and psychological bonds based on a common history and values are eroded. However, without dismissing the serious implications of each new round of political reforms on both the delivery of services and terms of employment (Smith, 2012), it is worth remembering that health and social care services have been subject to almost continuous social, political and economic pressures since the earliest days of collective welfare provision. These forces have required staff to continually reinvent and reposition themselves and to reshape their professional and workplace identities.

Furthermore, although changes to the requirements of participation in employment represent challenges for workers, claims that they *necessarily* constitute increasing disempowerment, marginalisation and the corrosion of identity may be overstated (Billett and Pavlova, 2005). Although this needs to be placed in the context of the empirical work cited earlier (Dyer et al., 2008), the suggestion that change can have positive impacts on personal and workplace identities is helpful. In the health and social care sector this includes the shifting conceptualisation of the service user, from passive 'lay person' to a more equal footing with professionals. As Coulter (2011) suggests, service user involvement has moved centre-stage in all forms of welfare provision. The rise of the 'expert patient', who is knowledgeable about their own condition and an equal partner in their own health, and the spread of personalisation within social care reform, has reconfigured relationships with service users. Arguably, this has redressed inequalities between service users and providers and challenged providers to consider the nature of the care they deliver and their own identity as the 'expert' in ways which have positively transformed services (Florin and Coulter, 2001). Other opportunities arise from the increased globalisation of the health and social care workforce and the employment of staff who bring with them different understandings and expectations of practice and workplace norms (Vertovec, 2006). In addition, the educational and employment opportunities which have opened through non-traditional routes confront traditional classed distinctions whereby, for example, doctors and registered nurses were historically drawn from the upper and middle classes. This represents important shifts in power, skills and knowledge which challenge the notion of fixed (and gendered and classed) professional identities.

Managers are also finding their roles increasingly redefined with reorganisation across the sector bringing new challenges both to the ways in which services are delivered and their own role as leaders and managers. For example, John Clark, a senior fellow with The King's Fund, suggests that managers are now having to cope with a shift in the balance of power. Instead of running organisations, they now work to support practitioners at the front line in setting priorities and leading change (Stephenson, 2012). These factors suggest that, rather than being stable and enduring, workplace identities are in constant flux with workers and professions (and workplaces and their managers) in continuous and reflexive negotiation about the nature of the organisation, the constitution of work, and their roles within it. While there are numerous benefits to such flexible and changing workplace identities, this process is not without its stresses. Rather, as Chapter 5 considered, the emotional cost of change and uncertainty can be immense. Moreover, as Haslam and van Dick (2010) suggest, shared social identity (that is, a sense of common values, purpose and shared norms) can provide an important source of material, emotional and intellectual support, while its absence is associated with high levels of stress and anxiety.

The next section draws on a psychoanalytically informed approach to understanding workplace identities and the implications for leaders and managers.

6.3 Defended identities – psychosocial approaches to workplace identities

A useful place for understanding workplace identification is the work of Anton Obholzer (1994). A psychoanalyst and organisational consultant, Obholzer's influential work draws on psychoanalytical theory to understand workplace identities and the psychological processes underpinning them. He proposes that public sector organisations are defensive structures (or containers) for the attendant anxieties generated by proximity to illness, distress and death. For the containing structures to operate effectively, there needs to be not only agreement about the primary task of the organisation (the care of vulnerable, sick or dying people) but also effective systems for keeping in touch with the nature of the anxieties projected (fear of death and disease). Taking responsibility for the latter is a key leadership and management task, but one that Obholzer suggests is routinely threatened by top-down management structures, which create psychological distance between managers, staff and service users. In nursing, this can be exemplified by ritualised, task-oriented care, an emphasis on emotional detachment, and a denial of feelings which inhibits the development of authentic relationships between patients and staff (Menzies, 1960).

Menzies' reflections on the nurse–patient relationship can help to make sense of Karen's defensive reaction to Jasmine's request (described in Case study 6.1). Seen through this lens, Jasmine's suggestion – that ward rounds might be more patient-centred – represents both a potential collapse of the ritualised distancing work of the ward round and a direct challenge to Karen's management style. However, by refusing to consider change, Karen's actions have a damaging effect on Jasmine's sense of professional identity and any sense of contributing to the organisation's vision. Moreover, Karen's actions reinforce a bureaucratic style of management which thwarts Jasmine's developing leadership, reaffirming hierarchies between management, staff and patients.

More positively, Obholzer (1994) suggests several ways in which managers can work with staff to improve services in ways which are psychologically beneficial for the organisation and individual staff. These include being clear about the organisation and task and ensuring that staff are given opportunities to contribute. In addition, he suggests there is a need for:

- psychologically informed management
- awareness of the (psychological) risks to staff
- openness towards service users.

In what ways do Obholzer's suggestions reflect the four building blocks of the fully rounded caring manager?

As Figure 6.3 illustrates, Obholzer's approach prioritises a psychologically informed approach to management which promotes the wellbeing of staff, service users and organisations, and demonstrates opportunities for leadership at all levels.

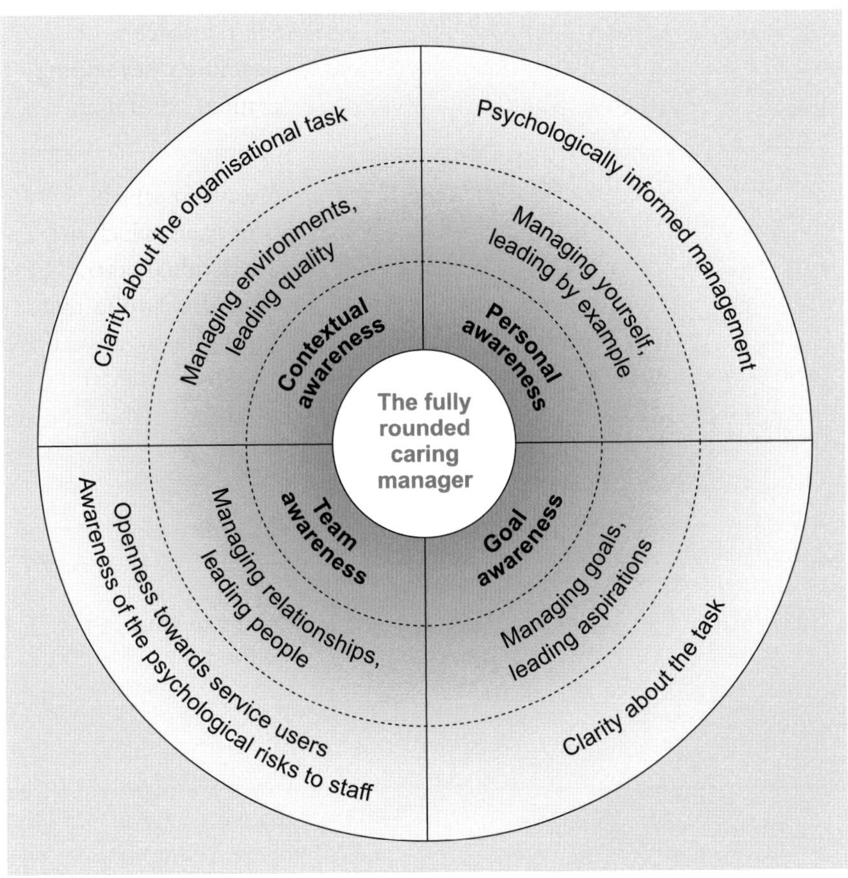

Figure 6.3 The psychologically informed manager

As this section has elaborated, a key element of a psychoanalytically informed approach to leadership and management is to recognise the psychological processes underpinning the relationships between managers and staff and the ways in which these can help or hinder the delivery of care. This approach enables us to make sense of Karen's response to a situation (which she found threatening) and the ways in which it was, ultimately, unhelpful for both Jasmine's sense of workplace identification and the wider organisation. The next section continues this focus on the importance for leaders and managers of understanding workplace identities and relationships.

6.4 Narrated identities

There is no substitute for dialogue in understanding where people are 'coming from'. Do you agree?

> [N]arrative is present in every age, in every place, in every society; it begins with the very history of mankind and there nowhere is nor has been a people without narrative.
>
> (Barthes, 1977, p. 79)

The importance of narrative in the constitution of workplace identities is suggested by Albert and Whetten (1985) and by Dutton et al.'s (2010) proposal that organisational identity is made visible in the stories it tells about itself. As they suggest, each organisation has a repertoire of stories which are observable in the way it represents itself publicly (Figure 6.4) but also in the private conversations of managers and staff.

Figure 6.4 Who says what and what does it mean for managers?

One of the most useful approaches for leaders and managers in health and social care is provided by Barbara Czarniawska (2000). By applying narrative theory and methods (Mishler, 1986), she explores the form which stories take and how they operate within different organisational contexts. Drawing on the example of a third-sector leader tasked with institutional reorganisation, Czarniawska explores how the chief executive officer (CEO) abandons a hierarchical change management approach, focusing instead on taking time to talk with staff about their values and beliefs. She argues that this focus gave him new perspectives on organisational and staff identities from which he was in a stronger position to work *with* staff in order to manage change effectively. The CEO's focus on people and relationships, and the ways in which leaders might work with them to enhance organisations, individuals and teams, is an important feature of a transformational model of leadership (Northouse, 2010; National Skills Academy, 2011; also, see Chapter 3).

Czarniawska's analysis has particular relevance for managers and leaders in health and social care who are facing a level of organisational change which threatens to disrupt individual and organisational histories and identities. As Czarniawska (2000, p. 13) elaborates, 'long-lived narratives are sediments of norms and practices, and as such deserve careful attention'. From this perspective, narratives are seen to make visible the dominant and residual stories of individuals and organisations which define and constitute identity over time (Strangleman, 2012). For Strangleman, these narratives are important ways in which people articulate and make sense of change, conflict and dissonance. The important work of storytelling in helping individuals to make sense of and maintain a coherent sense of identity is considered next.

The value of listening within a leadership framework

In the next case study, a new mother, Laura, describes how talking with her midwife, Jane, about her anxieties for the impending birth enabled her to reconcile her fears for the birth she had planned. As the case study explores, open dialogue, framed by a person-centred approach, can provide important opportunities for staff to transform care.

'Authentic leaders have the capacity to open themselves up and establish a connection with others. They are willing to share their own story with others and listen to others' stories (Northouse, 2010, p. 213).

Case study 6.2: Leading for woman-centred care

Laura was pregnant with her second child and increasingly uneasy about the imminent birth. She confided her anxieties to her midwife, Jane, who responded by listening to Laura's description of 'dark, terrifying dreams' and recent unsettling experiences of a close friend's traumatic delivery, enabling Laura to express her fears for the birth. Moreover, in reciprocating with her own birth stories and the skills she uses to deliver babies safely, Jane validated (rather than dismissed) Laura's concerns and opened up a space for emotional connection.

For Laura, her appointment with Jane was one of the most healing and honest that she had ever experienced; it enabled her to reconcile her anxieties and continue with her plans for a home birth.

'Person-centred care cannot happen without sound leadership' (Lynch et al., 2011). Do you agree?

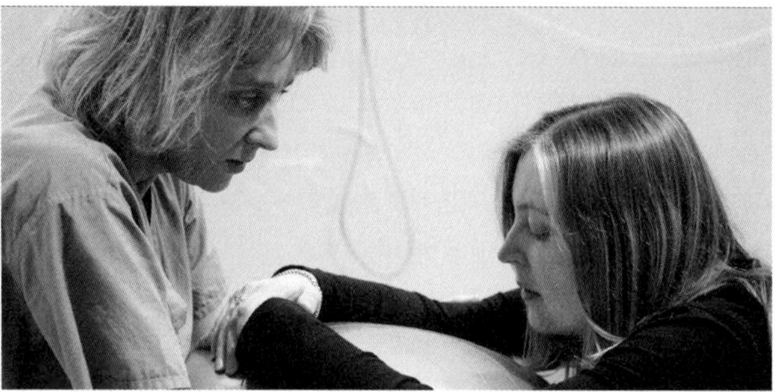

Figure 6.5 Making a space to listen

Jane's actions indicate that she was a skilled listener with a high level of emotional intelligence. She was able to recognise Laura's distress and to manage her own response, facilitating a positive outcome for Laura. Of relevance to leaders and managers is the way in which a seemingly ordinary act transformed Laura's experience, putting 'humaneness' at the heart of care (Coulter, 2011). By hearing Laura's story, Jane was able to incorporate this with her own professional narrative about safe deliveries, allowing both women to see the situation in a different way. In the busy and stressful environment of daily health and social care work, such moments are not always easy to manufacture (Figure 6.5); however, they are essential for someone wishing to manage and lead with care.

As the next section discusses, such emotional intelligence is an important attribute of transformational leadership, and one which can be facilitated by an authentic leadership model.

6.5 Authentic leadership – a relationship based on integrity

> Authentic leaders understand their own values and behave toward others based on those values.
>
> (Northouse, 2010, p. 213)

Jane has many of the attributes of an authentic leader (George, 2003). She is accessible, open and transparent; she has a clear sense of her own values and behaves towards other people accordingly; she is passionate about delivering woman-centred care; and she prioritises relationships.

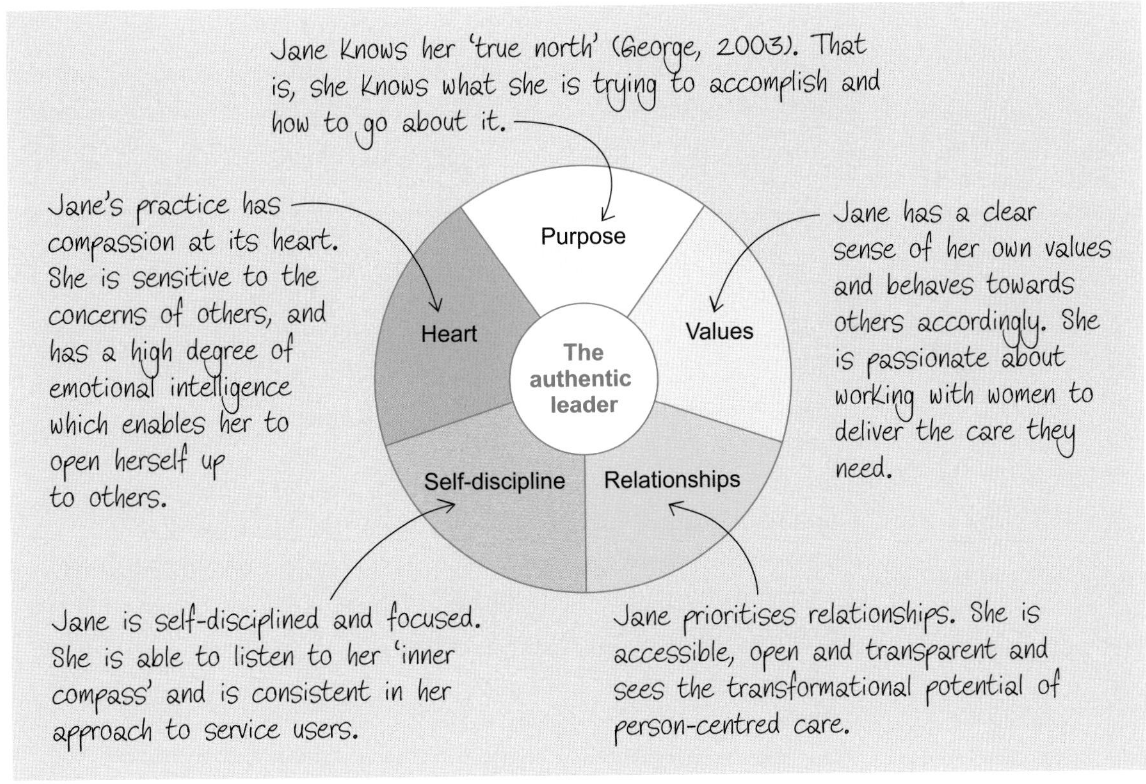

Figure 6.6 Authentic leadership and individual values (based on George, 2003)

'[T]he greatest leaders mobilize others by coalescing people around a shared vision' (Lynch et al., 2011, p. 1062).

However, as you saw with Jasmine's unsatisfactory experience in Case study 6.1, Jane is likely to struggle to enact this approach unless supported by an organisational culture and a leadership style which supports and nurtures her approach. This suggestion is borne out by McCormack and McCance (2010) in their analysis of the relationship between the organisational culture in which care is delivered and the type of care offered, suggesting a strong relationship between the two. These ideas are discussed in the next section which explores in more depth how Jane is supported by a particular style of leadership. As the section shows, analysis of the organisational and management culture of the birth centre in which Jane works makes clear that there is a strong correlation between Jane's commitment to 'caring about' the centre's values and the style of leadership.

Characteristics of a transformational organisation

Case study 6.3: Leading for woman-centred care (continued)

The birth centre where Jane works has a reputation for high-quality woman-centred care, characterised by a culture which values soft skills such as listening and feeling. But more than this, Jane's team is led by a visionary leader, Briana, who is committed to achieving woman-centred care and working *with* her team to achieve this. A transformational leader, Briana rejects hierarchical management structures and surveillance-oriented management practices, trusting her staff to support women to achieve their goals. Briana's commitment to autonomous practice enables staff to take risks (including emotional risks, as Laura's story revealed) in order to serve others. She also takes risks herself and is prepared to challenge threats from the hospital executive in order to maintain the centre's commitment to a vision of safe, women-centred care.

Briana places a high value on workplace relationships and supports her staff's relationships with service users, making time to listen to them to ensure that the centre is meeting its objectives. In recognition of the emotional burden of the work that staff do in caring for mothers and babies, Briana has created opportunities for regular staff debriefing.

This means that, unlike Jasmine, Jane has an emotional 'safety net' to maintain her energy reserves and prevent burn-out. A **fully rounded caring manager**, Briana's leadership style is based on spiritual qualities, a clear sense of purpose, and a commitment to inspiring other people.

Jane's alignment with the organisational culture is no accident. Research indicates that successful organisations select staff who fit their values (Northouse, 2010); analysis by Goleman (2004) explores the ways in which the emotional temperature of an organisation circulates through an organisation from leaders to the 'bottom line', suggesting that a leader's emotional intelligence is critical for a caring environment in which trust and healthy risk taking can flourish. However, managers cannot force their values on staff; rather, as Briana's model of leadership suggests, they need to work with staff to develop a shared vision in ways which recognise and support their own capacity to lead and build on their personal power and self-esteem (Wong, 2003).

The **personal awareness tool** can be helpful for reflecting on the fit between your personal values and those of the organisation you work in, and to develop your emotional intelligence as a leader.

Jane's experience of care demonstrates the important (but often invisible) processes that support high-quality patient-centred care. In common with research on person-centred care (Lynch, 2011) and health system innovation (Hendy and Barlow, 2012), leaders and managers who are successful in this regard:

- make time to listen to and appreciate the identities of their staff
- actively seek to understand the unique culture of their organisations
- take steps to positively enhance the delivery of care in ways which recognise the value of individuals, both staff and service users
- are compassionate, passionate and self-disciplined (George, 2003).

Do you think leaders can develop compassion and 'learn' to be authentic?

Jane has an inbuilt sense of compassion, born from her passion for woman-centred care. However, as George (2003) suggests, leaders can develop these qualities by getting to know the people they care for and work with. As both Jane and the third-sector CEO experienced (Section 6.4), a powerful way to do this is through listening. This process helps to facilitate a transformational style of leadership, and is an important means of developing **team awareness** – one of the essential elements of the **fully rounded caring manager** (Chapter 1).

The final section of this chapter builds on this perspective in order to explore how managers might lead effective workplace dialogue. It draws on a model of transformational leadership to develop creative workplaces in which both individuals and organisations can flourish.

6.6 Connecting conversations – managing identity challenges and collisions

Enabling people to speak freely and purposefully with each other is at the heart of effective leadership and management of high-quality health and social care services. Managers who are prepared to listen actively can achieve a more effective workplace in which staff have a sense of purpose and find value in their work (as Chapter 5 shows, this can be an important factor in maintaining wellbeing). In Jane's case, this meant working towards the birth centre's vision of woman-centred care, which gave her a meaningful connection with work and a positive self-identity. However, this case study does not make clear how managers and staff cope with *difference*. How do managers work with others who do not share their values in ways which are conducive to the delivery of quality services? You saw earlier how organisational cultures in which staff are not valued can be damaging to individual members of staff and contribute to the 'othering' of service users (Johnson et al., 2004). Recent high-profile cases, such as the scandal at Winterbourne View Hospital, suggest that poor leadership – including a failure of leaders and managers to challenge staff values and attitudes – can lead to escalating levels of challenging behaviour and, ultimately, a culture of abuse (Flynn, 2012; Jones, 2012; Figure 6.7).

Figure 6.7 Poor leadership is often a factor in cultures of abuse

Davis (2000) argues that models of collaborative working, rather than being based on sameness, should welcome and value difference. Drawing on the experiences of a social services department which sought to include people with learning difficulties in decision making, she argues that understanding 'the other', and valuing different perspectives, can enhance services:

> Affirmations, acknowledgement, and recognition are important, but *it is the questions and challenges that arise from the differences that are vital.* A diverse group can arrive at a place no individual and no like-minded group would have reached.
>
> (Davis, 2000, p. 1021, our emphasis)

However, as Davis (2000) notes, this is no easy task. Differences of professional status, occupational hierarchies and organisational culture can make it difficult for some professional and service user voices to be heard, as the next case study explores.

Can you see how the **stakeholder mapping tool** might be helpful in understanding the way different identity groups might approach a particular issue?

Case study 6.4: Managing difference

Susan is an experienced ward sister who was given the responsibility of managing a newly established patient reference group. The hospital executive anticipated this group would give a 'patient perspective' on services. Initially excited about this opportunity, Susan very quickly felt out of her depth. Almost immediately she experienced conflict between her expectations of the group's role and what she considered to be its questioning and combative style. The group seemed to want to know the evidence base for everything and, at the same time, were constantly stalling discussion with what she felt were unnecessary accounts of their own experiences of services. This was compounded by the negative experiences of staff tasked with working with the group. Nursing staff in particular complained to Susan that some of the older male members were 'overly challenging', undermining their professional knowledge about what was 'best for patients'.

Davis's ideas about managing diversity are helpful here, suggesting that the effective operation of this group was impeded by the occupational and gendered assumptions of both nurses and patients.. This can be seen in the ways in which the reference group readily deferred to doctors – whom they perceived to be higher status – and routinely challenged nurses, whom they considered occupationally and socially inferior (Grimshaw and Rubery, 2007). The group's devaluing of the (female) nurses mirrors a wider cultural valuing of men's work over women's work and their continued underrepresentation in strategic and leadership roles in both the private and public sectors (Dunn-Jensen and Stroh, 2007; Broadbridge and Hearn, 2008). The nurses too had their own assumptions – based on gendered and ageist identity categories – which enabled them to dismiss the largely elderly patients who made up the group's membership as 'troublemakers' with 'little understanding of the realities of managing a ward'. Negative reactions from nurses were particularly notable when members of the reference group attempted to raise their personal experiences of care (which included dirty wards, poor quality food and missing bed linen). These narratives were dismissed by nursing staff as 'personal and subjective interruptions' that disrupted the 'business' of the meetings.

Thinking about the work of Menzies (1980) on defended practices, how might you interpret the nurses' responses to patients?

A psychoanalytically informed reading of the nurses' responses might suggest that the patients' accounts threatened the nurses' sense of professional identity. The patients' suggestions endangered the nurses' status as experts who 'know best' about caring for patients, disrupting the boundaries and defences represented by the ritualised management of meetings. In this way, rather than fostering a sense of shared identity, common purpose and vision, meetings served instead to exacerbate and entrench differences between staff and service users.

Which model of leadership might be effective in enabling patients and staff to achieve a shared vision?

Shared agendas – hearing stories

Resolution was achieved in Case study 6.4 once the nursing staff realised the importance of working positively with difference and recognised the power of narrative to forge a collective vision. This was accomplished by scheduling a narratives discussion (Lawler, 2008), which enabled group members to share their experiences of care and set an agenda for action. The meeting was successful as it enabled members to voice their own situated and experientially based agendas. But it also had a fundamental impact on staff, forcing them to revisit some of their assumptions about how to engage with service users, and to question their earlier assumptions about the reference group being disruptive.

The way in which the lead nurse, Susan, brokered this relationship between staff and the patient reference group is important for managers. Drawing on key elements of transformational leadership, she was able to create a safe space for patients to describe their experiences while also recognising the ways in which these stories, which were sometimes accompanied by much anger and grief, might threaten staff identities. As Czarniawska (2000) elaborates, listening to stories is not about arbitrating between accounts; it is about ensuring that the multiple perspectives of speakers are heard. As this case study exemplifies, these can give managers and leaders a powerful insight into organisational culture, workplace relationships and identities. By making these different perspectives and values visible, Susan could create a collective vision of service based on 'power-from-within' (Wong, 2003).

6.7 Conclusion

This chapter has explored workplace identity and its intersections, suggesting that an understanding of the processes of identification is essential for leaders and managers seeking to work effectively with staff in health and social care. Drawing on concepts from psychoanalysis, the chapter has explored the ways in which staff and managers, sanctioned by organisations, defend themselves against anxiety in ways which can be detrimental to the organisation, its people and its goals. Drawing also on the notion that work identities are ongoing projects shaped by individuals' embodied engagement with work over time, and the suggestion that what develops is a sense of 'moral ownership' which can be threatened by change, the chapter has proposed that – within this context – the idea of 'narrated identities' is potentially of great value to managers and leaders.

Through a process of listening and observing, managers can access the different faces of an organisation, gauging its emotional temperature and so offering the possibility of working positively with staff in ways which are meaningful to them. If the predictions of Beck (2000) and Bauman (1998) about increasing occupational uncertainty are accurate, these leadership skills are likely to become an increasingly necessary part of a manager's role.

Key points

- People bring a mixture of social identifications derived from occupation, gender and class to actively shape meaningful workplace identities.
- Workers may face challenges in constructing positive workplace identities in organisations which do not value their contributions. Recent health and social care reforms have intensified these pressures.
- Theoretical approaches, such as Obholzer's model of psychoanalytically informed management, can be helpful in understanding how leadership practices can enable individuals to flourish within organisations.
- Narrative can be a useful way for managers to understand the perspectives of service users and staff, offering an important means of valuing other people and enabling staff to do the same. This requires a transformational style of leadership.
- A leader's emotional intelligence is critical for nurturing a caring environment in which trust and healthy risk taking can flourish.
- Managers who are successful in this regard: make time to listen to and appreciate staff; actively seek to understand the unique culture of their organisations; and take steps to positively enhance the delivery of care in ways which recognise the value of individuals. Such a manager is an authentic leader.

References

Albert, S. and Whetten, D.A. (1985) 'Organizational identity research', *Organizational Behaviour*, vol. 7, pp. 263–95.

Albert, S., Ashforth, B.E. and Dutton, J.E. (2000) 'Organizational identity and identification: charting new waters and building new bridges', *Academy of Management Review*, vol. 25, pp. 13–17.

Barthes, R. (1977) *Image, Music, Text*, London, Fontana.

Bauman, Z. (1998) *Work, Consumerism and the New Poor*, Buckingham, Open University Press.

Beck, U. (2000) *The Brave New World of Work*, Cambridge, The Polity Press.

Billett, S. and Pavlova, M. (2005) 'Learning through working life: self and individuals' agentic action', *International Journal of Lifelong Education*, vol. 24, no. 3, pp. 195–211.

Broadbridge, A. and Hearn, J. (2008) 'Gender and management: new directions in research and continuing patterns in practice', *British Journal of Management*, vol. 19, pp. 38–49.

Bucher, R. and Strauss, A. (1961) 'Professions in process', *The American Journal of Sociology*, vol. 66, no. 4, pp. 325–34.

Coulter, A. (2011) *Engaging Patients in Healthcare*, Buckingham, Open University Press.

Czarniawska, B. (2000) *The Uses of Narrative Theory in Organisational Research*, Göteborg, School of Economic and Commercial Law, Göteborg University.

Davis, C. (2000) 'Getting health professionals to work together', *British Medical Journal*, vol. 320, no. 7241, pp. 1021–2.

Dunn-Jensen, L.M. and Stroh, L.K. (2007) 'Myths in media: how the news media portray women in the workforce', in Bilimoria, D. and Piderit, S.K. (eds) *Handbook on Women in Business and Management*, Cheltenham, Edward Elgar.

Dutton, J., Morgan Roberts, L. and Bednar, J. (2010) 'Pathways for positive identity construction at work: four types of positive identity and the building of social resources', *Academy of Management Review*, vol. 35, no. 2, pp. 265–93.

Dyer, S., McDowell, L. and Batnitzky, A. (2008) 'Emotional labour/body work: the caring labours of migrants in the UK's National Health Service', *Geoforum*, vol. 39, pp. 2030–8.

Felstead, A., Bishop, D., Fuller, A., Jewson, N., Unwin, L. and Kakavelakis, K. (2009) 'Working as belonging: the management of personal and collective identities', in Ecclestone, K., Biesta, G. and Hughes, M. (eds) *Transitions and Learning through the Lifecourse*, Florence, Ky., Routledge.

Florin, D. and Coulter, A. (2001) 'Partnership in the primary care consultation', in Brooks, F. and Gillam, S. (eds) *New Beginnings: Towards patient and public involvement in primary health care*, London, The King's Fund, pp. 44–59.

Flynn, M. (2012) *Winterbourne View Hospital: A serious case review* [Online], South Gloucestershire Safeguarding Adults Board. Available at http://hosted.southglos.gov.uk/wv/summary.pdf (Accessed 15 January 2013).

George, B. (2003) *Authentic Leadership: Rediscovering the secrets to creating lasting value*, San Francisco, Calif., Jossey-Bass.

Goleman, D. (2004) *Emotional Intelligence: Working with emotional intelligence*, New York, Bloomsbury.

Grimshaw, D. and Rubery, G. (2007) 'Undervaluing women's work', *Working Paper 53*, Manchester, Equal Opportunities Commission.

Haslam, S.A. and van Dick, R. (2010) 'A social identity approach to workplace stress', in de Cremer, D., van Dick, R. and Murnighan, K. (eds) *Social Psychology and Organisations*, New York, Routledge, pp. 325–52.

Hendy, J. and Barlow, J. (2012) 'The role of the organizational champion in achieving health system change', *Social Science and Medicine*, vol. 74, pp. 348–55.

Hughes, E.C. (1956) 'The making of a physician – general statement of ideas and problems', *Human Organization*, Winter, pp. 22–3.

Jaros, S. (2009) 'Identity and the workplace: an assessment of contextualist and discursive approaches', paper presented at the Labour Process Conference, Edinburgh, Scotland.

Johnson, J., Bottorff, J., Browne, A., Grewal, S., Hilton, A. and Clarke, H. (2004) 'Othering and being othered in the context of health care services', *Health Communication*, vol. 16, no. 2, pp. 255–71.

Jones, J. (2012) 'Lessons from Winterbourne View: learning and development', *Community Care* [Online], www.communitycare.co.uk/Articles/18/09/2012/118530/lessons-from-winterbourne-view-learning-and-development.htm (Accessed 15 January 2013).

Lawler, S. (2008) *Identity: sociological perspectives*, Cambridge, The Polity Press.

Lucas, K. (2011) 'Blue-collar discourse of workplace dignity: using outgroup comparisons to construct positive identities', *Management Communication Quarterly*, vol. 25, no. 2, pp. 353–74.

Lynch, B.M., McCormack, B. and McCance, T. (2011) 'Development of a model of situational leadership in residential care for older people', *Journal of Nursing Management*, vol. 19, pp. 1058–69.

McBride, A. (2011) 'Lifting the barriers? Workplace education and training, women and job progression', *Gender, Work & Organization*, vol. 18, no. 5, pp. 528–47.

McCormack, B. and McCance, T. (2010) *Person-centred Nursing: Theory and practice*, Oxford, Wiley-Blackwell.

McDowell, L. (2009) *Working Bodies: Interactive service employment and workplace identities*, Chichester, Wiley-Blackwell.

Melia, K.M. (1987) 'Learning and working: the occupational socialization of nurses', in Mackay, L., Soothill, K. and Melia, K. (eds) *Classic Texts in Health Care*, Oxford, Butterworth-Heinemann, pp. 154–9.

Menzies, I. (1960) 'A case-study in the functioning of social systems as a defence against anxiety: a report on a study of the nursing service of a general hospital', *Human Relations*, vol. 13, pp. 95–121.

Merton, R.K., Reader, G.K. and Kendall, P.L. (1957) 'Some preliminaries to a sociology of medical education', in Mackay, L., Soothill, K. and Melia, K. (eds) *Classic Texts in Health Care*, Oxford, Butterworth-Heinemann, pp. 140–2.

Mishler, e.g. (1986) *Research Interviewing: context and narrative*, Cambridge, Mass., Harvard University Press.

National Skills Academy (2011) *Outstanding Leadership in Social Care*, London, National Skills Academy for Social Care.

Northouse, P.G. (2010) *Leadership: Theory and Practice* 5th edn, London, Sage.

Obholzer, A. (1994) *The Unconscious at Work*, London, Routledge.

Olesen, V.L. and Whittaker, E.W. (1968) 'The silent dialogue: a study in the social psychology of professional socialization', in Mackay, L., Soothill, K. and Melia, K. (eds) *Classic Texts in Health Care*, Oxford, Butterworth-Heinemann, pp. 148–50.

Sennett, R. (2008) *The Craftsman*, London, Allen Lane.

Smith, R. (2012) 'NHS staff who don't agree to pay cut face sack', *Daily Telegraph*, 16 July [Online], www.telegraph.co.uk/health/healthnews/9401258/NHS-staff-who-dont-agree-to-pay-cut-face-sack.html (Accessed 15 January 2013).

Stephenson, J. (2012) 'The health service needs a new breed of leader', *Guardian Professional*, 20 June [Online], www.guardian.co.uk/healthcare-network/2012/jun/20/health-service-new-breed-leader/print (Accessed 26 July 2012).

Strangleman, T. (2012) 'Work identity in crisis? Rethinking the problem of attachment and loss at work', *Sociology*, vol. 46, no. 3, pp. 411–25.

Tajfel, H. and Turner, J.C. (1979) 'An integrative theory of intergroup conflict', in Austin, W.G. and Worchel, S. (eds) *The Social Psychology of Intergroup Relations*, Monterey, Calif., Brooks/Cole, pp. 33–47.

Tew, J. (2006) 'Understanding power and powerlessness: towards a framework for emancipatory practice in social work', *Journal of Social Work*, vol. 6, no. 33, pp. 32–50.

The King's Fund (2011) *The Future of Leadership and Management in the NHS: No more heroes*, London, The King's Fund.

Vertovec, S. (2006) 'The emergence of super-diversity in Britain', *Working Paper no. 25*, University of Oxford, Centre for Migration, Policy and Society.

Wong, K.-H. (2003) 'Empowerment as a panacea for poverty – old wine in new bottles? Reflections on the World Bank's conception of power', *Progress in Development Studies*, vol. 3, no. 4, pp. 307–22.

Chapter 7 Managing the team

Julie Charlesworth

7.1 Introduction

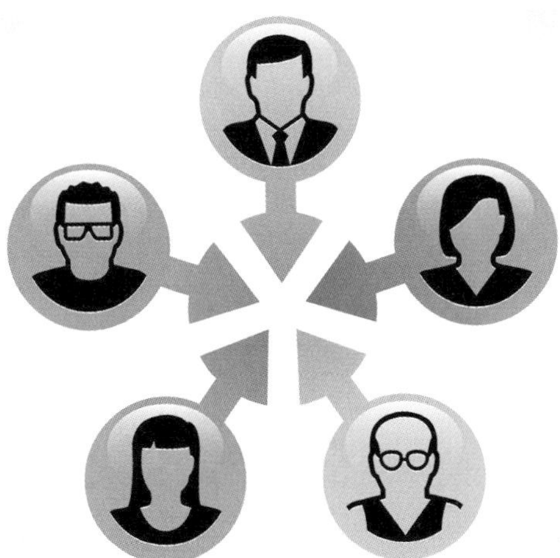

Figure 7.1 Team awareness is one of the basic building blocks of a fully rounded caring manager

The language of 'teams' and 'teamwork' is everywhere in health and social care, and working in multidisciplinary teams is often presented as the only way to deliver effective and integrated services (GMC, 2006; DH, 2008a, b). Indeed, the failure to work in teams has been cited as a risk to patient safety: for example, in the Bristol Royal Infirmary Inquiry (2001). However, bringing together different, and often diverse, professional groups into cohesive teams and breaking down traditional, and often powerful, barriers can be challenging for both managers and team members. Furthermore, there is also a need to involve service users and carers in these teams, as part of the emphasis on partnership working. This can add another layer of complexity for managers in ensuring a positive experience for all members of the team.

Both leadership and management have key roles to play in working with and building successful teams.

Given that many service users in health and social care now experience being cared for by teams and not individuals, it is crucial that the team functions effectively. The manager's role is to facilitate a team's development over time, particularly through the difficult early stages of formation. It is not a one-off exercise (for example, on an 'away day') but an integral and ongoing part of the work of any manager or team leader (Ward, 2003). Complex teams also need strong leadership, particularly through the early stages of development, in creating a shared vision for the team and in encouraging all team members to take responsibility for this.

This chapter looks at why teams have emerged as such a central feature of caring work, discusses what teams are, and explores some of the challenges associated with managing and leading teams. **Team awareness** is one of the key building blocks of the **fully rounded caring manager and leader** (Figure 7.1). Essentially, it is about managing relationships within the team and the team's relationships with other people. This chapter therefore relates specifically to this building block. However, in managing or leading a team, it is important also to maintain your focus on the other building blocks: keeping an eye on the team's goal; being sensitive to the wider context; and being aware of your own influence on team dynamics.

This chapter focuses particularly at the micro level, that is, on the day-to-day team rather than the more complex type of team – a partnership – which is explored in Chapter 8. Therefore, this chapter addresses the following core questions.

- What is a team and why do teams matter?
- How is a team 'built' and maintained, and what is the manager's role in this?
- What role does leadership play in teamwork?

7.2 What is a team and why do teams matter?

'There are a number of reasons why people prefer to work in groups, including for affiliation, to gain a sense of identity, to help each other to make sense of the world, to protect their own interests and to get things done' (Martin et al., 2010, p. 296).

Teams have emerged as a permanent feature and are almost taken for granted in health and social care work. Understanding how teams work is therefore crucial for any manager or leader. At the simplest level, teams are often composed of a range of different people with unique skills, insights and strengths. This diversity can help to ensure that complex care is delivered effectively in a way that a single individual or a disparate group of people could not achieve. Teams also matter because people matter and because teams are now the main way in which people are organised into getting the work done, and where they may expect some support for their work. They are also the principal way in which many service users now experience their care (DH, 2008a, b).

It is argued that teamwork contributes to best results in terms of productivity and efficiency, as well as on the more human dimensions of staff morale and reduced absenteeism (Procter and Mueller, 2000). Furthermore, the language of teamwork, such as 'belonging to a team' and 'membership', are certainly appealing to health and social care settings with complex occupational hierarchies and imbalances of power (Finn et al., 2010). But this is only achieved if the team is effectively managed. Popular images of teams are so positive that the word 'team' is often used to describe any arrangement in which staff are nominally grouped together, irrespective of whether they actually work together as a team. In fact, groups which do not work collaboratively may be called teams, perhaps to hide this fact, or in the hope that greater collaboration will result. So whereas government policy and much management literature highlights the advantages to teams, many sociologists researching teams in action focus on a more critical view of teamwork and attempt to get behind the rhetoric (Martin and Finn, 2011).

Defining the team

The meaning of 'team' and 'teamwork' is both contested and controversial.

Different definitions of teams stress requirements such as coordination, mutual accountability, diverse professional backgrounds and synergy (the idea that more can be achieved collectively than by individuals acting alone). Some researchers have also highlighted that teams 'feel' different in different organisational contexts and, in particular, that variations in context can impact on existing professional structures; that is, whether they carry on as before or are transformed into a new, more egalitarian way of working (Currie and Procter, 2003; Finn et al., 2010).

Question: When is a team not a team? Answer: When it lacks **goal awareness**.

The definition used here is: *a team is a group of people who work together towards a common goal.* An emphasis on the team as a group underpins this chapter. Whether or not the team regularly meets as a group, it can be argued that it still behaves as a group – in the sense that group processes involve a need for both a *shared purpose* and an understanding of how people *feel* about being part of the team (Ward, 2003). It has been increasingly recognised that appropriate management and leadership are needed to facilitate these processes in order to create effective teams. This has been described as moving from 'cop to coach' (Currie and Procter, 2003); that is, moving from an authoritative and directive leadership style to one which is more enabling, supportive and distributed.

The criteria used to decide who is in the team and who is not may produce different results. For instance, people's contracts and a list of their responsibilities may contrast with who actually attends the team meetings, who uses the same room or building, or who contributes to getting the work done. Also, as the following three diverse cases show, different types of team exist in different settings and can sometimes extend over a wide geographical area.

Case study 7.1: Three types of team

Team 1 Adam's surgical team

This is a closely knit team which interacts regularly within the operating theatre in a large city hospital. The core team members are surgeons, anaesthetists, nurses (both theatre and scrub), operating department practitioners and runners. On the periphery of the core team there are ancillary staff such as the consultants' secretaries, booking clerks and porters. This team is an example of a traditional healthcare team, its core team members each representing a profession with its own history and identity and sets of hierarchical and power relationships.

Team 2 Parvati's youth offending team

Youth offending teams (YOTs) are multi-agency teams in England and Wales, which were set up after the Crime and Disorder Act 1998 was passed. This team comprises a police officer, a health worker, an education worker, a social worker and a probation officer. Their role is to work with children and young people involved in offending or at risk of offending. The team is one of three within its locality, all of which are managed by a centralised management services team as part of the local authority. YOTs are complex teams of individuals representing different organisational and professional identities and working closely together to deal with individual referrals but also at a partnership level in feeding into wider issues of crime and disorder in a locality.

Team 3 Shuana's meals-on-wheels team

Meals-on-wheels is a social service which delivers meals to people unable to provide a hot and nutritious meal for themselves. This team comprises a small core of paid local authority staff managing the centres and assessing referrals, which involves working closely with other health and social care professionals and cooks preparing the meals, as well as a large team of volunteer drivers and kitchen helpers. Volunteers give a time commitment ranging from a day per week to just a few hours now and again. Managing volunteers and ensuring they feel part of the team can be challenging: communication is often difficult with a large and geographically dispersed group and the service is subject to considerable change due to budgetary constraints.

Individuals from different disciplines and organisations may operate as one team but also have loyalty to a 'home base' (Ward, 2003). Some teams may have to make decisions with far-reaching consequences beyond their professional boundaries, perhaps in terms of commissioning services. As Ward suggests, such situations can easily cause rivalries, tension and conflict. Consider also that multidisciplinary teams often include service users, carers and volunteers, some of whom may not be used to working in this type of environment. Alternatively, they may come from backgrounds where they have had considerable experience of decision making as well as leading teams and they may want to have a greater say in what the team does.

Another type of team – the 'virtual' team – is becoming an increasingly common way of bringing together a diverse and dispersed group of people. A virtual team relies on technology to make up for the lack of face-to-face meetings, using instead email, voicemail, video-conferencing, the internet, the intranet and other collaboration platforms (Daft, 2006). Given the potential for saving both cost and time, this type of team could become more common in cash-strapped health and social care environments. However, such teams also require different forms of management (see Chapter 20 for more on integrating information technology and virtual communication in the health and social care workplace).

All of this shows that teams are complex and how it is important to think carefully about who is in the team, what their conflicting identities might mean, and how to support more remote members.

For example, it would be easy for Shuana, as manager of the meals-on-wheels team, to focus on the core of paid staff when arranging team meetings and discussing new ways of working. It would be very difficult to find a meeting room or suitable time to involve every volunteer.

How do the four building blocks relate to who is included in the team?

7.3 How do managers and leaders 'build' a team?

Figure 7.2 Building a team is a collaborative effort

As mentioned above, one of the four building blocks of the **fully rounded manager** is **team awareness**, underpinned by managing relationships and leading people. Skills in this regard are therefore important in nurturing a team to motivate it to work effectively (Figure 7.2). Managers may have been promoted from within the team or moved from another part of the same organisation, or even appointed from outside the organisation. So the history of how they joined the team and how the team came together will affect how people view the manager and the manager's relationships with the team members (Ward, 2003). Returning to the three case study teams, as you read the managers' promotion histories outlined below, think about how these experiences might influence relationships in these teams.

Case study 7.2: Team leaders' promotion histories

Team 1 Adam's surgical team

Adam was new to the region when he was appointed as the consultant surgeon and leader of the surgical team. The existing team was clearly split. There was still much loyalty to the previous (and very charismatic) surgeon, who had left some months before, but there was also loyalty to the locum surgeon, who had held the team together through the difficult transition. Adam sensed that, although people seemed keen to make a new start with him as their new leader, deeper down there seemed to be a longing to return to the 'golden age' of the original charismatic leader. He felt it was going to be hard to get past this and convince the team to consider doing things differently.

Team 2 Parvati's youth offending team

Parvati was the newly promoted manager of the youth offending team. She had worked in the team for five years, having originally joined during a period of great stress and high staff turnover. In those early days, despite not being the manager, she had helped to 'steady' morale in the team by showing patience, resilience and support for the leader. As the manager, she continued to remind people of the importance in their work of balancing the needs of the local community, the young people they were helping, and the challenges they themselves faced around multiprofessional working.

Team 3 Shuana's meals-on-wheels team

Shuana became the deputy manager of the meals-on-wheels service when Malcolm, the manager, was instructed to appoint her by his senior management team at the local authority. She had been managing a small social care project locally, which had closed at short notice as a result of funding cuts, and Shuana felt she had not been well supported by senior management. She was transferred to the meals-on-wheels service at only two weeks' notice, and the sudden change upset her, Malcolm and the rest of the team.

(Based on Ward, 2003)

The positive history of Parvati's involvement in the team contributed to the welcome which all team members gave her when she was appointed as manager, and she had a good understanding of the team already. In contrast, Shuana's appointment was problematic from the start, causing anxiety for everyone. Malcolm felt imposed on and resentful at the way in which she had been brought in, and he felt his role as manager was undermined by having effectively no choice in the appointment of such a key role as deputy manager. However, despite such a rocky start, Shuana ultimately proved herself in the new setting, showing that people are not trapped or limited by their histories. However difficult the circumstances surrounding her appointment had been, she herself had much to offer in the post and proved herself over time to the team.

Becoming the manager of a team involves a transition, for both the manager and the team members.

In Adam's case, he had the difficulty of promoting new ideas to a team still wedded to old ways. He wanted the team to work in new and more responsive ways; meanwhile, the rest of the team thought they knew how the job should be done and they just wanted to be allowed to get on with it as they always had done.

Being promoted to be a manager in your own team, as in Parvati's case, can be difficult. It could have taken some time for her former peers to accept she now had authority over them. Likewise, she may have felt awkward about asserting authority over people who were also her friends (Ward, 2003). However, her positive working relationship with the team, resulting in good **team awareness** and wider **contextual awareness**, helped to ease this transition. The important point for any manager is to understand the existing team dynamics.

How would a manager's sense of contextual awareness enhance their ability to work with a new team?

Understanding team dynamics

When putting a team together, the manager probably needs to think primarily in terms of which professions and functional skills are needed and, in the case of more complex arrangements, which other organisations and external members should be represented on the team. Therefore, while keeping a focus on the needs of the team, a wider **contextual awareness** is also crucial.

Beyond the professional role of individual members, any team, whether in health and social care or not, also has particular dynamics, in terms of which roles individual members play in the team process. There are perceived to be common team roles across all teams and these team roles are much more about people's personalities and team dynamics than about professional representation or skill sets (Belbin, 2010). So, for example, is one member good at the detail of planning? Is another good at networking outside the team? Until the team starts functioning, it is not always clear who fulfils the different roles or even whether you have a mixed and well-balanced team. Of course, a problem can arise if all the team members have similar personalities and approaches: for example, if none of them is good at finishing tasks or attending to detail!

Using coaching (see Chapter 10) or appropriate continuing professional development (see Chapter 9), the team leader can encourage or nurture team members to take on different roles in order to build their confidence, skills and abilities.

A key part of **team awareness** is also understanding how teams function, and how to manage a team through the different stages of team development. If a manager is tasked with putting together a brand new team, or establishing their role within an existing team, it might be helpful to be aware of the different stages a team might work though. Bruce Tuckman (1965) developed a framework for understanding how small groups work together, which was further developed by Tuckman and Jensen in 1977. He suggested that they usually go through a series of stages which help them deal with challenges, find solutions and work together more effectively (see Box 7.1). Although this framework has been widely criticised, it is still useful today for understanding how a team might grow and develop, shifting and changing over time.

Box 7.1: Tuckman's framework of group development

Forming – in the early stages, the team is a collection of individuals. Their work is characterised by general talk about the purpose, identity, composition, lifespan, leadership and working arrangements. Individuals are often keen to make an impression on the others and establish their own personal identities at this stage. It can be difficult for a manager, like Adam or Shuana, to come in after this crucial stage. For a caring manager, it is helpful to support each individual in developing and reflecting on their own **personal awareness** at this stage, so that they are aware of what part they are playing in the forming stage.

Storming – most groups go through a period of conflict after an initial superficial consensus. At this stage, the purpose of the group and roles within it, working patterns and behaviour may all be challenged and some interpersonal conflict is to be expected. A strong leader can emerge at this stage, like Parvati as she moved from being a supportive team member to actually managing the team. If successfully managed, this can help to develop trust across the team, which can lead to the formulation of more realistic goals and more effective working.

Norming – this stage is characterised by the establishment of the norms and patterns of work under which the team will operate; for example, how it should work, how decisions are taken, and what degree of openness, trust and confidence is expected among members. People will be testing feelings and opinions within the group and establishing their level of commitment.

Performing – once the previous three stages have been completed, the group should be fully productive. Much energy will have gone into resolving group processes and exploring individual objectives and roles. These measures are often never fully resolved with groups that meet infrequently and may continue to hinder the group. If conflict continues, it is worth exploring structured ways of dealing with it (see Chapter 17 on managing conflict).

Adjourning – many teams disband or re-form into other groupings once a task has been completed. People can find this stressful and this is where managers can help by giving supportive feedback and encouraging team members to continue networking. Social events to mark the end of the team's work can be valuable in helping the transition (see Chapter 5 on managing transitions).

(Based on Tuckman, 1965; Tuckman and Jensen, 1977)

The framework is a useful device for reflecting on why a team may be working in a particular way at a particular time, and it is still used widely. However, it should not be accepted uncritically. Knight (2006) suggests that not all stages are necessarily experienced by all teams, and the reality is rarely the simple linear process implied. Clearly, the context and the purpose of the team will be important here: for example, it may be a new team but the people may know each other from other work or team contexts. In such situations a focus on **goal awareness** can help to reorientate people around the new task. Furthermore, the complexity of many working environments, where tasks are frequently defined by the wider organisational context and membership may change frequently, means such a framework often has limited application (Payne, 2000; Ward, 2003).

How might Adam, Parvati and Shuana have used Tuckman's framework to manage the transition into their teams? Would it have been more useful to reflect on the four building blocks of the caring manager?

Not all teams have the time and resources to dedicate to elaborate team-building events, but there is usually scope to have some time to stop and think about how team members are relating to each other and how this impacts on their functioning. It can be helpful here to reflect on something like Tuckman's framework, in addition to the four building blocks of caring management. **Team awareness** also involves reflecting on the composition of a team: for example, people's age, gender and length of service, or the ethnic mix of the team (Ward, 2003; see also Chapter 6 on managing identities). Even if a team is fairly well established, changes in the wider environment, such as service reorganisation and budget cuts, will affect team dynamics and relationships. All teams will face change, and how the team recognises and responds to these changes will determine how well those changes are weathered (Ward, 2003). As described in Chapter 4, the notion of change and how it is handled is complex and challenging, so the manager or leader of any team must also understand the nature of change.

7.4 Managing and maintaining the team to get the work done

Much of the discussion so far has been about the 'expressive' function of teams and their managers – that is, the way teams work together. However, there also needs to be a focus on the 'instrumental' function because teams are ultimately brought together to get the work done (Ward, 2003); they have to stay 'goal aware'. In managing and maintaining a team, therefore, the manager needs to maintain **goal awareness**, to ensure the team functions effectively to get the assigned tasks done, and that each member does what they are assigned to do (Figure 7.3).

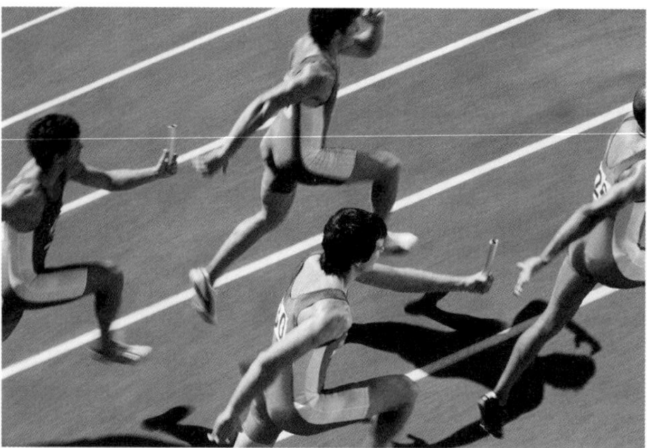

Figure 7.3 Keeping on track is fundamental to good teamwork

Allocation and delegation

An essential part of 'getting the work done' is the allocation of work tasks and responsibilities. The purpose of delegation is to ensure that there is an appropriate distribution of work across a team. Any team working in health and social care probably has a mix of skills and abilities as well as different preferences. Effective delegation not only ensures that the tasks attributed to various team members play to their strengths but also provides opportunities for less experienced members of the team to take on new tasks, while ensuring that the team leader is not overburdened. Delegation also gives the message to team members that their leader trusts them to take on various responsibilities.

However, delegation can be misused when complex tasks are delegated to inexperienced team members, or if the appropriate resources are not in place to support a team member taking on a new task. An effective team leader will ensure that team members are aware of the rationale behind the decisions being made. They will also seek feedback on the success of a new or an inexperienced team member who has been tasked with taking on a new challenge. The **ten-step delegation tool** can help to ensure safeguards are in place to make sure the *right* person is delegated an *appropriate* task and *supported* to complete it successfully.

A team manager needs to have the leadership skills to do this – to oversee the work of the team and to delegate effectively. For example, a manager in a care home will monitor all new admissions, but will not necessarily admit each new resident. Other members of the team will be competent to do so safely, therefore this task should be delegated.

By doing so, the care home manager demonstrates leadership skills in trusting the team to carry out tasks of high importance and therefore motivates them to deliver a high standard of care.

In allocating work across a team, the onus on the manager or leader in health and social care is to always maintain a balance between the individual, the team and the goal (see Adair's model of leadership in Chapter 3, Section 3.4). By taking a proactive approach in allocating work, the manager will use their emotional intelligence and their awareness of each member's skills and competences to match the tasks that have to be achieved to the strengths within the team. Being seen to be fair is important to the individual team members. Therefore, ensuring that unpopular tasks are rotated is important, as well as ensuring that the team as a whole can see the value of the goal they are working towards – providing the best possible care at all times.

Negotiating workloads

Case study 7.3: Looking at workloads

In Parvati's youth offending team, one member sat silently through allocation meetings, never offering to take on any work. Week after week, other members took on new cases, until the realisation dawned that this colleague was not taking a fair workload and his tactic of silence was a success. Parvati did not appear to be responding to this, so the rest of the group stopped volunteering for new work. The allocation pile grew and team meetings got tense. Eventually, an experienced worker said, 'You can't expect the rest of us to take on new work while George never offers to take on anything.' This forced the situation into the open and led to a discussion of workload.

(Based on Ward, 2003)

In balancing goals, fair distribution across the team, and personal strengths and weaknesses, a manager must also think about the question of workloads. Different team members can appear able to cope with different amounts of pressure but, if this is not managed fairly and transparently, problems and resentment can arise. In the YOT, the team members might have preferred it if Parvati dealt with the issue of fair workloads from the start and, when the problem arose, perhaps she should have addressed it sooner by talking to George in private. The situation caused disquiet in what had previously been a smooth-running team. The team manager has an important responsibility, therefore, in promoting openness and tolerance within the team. If this is not done, it can lead to serious conflict.

While 'not pulling your weight', like George, can cause upset, doing *too much* work can also be viewed negatively by the team (Shepard, 2010). This is because teams may develop expectations about team members' and managers' behaviours and thus a set of 'norms' about the team and how much effort is appropriate. An example from the meals-on-wheels team illustrates this.

Case study 7.4: Doing *too* much

Dan is a new and enthusiastic volunteer who would stay and chat to clients after delivering their meals. This was part of the general role, and he had been impressed with how much time he saw Shuana dedicating to clients, but the amount of time he spent on it meant it was slowing down his delivery rate. Also, other members of the team started getting asked by clients why *they* didn't stay and chat for as long as 'the lovely Dan'. Eventually, Dan became stressed by the extra hours he spent at work and the rest of the team felt their effectiveness was being called into question, simply because they could not spend so much time chatting with clients.

In this situation it was up to the team manager to provide realistic expectations about what was expected from the volunteers. Dan's approach was unsustainable but was perhaps partly spurred on by following Shuana's lead.

What would you have done as a manager in the two cases of George and Dan?

As discussed in Chapter 5, working in health and social care is stressful simply because of the nature of the work: dealing with vulnerable people when they are in need of individualised care and compassion. There is unpredictability about the work, and very often pressure to 'do more with less'. Added to this are the almost constant changes faced within health and social care organisation and service delivery (see Chapter 4). If teams are to function well in such circumstances, they cannot just rely on 'common sense'. Members have a professional responsibility to be aware, both individually and as a group, of how they can work together effectively. They also need to pay attention to what has to be done to keep their communication and collaboration going. This awareness and commitment to maintain a well-functioning team needs to be everyone's responsibility, and not just the manager's.

Maintenance, repair and rebuilding

It might be tempting to think that, once established, a team can run itself. However, as you saw with the case of George, even apparently well-functioning teams can face problems. In a small team whose members are collaborating closely for most of the time, keeping an eye on the way the team functions should not be too difficult, although it takes some collective self-discipline (Ward et al., 1998). The functioning of a team can become more challenging as the team expands, or in a team that has more complex methods of communication, perhaps because it is spread across sites or includes community working. The leaders of such teams will need to be conscious not only of the team and the task but also of ensuring that the identity of individuals as team members is maintained, to ensure they stay personally committed to the group aims (Adair, 2002).

An effective team leader will therefore carry out 'team maintenance', by being aware of the team dynamics and proactively facilitating opportunities for the team to work in a cohesive way and for each individual to take an active part in sustaining team cohesion.

Alternatively, the team might want to consider a very different approach, distinct from the regular 'business' of the team. One increasingly popular way of doing this is by following Open Space Technology (see Box 7.2).

Box 7.2: Open Space – four principles and one law

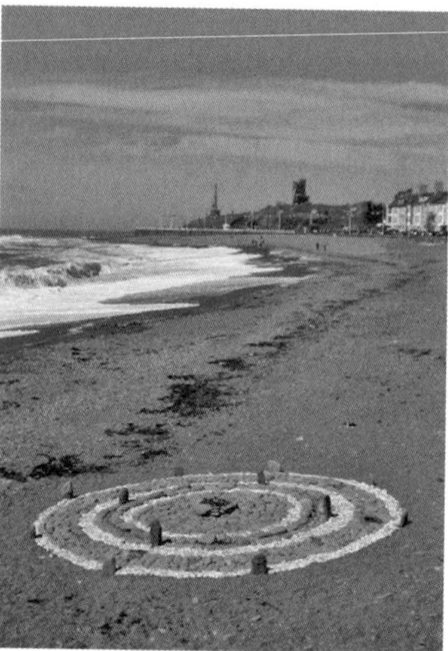

Figure 7.4 A circle provides the geometry for open communication

Following a method devised by organisational consultant Harrison Owen, Open Space meetings take place in a circle (Figure 7.4) and follow the basic principles below.

Whoever comes is the right people	There is little point in worrying about all those who should have come, might have come, but didn't come. Concentrate on those who are there; the group present is always the right group.
Whenever it starts is the right time	Conventional wisdom says that if you want to get something done, you must start on time. Open Space events have a beginning and an end, but everything in the middle must be allowed to run its own course. Spirit and creativity do not run on the clock.
Whatever happens is the only thing that could have	Focus on the here and now, and eliminate all of the 'could-have-beens', 'should-have-beens' or 'might-have-beens'.
When it's over, it's over	You never know how long it will take to resolve an issue, but whenever the issue or conversation is finished, move on to the next thing.

The Law of Two Feet	If you have two feet, you must be prepared to use them. If you find you are neither learning nor contributing, use your two feet and go somewhere you can make a difference. Indicate that you have nothing further to contribute, wish them well, and go and do something useful.

(Based on Owen, 2012)

Open Space meetings can be used to encourage a different way of thinking in a team. In the case of the hospital surgical team, the previous team leader had adopted quite a directive approach to meetings and often made decisions with little consultation. Team members liked his businesslike approach but also had an underlying feeling that not all problems were being discussed in a fair and democratic way. Adam thought holding an Open Space session would be a way to air issues and move on.

Case study 7.5: Embracing Open Space

The team members arrived at the room to find the chairs arranged in a circle with blank flipcharts and sticky notepads on the floor. Adam welcomed everybody and explained that the team needed to come up with the agenda based on the burning issues facing the team. He then stepped back and invited them to start identifying ideas. At first, they were surprised at such an unstructured approach but soon realised they had many ideas and issues they wanted to explore. By the end of the session, they felt really energised.

Although it was going to be difficult to operate such meetings regularly due to time and shift constraints, the team agreed that they could also meet virtually on specially constructed online forums, which could stretch the time frame and allow these discussions to flow asynchronously over a week or more.

Effectively maintaining a functioning team through fostering collective **team awareness** – and perhaps using the sort of Open Space approach adopted by Adam – facilitates an organic approach to teamwork. It does not necessarily mean doing different things from normal but, rather, doing some of the same things differently. For example, Ward (2003) suggests staff supervision or staff meetings can be used not just for the instrumental business of ensuring that all responsibilities and tasks are carried out appropriately, but also they can be adapted to include a focus on the expressive side of the team's work. Time spent doing this can prevent problems occurring, thereby saving time in the long run.

However, even in the best-run organisations, things sometimes go badly wrong, and the effective leader and proactive manager needs to recognise this, be aware of potential problems brewing, and do something about it should they occur. An effective leader will recognise the potential for conflict within a team, and be able to use their emotional intelligence (see Chapter 2) to pick up on any tensions arising. Intervention is needed at this point *before* it develops into a conflict. However, it is not always possible to intervene early and the team leader will be required to act as mediator when conflict arises within a team (see Chapter 17 for more on dealing with conflict). This might reveal that it is something the manager is 'getting wrong'.

If the team leader or manager is part of the problem, the best way forward may be to bring in an outside adviser or consultant, preferably someone without line management responsibilities to the team. This can 'free up' communication and enable both people to speak and difficulties to be aired in a safe environment (Furnivall, 1991). It can be challenging for a leader to 'let go' in this way, but it is also often the mark of strong leadership underpinned by good **personal awareness**.

7.5 Leading the team

> [C]reating a culture of engaging leadership is critical, since it not only predicts the performance of teams, it also predicts a range of positive affective outcomes, including high levels of motivation, job satisfaction, job and organisational commitment, as well as wellbeing indicators …
>
> (Alimo-Metcalfe et al., 2008, p. 595)

Putting your best foot forward

The role of the team leader is often challenging, but it can also be rewarding when effective leadership leads to individual team members feeling that their contribution to the overall working of the team is worthwhile, recognised and appreciated. Chapter 3 shows that, by working towards a shared vision, through distributed leadership, teams are likely to be more effective in achieving their goals. Thus, the 'whole' team can be seen as potentially much greater than the sum of its parts, because it can enable individuals to discover or develop new talents in a supportive environment where everyone is working towards the same end. Ward (2003) suggests the role of the team leader or manager can then be seen as similar to an orchestral conductor: bringing out the best in individuals to enhance the performance of the whole group and stimulating individuals further to give of their best and reach new heights (Mintzberg, 1998). The team leader 'as conductor' might focus on the interpersonal dynamics of leadership: thinking about how to inspire people and encouraging them to inspire each other.

Recalling Chapter 6, how can team leaders nurture team identity?

Leading a team also requires awareness that there may be resistance to being part of that team, and team members may not identify with the external image of the team or that preferred by management. Learmonth (2009) carried out an ethnographic study in a hospital and found that the 'discourse' of teams was resisted by some staff who had created alternative identities for themselves (see Box 7.3).

Box 7.3: Are we a team?

The official hospital literature was replete with such terms as teams and teamwork, which managers used in routine and unnoticed ways. The monthly meetings that all staff attended were designated 'team briefings', for example, and job advertisements typically used the description 'team player' to portray the kind of employee being sought. Indeed, *Join The Team And Make A Difference*, a slogan taken directly from a national government recruitment campaign for NHS staff, was the screensaver on all the hospital staff members' computer terminals. However, the people with whom I spent most of my time during the field work – filing clerks in the medical records department, workers who maintained the paper records of patients' clinical details – rarely used the term spontaneously. They much preferred referring to one another as 'the girls'.

(Learmonth, 2009, p. 1888)

In their research on an operating department team, Finn and colleagues (2010) found that surgeons and anaesthetists used the discourse of teams to 'reproduce and legitimate their privileged position, while nurses and ODPs [operating department practitioners] mobilized team discourse in order to challenge medical privileges' (p. 1152). Therefore, the discourses of teams can clearly be used in different ways, whether to subvert a supposed team identity or to maintain existing power relationships. This highlights the fact that teams are based on interpersonal relationships which, as Wong (2003) emphasises, have an inherent power dynamic. Anyone trying to 'conduct' a team will need to be attentive to such dynamics which might work to undermine or subvert their plans.

What power imbalances might there be in the meals-on-wheels team between volunteers and paid members of the team? In the youth offending team, how might the different professions involved lead to power struggles?

The manager carries a specific responsibility to cultivate awareness and commitment, and to demonstrate and model it in action. However, if this responsibility just stays with them, it is less likely to be 'owned' by other team members or the team as a whole. Part of what the team manager has to do, therefore, is to promote and foster people's 'team membership skills' and this involves good leadership. A core part of what makes teamwork 'work' concerns the more intangible qualities of effective collaboration, such as a supportive atmosphere, a positive culture and mutual respect among team members. Qualities such as these can seem elusive and hard to achieve if they are missing, but a manager with good **personal awareness** and **team awareness** can facilitate their development by understanding the interpersonal dynamics of their team and how best to foster mutual support and a collaborative identity across it. Often, therefore, getting this right relies on not only efficient management but also effective leadership.

7.6 Conclusion

Teams matter in health and social care because people at work need to be able to communicate and collaborate if they are to provide safe and effective care. The way teams operate is complex and variable, and needs to incorporate and adapt to continual change. It is important, therefore, for a manager to be aware of the expressive aspects of a team – how people feel about the team and their place in it – as well as the instrumental task of getting the work done in an appropriate, safe, fair and transparent manner.

This chapter covered some of the ways in which managers can develop their **team awareness** to promote and support better communication and collaboration in the everyday management of their teams. Chapter 8 on partnerships develops these issues in more depth.

Good **team awareness** can help to keep the team on track under the pressures and demands of everyday work (team 'maintenance') and help to deal with difficulties as they arise (team 'repair' and 'rebuilding'). These are core responsibilities of the team manager, but this chapter also explored how important strong leadership can be in achieving this. Effective leadership means each team member is seen as an individual with strengths and weaknesses, as well as someone contributing to the overall team performance. While the team leader will always have one eye on the end goal they must never forget, therefore, that the people in their team are the key to achieving it!

Key points

- Teams matter because they are the main way in which the service user experiences health and social care.
- Multiprofessional teams are complex and, if managed effectively, provide the opportunity to bring a variety of skills and experiences to tackling a problem or task.
- Team managers have to keep a constant focus on both the instrumental *and* the expressive aspects of the work: the task that has to be achieved and the way in which the task is achieved.
- Teams benefit from strong leadership to negotiate the different stages of development and to foster and support their expressive function.
- An effective team leader is aware of how power dynamics affect team morale and the way in which their team functions.

References

Adair, J. (2002) *Effective Strategic Leadership*, London, Macmillan.

Alimo-Metcalfe, B., Alban-Metcalfe, J., Bradley, M., Mariathasan, J. and Samele, C. (2008) 'The impact of engaging leadership on performance, attitudes to work and wellbeing at work. A longitudinal study', *Journal of Health Organization and Management*, vol. 22, no. 6, pp. 586–98.

Belbin, R.M. (2010) *Team Roles at Work* (2nd edition), Oxford, Butterworth-Heinemann.

Bristol Royal Infirmary Inquiry (2001) *Learning from Bristol*, London, The Stationery Office.

Currie, G. and Procter, S. (2003) 'The interaction of human resource management policies and practices with the implementation of teamworking: evidence from the UK public sector', *International Journal of Human Resource Management*, vol. 14, pp. 581–99.

Daft, R.L. (2006) *The New Era of Management*, London, Thomson.

Department of Health (DH) (2008a) *NHS Next Stage Review: A high quality workforce*, London, The Stationery Office.

Department of Health (DH) (2008b) *NHS Next Stage Review: High quality care for all*, London, The Stationery Office.

Finn, R., Learmonth, M. and Reedy, P. (2010) 'Some unintended effects of teamwork in healthcare', *Social Science and Medicine*, vol. 70, pp. 1148–54.

Furnivall, J. (1991) 'Peper Harrow – consultancy – a customer's view', in Silveira, W.R. (ed.) *Consultation in Residential Care*, Aberdeen, Aberdeen University Press, Chapter 2.

General Medical Council (GMC) (2006) *Good Medical Practice*, London, GMC.

Knight, P.J. (2006) *Small, Short Duration Technical Team Dynamics*, Fort Belvoir, Va., Defense Acquisition University Press.

Learmonth, M. (2009) '"Girls" working together without "teams": how to avoid the colonization of management language', *Human Relations*, vol. 62, no. 12, pp. 1887–1906.

Martin, G.P. and Finn, R. (2011) 'Patients as team members: opportunities, challenges and paradoxes of including patients in multi-professional healthcare teams', *Sociology of Health and Illness*, vol. 33, no. 7, pp. 1050–65.

Martin, V., Charlesworth, J. and Henderson, E. (2010) *Managing in Health and Social Care*, London, Routledge.

Mintzberg, H. (1988) 'Covert leadership: notes on managing professionals', *Harvard Business Review*, November–December, pp. 140–7.

Owen, H. (2012) *Opening Space for Emerging Order* [Online]. Available at www.openspaceworld.com/brief_history.htm (Accessed 22 November 2012).

Payne, M. (2000) *Teamwork in Multiprofessional Care*, Basingstoke, Macmillan.

Procter, S. and Mueller, F. (2000) *Teamworking*, London, Macmillan.

Shepard, J.M. (2010) *Sociology* (10th edition), Belmont, Calif., Wadsworth Cengage Learning.

Tuckman, B.W. (1965) 'Development sequence in small groups', *Psychological Bulletin*, vol. 63, pp. 384–99.

Tuckman, B.W. and Jensen, M.A.C. (1977) 'Stages of small group development revisited', *Group and Organisational Studies*, vol. 2, pp. 419–27.

Ward, A. (2003) 'Managing the team', in Seden, J. and Reynolds, J. (eds) *Managing Care in Practice*, London, Routledge/The Open University, pp. 33–56 (K303 Set Book).

Ward, A., McMahon, L., Cain, P. and Howard, T. (1998) 'The function of the ward meeting', in Ward, A. and McMahon, L. (eds) *Intuition Is Not Enough: Matching learning with practice in therapeutic child care*, London, Routledge.

Wong, K.-F. (2003) 'Empowerment as a panacea for poverty – old wine in new bottles? Reflections on the World Bank's conception of power', *Progress in Development Studies*, vol. 3, no. 4, pp. 307–22.

Chapter 8 Managing partnerships

Julie Charlesworth

8.1 Introduction

Figure 8.1 'Coming together is a beginning; keeping together is progress; working together is success.' (Henry Ford, 1863–1947)

> I'm trying to persuade people that this partnership working isn't something that you do in addition to your day job. Partnership working becomes the way you do your day job.
>
> (Local authority policy officer, quoted in Charlesworth, 2002)

Partnership working usually occurs because there is a need to go beyond involving known individuals or professionals to invite wider representation and expertise (Figure 8.1). This may be because of government guidelines, or because there is a realisation within the organisation that previous policies have been unsuccessful owing to limited resources or expertise. Often, collaboration is initiated because one organisation needs the input – and invariably resources – from another sector, such as voluntary and community groups or private sector investment.

In theory, the reasons for working in partnership in health and social care make perfect sense: people increasingly have complex needs that do not fit neatly into the categories or organisational boundaries within which it is convenient to provide services. Therefore, a more holistic approach involving different organisations and professions is required to understand this intersection of health and social care needs. Furthermore, in times of substantial change and financial restrictions, managers and leaders need to be even more innovative in finding ways to pool resources and work successfully with other organisations in order to maintain quality services.

As outlined in Chapter 7, many service user needs are addressed, and often improved, by professionals working in multidisciplinary teams. However, partnerships go beyond these teams and are much more complex. By their very nature of involving numerous organisations from different sectors and organisational cultures, they require careful leadership and management. A 'successful' partnership is often one where the end result is a new and fully integrated service or organisation created from an initial set of fragmented arrangements, which requires strong management and leadership from start to finish.

Since the 1970s, numerous directives and initiatives have been designed by both central government and local agencies in order to stimulate joint working and to emphasise its role in effective service delivery. In many policy areas, working in partnership is now mandatory. This does not mean, however, that all partnerships are necessarily successful; in many cases, managers are increasingly unsure what the criteria for success actually look like. Indeed, commentators on the extensive literature on partnership working are increasingly critical about the focus on *process* rather than *outcomes* (for example, Dickinson and Glasby, 2010). In other words, does working in partnership really deliver better outcomes for patients and service users?

Thinking about partnership working raises several difficult questions about the challenges of operating and managing collaboratively:

- How do you lead a complex team made up of different professions and organisations and create shared aims and vision?
- What skills are required to be a participant in, or a manager of, a partnership?
- How do managers evaluate the success of a partnership?

Generally speaking, collaboration is not easily viewed as a stand-alone topic for front-line managers. It pervades all aspects of managers' work (for example, managing teams, monitoring and audit, service user consultation, managing change and conflict). It also draws on a range of management skills and knowledge, particularly leadership, but also decision making, communication, negotiation, developing strategy, and managing information and finances. In addition, managers need a good awareness of other organisational and professional cultures and ways of working, as well as an understanding of how partnership has functioned locally in the past.

The literature on partnership working can be confusing – much of it has a 'feel-good' approach, emphasising the benefits of partnership working, but often lacks a credible evidence base for this. Other literature is overly negative and pessimistic for the prospects of successful collaboration. The reality is that partnership working is here to stay, so this chapter focuses on some key issues and debates in managing and leading partnerships; and, given that working collaboratively is both well established and in many cases mandatory, what managers can do to ensure inclusive, accountable and effective structures for improving outcomes for their staff and service users.

The core questions addressed in this chapter are:

- What are partnerships and why bother to collaborate if it is difficult?
- What is the role of power in partnerships?
- What are the sources of conflict and difference?
- How do managers lead and evaluate successful partnership working?

8.2 What is partnership working and why bother?

Although partnership working is in many instances mandatory and deemed good practice, organisations have often developed their own initiatives or interpretations of government policy. Consequently, there is considerable variation between localities in terms of how organisations and managers work together across traditional boundaries (Figure 8.2). The history of joint working in a locality can also continue to influence current arrangements: for example, past negative experiences play a part in organisational memory and individuals' willingness to engage with other organisations (Charlesworth, 2001).

Before continuing, it is useful to consider what 'partnership working' means and how it differs from teamworking (see Box 8.1).

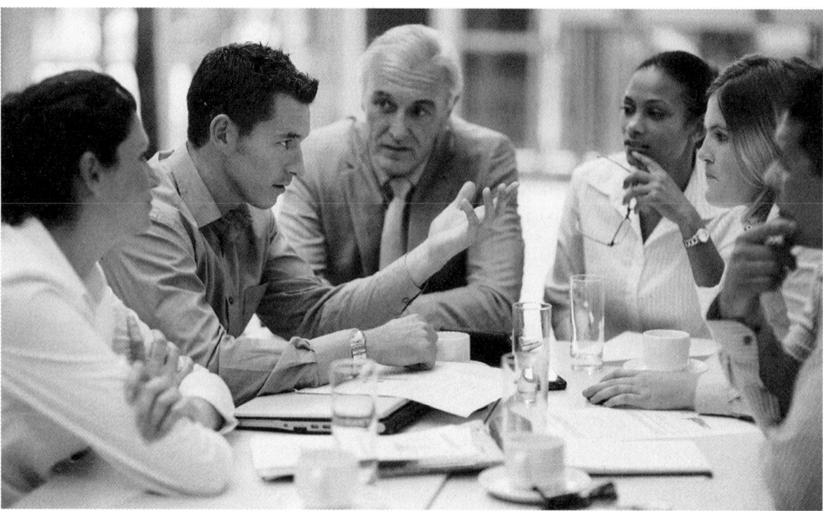

Figure 8.2 How can you recognise partnership?

Box 8.1: Defining 'partnership working'

Different terms are used to describe working across boundaries, including: joint working, collaboration, partnership, interorganisational relationships, networking, joint venture, consortium, alliance, coordination, and cooperation. In a sense, a partnership is a team – admittedly a very complex team – but it usually means that different organisations and/or sectors are involved and not just different professions. In health and social care, we might refer to a multidisciplinary team dealing with an individual patient or a group of service users. However, partnership working is generally more visible and distinct, often at a strategic level: for example, in planning and decision making, in wider consultation, in public involvement, or in change initiatives or specific projects.

Partnerships may also be more formal than many regular teams: for example, they might involve dedicated resources, have their own budget and partnership board, or get a group of people from different organisations together once every few months to develop a joint strategy or project proposal. The concept of partnership generally does not include relationships that are very clearly contractual; for example, buying a product or service from a private sector supplier (with the exception of some public–private initiatives in health care).

Nor does it include organisations that have merged with or taken over another organisation, although clearly these may have begun as partnerships and become a fully integrated single organisation (for example, some health and social care trusts).

Essentially though, a partnership is a way of working jointly where there is shared commitment, an interest in positive outcomes, and a desire to overcome the inflexibilities of boundaries (Sullivan and Skelcher, 2002).

Clearly, partnership working does not just happen overnight; even where it is mandatory, individuals and the organisations they represent often progress through different stages of collaboration. In the past, commentators have suggested that organisations work in a linear fashion towards partnership (for example, Hudson et al., 1998; see Figure 8.3).

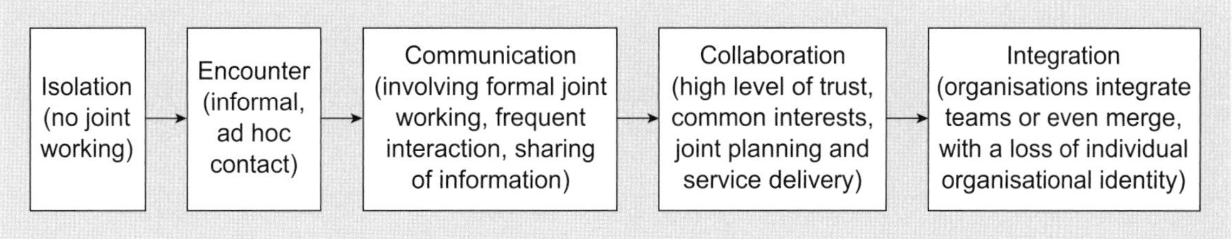

Figure 8.3 Steps towards partnership working (based on Hudson et al., 1998)

However, it is not always such a linear process. Glasby and his colleagues (2011) discuss degrees of partnership in terms of the *depth and breadth* of the relationship and what options are available, depending on the desired outcomes, strengths and limitations of the organisations. Depth refers to sharing information, consulting each other, coordinating activities, joint management, partnership organisation or formal merger. Breadth refers to which organisations and communities need to be engaged. The relationship can then be expressed as a matrix chart to help organisations assess where they are now and where they want to be in the future (Figure 8.4).

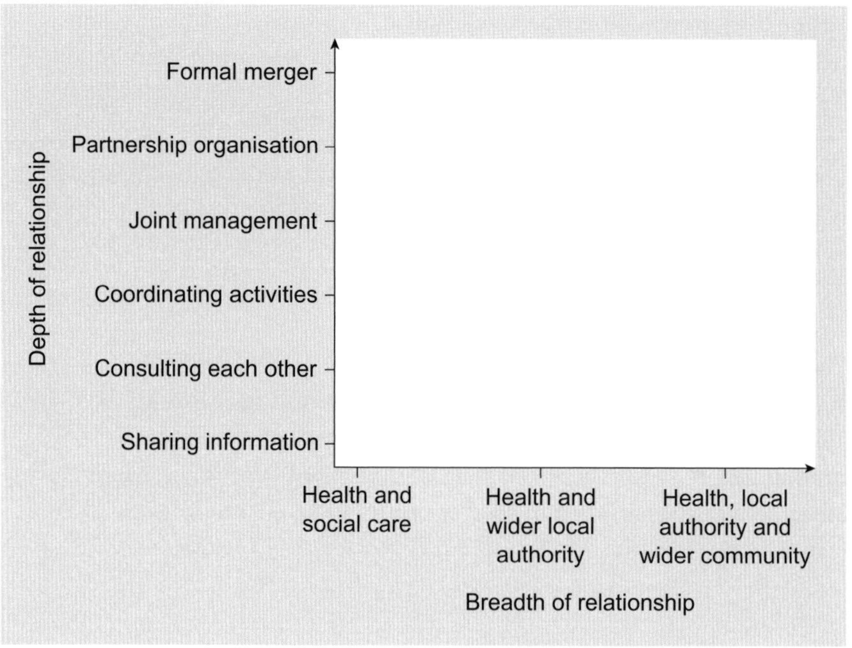

Figure 8.4 Depth versus breadth in partnership working (Glasby et al., 2011, p. 5)

Chapter 7 describes how managers can use Tuckman's framework of team development to understand how their team develops and functions over time. How useful do you think this would be in understanding how partnerships develop and the implications for managing them?

This section has started to explore what partnership means and the sheer complexity involved. So why do organisations bother with it?

Why collaborate?

> If we don't have partners to work with … we wouldn't be able to do our job properly. We would be limited in what help we could offer. We would be doing a disservice to service users. We would be limiting their opportunities.
>
> (Shirley Findley, regional service manager for Safeguarding Communities: Reducing Offending, Scotland, 2012)

The government agenda set the pace for collaboration during the 1990s but it was based on a history of interprofessional and interagency working across different services, and the drive to improve services, reduce costs and duplication, add value, increase accountability, and respond to the complexity of service users' needs. Governments and organisations themselves have recognised that there are cross-cutting issues, which do not fit neatly under the remit of one organisation, and that, in fact, they fall into the 'interorganisational domain'. This is a policy space where the only means of dealing with such issues successfully is through collaboration between organisations, perhaps with one organisation acting as a 'strategic bridge' to bring them together (Huxham and Vangen, 2005).

In the past, statutory organisations often took on the role but it could easily be a voluntary or private sector organisation. This also highlights the need for an appropriate individual from the bridging organisation to take on a key leadership role: after all, it is not organisations which lead but *people* and they can make a difference not only to the process but, more importantly, to improving outcomes for patients and service users.

'Expert facilitation is reliant on leaders knowing when collaboration is and is not appropriate …, being able to act strategically in identifying who needs to be brought to the table and for what and being able to build trusting and productive relationships between partners' (Sullivan et al., 2012, p. 55).

Huxham and Vangen (2005) have extensively explored the concept of *collaborative advantage* as a prime reason for organisations seeking to work together. This is primarily concerned with creating synergy between collaborating organisations and the outputs of collaboration that could not have been achieved except through collaborating. However, partnerships often fail and this is termed *collaborative inertia* to describe 'when the apparent rate of work output of a core group is slowed down considerably compared to what a casual observer might expect the group to be able to achieve' (Huxham, 1996, p. 241). This highlights the importance of maintaining a clear focus on the potential results attainable through collaboration, and not regarding joint working as something that will automatically generate results just because it is 'a good thing' to do. It also illustrates the importance of management and leadership in working through any degree of collaborative inertia and how **goal awareness** (one of the four building blocks of the **fully rounded caring manager**) could be the key to successful collaboration.

Therefore, closer working together could include the following benefits.

- Developing a shared vision, aims and objectives, in order to deliver an integrated strategy or services better able to meet the needs of service users.
- Involving a wider range of people and organisations in decision making to ensure a more participative way of working.
- Improving communication between organisations.
- Pooling resources such as funding, staffing, equipment, office space and access to training.
- Sharing expertise from organisations and individuals working in a similar (or a different) field.
- Enabling both staff and unpaid workers from different organisations to encounter different organisational cultures and ways of working, share good practice, and learn from the experience to deliver better outcomes for service users.

The bottom line, however, should be a focus on outcomes: that is, does partnership working make any difference to service users (Glasby and Dickinson, 2008)?

In reality, the reasons for working in partnership may shift over time in response to different external and internal pressures and conflicts. Furthermore, an organisation may have different views on partnership working, depending on the policy area. Managers themselves may feel differently towards the various partnerships in which they are engaged, perhaps because of the personality of individuals involved, how strong the leadership is, the size of the budget, and so on. Therefore, context is extremely important in understanding people's experiences of partnership working.

Although there are many examples of best practice and services where the philosophy of joint working is embedded, there are also many examples of failure. Yet government agendas have increasingly made collaboration 'core business' across health and social care and something organisations and managers cannot ignore.

The local authority policy officer quoted at the beginning of this chapter encapsulates this philosophy: it is an integral element of the manager's day job.

So, how can managers ensure that collaboration produces successful outcomes and is inclusive and accountable? What factors contribute to the success or failure of partnership working? There is literature on why collaboration fails in research on public, voluntary and private sector organisations (see Huxham and Vangen, 2005; Dickinson and Glasby, 2010). Although there may be some context-specific factors, many of the issues raised apply to all types of collaboration. For example, similar issues occur whether the initiative is between a local authority and a voluntary organisation or between different multinational companies! Therefore, participants in failing partnerships cannot use the excuse that they 'failed' through lack of resources, size or input from powerful individuals.

The fact is that partnership development is extremely complex and variable with organisations subject to many different internal and external pressures. For example, there may be a specific local and historical context, where previous negative or positive experiences of working together may affect the pace of progress. Furthermore, even if organisations have worked together well in the past, different individuals may now be involved from those organisations, and they may have less experience of partnership working or a different style of leadership. Partnerships are teams of individuals and working with other people is difficult, particularly if the team members sitting around the table represent different professions, sectors, levels of seniority and expertise – and, of course, personalities. All public services and the voluntary sector are under pressure through wider political imperatives and constraints, organisational restructuring, and pressures on budgets – all of these factors can be reflected in organisations' expectations for the partnership.

The rest of this chapter concerns the practical implications of collaborative working for managers and leaders. It explores how they might anticipate and address the problems and challenges outlined here on a daily basis, in order to lead and manage a successful partnership in health and social care.

8.3 Managing power relationships

> [W]hatever our status or our background we all have something different to contribute.
>
> (Robinson, 2004, p. 9)

'Power and hierarchy in professional and managerial relationships can stultify effective partnerships' (Joint Improvement Team, 2009, p. 5).

There is much rhetoric about collaboration – from both central government and local organisations themselves – but, in reality, it can be difficult and many people have experienced failed partnerships. Experiences of the same initiative can be mixed: for example, statutory agencies may proclaim a particular initiative a success but representatives from voluntary organisations, service users and carers may feel they have not played an equal role in it, or that they have been failed by a lack of communication. This type of experience could make people wary of future proposals and unhappy about contributing time and effort if their views are deemed subordinate to those of other partners. This highlights one of the main challenges in partnership working: the role of *power.*

Power relationships cut across all aspects of partnership working. There is a paradox, however: they are the reason why partnership working happens – to make the planning of services more inclusive and accountable by reducing power imbalances between organisations and with service users. However, if the imbalances persist, the partnership can fall apart. Furthermore, gender, socio-economic group, ethnicity and disability inevitably cut across power relationships and affect different people's capacity to participate fully in partnership working. The following quotation, which concerns regeneration partnerships but is equally applicable to the health and social care context, considers the issue of power in organisational terms.

> [P]ower imbalances apply to the relations between partners – from the public, private, voluntary and community sectors. However, they can also apply to relations within the sectors engaged in partnerships – between one grouping within a community and another, between representatives and those they are supposed to be representing, between majority groups and minority interests,

> between those with the most extensive networks and those with the least extensive.
>
> (Mayo and Taylor, 2001, p. 40)

What are the sources of power imbalance in a partnership context?

There are many potential sources of power imbalance in partnership working. First, different professions have views on their own and others' status and position in a perceived hierarchy. One professional group may feel that they should lead the partnership, given their history in leading initiatives. This can create difficulties when trying to encourage new occupational groups (such as nurses) to take an enhanced role in management structures, or to take on new responsibilities, which might lead to much personal stress (see MacKian et al., 2003).

Second, the differences between sectors have traditionally had an impact on new partnership working. Voluntary and service user organisations have felt they had lower status and power than statutory organisations. They have expressed concern that they do not have the same position in the collaboration because they do not have equal financial power and they often think their position is 'tokenistic'.

Third, the differences between organisations and professional groups potentially create communication problems, particularly through using different jargon, which can be confusing enough for the professionals and managers in statutory service but may be completely bewildering for the service users and voluntary organisation representatives, making them feel excluded from discussions.

Technical language and expert knowledge have traditionally been used to create authority and power for some individuals, professions and organisations, thereby attempting to exclude others. There is increasing awareness of this problem and attempts are being made to change these factors in new partnership arrangements. Clarke and his colleagues (2007) explored the relationships between knowledge and power in their research on involving citizens more in decision making in public services. Their interviewees were managers, professionals, service users and local people who frequently spoke about tension around power and the role of tradition and hierarchy:

> [Their interviewees] point to ways in which public services are considered to be a site of hierarchically organised professional knowledge and power that has become unsettled and tangled into new knots as other forms of knowledge are asserted and other claims to power – or empowerment – are made. Managers and senior professionals … see themselves as responsible for undoing the 'knowledge/power knot' and reconstructing the relationships between staff and users. Organisations, embodied in the authority of managers, have been trying to find new configurations of knowledge and power that would take account of a more active, participating, competent public.
>
> (Clarke et al., 2007, p. 117)

How can the web of power (Wong, 2003; see Chapter 1) help to understand people's experiences of partnership working?

Lukes (1974) provided one of the most frequently cited discussions of power. His concept of 'non-decision making', whereby issues are kept off the agenda, was applied by Mayo and Taylor (2001) to partnership. They suggest that powerful partners (government departments, private sector organisations) influence outcomes through setting agendas and deciding what will, and what will not, be discussed. This is an example (similar to Wong's argument) of statutory organisations having subtle power over others.

Distributed leadership (see Chapter 3), which harnesses the motivation of staff at all levels of an organisation, is needed to promote working in unison towards a partnership vision.

As Huxham and Vangen (2005) report, the very nature of collaboration means organisations have different aims, objectives and reasons for being involved in working with others. This is also the source of strength of the interaction. They further suggest that there are two types of goal: first, *meta-goals*, which are goals for the collaboration and the reason why it exists. However, there is an inherent contradiction with setting these meta-goals: they need to be explicit but the more rigid they are, the less likely organisations are to sign up to them. Second, there are *organisation-specific goals*, which each organisation wants to achieve through the collaboration but are separate from the goals of the collaboration, such as raising their own organisation's profile.

Both types of goal may need to be addressed in order to achieve a successful partnership. However, the presence of different aims and objectives can create difficulties in building trust and concerns around conflicting agendas.

How can a manager ensure that both types of goal are met satisfactorily? Does thinking about the four building blocks of the caring manager help?

Huxham (1996) suggests that when people embark on cross-boundary working without a clear idea of what they want to achieve, and who they are working with, it is doomed to fail. People are often too busy to attend meetings and commit resources to a new initiative that lacks a clear focus. This therefore highlights the need for clear leadership and the development and ownership of a clear and shared vision for the group (see Chapter 3 for more on why vision is so important).

Research by the Institute for Voluntary Action Research on voluntary sector involvement in partnerships found that there was often a lack of understanding about why they were expected to work with staff from other organisations, the purpose of the partnership, and the particular programme within it. This suggests that **goal** and **contextual awareness** were absent. As one interviewee stated: 'The bid was put together by the partners, but no-one owned it. Everyone had a different interpretation of the main thrust of the bid' (IVAR, 2011, p. 25).

Where a partnership was successful, it was usually supported by a shared vision of developing high-quality services. For example, in a partnership between a children's centre and a city council:

> Both parties understood their need for the other in order to succeed in this aim, and recognised that they would both gain something that neither could achieve in isolation. Their shared goals helped them focus on the longer-term aim and deal with detailed negotiations over buildings and finance in an open and positive manner.
>
> (IVAR, 2011, p. 30)

Furthermore, IVAR's studies showed that communicating rationale, vision and potential outcomes within the partner organisations tackled concerns about loss of status, identity and organisational culture. However, even when a strong shared vision is in place, it is not always the most obvious of identity or power struggles which might undermine someone's efforts to be involved in successful partnership working, as the following case study shows.

Case study 8.1: Time for partnership?

In a local partnership working to improve maternity services, Susan, a service user representative, was facing difficulties in securing expenses for her involvement. The partnership manager, Eva, took this to be an issue of 'power' and suggested it was a case of Susan not recognising her own 'clout'. She tried to reassure Susan, telling her she had the authority and right to demand adequate recompense from the appropriate channels. However, for Susan it wasn't a question of power, but a practical one – as each hour spent chasing up the issue involved costly child care and a loss of earnings.

This wasn't a case of a lay person not thinking she had the same weight as a professional committee member; it was the simple practicalities of devoting time to chasing up side issues outside the main work of the partnership. The manager, Eva, in assuming it was because the lay person felt less powerful, overlooked other issues which needed to be addressed, such as better management of financial support.

For partnership to work, all parties need to have an equal voice, be able and willing to share power, and be able to operate on an equal footing. Voluntary organisations do have a source of power because they are needed by statutory agencies for their views and contact with service users; and service users have power because, without them, there would be no service in the first place. If the purpose of partnership is to empower groups outside the statutory agencies to provide better services, managers need to be aware of power structures and imbalances, and find appropriate ways of overcoming them, to lead everyone towards the same core vision. One way of doing this could be to ask a representative from a voluntary organisation or service user group to have a prominent role in a partnership, supported where necessary. However, this must always be done in a way which is sensitive to people's contexts – which may make equal participation difficult.

8.4 Managing change, conflict and difference

> [We've got] all these drivers on performance targets and they want to see outcomes, they want to see things that make a difference, but that is a really difficult, rigorous systematic process to go through when you're trying to engage partners. Traditionally, when we've done partnership working, we've looked for people to come together to begin to work through things and ideas begin to grow. Now the whole driver is a much more kind of disciplined approach from government. It's very difficult to put that across to people who might not have been involved at all in the subject.
>
> (Local authority assistant chief executive, quoted in Charlesworth, 2002)

The need to manage change is a constant factor in all areas of public services but particularly in health and social care (see Chapter 4). Managers say that this makes partnership work difficult and can create conflicting views on what, and how, to prioritise. Pressures to meet performance targets can put a strain on successful collaboration and limit organisations' wider vision. The types of conflicting issues which can arise include:

- Organisations within a partnership relationship are probably competing for the same resources from central government or other funders.
- They may also have to deliver complex policy outcomes within the partnership at the same time as trying to meet the performance requirements placed on their 'own' organisations.
- There are difficulties in managing the interface between different conceptions of 'what works' – especially where a manager's own professional view of good practice conflicts with a policy arising from a different evidence base.

These pressures inevitably impact on partnership working and can be exacerbated where the philosophy that partnership is 'the way you do your day job' is not fully embedded. Dealing with the pressures of change can mean individuals and organisations think they can jettison anything they consider superfluous and/or difficult, as described by Vivian McConvey, who leads the voluntary organisation Voice of Young People in Care:

> Because what happens midway through a project, something within their job becomes a bigger priority and the partnership work or the project we're working on gets a lower priority and they start to disappear. People who see it as integrated into their work and a way of getting business done – you will find that they approach meetings differently. They approach a relationship differently. They have different conversations with you. That they engage with you as someone who is really integral to getting the actual outcome that's required.
>
> (Vivian McConvey, chief executive of VOYPIC, 2012)

How might a manager ensure that partnership is integrated into people's approach to work even when they are facing other challenging changes?

Successful joint working does not happen overnight, partly because collaboration is a lengthy and painstaking process even under ideal conditions. However, it becomes even more difficult where managers are operating within an environment of new and/or changing structures and tight resource constraints. Even where organisations manage to begin partnership working, coping with new and changing organisational and team structures can be both exciting and frightening at the same time.

Does partnership working mean losing professional identity?

As shown in Chapter 7, multidisciplinary working can be difficult. Each professional group traditionally had its own identity, culture, training, and accreditation and allegiances beyond the workplace to national professional bodies. In the following quotation, a manager talks about these difficulties when first bringing together a health team and a social care team in a joint workshop to look at their future collaboration.

> [The workshop] raised a lot of issues about how people felt about the other team. In general, the health teams felt they had got more status: they worked alongside nurses and they felt they were going to lose that. They felt the social care teams didn't have as much status as they were managed by social care staff who weren't qualified. We knew we wouldn't get over that in a workshop but we felt it was a useful forum for actually raising these issues in front of each other and, while you can't address a lot of them, knowing about them was a first step.
>
> (Martin et al., 2010, p. 10)

Figure 8.5 Working in partnership can challenge identities

How can such knowledge be put to practical use to become a positive, rather than a negative, source of power?

People bring different backgrounds, experiences and traditions of working to multidisciplinary partnership working. Also, there is often talk of the strong cultural differences between organisations – such as between health and local government – many of which arise from their different management structures. This may be less of a problem at front-line manager level but there have traditionally been variations in the degree of autonomy that local authority managers have compared with health authority managers. Some managers may not be empowered to make decisions or commit resources at the time of a meeting, which can delay moving forward and spoil the momentum of enthusiastic joint working. It may also be disconcerting when decisions agreed in partnership meetings have to be ratified in, or are thrown out of, local authority committee meetings.

When a partnership has led to an integrated organisation, differences between organisations and professionals may be amplified. For example, some organisations have brought together a range of professional groupings, all with different pay and conditions, employment status, experience of line management structures, and ways of working. This may lead to tensions between staff, which managers need to resolve, but the differences could also foster feelings of loss of identity (Figure 8.5). In an integrated organisation where traditional roles and responsibilities become blurred or posts are funded by different organisations, workers may question their new role. 'Which organisation do I belong to?' 'Will staff with different professional backgrounds accept my role?' 'Do I still feel affiliated to my national professional body?' Staff are often concerned about threats to their professional identity and whether their jobs and roles will be merged. In practice, however, closer working can strengthen people's understanding of each other and lead to a heightened defence of their different professional identities.

Clearly, some people find interagency and interprofessional working potentially threatening, particularly those who fear change. Skills in managing change are useful attributes in this context (see Chapter 4 for more about managing change in health and social care). Managing complex relationships and identities in diverse partnerships is likely to be an ongoing process and it is important to remember to always communicate information to team members and enable others to discuss their concerns as they arise (see Chapter 6 for more on managing identities in the workplace).

8.5 Bringing it all together: leading and managing successful partnerships

> [We] want people with good analytical skills … You need skills in dealing with the community, speaking the same language, because they have a different set of languages to the professionals, and then you need skills of diplomacy, negotiation, empathy with partners, being able to look at the broad horizon and short-term project management … But the interpersonal skills are probably the most important because you get people who in an organisation progress from being a professional to being a manager … If you're constructive and positive and you recognise that you have a personal relationship, they're much more likely to help you and be someone you can call on if things go wrong, or if you upset them, they'll probably be prepared to live with it … Command and control might deliver a project by pushing people to get things done by a certain date but it's probably [more] the ability to be able to use a menu of different skills on appropriate occasions.
>
> (Local authority senior manager, quoted in Charlesworth, 2002)

Figure 8.6 'The whole is greater than the sum of its parts.' (Aristotle, 384–322 BC)

This quotation highlights well the importance of reflecting on the **four building blocks of a caring approach** to management and leadership and how they can be used to take a positive stance towards some of the dilemmas faced by managers when working in partnership with other organisations. You may be wondering at this point whether the problems are insurmountable. Managers need to be constantly aware of what might be causing a barrier or resistance; what the cultural differences are between different organisations and staff and why these persist; what power imbalances are at work; and how they can ensure accountability, representativeness and cultural change.

This seems quite an ambitious list but many managers already have such skills and attributes that they have developed working with their own team. There are also many management tools that can support **contextual** and **team awareness** in partnership working. For example, stakeholder mapping helps identify those who have influence in a particular project, and SWOT analysis identifies strengths and weaknesses, opportunities and threats. Both of these tools have been in wide circulation for many years and are considered management staples, so **stakeholder mapping** and **SWOT analysis** are two of the tools included in the toolkit for this book.

Obviously, not everyone involved in partnerships is a manager: service users, volunteers and elected members often take leading roles in collaboration. Therefore, arranging a joint training programme, however brief, for partnership representatives is often useful in terms of learning new skills and networking with other participants during the training. Valuable skills and attributes include: being able to communicate and use appropriate language; negotiation; listening; empathy with partners; and understanding and respecting difference. Ways of 'learning' these skills vary and often team members find it useful to learn together and, in the process, build a partnership team identity. The use of an Open Space approach, as described in Chapter 7, could be useful here.

Building trust

Trust, loyalty and justice are the central tenets of transformational leadership (see Chapter 3).

The ability to build trust is crucial in achieving successful collaboration but it is extremely difficult, particularly where there is no history of partnership working or there is a legacy of poor relationships (Huxham and Vangen, 2005). Stereotypes of other professionals may get in the way, as will unrealistic expectations of what each partner can contribute. Building trust is a reinforcing process, in that it is needed at the beginning of collaborations to establish good working relationships, but successful outcomes are also required so that the trust is developed further and collaboration is advanced (Hudson et al., 1999). Of course, it is also a two-way process: you need to trust others and they need to trust you. In addition, there needs to be interorganisational trust (and internal organisational cultures receptive to partnership), so that when key individuals leave, the collaboration does not fall apart.

In addition to considering ways of improving communication, trust and team building, issues of leadership clearly need attention, which might be most appropriate in teams with strong differences in organisational and professional cultures and, therefore, potential sources of conflict. IVAR (2011) found that successful partnerships had at least one 'collaboration champion' – someone with 'enthusiasm for change through collaboration' who can 'scan the environment, recognise collaborative opportunities and have the skills and charisma to bring together appropriate partners' (p. 31).

Leadership and vision are required in order to keep a strong focus on the aims and objectives of the partnership. Therefore, the situational leadership model (see Chapter 3), where the direction and support of a team might be adjusted once the manager has got to know the members, could be appropriate in building trusting relationships in a partnership setting. Partnership is also an ideal opportunity to encourage leadership in other people. This is important in a multi-agency environment, where people outside statutory agencies should be encouraged to chair meetings and lead on key strands of the project. This might be a new and challenging approach to leadership for some managers.

Alban-Metcalfe and Alimo-Metcalfe (2010) highlight how the concept of 'integrative leadership' might be important in partnership working as it emphasises leadership as a shared activity with shared responsibilities. They describe integrative leadership as a communal form of leadership 'whereby individuals succeed, through working collaboratively with one another' (p. 4), as opposed to autonomous, autocratic styles of leadership. Box 8.2 summarises their 'new paradigm' for leading partnerships.

Box 8.2: Integrative leadership

Integrative leadership constitutes a *new paradigm*, which requires the adoption of a different kind of mindset, in which the effective functioning of a team, acting as a whole, is the goal. The practical implications of this include that:

- the leadership of the team involves shared responsibility of team members
- integrative leadership in different contexts requires different sets of skills or competencies
- fundamental to its success, in all contexts, is the ability of a team to fully engage all team members, and those with whom the team interacts
- integrative leadership will be most effective where relevant leadership competencies are enacted in an engaging way
- the different perspectives that members of a team, working collaboratively, can bring will enable teams to tackle even wicked problems most effectively
- leadership development should be context-relevant, and result in an increase in social as well as human capital.

(Alban-Metcalfe and Alimo-Metcalfe, 2011. p. 11)

Social capital relates to the collective benefits derived from people interacting and cooperating with each other. *Human capital* refers to the skills, knowledge and experience of people.

How practical do you think this concept of integrative leadership is for partnership working, given the constraints and pressures outlined in this chapter?

Integrative leadership may sound like a rather ideal end result, but developing working relationships based on trust, while maintaining an awareness of **the four basic building blocks of the caring manager**, can certainly help to move towards it.

8.6 Conclusion

> Sometimes this is about developing good services in conjunction with a partner agency and realising where your role ends and their role begins. But there's a cohesive bit. You know we're not opposite polar ends, we're actually working together and it's your best seamless transition. And at the end of the day it's the service user that matters.
>
> (Shirley Findley, regional service manager for SACRO, Scotland, 2012)

All front-line managers can probably expect to be involved in partnership working and this chapter described some of the complexities that might be encountered during the process. It also highlighted the reasons why this way of working is considered so important. First, a lack of communication and coordination between agencies has serious implications for quality care. Second, different agencies can play a role in planning and delivering services; and finally, improved care services result from true partnership between providers and service users. However, it is rarely a smooth process, so there is a key role for managers and leaders to play.

The examples used in this chapter show how managers can help ease the process but, sometimes, even the most experienced managers can face resistance from their team members. This is perhaps a reminder that interagency and interprofessional working can be slow and often draws on a variety of management and leadership skills as well as a lot of patience. In particular, it is important that everyone is encouraged to work towards a shared vision – whether this is facilitated by careful strategic and practical management, by inspired distributed and integrative leadership or, it is to be hoped, by a mixture of both.

Learning from experience – both negative and positive – is an effective way to progress. The examples in this chapter should raise some questions, such as:

- How would *you* do things differently?
- How can *you* lead a successful partnership and inspire leadership in other people?

- What kind of improvements in outcomes can service users and carers expect?
- How can managers aid communication and coordination?

Partnership working happens at different levels and there is much scope for 'bottom-up' initiatives on partnership. This is where front-line managers have a key role to play, bringing together different professional groups and identities, and involving service users in an empowering and facilitative environment for effective collaboration (see Chapter 13 for more on involving service users and carers). The challenges here are big, but the potential rewards are bigger still.

Key points

- Partnership working is needed in health and social care because service users have complex needs which do not fit into neat categories. Therefore, partnership is now regarded as core business and the main way to deliver better outcomes for service users.
- Partnership working has a long history in public services but is still often perceived by staff as a complex, difficult and lengthy process.
- Power relationships play a key role in partnership working and require careful management. It takes time to work through organisational and professional differences.
- Being clear about agendas and what different people hope to achieve from collaboration can help success rates. It is important to be clear about the purpose of partnership and why different organisations are involved.
- By honing their skills in leadership, building trust and managing change, managers can facilitate the partnership process. In particular, models of distributed, situational and integrative leadership can be useful.

References

Alban-Metcalfe, J. and Alimo-Metcalfe, B. (2010) 'Integrative leadership, partnership working and wicked problems: a conceptual analysis', *The International Journal of Leadership in Public Services*, vol. 6, no. 3, pp. 3–13.

Charlesworth, J. (2001) 'Negotiating and managing partnership in primary care', *Health and Social Care in the Community*, vol. 9, no. 5, pp. 279–85.

Charlesworth, J. (2002) *Redefining Roles through Partnership Working*, unpublished discussion paper, Milton Keynes, The Open University Business School.

Clarke, J., Newman, J., Smith, N., Vidler, E. and Westmarland, L. (2007) *Creating Citizen-Consumers: Changing publics and changing public services*, London, Sage.

Dickinson, H. and Glasby, J. (2010) 'Why partnership working doesn't work', *Public Management Review*, vol. 12, no. 6, pp. 811–28.

Findley, S. (2012) Interview for K313 video, Milton Keynes, The Open University.

Glasby, J. and Dickinson, H. (2008) 'Greater than the sum of our parts? Emerging lessons for UK health and social care', *International Journal of Integrated Care*, vol. 8. Available online at www.ijic.org.

Glasby, J., Dickinson, H. and Miller, R. (2011) 'Partnership working in England – where we are now and where we've come from', *International Journal of Integrated Care*, vol. 11. Available online at www.ijic.org.

Hudson, B., Exworthy, M. and Peckham, S. (1998) *The Integration of Localised and Collaborative Purchasing: A review of literature and a framework for analysis*, Leeds, Nuffield Institute for Health.

Hudson, B., Hardy, B., Henwood, M. and Wistow, G. (1999) 'In pursuit of inter-agency collaboration in the public sector: what is the contribution of theory and research?', *Public Management*, vol. 1, no. 2, pp. 235–60.

Huxham, C. (1996) 'Advantage or inertia? Making collaboration work', in Paton, R., Clark, G., Jones, G., Lewis, J. and Quintas, P. (eds) *The New Management Reader*, London, Routledge/The Open University (B800 Set Book).

Huxham, C. and Vangen, S. (2005) *Managing to Collaborate: The theory and practice of collaborative advantage*, London, Routledge.

Institute for Voluntary Action Research (IVAR) (2011) *Thinking About … Collaboration: A ten year research synthesis*, London, IVAR.

Joint Improvement Team (2009) 'Chapter 4: Barriers to Partnership Working', Health, Social Care and Housing Partnership Working, *Briefing Notes for Practitioners and Managers*, August, London, JIT.

Lukes, S. (1974) *Power: A Radical View*, London, Macmillan.

MacKian, S., Elliott, H., Busby, H. and Popay, J. (2003) '"Everywhere and nowhere": locating and understanding the "new" public health', *Health and Place*, vol. 9, no. 3, pp. 219–29.

Martin, V., Charlesworth, J. and Henderson, E. (2010) *Managing in Health and Social Care* (2nd edition), London, Routledge.

Mayo, M. and Taylor, M. (2001) 'Partnerships and power in community regeneration', in Balloch, S. and Taylor, M. (eds) *Partnership Working: Policy and Practice*, Bristol, The Policy Press, pp. 39–56.

McConvey, V. (2012) Interview for K313 video, Milton Keynes, The Open University.

Robinson, D. (2004) *Unconditional Leadership: A principle-centred approach to developing people, building teams and maximising results*, London, Community Links.

Sullivan, H. and Skelcher, C. (2002) *Working across Boundaries: Collaboration in public services*, Basingstoke, Palgrave Macmillan.

Sullivan, H., Williams, P. and Jeffares, S. (2012) 'Leadership for collaboration', *Public Management Review*, vol. 14, no. 1, pp. 41–66.

Wong, K.-F. (2003) 'Empowerment as a panacea for poverty – old wine in new bottles? Reflections on the World Bank's conception of power', *Progress in Development Studies*, vol. 3, no. 4, pp. 307–22.

Chapter 9 Managing continuing professional development

Chris Kubiak

9.1 Introduction

Figure 9.1 'Knowledge does not keep any better than fish' (Whitehead, 1932, p. 147)

In 1932, the philosopher and mathematician Alfred Whitehead (1861–1947) wrote that 'Knowledge does not keep any better than fish' (p. 147; Figure 9.1). He was, in part, arguing for the need for individuals who go into practice with new ideas and fresh insights into the world around them. His description of knowledge as needing constant refreshing and reconsideration in its application to new situations highlights the importance of ongoing continuing professional development (CPD) in the constantly changing world of health and social care.

This chapter explores the management of CPD arising from both everyday work activity and through the more formal processes of induction, supervision and appraisal. A 'leading learning model' is described as a tool to guide the management of CPD.

This chapter addresses the following core questions.

- What drives the need for CPD?
- How is CPD managed and led?
- What are the common methods of CPD?

9.2 Leading learning

Case study 9.1: Steve

Steve had worked for five years as a support worker for people with mental health problems. He recently changed jobs to work with people with profound physical and learning disabilities. Although he felt confident with most aspects of his work, some of the people had epilepsy and he did not know how to respond appropriately should someone have a seizure.

Steve's situation raises several questions about his professional development. As a new member of staff, how should he be inducted into the organisation? Does his manager know he needs training in epilepsy? Are there appraisal or supervision processes in place to capture this information? Thinking more broadly, what does Steve think he needs to learn and what does the role demand of him? If he is not confident or knowledgeable enough to work with people who have epilepsy, are there enough staff members with this skill to ensure that all can be safely supported? These questions about managing the direction and nature of CPD are the focus of this chapter.

From a manager's perspective, the direction and nature of Steve's CPD will be influenced by a complex set of driving forces. His learning should improve service user outcomes and reflect the expectations of service user groups. Service users are not the only interested party, though. Service regulators, who ensure government standards are met, are interested in Steve's CPD and the quality of his care. Although Steve is unlikely to be registered, professional regulators require many practitioners to adhere to standards of conduct and professional development.

Should he go on to study a pre-registration training programme, his professional body would require certain standards of ongoing development. Steve's employing organisation may also operate a framework of expected capabilities for practitioners as well as processes for CPD that will shape his learning opportunities. Steve himself probably also has personal development and career goals in mind.

Managing CPD in health and social care involves a complex landscape incorporating legal, professional and organisational requirements as well as the needs of the individual concerned. However, the need for CPD is ever-changing. Not only do standards and expectations change but no one's initial training is sufficient for a lifetime of practice. Advances in medical techniques, shifting philosophies, the varying needs of service users, and newly discovered solutions to long-standing problems all demand ongoing CPD. Managing CPD therefore involves a nuanced sense of awareness: of **context** (legal, professional, organisational); of **goals** (care outcomes); of the **team** (balance of competences and skills) and **personal** needs (goals, ability).

The leading learning model shown in Figure 9.2 (see Box 9.1) helps characterise this array of interests and drivers as well as provide focus for the **contextual awareness** of managing CPD. In leading learning, the manager needs to balance organisational requirements with the personal learning needs of each employee and the demands of managing a team (Peel, 2003). These different levels can also offer resources to support learning that can be tapped by managers in their promotion of CPD. Although the leading learning model resonates with the multitiered perspective of human resource methodologies such as learning needs analysis, a fourth dimension also needs to be taken into account – the way in which specific work roles require particular competences (Barbazette, 2006).

Box 9.1: Introducing the leading learning model

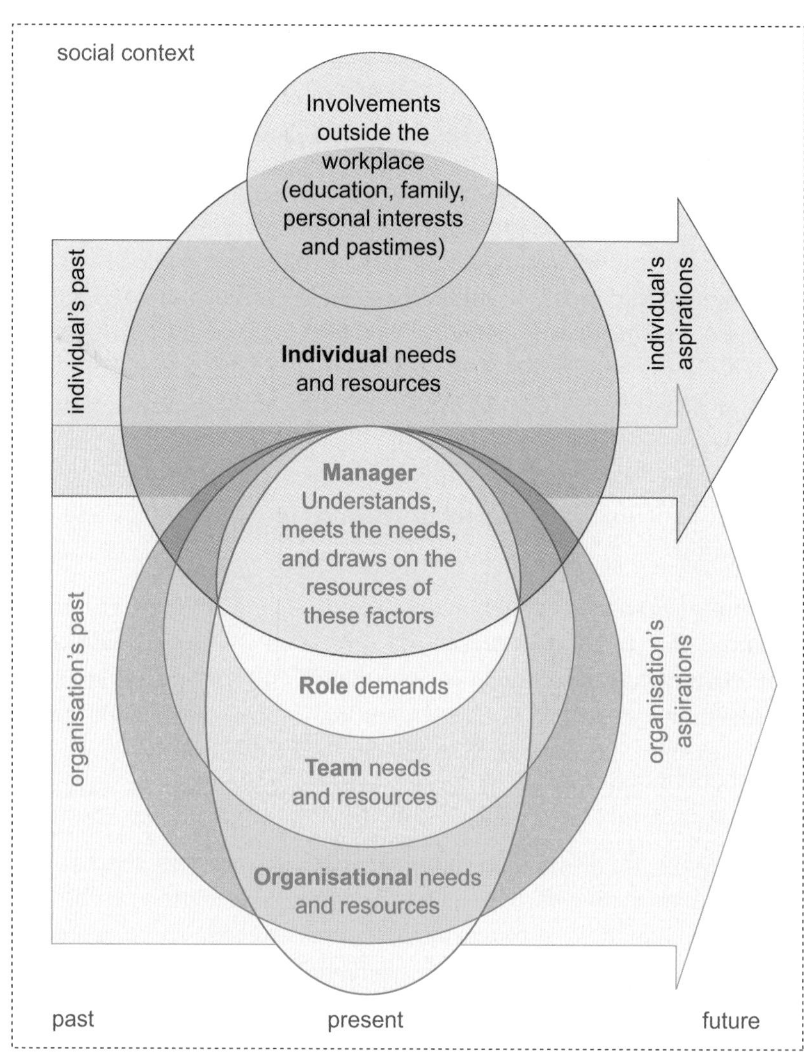

Figure 9.2 The leading learning model

The four levels of need in this model are as follows.

1 **Organisational needs and resources:** organisations require staff to attend standard training on subjects such as equal opportunities or health and safety laws. Some of these needs emerge out of the ephemeral nature of the political, economic and social context. An organisation's operation may be shaped by the austerity measures associated with a recession or the current emphasis on patient or service user involvement. All of

these factors will influence the organisation's budget priorities, goals and strategic plan as well as particular protocols and policies to deliver on the promise to the service user. At the same time, organisations offer resources to support learning such as funding to study at university, centralised training courses, or policies setting out an induction programme.

2 **Team needs and resources:** the manager will also be leading a department or a team which requires practical decisions about allocating the training budget fairly or ensuring cover when staff members attend a course. There will also be strategic demands. Does the team have the right skill mix to meet service user needs or address service weaknesses? Managers must ensure fairness of access to development opportunities, link CPD to collective goals and ensure that the team members can work together. At the same time, the team is a resource for learning in that experienced practitioners can mentor newcomers, group discussions in staff meetings can build understanding of particular issues, and co-working can model different approaches to practice.

3 **Role demands:** learning needs arise out of the particular nature and demands of the role (Barbazette, 2006). A work role implies particular responsibilities, tasks and standards of performance which can only be accomplished with particular skills, knowledge and attitudes (CIPD, 2006). Therefore, managers need to understand role requirements. Understanding of the role also includes the more amorphous qualities such as compassion, empathy, responsibility and respect (CIDC, 2012).

4 **Individual needs and resources:** individuals have their own needs for growth, career progression and personal fulfilment. Identifying and harnessing each individual's strengths for both individual and organisational benefit can have a powerful impact on staff. Engaging in CPD will increase staff retention (Cornes et al., 2010). It will also shape motivation and involvement in the service (Royal College of Nursing, 2007).

Although the need to develop your capacities to their fullest is a basic human drive (Maslow, 1954), not everyone will engage in available learning opportunities. Management's view of what should be learned may not match that of the individual (Billett, 2010). Workers can be ambivalent about learning opportunities such as new responsibilities (Eraut, 2004). They may resist CPD if it is associated with practice they feel uncomfortable with (Rainbird et al., 1999). As Figure 9.2 shows, each worker is likely to have had a history in other settings which will have shaped their competence, concerns and interests. They may have aspirations for roles that lie outside their current workplace. They are not just concerned with their work role but also with the quality of their life outside work and may resist claims on that time. Therefore, a worker's concerns and interests are only ever partly those of their workplace. Nevertheless, such factors will shape how they construe their work and CPD. The manager's role, then, is to understand and respond to an individual's potential and values as well as their aspirations and wider concerns.

You might have also noticed that Figure 9.2 suggests that organisations and teams have a history and aspirations. A team or an organisation's past practice can exert a powerful influence on how things are done. Changes to practice can be difficult to make when tradition and routine are well established. Equally, organisations have aspirations and goals that practitioners need to achieve. A goal to establish a new practice such as person-centred care may demand CPD too.

Consider Steve's situation in Case study 9.1. What are the individual, role, team and organisational issues in play?

In terms of the organisational tier, service regulation often requires an induction covering specific topics within a certain time frame. Also, organisational resources may mean that an induction course may be unavailable because, for example, sessions are only economical with ten inductees or more. The team tier may be a resource in that it is a source of mentors or experienced practitioners to shadow but, until Steve can manage seizures, some of his duties may have to be handled by colleagues. That is, his development and performance impacts on team resources. Steve's manager will need to understand what work he performed in the past, to understand what he is capable of now, as well as his career aspirations. Such issues are important to making relevant developmental opportunities available.

The emphasis of the leading learning model on organisational, team and individual factors is closely related to the four building blocks introduced in Chapter 1. The manager's capacity to support CPD depends on understanding the requirements of an organisation as well as the resources for learning available through a team of experienced practitioners who can offer guidance and insight. However, by incorporating the organisational tier, the leading learning model, like the building blocks of the caring manager, has a wider focus. Managers must be aware of the way in which learning arises out of the interaction of these tiers and balance their demands. For example, an oversubscribed and under-resourced service may adopt an organisational strategy to train healthcare assistants to perform some nurses' tasks. However, the nurses in the team may feel their role is being eroded by this development and resist it (Spilsbury and Meyer, 2004). Some healthcare assistants may embrace their role expansion for the way it makes their role more interesting. Others may resist it because they are content with their responsibilities, want more money for extra work, or believe that such tasks belong to nurses (Hancock et al., 2005).

The leading learning model does not imply that practitioners should acquiesce to organisational goals. Managers may, as Harris et al. (2006) found, draw out practitioners' talents and use these to develop new aspects of the service – that is, individuals are resources as much as demands. Managers may also challenge their organisations' strategies and priorities based on their understanding of what the practitioners' role means for, and demands of, staff. This may mean protecting staff from overwhelming demands that erode opportunities for ongoing learning. The leading learning model is central to the conceptualisation of CPD in this chapter and it is revisited throughout the following discussion.

Leading learning will involve trade-offs and compromises but it can also incorporate inspiration and creative decision making, leading to the development of a better service.

9.3 Learning as a by-product of everyday practice

Many definitions of CPD imply that learning arises out of specific time set aside for activities such as course attendance or personal study days. These formal opportunities are only one aspect of learning. Practitioners often report that learning through everyday work experience is one of the richest and most significant aspects of CPD (Eraut, 2011). So, for example, although Steve had not attended training, he started learning on his first day. We now continue with his story.

Case study 9.2: Steve (continued)

In his first week, Steve read service user files and shadowed his colleagues. By week two he was working with 'less complicated' service users. Colleagues were available to answer questions and periodically offered 'a quiet word in your ear' if he seemed to be having difficulties.

Steve soon stopped feeling like a newcomer and just joined in with daily working life – discussing problems at handover meetings, making plans for the day, and taking decisions.

Steve learned a lot about epilepsy too. Throughout the day, colleagues pointed out when they thought someone was about to have a seizure. When a service user had a seizure, Steve observed his colleagues monitoring breathing, administering medication and supporting recovery. His colleagues always discussed the seizure afterwards, giving Steve an opportunity to ask questions. After a month, Steve attended induction and then a training course on epilepsy. With his experience, he already understood something about the topic but the theory consolidated what he knew. Experience and training left him feeling confident in his knowledge.

What experiences contributed to Steve learning about epilepsy?

Steve's growing competence and confidence only partly involved formal learning activities. Much of his learning came out of daily practice. The educational researcher Michael Eraut spent over a decade interviewing and observing practitioners in practice, returning to some over several years to track their development. In 2011, Eraut concluded that much learning is a by-product of work arising out of engagement in work tasks, tackling challenges and interacting with colleagues and service users. There are resonances here with Steve's experience of observing practice, asking questions and receiving feedback. These activities allow him to see how a colleague reads situations, monitors them and takes decisions (Eraut, 2011).

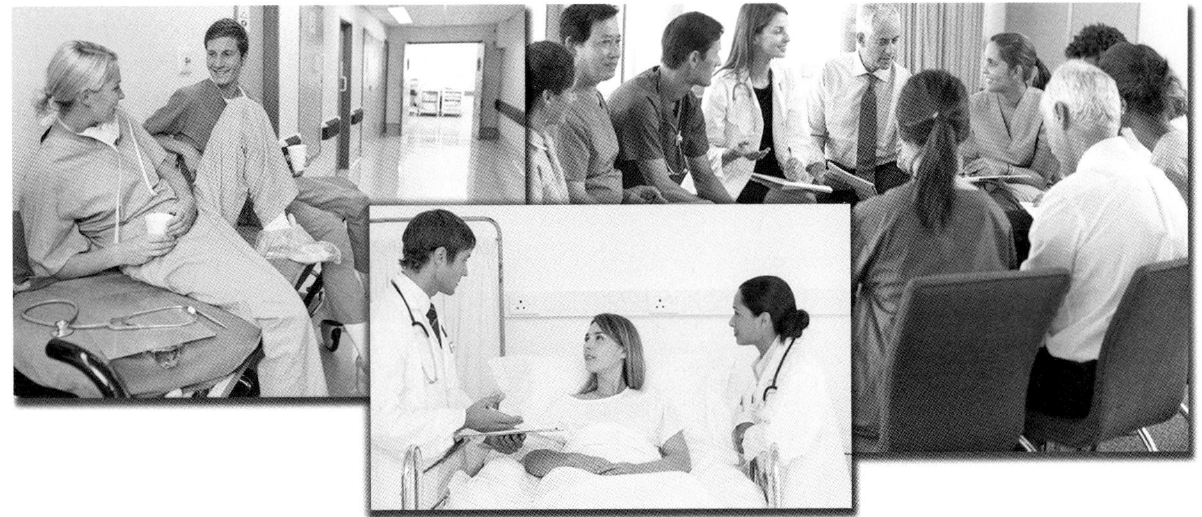

Figure 9.3 Tea breaks, meetings and watching other people at work can be powerful learning experiences. How can you organise the workplace to maximise these opportunities?

Interactions with colleagues are intertwined with the working day – a chat over coffee, advice while in action, interpreting a patient's or service user's behaviour, or problem solving (Figure 9.3). The significance of learning through practice is not new or radical. Many accounts stress ongoing human learning regardless of place or activity (Billett, 2010). Kolb's experiential learning process illustrates how observing or reflecting on the experiences of practice leads to new understandings or principles which are tested in subsequent activity (Figure 9.4) (Kolb, 1984).

Although this model is very well known, it can be challenging to suggest non-formal learning is as robust and valuable as that taking place through formal training or study (Billett, 2010). Managers may be troubled that Steve's account involves learning things that are outside any formally sanctioned approach to practice. What is to stop him picking up bad practice?

The experiential learning process describes how people reflect on and form new understandings of practice. However, it overlooks non-reflective learning in which people develop with little awareness of doing so, memorise by rote, or acquire basic skills through repetition with little thought (Jarvis, 2006).

By being aware of the importance of experiential learning, and incorporating it in the leading learning model, managers can design roles or organise team processes to maximise on-the-job learning (Felstead et al., 2009). Eraut (2006) argues that the following features of the workplace context can enhance opportunities for learning.

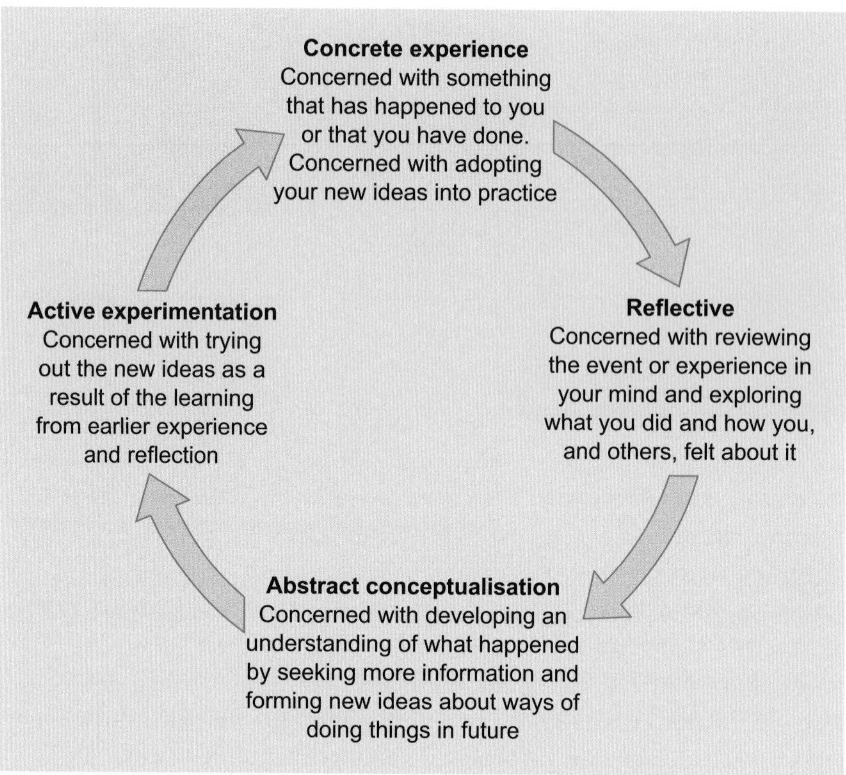

Figure 9.4 Kolb's learning cycle (adapted by McClure, 2005, p. 6)

- **Human and physical environments:** can be designed to support contact between practitioners, shared working and opportunities to recognise when a colleague can give some help or advice. This includes private spaces to discuss service users, take advice, coach or mentor in practical skills and shared decision making (see Chapter 11 for more on managing in the caring environment).
- **Practitioners' relationships at work:** as practitioners learn much from their colleagues, relationships of mutual trust underpin their willingness to discuss concerns, mistakes and ethical issues, and to share their practice in complex, uncertain or challenging circumstances.
- **Patterns, conditions and allocations of work:** the allocation and organisation of work determines opportunities to take on more complex tasks and work alongside other people from the team or other areas – all factors which stretch people and foster understanding. Work is allocated to match the practitioner's level of competence so that new challenges drive their learning but do not, as Eraut (2011) argues, overchallenge them so they feel exhausted or

overwhelmed. Pressures of work limit opportunities to consult, discuss a problem together, receive feedback and stop to think, all of which foster learning. Good managers may be able to redirect resources in a crisis.

- **Culture:** all practitioners are inducted into the culture of their teams which reflects attitudes to learning and what is considered good practice as well as the preferred image, goals and purposes of the practitioners. Culture will shape what can be said and not said as well as the ideals and justifications for practice. (You can read more about organisational culture in Chapter 12.)

However, these factors will not guarantee learning. Practitioners vary in how they respond to learning opportunities (Billett, 2010). For example, in the case study, Steve valued his time shadowing colleagues while someone else may see it as irrelevant. Some learning opportunities may be ignored or rejected – an issue which is not captured by the experiential learning process in Figure 9.4 (Jarvis, 2006). A leader can act as a broker between the needs of the new learner and the opportunities for learning available in their unit, matching one with the other. As the leading learning model suggests, understanding individual needs, and how to manage them, is therefore centrally important.

How would your management practice change if you reframed your staff members' everyday tasks as learning activities?

9.4 Managing formal learning opportunities

In discussions of CPD, non-formal learning receives much less attention than formal methods. The predominant concern is with evaluating learning needs, planning to meet them, staff appraisals, the use of documentation to prioritise and monitor progress, the need for supervision or for training courses (see, for example, Royal College of Nursing, 2007, 2009; Gumus et al., 2011). Overlooking the breadth of Steve's non-formal learning in favour of formal learning will lead to an understanding of CPD as an activity that primarily occurs away from the job. This view may distract managers from finding ways to make learning a daily occurrence through thoughtful organisation of the work environment and role.

The standardisation of formal CPD does have its advantages, though. Formalisation can connect practitioners' learning opportunities with the strategic directions and priorities of the service. Formalisation also meets the needs for audit and accountability in which governmental, regulatory and funding bodies need assurance that workers are being suitably scrutinised and regulated (Cole, 2004). The availability of CPD is typically part of any formal assessment of service quality (Staniland et al., 2011). Formal CPD, with its measurable inputs and outputs, assessments and certificates, is more suited to such ends.

Formal learning, such as training courses, can enable practitioners to consider alternative perspectives, to critique and to challenge practice. For example, students on university courses report developing greater reflectiveness and understanding of their work which led to a desire to challenge work practices (Forrester-Jones and Hatzidimitriadou, 2006). Training courses make practitioners aware of pitfalls in their practice, review existing evidence and collect new evidence in ways that avoid difficulties (Eraut, 1994).

It is important to note as well that practitioners' access to learning opportunities can be inequitably distributed (Billett, 2004). Hughes (2005) investigated nurses' access to CPD, and suggests that who you are, what you do and where you work influences the likelihood of access to CPD opportunities. The formalisation of CPD can help ensure (but not guarantee) that all workers gain fair access to learning opportunities.

So, as important as non-formal learning is, it should coexist with formal methods. The rest of this section considers three formal CPD processes – induction, supervision and staff appraisal.

Managing staff induction

All services need to support the entry of new staff into the organisation and help them understand their role. Thomas et al. (2008) argue that even experienced practitioners encounter 'newness' when they move workplaces to start a new job – different levels of autonomy, approaches to line management, teamworking style or culture. So, although a newly qualified practitioner may feel 'scared to death' in their first job, experienced workers may also have the culture shock of starting a role in a new team. So, despite having several years of practice under his belt, Steve's transition to his new job needed careful attention.

As the leading learning model suggests, managers need to understand the individual needs of new members of staff (Bates et al., 2010). Peel (2003) argues that managing a new member of staff's induction is partly a process of aligning their past experience to the requirements of the post. If this is done poorly, it can have a negative effect on worker retention.

The manager will also be attempting to ensure that the induction of newcomers meets organisational demands. Usually, regulatory agencies such as the Care Quality Commission (2010), professional bodies (Bates et al., 2010) and organisations themselves have specific induction requirements for workers to understand key policies, procedures and philosophies. These processes must be matched to individual needs in a meaningful way and, at the same time, be carried out in the specific context of the organisation with its particular resource limitations. Team members themselves will need to guide, support and mentor newcomers, which also has resource implications.

Apart from sending new team members on an induction course, what else can be done to manage their entry into the organisation?

Managers need to structure and plan each worker's induction, ensuring that new team members are not overwhelmed by their responsibilities and the culture shock of a new post (see Box 9.2).

Box 9.2: Miller and Blackman's research

Miller and Blackman (2003) studied the first three years of life as a practising nurse. One newly qualified nurse was assigned a mentor and had an education package with clearly stated competences to attain. However, not having received any feedback on his performance, he did not feel supported at all:

> I feel the department have let me down ... because they haven't really been supporting me, I didn't feel that they'd been supporting me but they felt ... that they didn't have to because they felt I was too confident, well not too confident, they felt I was exuding so much confidence that I was ... coping well when in reality I wasn't …
>
> (Miller and Blackman, 2003, p. 22)
>
> This nurse's colleagues were surprised that he felt unsupported. Misinterpreting his confidence, they did not think that he needed feedback. The fact that nobody had said anything meant that he felt undermined and lost his confidence.

This example shows several processes that should support transition into an organisation – a strong network, clear expectations of the necessary skills and mentorship. Miller and Blackman (2003) suggest that mentors can enhance induction if they spend time working with the newcomer and support them to practise their skills in the new environment. They need to show an interest in the newcomer's development and have a role in answering questions and actively questioning the newcomer to encourage reflection on their practice. Managers should assume that any new staff member needs support to make the transition into an organisation (Peel, 2003). In the example above, the nurse's confidence may have been a reflection of anxieties about appearing incompetent and did not suggest that support was unneeded. Miller and Blackman (2003) describe the awkwardness of novice nurses who, wanting to build credibility, may not want to be seen as not coping, even though they know they can ask for help.

Several authors have made recommendations for effective induction, although often in the context of novice practitioners. Jack and Donnellan (2010) suggest that induction for social workers includes:

- additional supervision with a focus on career development and opportunities for reflection
- discussion of ongoing training needs
- a clear definition of what constitutes a protected workload while settling in
- opportunities for shadowing and co-working.

Miller and Blackman (2003) emphasise non-formal learning, suggesting:

- demonstrations of procedures with opportunities to practise skills
- explicit statements about required tasks and performance
- regular feedback and challenging tasks
- exposure to different areas of practice
- help with prioritising
- encouraging requests for help.

It is clear from such recommendations that good induction is closely related to supervision, appraisal and CPD plans. Supervision is discussed next.

Supervision – from luxury to staple

Health and social care work is characterised by its uncertainty and complexity. Practitioners need opportunities to reflect on the fraught and challenging moments of practice. Starting in his new role, Steve encountered a different service user group with an unfamiliar health condition. Operating at the edge of his competence, Steve needed what Bishop (2007) refers to as an opportunity to 'play back' – reflect on practice and self-critique. He needed feedback. Maybe he also needed someone to gently challenge the appropriateness of his practice? He needed 'supervision'.

In recent years, supervision has shifted from a luxury item in the health and social care workplace to a basic need, central to practice and development (Driscoll and O'Sullivan, 2007). Yet Rouse (2007), reviewing the literature on supervision, found considerable diversity and lack of clarity in definitions and approaches. This lack of clarity may reflect the unfamiliarity of supervision to some occupational groups (Driscoll and O'Sullivan, 2007); for example, it was practically unheard of in nursing in the UK in the 1990s (Bishop, 2007).

Also, different views of supervision can reflect the multidisciplinary workplace. Some practitioners come from traditions such as social care where it is seen as an opportunity for reflection and support, while others will expect a more instrumental approach (Peel, 2003). In contrast, supervision was more readily established in mental health nursing and health visiting where listening and talking were more common practices.

Practitioners with heavy workloads may not see the value of taking time out for supervision and would prefer to just 'get on with the job'.

These different definitions have practical implications for managers, who may find that their staff's varied experiences and expectations have led to quite different understandings of the process (Peel, 2003). Proctor's model in Figure 9.5 can be used to clarify the core purposes of supervision.

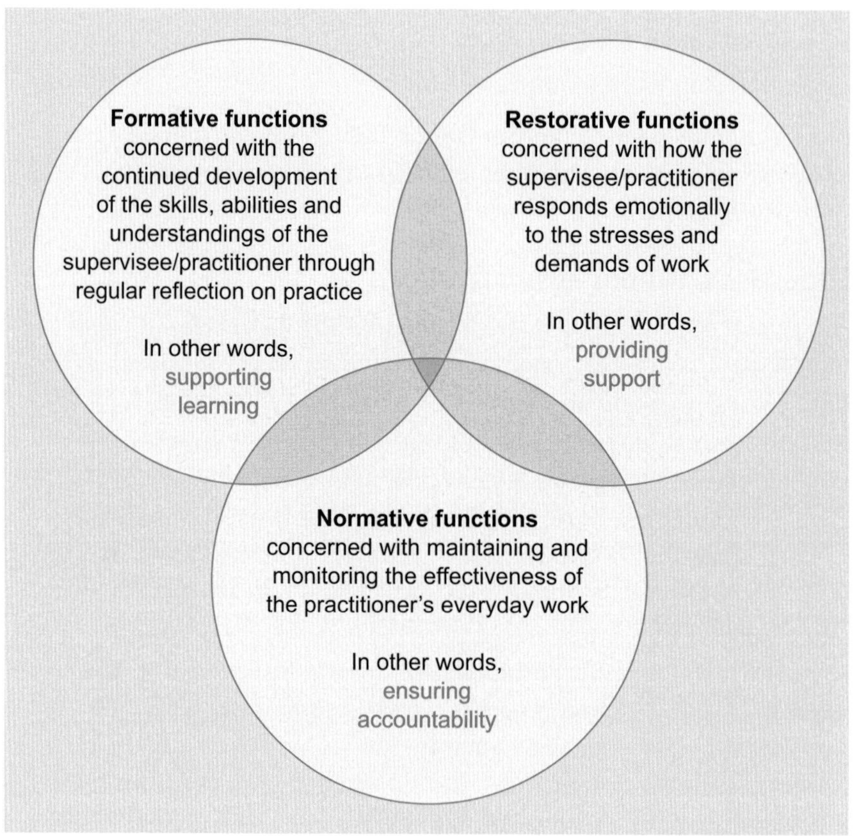

Figure 9.5 Proctor's model of supervision (Driscoll and O'Sullivan, 2007)

The anonymised supervision record below (Figure 9.6) is for Mel J., an occupational therapist who has recently taken up the post of Stroke Clinical Specialist. The text in brackets identifies which function from Proctor's model is being addressed.

Supervision record – 16th November

Name: Mel J. (Stroke Clinical Specialist)
Manager: Manju P. (Neuro-rehabilitation Services Manager)

Mel is assessing all referrals within the required six weeks. [ensuring accountability] Has had no training in the assessment method and finds the process cumbersome. Manju to put Mel in contact with colleague with same role to develop her technique. [supporting learning]

Mel discussed a service user who had a stroke at a young age and had been placed in a residential care home. As he had been discharged from the service, Mel was not sure if he should remain on her caseload. Manju suggested that, as there is no one else available to address his needs, he should remain on her caseload. [ensuring accountability] Mel felt the home's activities did not reflect his interests and they lacked a rehabilitation focus. Was not sure of best way forward. Discussed making referral to the consultant for a review and to discuss with the social worker about funding available for further rehabilitation. [supporting learning]

Mel is anxious about facilitating the stroke support group. [providing support] The group seems to lack direction. One member is very difficult to deal with. Discussed how problems could be addressed by re-establishing group focus and setting ground rules. [supporting learning] Group is poorly attended and Mel was encouraged to expand membership. [ensuring accountability]

Figure 9.6 Mel J.'s supervision record

Although not all supervision sessions will attend to all three functions, Proctor's model can be used to help managers and supervisees understand and prepare for supervision. It also connects with the leading learning model, as it suggests that managers should find out what each individual staff member wants from supervision. Supervision involves balancing the individual's need for support with the organisation's demand for accountability by enabling learning opportunities that help people perform as the role demands.

Are managers always the best people to carry out supervision?

Sometimes, managers should not be involved in some aspects of supervision. Even when specialist knowledge is not needed, the particular balance of the different purposes of supervision may be compromised by managerial concerns (Peach and Horner, 2007). Discussing social workers, Peel (2003) argues that practitioners want emotional and professional support while managers may prioritise monitoring performance. He implies that, in a climate stressing tighter management and monitoring of staff, supervision can become preoccupied with ensuring quality and regulating working practices.

In the spirit of meeting these different needs, Proctor's model offers a way to systematically set an agenda for supervision and think strategically about who is best placed to serve its purposes. A senior practitioner may be most suited to supporting the formative and restorative functions, while managers may find that they are best placed to address the normative function (Driscoll and O'Sullivan, 2007). The model may also provoke personal reflection among managers who could use it to consider how effectively they fulfil all three processes.

Effective supervision just does not happen in some organisations. Why do you think this might be?

Establishing supervision as a regular practice in the workplace can be difficult. There can be practical problems, such as staff shortages, overburdened staff or lack of funds and facilities. However, Bishop (2007) argues that these are all reasons for why it is all the more necessary. Similarly, it can be difficult to establish regular supervision because potential supervisors feel they lack the necessary skills.

Supervisees too may not know quite how to go about being supervised or they may think it is a pointless activity, arguing that 'I can't change anything' or 'What difference will it make?' They may also fear being judged, assessed or criticised by a superior.

However, even when formal supervision is not in evidence, Driscoll and O'Sullivan (2007) argue that many aspects of supervision take place in workplaces in an informal rather than a formal fashion (Figure 9.7).

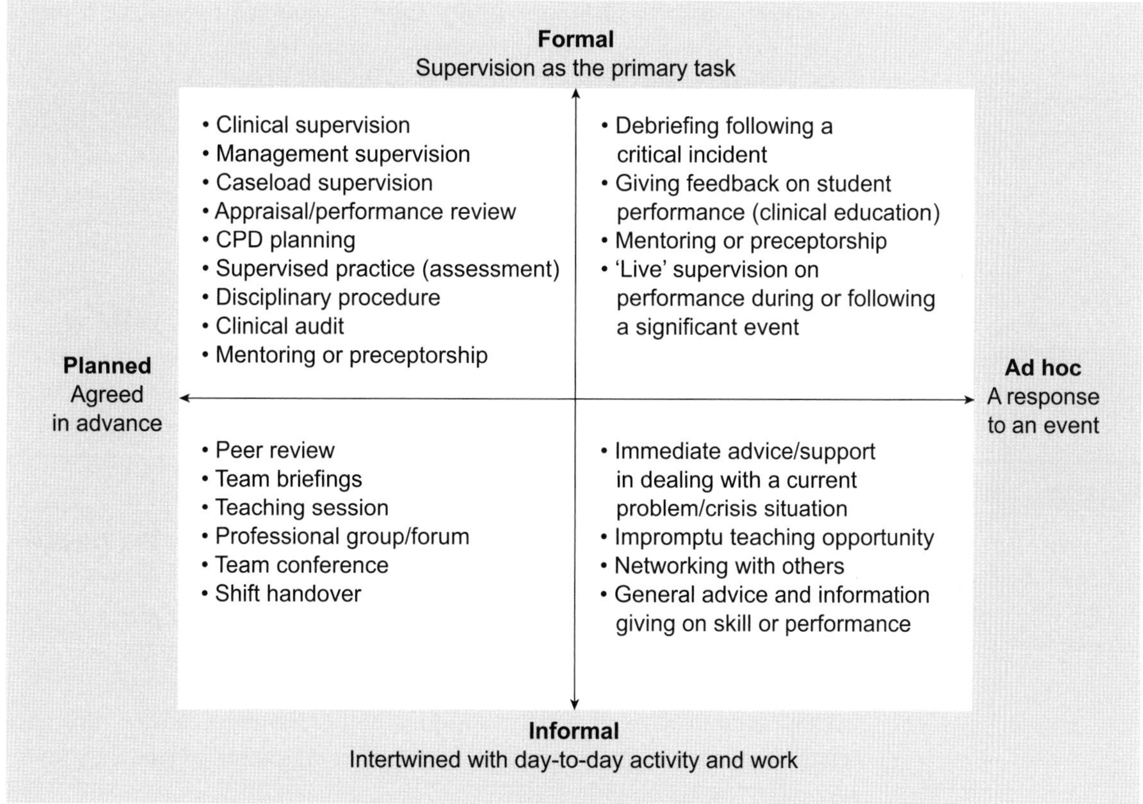

Figure 9.7 Two dimensions of supervision (based on Driscoll and O'Sullivan, 2007)

With supervisory activities permeating workplaces in a variety of forms, managers have much to build on in establishing supervision as a worthwhile practice (Driscoll and O'Sullivan, 2007). The danger is that practitioners and managers may feel that, as they are 'doing it anyway', there is little need for formal sessions. However, if supervision sessions are given a permanent slot, it may be more difficult to quietly forget about it.

Appraisal

In the case of Mel above, supervision was an opportunity for support with and learning from the daily challenges in her role. However, as valuable as such supervision is, it is not suitable for taking stock of her performance overall and where she is going in her career. Appraisal, on the other hand, takes a much longer view. Appraisal is a process of reviewing performance, focusing workers' attention on the achievement of organisational objectives, and planning for long-term personal and career development (Tourish, 2006). Free of the need to deal with day-to-day issues, the appraisal interview is a space for the employee to reflect on their role, their competence and their place in the organisation. It is also about where they are going in their life – their career and possible goals for the future (Staniland et al., 2011). Mel is unlikely to have time to discuss her career plans in supervision, but appraisal should provide a space for this conversation.

Appraisal offers a space to think about short- and long-term goals.

Considered within the leading learning model, appraisal is not just about individual needs. It is focused on organisational needs too, enabling managers to assess worker performance so that individuals can direct, correct and improve their practice to meet the organisation's goals (West et al., 2002). Appraisal should yield action plans for development for the next year through which targeted training and support can be identified (Bentley and Dandy-Hughes, 2010). The danger is that individuals can feel that their personal needs are overlooked in favour of organisational requirements (Spence and Wood, 2007). Positive performance may be ignored and amorphous factors, such as motivation, creativity, team spirit, responsibility and loyalty, go unmeasured (Tourish, 2006). Appraisal can become a top-down bureaucratic process in which the individual's learning needs, as they relate to their own priorities, goals and sense of career trajectory, are secondary or go unaddressed.

With these tensions, appraisal is a communication event that can provoke anxiety and, therefore, needs to be carefully managed (Spence and Wood, 2007). Tourish (2006) is extremely critical of the efficacy of appraisal, describing it as fraught, with biases of perception and ineffectual feedback. Managers tend to exaggerate individual contributions to failures and underestimate organisational causes. Individuals can be poor at receiving criticism, tending to overestimate their abilities, and see a relatively few negative comments as dominating the entire appraisal. The process can be conflictual and stressful. Add to this the link with salary level (Bentley and Dandy-Hughes, 2010), or the inequality between the manager and the employee (O'Connor and Lee, 2007), and appraisal can be a difficult experience. In short, it takes the skills outlined in the four building blocks of a **fully rounded caring manager** to 'get it right'.

As you read the examples in Box 9.3, reflect on what shaped these people's experiences of appraisal.

Box 9.3: Experiences of appraisal

Gary

I felt it was fair … She [the charge nurse] will roster herself a day shift so you can spend 12 hours working with her … I respect her as a nurse and my perception of her as a manager is that she has a genuine concern for the welfare of her staff.

Lilly

Some of the comments weren't professional. They were personal opinions and I didn't know where they were coming from … like 'Well you have a strong personality' and that was left hanging. I didn't know whether it was positive or negative. If she had qualified it, it would have been fine but I was left without meaning … I felt I had to justify my practice and how I was as a person.

Penny

It didn't in any way reflect my own feelings about not being competent in the job … To be given a very positive appraisal is nice but at the same time it makes me feel that huge amounts are being expected of me and that can be more disconcerting than having a realistic appraisal. I am very much a novice.

(Spence and Wood, 2007, pp. 57, 58)

These examples suggest the perceptual differences, complex emotions and relationship dynamics associated with appraisal. Gary's positive experience arises out of his sense that the appraisal was fair as well as respect for his manager and her concern for his performance. A fair appraisal system and trust are conditions for a non-threatening and non-judgemental appraisal (Peel, 2003). Gary's charge nurse observed him for 12 hours to capture authentic feedback. The manager's commitment to the process is important (Redshaw, 2008). If employees do not trust appraisal information, they will discount its usefulness and will not act on it to improve performance (Tourish, 2006).

In Lilly's case, she was unsure what her feedback actually meant, while Penny felt it was not accurate. Practitioners such as Penny, who feel insecure about their abilities, may find appraisal particularly stressful (Bentley and Dandy-Hughes, 2010). Feedback can be fraught with biases. You may be aware of the way in which your expectations or assumptions can influence what you see in daily life. Similarly, in appraisal there can be assumptions that strengths or weakness in one area will also recur in other areas, and a focus on information that confirms first impressions or personal feelings about the person influencing the appraisal (Tourish, 2006). This is unhelpful, as neither Penny nor Lilly was left in a position to improve their performance.

However, appraisal, if done well, can give a voice to the individual's contribution to the workplace and raise their self-confidence (O'Connor and Lee, 2007). It can help people feel valued and recognised (Spence and Wood, 2007). However, if handled poorly, it can be worse than no appraisal at all. It can have a negative effect on motivation, job satisfaction, commitment, and trust between managers and employees (Tourish, 2006; Redshaw, 2008).

Someone practising 'situational leadership' (Chapter 3) matches their style of leadership to the amount of direction and support staff require. This could be particularly applicable in relation to CPD.

9.5 Conclusion

Continuing professional development (CPD) can be understood as the reconciliation of the needs of each practitioner with the ever-changing needs of the team, organisation and role. It should therefore be understood as being at the heart of balancing the four building blocks of the caring approach to management and leadership. Induction, supervision and appraisal are mechanisms for the manager to mediate the demands of these needs.

Induction focuses on supporting practitioners' transition into the organisation and demands acute awareness of the needs of each individual, regardless of experience. Supervision, with its concern with balancing an individual's needs for support and personal development with the organisation's demands for accountability, is another form of mediation that gives rise to learning. Appraisal also has a mediatory role in its concern with organisational accountability and the individual's sense of personal performance and future. Supervision, appraisal and induction can deal with deeply personal or difficult matters and must be handled with thoughtfulness and care. Leadership skills in motivating and inspiring are key here, as is emotional intelligence (see Chapter 2).

However, much learning is intertwined with daily work, sometimes occurring outside the practitioner's awareness. Managers in their leadership role have a part to play here, too, in the way in which they try to shape the work environment by: facilitating opportunities for practitioners to talk and build trusting relationships; allocating work to stretch but not overwhelm or overload; and supporting the establishment of cultures of good practice and learning.

Key points

- Leading learning involves balancing organisational needs (strategic, governmental, regulatory, legal, political and economic factors), individual needs for growth, personal fulfilment and career progression, team needs for coordination and the demands of the practitioner's role.
- Much learning occurs through day-to-day practice and can be fostered through paying attention to the environment, relationships, conditions and allocation of work, and team culture.

- All practitioners, regardless of experience, need induction. Effective induction is supported by supervision, mentoring, opportunities to shadow, regular feedback, and the explicit expression of requirements.
- Supervision can be planned or ad hoc, formal or informal. It can involve attention to supporting learning, providing support and ensuring accountability.
- Appraisal is a process of reviewing performance, focusing worker attention on the achievement of organisational objectives and planning for personal development. As a communicative event, it requires careful planning and skilled execution.
- A caring approach to CPD encompasses both careful management of the necessary processes and strong leadership dedicated to creating a learning environment for everyone.

References

Barbazette, J. (2006) *Training Needs Assessment: Methods, tools and techniques (Volume 1)*, San Francisco, Calif., Pfeiffer.

Bates, N., Immins, T., Parker, J., Keen, S., Rutter, L., Brown, K. and Zsigo, S. (2010) '"Baptism of fire": the first year in the life of a newly qualified social worker', *Social Work Education*, vol. 29, no. 2, pp. 152–70.

Bentley, J. and Dandy-Hughes, H. (2010) 'Implementing KSF competency testing in primary care. Part 2: evaluation of the pilot of an appraisal tool', *British Journal of Community Nursing*, vol. 15, no. 11, pp. 553–60.

Billett, S. (2004) 'Co-participation at work: learning through work and throughout working lives', *Studies in the Education of Adults*, vol. 36, no. 2, pp. 190–205.

Billett, S. (2010) 'Learning through practice', in Billett, S. (ed.) *Learning through Practice: Models, traditions, orientations and approaches*, Dordrecht, Springer, pp. 1–20.

Bishop, V. (2007) 'Clinical supervision: what is it? Why do we need it?', in Bishop, V. (ed.) *Clinical Supervision in Practice: Some questions, answers and guidelines for professionals in health and social care*, Basingstoke , Palgrave Macmillan.

Care Quality Commission (2010) *Essential Standards of Quality and Safety*, London, CQC.

Chartered Institute of Personnel and Development (CIPD) (2006) *Identifying learning needs in organisations* [Online]. Available at www.cipd.co.uk/NR/rdonlyres/BAE22874-1D3C-4912-BBD9-1C14803E8A44/0/1843981645sc.pdf (Accessed 8 September 2012).

Cole, M. (2004) 'Capture and measurement of work based and informal learning: a discussion of the issues in relation to contemporary healthcare practice', *Work Based Learning in Primary Care*, vol. 2, no. 2, pp. 118–25.

Commission on Improving Dignity in Care (CIDC) (2012) *Delivering Dignity: Securing dignity in care for older people in hospitals and care homes. A report for consultation* [Online]. Available at www.nhsconfed.org/Documents/dignity.pdf (Accessed 13 March 2012).

Cornes, M., Gill, L., Armstrong, S. and Bowes, M. (2010) *Impact on staff retention rates in four diverse social care provider organisations in Cumbria* [Online]. Available at www.kcl.ac.uk/content/1/c6/06/75/94/Cornesetal2010Personal.pdf (Accessed 22 August 2011).

Driscoll, J. and O'Sullivan, J. (2007) 'The place of clinical supervision in modern healthcare', in Driscoll, J. (ed.) *Practising Clinical Supervision: A reflective approach for healthcare professionals*, Edinburgh, Ballière Tindall Elsevier.

Eraut, M. (1994) *Developing Professional Knowledge and Competence,* London, The Falmer Press.

Eraut, M. (2004) 'Learning to change and/or changing to learn', *Learning in Health and Social Care*, vol. 3, no. 3, pp. 111–17.

Eraut, M. (2006) Editorial: 'Learning contexts', *Learning in Health and Social Care*, vol. 5, no. 1, pp. 1–8.

Eraut, M. (2011) 'Informal learning in the workplace: evidence on the real value of work-based learning (WBL)', *Development and Learning in Organizations*, vol. 25, no. 5, pp. 8–12.

Felstead, A., Fuller, A., Jewson, N. and Unwin, L. (2009) *Improving Working as Learning*, Abingdon, Routledge.

Forrester-Jones, R. and Hatzidimitriadou, E. (2006) 'Learning in the real world? Exploring widening participation student views concerning the "fit" between knowledge learnt and work practices', *Assessment and Evaluation in Higher Education*, vol. 31, no. 6, pp. 611–24.

Gumus, G., Borkowski, N., Deckard, G.J. and Martel, K.J. (2011) 'Healthcare managers' perceptions of professional development and organizational support', *Journal of Health and Human Services Administration*, vol. 34, no. 1, pp. 42–63.

Hancock, H., Campbell, S., Ramprogus, V. and Kilgour, J. (2005) 'Role development in health care assistants: the impact of education on practice', *Journal of Evaluation in Clinical Practice*, vol. 11, no. 5, pp. 489–98.

Harris, A., Kubiak, C. and Rogers, A. (2006) 'Building firm foundations: an evaluation of a work-based foundation degree programme for mental health workers', Paper presented at European Conference for Educational Researchers, University of Geneva, 13–16 September 2006.

Hughes, E. (2005) 'Nurses' perceptions of continuing professional development', *Nursing Standard*, vol. 19, no. 43, pp. 41–9.

Jack, G. and Donnellan, H. (2010) 'Recognising the person within the developing professional: tracking the early careers of newly qualified child care social workers in three local authorities in England', *Social Work Education*, vol. 29, no. 3, pp. 305–18.

Jarvis, P. (2006) *Towards a Comprehensive Theory of Human Learning*, Abingdon, Routledge.

Kolb, D.A. (1984) *Experiential Learning: Experience as the source of learning and development*, Englewood Cliffs, NJ, Prentice Hall.

Maslow, A.H. (1954) *Motivation and Personality*, New York, Harper.

McClure, P. (2005) *Reflection on Practice* [Online].Available at http://cw.routledge.com/textbooks/9780415537902/data/learning/8_Reflection_in_Practice.pdf (Accessed 7 November 2012).

Miller, C. and Blackman, C. (2003) *Interim Report for Nursing*, London, Economic and Social Research Council, Teaching and Learning Research

Programme. Available online at www.tlrp.org/dspace/retrieve/131/report_nursing.pdf (Accessed 2 September 2012).

O'Connor, M. and Lee, S. (2007) 'Authentic performance appraisal: when home is the workplace', *International Journal of Palliative Nursing*, vol. 13, no. 12, pp. 606–9.

Peach, J. and Horner, N. (2007) 'Using supervision: support or surveillance', in Lymbery, M.E.F. and Postle, K. (eds) *Social Work: A Companion to Learning*, London, Sage Publications Ltd.

Peel, M. (2003) *Managing Professional Development*, London, Routledge.

Rainbird, H., Munro, A., Holly, L. and Leisten, R. (1999) *The Future of Work in the Public Sector: Learning and workplace inequality*, Northampton, Centre for Research in Employment, Work and Training, University College Northampton. Available online at www.leeds.ac.uk/esrcfutureofwork/downloads/workingpaperdownloads/fow_paper_02.pdf (Accessed 3 March 2007).

Redshaw, G. (2008) *Improving the Performance Appraisal System for Nurses* [Online]. Available at www.nursingtimes.net/nursing-practice-clinical-research/improving-the-performance-appraisal-system-for-nurses/1314790.article (Accessed 19 August 2011).

Rouse, J. (2007) 'How does clinical supervision impact on staff development?', *Journal of Children's and Young People's Nursing*, vol. 1, no. 7, pp. 334–40.

Royal College of Nursing (2007) 'A joint statement on continuing professional development for health and social care practitioners', London, RCN.

Royal College of Nursing (2009) *HCA Toolkit: Unit 4 – Personal and professional development of health care assistants* [Online]. Available at www.rcn.org.uk/development/health_care_support_workers/learning_and_development/hca_toolkit/unit_four (Accessed 8 August 2011).

Spence, D.G. and Wood, E.E. (2007) 'Registered nurse participation in performance appraisal interviews', *Journal of Professional Nursing*, vol. 23, no. 1, pp. 55–9.

Spilsbury, K. and Meyer, J. (2004) 'Use, misuse and non-use of health care assistants: understanding the work of health care assistants in a hospital setting', *Journal of Nursing Management*, vol. 12, no. 6, pp. 411–18.

Staniland, K., Rosen, L. and Wild, J. (2011) 'Staff support in continuing professional development', *Nursing Management – UK*, vol. 18, no. 1, pp. 33–7.

Thomas, H., Hicks, J., Martin, G. and Cressey, G. (2008) 'Induction and transition in the National Health Service for four professional groups', *Learning in Health and Social Care*, vol. 7, no. 1, pp. 27–36.

Tourish, D. (2006) 'The appraisal interview reappraised', in Hargie, O. (ed.) *The Handbook of Communication Skills* (3rd edition), London, Routledge, pp. 505–30.

West, M.A., Borrill, C., Dawson, J., Scully, J., Carter, M., Anelay, S., Patterson, M. and Waring, J. (2002) 'The link between the management of employees and patient mortality in acute hospitals', *The International Journal of Human Resource Management*, vol. 13, no. 8, pp. 1299–310.

Whitehead, A.N. (1932) *The Aims of Education and Other Essays*, London, Williams and Norgate Ltd.

Chapter 10 Developing a coaching style of management

Joan Simons

10.1 Introduction

Catch a man a fish
Feed him for a day
Teach a man to fish
Feed him for life

Figure 10.1 Coaching can last a lifetime

A survey carried out by the Chartered Institute for Personnel Development found that 47 per cent of managers were using coaching in their work (CIPD, 2007). Yet 'the manager as coach' is a relatively new concept (Ellinger et al., 2010). It gained currency with the work of Evered and Seleman (1989), who identified coaching as a core managerial activity. It is now widely recognised that it can be useful for managers to add an understanding of coaching to their repertoire of skills in leading and empowering their staff to maximise their potential. In health and social care, coaching is seen as one way to maximise delivery at the point of service (Foster-Turner, 2006).

Coaching can be defined as:

> [A] human development process that involves structured, focussed interaction and the use of appropriate strategies, tools and techniques to promote desirable and sustainable change for the benefit of the person being coached and potentially for other stakeholders.
>
> (Bachkirova et al., 2010, p. 1)

In health and social care, the benefits may relate to colleagues, patients and/or service users. Human resource practices have been gradually devolved to line managers alongside a growth in the expectation of employees about their personal development. A generation ago, people expected to have a job for life. Today, the indications are that the average person will have four changes in career or direction in their working life. Such change impacts on an individual's expectations of their manager's role in fostering and facilitating their progress within any given post.

Despite the recognised need and apparent benefits of managers coaching their staff, Peterson and Little (2005) acknowledge the lack of resources aimed at specifically helping managers to coach people better. Therefore, managers and leaders in health and social care need to gain an understanding of what coaching is, how they might add it to their repertoire of skills and, more importantly, how to develop a culture at work that encourages coaching.

This chapter addresses the following core questions.

- What is coaching and how does it differ from mentoring?
- What are the benefits and the limitations of coaching?
- How can coaching be used to induct new staff, achieve work-related goals, and deal with conflict?
- What skills are necessary to develop a coaching style of management in health and social care?

For simplicity, the examples in this chapter focus on one-to-one coaching, but the format of both team coaching and self-coaching is the same.

The similarities and differences between coaching and mentoring

For some time there has been confusion over the differences and the similarities between coaching and mentoring. So it is helpful to identify some clear differences between them.

The word 'mentor' comes from Greek mythology, when Odysseus asked his old friend, Mentor, to watch over his son while he went to fight in the Trojan War (Hope Moncrieff, 1992). Odysseus asked Mentor to teach his son all he knew. As a result, the word 'mentor' means 'teacher', and involves a one-way flow of knowledge from the more experienced mentor to the inexperienced mentee. Both mentoring and coaching enable personal growth. They both facilitate the acquisition of new knowledge. They both involve building rapport between two people. However, there are some fundamental differences in key skills and methods.

- A mentor gives advice to their mentee; a non-directive coach never gives advice to their client.
- A mentor comes from a position of being more knowledgeable than their mentee; a coach comes from the perspective of not needing to be an expert in the field because the person being coached holds all the answers to how they can achieve their goal.
- A mentor's task is accomplished when they have imparted all the necessary knowledge to a mentee to enable them to be competent in their role; a coach's job is done when the person being coached achieves their goal, by working out how to get there through using skilled, targeted questioning, and increasing self-awareness.

Coaching is a form of personalised, supported learning used to accomplish goals in a chosen area of focus, either personal or professional. It has the benefit of increasing self-awareness and consciousness in individuals by identifying strategies and resources within themselves to achieve their goals and those of the organisation. A survey for the journal *Coaching at Work* and The Association of Coaching found that the majority of respondents felt that meaning and purpose in life was integral to coaching (North, 2009).

Effective coaching requires a predominantly 'non-directive' approach (Downey, 2003) in which learning is intrinsic and satisfaction derives from the pursuit and achievement of meaningful goals. This is what effective coaching can be. Working in health or social care, it may be quite a challenge to take a non-directive stance, especially in a leadership or management role. These roles require decisiveness and delegation and they need to provide advice or even instruction on a daily basis, none of which could be called non-directive. However, the premise of non-direction in coaching is based on the belief that individuals have within them the ability and the means to identify their goals and, with help from a coach, they can find a realistic way forward to achieving their goals. The power of this type of coaching is in the person being coached themselves identifying their options, their potential obstacles and their support mechanisms. The resulting action plan to achieve their goal is much more likely to be realistic and achievable as they own it.

What obstacles can you see to developing a coaching style of management in your workplace?

There are various approaches to coaching and to be an effective coach requires specific training. In the UK, such training is offered in several institutions, the largest being The Coaching Academy in London. None the less, a coaching style of management and leadership can be developed which is built on the basic philosophies behind coaching. The rest of this chapter explores three specific approaches to coaching and how they might be applied in the context of health and social care.

10.2 The First 90 Days approach

Case study 10.1: A new job

Michael had just been appointed as a new manager in the housing department of Dexter Council. He felt passionately that housing should always be a priority for improving outcomes for people who use services. Therefore, Michael was quite anxious to make a success of this new job. He felt confident that he had the right experience, background and skills but was worried that he had so much to learn and did not really know where to start. He had to relocate to this borough to take up his new role and had to get to know the staff he would be working with.

On his first day in the job, Michael's line manager offered him a series of coaching sessions to help him in his transition through the first 90 days in his new role. At first, Michael was worried when he was made this offer – did his manager think he was not up to the job? Was this some kind of extra support the council thought he needed because of some inadequacy? Michael reluctantly accepted the offer but was then more worried than ever and felt he had got off on the wrong foot in his new job.

New leaders or managers have a limited time frame in which to capitalise on their new role in order to become effective. Watkins (2003) suggests that this time frame is 90 days long, after which if the new manager or leader has not grasped the opportunities, it will be too late. Watkins' model is underpinned by five core principles.

1 A new manager's success or failure depends on their ability to evaluate their situation and identify its characteristic opportunities.
2 There are systematic methods that a new manager can use to both lessen the likelihood of failure and reach the break-even point.
3 Leadership is ultimately about leverage. Effective leaders use leverage – their ideas, energy, relationships and influence – to create new patterns in an organisation.
4 Transitions are a crucible for leadership development and should be managed accordingly.
5 Accelerating transitions makes sense: good people get bored after a few years and crave new challenges.

In the case study above, the offer to Michael of coaching in the early stages of a new job came as a surprise to him, and he initially felt undermined by the suggestion. The story now continues.

Case study 10.2: Michael's first 90 days

Michael's manager, John, explained that Dexter Council introduced coaching so that every new manager could be helped to be more effective in their new role quicker than if they had to work out things for themselves. Michael was the fourth person John had coached through the process in the last 12 months. On hearing this, Michael immediately relaxed, forgot his feelings of inadequacy, and wanted to hear more about this opportunity to help him maximise his potential in the first 90 days of his new job.

In his meetings with John over the next three months, Michael learned how to be systematic about what he needed to learn in his new role. He assessed what would make the role most effective and what success would look like. By evaluating his new role, he could see who were the other key people he had to work with. He consciously planned the conversations he would have with these key individuals and learned to manage the expectations of both his staff and peers.

Figure 10.2 Coaching can shed new light on a situation

After 90 days, Michael met John again, who asked him what difference the first 90 days of coaching had made to him. Michael said that when he started previous jobs he was always anxious about how it was going to work out. He felt that the first few months were a difficult time of adjustment, and that success was usually down to luck, not judgement. However, in this job, it was like someone had turned on a light in his head (Figure 10.2). He was functioning on a different level, taking control, doing things consciously, planning ahead, and working with more purpose than he ever did in the last 20 years of his career. He felt the coaching had helped him work out very clearly what he needed to achieve in his new job and who could support him to achieve it. He thought he had achieved more in his first 90 days in this job than he had done in a year in previous posts.

Hollenbeck and Hall's 'self-confidence formula', described in Chapter 1 (see Figure 1.7), works on the same principle as the First 90 Days approach.

It is clear from this case that the result of Michael's coaching by John enhanced his ability to be effective in his new job. It accelerated his learning and focused his energy on identifying just what success in the job meant, followed by pursuing that goal with clarity. The support that the coaching provided meant that he could set aside his anxieties about getting to know the job and the staff, as the coaching enabled him to identify a way forward. It reduced the interference his anxiety had created and allowed him to work towards maximising his potential in his new role. By growing in self-awareness and gaining increased clarity, people being coached develop increased self-confidence and grow in self-belief; they learn to ignore self-doubt or negative thoughts that might hinder them in achieving their goal.

In order to build in coaching as an integral part of their role, managers need to develop a mindset of 'manager-as-coach'. According to Hunt and Weintraub (2002), this entails the following characteristics:

- an attitude of helpfulness
- less need for control
- empathy in dealing with other people
- openness to personal learning and receiving feedback
- high standards
- a desire to help others to develop
- a theory of employee development that is not predicated on a 'sink-or-swim' approach
- a belief that most people want to learn.

Looking at the characteristics involved in a coaching mindset, what similarities are there to the characteristics of transformational leadership described in Chapter 3?

Through John's coaching, Michael managed to consider the meaning and purpose of his role, and its value for service users. This clarity gave Michael confidence in settling quickly into a new job by being focused on what he needed to achieve.

'Managers who coach their employees become known as good managers to work for, developers of talent, and achievers of business results' (Hunt and Weintraub, 2002, p. 39).

Rather than telling a person what to do, like a traditional manager might, the manager-as-coach uses a series of questions and probes to get the person being coached to think through their own performance and what might be interfering with it, and working towards their potential. Gallwey (2001) sums up this process in the equation:

performance – interference = potential

Recalling the case of Michael, what 'interference' was he dealing with on his first day in his new job?

Coaching can help reduce an individual's 'interference', allowing them to work towards their potential. Interference can take many forms, such as self-doubt or negative (often unfounded) self-beliefs that act as obstacles to working towards your potential. One way of reducing interference is to work with a particular model, as described next in another case study.

10.3 The GROW model of coaching

Case study 10.3: Nancy's need to GROW

Nancy worked as a senior physiotherapist in a large district general hospital. She had worked hard to get where she was and, five years ago, succeeded in gaining her current post, managing a team of physiotherapists. She loved the job and, in fact, had wanted it for several years, but recently she found it less fulfilling and was becoming restless. She could see that the service she and her team delivered was of a good standard, but she also recognised that there was more they could do for some of the elderly patients they worked with. She had read some very innovative research papers recently on increasing the effectiveness of physiotherapy by using a psychology-based approach to increase compliance with exercise. Nancy would love to go on such a course but knew the chances of it happening were very slight. Her colleague, Jim, had been having coaching to help with his time management and he suggested to Nancy that she should look for some coaching, which she did.

In her first session, the coach, Ben, explained that he would be using the GROW model and the coaching would be non-directive. Nancy was then asked to describe the background to why she was looking for coaching. She described her job, her lack of satisfaction, and being unsettled. Having heard this, Ben reflected back to Nancy what he had heard, and summarised it by saying, 'You strike me as being bored'. At first, Nancy was quite taken aback by this comment, but quickly realised it was true, and agreed – with some relief – that she *was* bored, but she did not want to change her job; she just wanted more out of it. Having agreed that she was bored, Nancy was very receptive to working towards a goal that would help her alleviate the boredom.

Many coaches use a model to structure their coaching. One popular model is the GROW model (Whitmore, 2009), which consists of four stages:

Goal identification

Reality

Options

What will you do?

You can find the full details of the **GROW model** in the toolkit. This is how Nancy's coach used the model with her.

Case study 10.4: Coaching for career development using the GROW model

Figure 10.3 Know your target

The next stage Ben worked on with Nancy was identifying her goal (Figure 10.3). Nancy was quite tentative about clearly stating her goal, as she saw it as more of a dream than a goal: that is, to go on a one-year postgraduate psychology course to help her develop enhanced compliance in elderly patients. Ben asked Nancy who the course would benefit, and how increased compliance in elderly patients would help them.

Nancy replied that for some it would mean returning home from hospital rather than going to a nursing home, maintaining their independence and, in fact, their quality of life.

This line of questioning made Nancy realise that what she thought was a very personal, almost hidden, goal had real professional significance, which gave her the confidence to believe that she should commit herself to the goal of achieving a place on the psychology course. With help from her coach, she decided to ignore the 'negative mind chatter' that went on in her head, telling her this was a daft thing to want to do. With increased confidence and renewed enthusiasm, Nancy was coached for six months, working each time with Ben on her goal of getting a place on the course.

If you need to spend some time clarifying your goals before working with the **GROW tool**, the **goal-setting tool** might be useful.

Nancy's determination and motivation meant that, for every obstacle she encountered over the next six months, she could identify a way forward. Her coach, Ben, used the **GROW** model to identify each journey **goal** Nancy identified, such as finding a supervisor, obtaining funding, making the application, and attending the interview. He then ensured they worked through each of the stages by identifying the **reality** of each goal, looking for all the possible **options** available and who could provide support. Having considered all the options available, **what Nancy was going to do next** was identified at each coaching session, until Nancy was successful in achieving a place on the course. Looking back, she was very surprised by her success. Ben, however, pointed out that she had always had the resources within her to be successful; what coaching did was help remove the *interference* to allow her to reach her *potential.*

Can you identify ways in which you could use the GROW model in developing a coaching style of management?

Nancy's case demonstrates how having self-doubt, or lacking in confidence about a career aspiration, can create obstacles or interference to moving forward in achieving career goals. One aspect of Nancy's coaching that helped her move forward was realising that her goal was related to improving the quality of life of elderly people and not just a personal goal. This self-doubt was interfering with Nancy's ability to achieve her potential; however, once it was overcome, she managed to successfully achieve her goal.

Nancy's self-doubt and perceived obstacles may have been influenced by the concept of the Inner Game, where individuals have conversations with themselves that influence their self-belief, as explained in Box 10.1.

Box 10.1: The Inner Game

The thoughts people have and the things they tell themselves can be quite influential in their attitude to new challenges: for example, 'I'm not clever enough', 'I'm too old', or 'I'm not that type of person'. Tim Gallwey (2001) developed a concept called 'the Inner Game' to describe the capacity of people to have conversations with themselves. These conversations are notable for the criticism, judgement and condemnation that individuals heap on themselves. Gallwey asks the question 'Who is talking to whom?', indicating two separate entities within the one person's mind. He suggests that there are two 'selves' which, in relation to playing tennis, are the 'teller' and the 'doer'. One gives instructions and the other seems to perform the action. Myles Downey took this concept forward in relation to coaching, naming the two selves 'Self One' and 'Self Two', and suggesting that:

- Self One is the internalised voice of our parents, teachers and those in authority. Self One seeks to control Self Two and does not trust it. Self One is characterised by tension, fear, doubt and trying too hard.

- Self Two is the whole human being with all its potential and capacities including the 'hard-wired' capacity to learn. It is characterised by relaxed concentration, enjoyment and trust.

(Downey, 2003, p. 45)

As a coach, the aim is to operate from Self Two. This is where a coach can do their best and most rewarding work. When coaching, the aim is to get the person being coached into, and staying in, Self Two. In this way, a person being coached can be more insightful, objective, intuitive and creative.

Helping the person being coached to be in Self Two in everyday life, and particularly in the critical moments such as key meetings and presentations, is arguably part of the coach's or line manager's role. More than 30 years after they first launched modern coaching and Inner Game thinking, Tim Gallwey and John Whitmore believe the approach has more to offer now than ever before (Gallwey and Whitmore, 2010). This is because of the increased demands placed on employees to be more flexible and take on new learning in the workplace to increase efficiency.

Can you identify your Self One and Self Two?

Coaches empower the person being coached by helping them to become more self-aware, identifying what they do with the time they have, and then choosing to take responsibility for their life. By taking responsibility, they can learn from a situation and move forward to what they want to achieve. They also realise they cannot control situations outside themselves, but they can control their reaction to the situations or people they work with.

Getting ready for coaching: setting the ground rules

For coaching to be highly successful, you need to prepare carefully and clarify expectations at the outset. As a manager in health and social care, coaching situations have many different guises: for example, a member of staff may clearly have potential but, through lack of experience, needs to build on their self-confidence; or a discrete project is to be carried out by a member of staff who needs support to successfully complete it on time. Both situations would benefit from coaching, but one is more predictable in the process needed. A member of staff who needs to build on their confidence will respond to a coaching style of management whereby the manager uses opportunities to help them grow in self-awareness, identify their goals, and work towards them gradually over time. In relation to completing a particular project, a more focused approach to coaching is required as there is a defined goal and an identified time limit to achieve success. The GROW model can be particularly successful in this sort of situation.

When starting one-to-one coaching, it should be agreed how many coaching sessions there will be, over how long a period, and when they should take place. This gives control to the person being coached and sets expectations from the outset. This initial understanding can be helped with an explanation and understanding of what coaching is and is not, to clarify that there are situations in which coaching is not appropriate. For example, a coach will not agree to pursue a goal that would involve dishonesty or breaking a professional code of practice because coaching has an ethical underpinning. (See Chapter 16 for more about morals and ethics in health and social care.)

The coach needs to build up rapport with the person being coached from the first session, to gain their trust and confidence in the success of the coaching outcome, and to enable them to open up about what might be a very personal topic, thus enabling honesty in the realities of the situation and the likelihood of success. A manager who is coaching a member of staff will already have a working relationship; however, clarity around the coaching relationship is still needed. Once these initial ground rules have been established, it is necessary to assure the person being coached of confidentiality, so that they feel comfortable exploring any sensitive issues.

One-to-one coaching depends on honesty, openness and sometimes exposing weaknesses, perhaps making the person being coached feel vulnerable. These coaching interactions are potentially life changing, as with the case of Nancy, who realised her dream to fundamentally alter the orientation of her career by carving out an identity in a new field allied to her role as a physiotherapist.

During coaching sessions many aspects of everyday work may be discussed. If the coach is also the manager, what are the implications for confidentiality?

So far, coaching has been proposed as a process for achievement and growth in self-awareness and self-confidence. There will be times, however, when a process is needed to deal with the more negative aspects of being a manager in health and social care, such as dealing with conflict.

The next section outlines a coaching model that focuses specifically on coaching an individual through conflict, starting with another case study.

10.4 A conflict coaching model

Case study 10.5: Maria's workplace conflict

Maria planned the shift patterns for the unit she worked on, delivering 24-hour care to adults with severe learning disabilities. There were occasional requests for certain shifts from staff who wanted to have a specific weekend off, or who had some family commitment they needed to attend. One new member of staff, Heather, put in requests every week and didn't want to work the unpopular late shift if at all possible. She preferred to work from 8 a.m. to 4 p.m. so that she could get home to her children. Maria, who didn't have children, thought that this was unfair because it meant other staff had to work more late shifts to make up for Heather's unwillingness to do them.

Rather than speak to Heather, Maria tried to do what she thought was fair, and only agreed to Heather's requests every other week. Heather was very unhappy about this and angrily confronted Maria, telling her she was being unreasonable not giving her the off-duty she requested because working on a late shift meant she spent most of her earnings on child care.

Maria felt very challenged by Heather's angry tone and aggressively pointed out that Heather was being unfair to her colleagues by not pulling her weight and that she shouldn't have taken on the job if she couldn't do it fairly. Heather was furious, and told Maria she was being thoughtless and uncaring as she didn't have children herself. Heather then threatened to resign if Maria didn't apologise for being unfair over the off-duty.

After this very heated exchange, Maria went to her manager, Gail, in tears as she thought she was doing a good job on the duty rota, trying to allocate shifts evenly, and was angry and frustrated with the patronising and insulting way Heather had spoken to her. She said she would apologise if necessary but didn't want to work with Heather any longer.

In any organisation there are times when conflict arises. This could be due to either a straightforward personality clash or staff competing for limited resources, or it could be a result of poor communication at a time of stress, such as when departments are moved or merged with other departments. There can also be conflict around different expectations, as in the case of Maria and Heather. Whatever the source of the conflict, very often a third party needs to help solve it. This responsibility is probably held by the manager or leader as their staff will expect them, because of their position, to recognise and defuse conflicts.

Tricia Jones and Ross Brinkert have worked in the field of mediation and coaching for many years. They devised the Comprehensive Conflict Coaching model, which is aimed specifically at resolving conflict (Jones and Brinkert, 2008; see Box 10.2). This model can be used with an individual who wants to resolve a conflict issue.

Box 10.2: The four stages of the Comprehensive Conflict Coaching model

1. Discovering the story
2. Exploring three perspectives:
   - (a) Identity
   - (b) Emotion
   - (c) Power
3. Crafting the best story
4. Enacting the best story

(Jones and Brinkert, 2008)

There are two underlying orientations to this model. First, it takes a communication perspective as being key to understanding conflict, focusing on the enactment of conflict and the analysis of verbal and non-verbal communication to identify patterns over time. Second, it also assumes that any conflict is contextual: that is, it develops as a result of people's situations and will influence current and continuing relationships.

The four stages of the model are explored in more detail below, by applying them to Maria's case.

Case study 10.6: Applying the conflict coaching model

1 Discovering the story

This stage allows the person in conflict to construct a coherent narrative of their experience of the conflict and to take the perspective of the other parties in it. At this stage, the coach concentrates on discovering as much of the story as possible, to get an adequate understanding of the conflict, the parties involved, and the context. This stage needs three levels of clarification: the initial story; refining the story; and testing the story.

The initial story provides information about how the individual sees important issues, people and opportunities in the conflict. Refining the story encourages the individual to provide more information pertinent to how other parties may be experiencing the conflict and focuses on how this is affecting other people in the organisation. A key aspect at this stage is that the coach is not challenging the story but encouraging the individual to provide the most comprehensive and coherent narrative.

Once the coach feels they have the full contextualised story, the next stage is to test the story. This involves testing the assumptions that the person being coached is making about the individuals involved in the conflict. In the conflict between Maria and Heather, Gail will need Maria to articulate what happened and acknowledge how she and Heather have been affected by the incident.

2 Exploring three perspectives: identity, emotion and power

The purpose of this stage is to help the person being coached understand the forces in the conflict, so they can understand what to change and how to change it. The three essential analytical elements in any conflict are: issues of *identity*; issues of *emotion*; and issues of *power*.

(a) Identity

Desired and damaged identity lies at the heart of conflict. Most people are in conflict because they believe someone or something is preventing them from being who they are or who they want to be. Maria believes Heather has accused her of being unfair, while Maria took those actions to be fair to all of her colleagues. People in conflict are often ignorant of how their actions are negatively impacting on the identity of the other person. The role of the coach is to clarify with the individual their current and desired identity, helping them to protect their identity while adjusting how they perceive the other person. Gail will want both Maria and Heather to feel they are being fairly treated and can therefore work together again.

(b) Emotion

Emotions are central to conflict: they serve as a measure of how important the conflict is to an individual and provide a way of understanding what needs to change to resolve the conflict. Understanding emotions gives an insight into why people act in certain ways. Exploring emotions helps the individual in conflict understand why they are motivated to deal with the conflict as well as understand why others have behaved in a certain way. In Heather's case, her weekly requests are due to her family responsibilities, and her need to make her job viable economically. Whereas Maria's priority is to see that all colleagues are treated the same, regardless of circumstances.

(c) Power

This perspective focuses on the ability of the individual in conflict to influence the current situation in a way that is favourable to them. Can they make changes to the current situation that will increase their ability to create their desired identity and cultivate more positive emotions? The coach can explore such issues as: what factors are in the way? What resources are needed to increase this influence? Who can help? What are the consequences of changing the power relationship?

One solution to this case study is that Heather seeks permission from Gail to formalise her shift patterns to suit her circumstances and allow her to work only one late shift. Maria then would not have to deal with off-duty requests every week, and make decisions about what is fair.

Chapter 1 describes Wong's web of power (Wong, 2003). Which expressions of power are being dealt with here?

According to Covey (2004), to begin with the end in mind is one of the habits of highly effective people.

3 Crafting the best story

Having established a coherent story, and viewed it from the three perspectives of identity, emotion and power, the next stage is to encourage the person being coached to identify and articulate what the situation would be like if the conflict were managed most effectively. Using the information gathered through the three perspectives, the coach helps the individual to craft a story of success – a journey with clear milestones that would meet the identity, emotion and power interests of the individual. In the case of Maria and Heather, the best story would be for Heather to have an agreement that she works only one late shift per week, and for Maria not to have to deal with weekly requests, and to appreciate that not everyone should be treated the same about their off-duty.

4 Enacting the best story

Do you know what your preferred style of dealing with conflict is? Chapter 17 explores this further with the conflict style model of Thomas and Kilman (1978).

Knowing what you want can help you identify what needs to happen to move you towards that end. At the final stage, the manager-as-coach works with the individual to consider options for a way forward. Once all of the options have been considered, decisions are made about what actions the individual will take to move towards resolving the conflict. By using the conflict coaching model, Maria and Heather's manager, Gail, can make both parties appreciate the other's point of view, identify a possible solution, and work towards it.

10.5 The benefits and limitations of coaching

Figure 10.4 Coaching has both pros and cons

Coaching potentially benefits not just individuals: the cumulative effect of individuals being coached and working towards maximising their potential is also likely, through synergy, to have a considerable overall positive effect on their organisation. The assumption behind coaching is that the coaching dialogue gives the person being coached the opportunity for reflection, and thereby to develop a deeper understanding of their behaviour and the impact of this behaviour on performance and their relationships with other people (Truijen and van Woerkom, 2008). The contribution of coaching to leadership development can be identified at both the individual and the organisational level (Simpson, 2010).

The coach's role is to discover, clarify and align with what the person being coached wants to achieve. However, not everyone wants to be coached, and the manager may not have either the time or the inclination to take on the role of coach. Therefore, there are several limitations to coaching which need to be recognised in relation to either the coach, the person being coached, or the purpose and function of the coaching (Figure 10.4).

Clearly, for coaching to be successful, the person being coached has to be ready for coaching, able to see the relevance of it to them, and motivated to work with a coach to achieve their goals. It is not enough for a well-intentioned manager to decide that they will coach their staff to increase their unit's effectiveness. On the other hand, not all managers can be effective coaches. In fact, to be a non-directive manager-as-coach may run contrary to a manager's natural style of delegating and advising their staff. Many managers spend much of their time being directive and giving advice. So it may be too much of a transition for them to adopt the non-directive stance required in coaching, where the coach enables the person being coached to identify for themselves how to achieve their goals. Meanwhile, the person being coached may not want to disclose too much to their manager, which may create barriers to the coaching being successful. Coaching requires trust between the manager-as-coach and the person being coached. If this cannot be established within that relationship, an independent coach might be the solution.

In the busy context of health and social care work, many managers may feel they simply do not have the time available to coach their staff. Specialist practitioners who are managers in health and social care may find it difficult to set aside their expert knowledge and take on a non-directive role to assume a coaching role (Truijen and van Woerkom, 2008). There will be times when expert advice is exactly what is needed rather than coaching. The challenge for the manager is to be able to identify when coaching is appropriate and when it is not.

10.6 Conclusion

This chapter provided an introduction to the concept of coaching. It focused on developing a coaching style of management in health and social care work. And it proposed that using a coaching approach can harness both individual and team potential to achieve goals more efficiently than in a more traditional approach.

Three approaches to coaching were explored which may relate to any manager in health and social care: the First 90 Days, which enhances the experience and contribution of a new member of staff; the GROW model, which can be aligned to staff development; and the Comprehensive Conflict Coaching model, which can be used to help resolve conflict.

Coaching can be a focused one-to-one intervention, as in the case of Michael and John, or an approach or a style that managers adopt more broadly as part of their repertoire of skills in dealing with everyday issues in the workplace, as in the conflict between Maria and Heather. At a superficial level, coaching helps people to clarify their goals, to plan their actions, and to succeed more readily both at work and in life. It helps people to learn and perform better by enhancing their awareness, responsibility, self-confidence and self-reliance. At a deeper level, when done well and responsibly, coaching helps people along their professional journey towards higher or deeper levels of themselves – to discover who they really are (Whitmore, 2008).

While there are many benefits to coaching, this chapter acknowledges that not everyone wants to be coached, and not every manager will feel comfortable taking on a coaching style of management. Being able to recognise when a coaching style is appropriate is a skill that managers need to develop. The essence of coaching is learning, either about yourself, or about how to carry out your work responsibilities more effectively. In the ever-changing world of health and social care, being adaptable through new learning – which can be facilitated and enhanced through coaching – has considerable currency.

'Only when coaching principles govern or underlie all management behaviour and interactions, as they certainly will do in time, will the full force of people's performance potential be realised' (Whitmore, 2002, p. 5).

Key points

- Coaching can be either a focused intervention with set boundaries, or a style or an approach used by managers or leaders to manage everyday situations in the workplace.
- Coaching is non-directive – it is based on the understanding that individuals are resourceful in themselves and, with help, can identify ways of achieving their goals.
- There is a range of situations in which coaching might be appropriate: for example, when someone starts a new job, when aiming for a specific goal, or when dealing with conflict.
- There are numerous approaches to coaching and three popular models are explored in this chapter.
- A manager can adopt a coaching style in their management and leadership roles which will help to support them and their team in developing their **personal awareness**, **team awareness**, **goal awareness** and **contextual awareness**.

References

Bachkirova, T. Cox, E. and Clutterbuck, D. (2010) 'Introduction', in Cox, E. Bachkirova, T. and Clutterbuck, D. (eds) *The Complete Handbook of Coaching*, London, Sage Publications.

Chartered Institute for Personnel Development (CIPD) (2007) *Coaching in Organisations*, London, CIPD.

Covey, S.R. (2004) *The 7 Habits of Highly Effective People*, London, Simon and Schuster Ltd.

Downey, M. (2003) *Effective Coaching: Lessons from the coach's coach* (2nd edition), Mason, OH, Thomson TEXERE.

Ellinger, A.D., Beattie, R.S. and Hamlin, R.G. (2010) 'The manager as coach', in Cox, E., Bachkirova, T. and Clutterbuck, D. (eds) *The Complete Handbook of Coaching*, London, Sage Publications.

Evered, R.D. and Seleman, J.C. (1989) 'Coaching and the art of management', *Organizational Dynamics*, vol. 18, pp. 16–32.

Foster-Turner, J. (2006) *Coaching and Mentoring in Health and Social Care*, Oxford, Radcliffe Publishing.

Gallwey, W.T. (2001) *The Inner Game of Work*, New York, Random House Trade Paperbacks.

Gallwey, T. and Whitmore, J. (2010) 'Inside out', *Coaching at Work*, vol. 5, no. 3, pp. 34–5.

Hope Moncrieff, A.R. (1992) *The Illustrated Guide to Classical Greek Mythology*, London, BCA Books Studio Editions.

Hunt, J.M. and Weintraub, J. (2002) 'How coaching can enhance your brand as a manager', *Journal of Organisational Excellence*, vol. 21, no. 2, pp. 39–44.

Jones, T.S. and Brinkert, R. (2008) *Conflict Coaching: conflict management strategies and skills for the individual*, Thousand Oaks, Calif., Sage Publications.

North, S.J. (2009) 'Generation why?', *Coaching at Work*, vol. 3, no. 6, pp. 22–4.

Peterson, D.B. and Little, B. (2005) 'Invited reaction: development and initial validation of an instrument measuring managerial coaching skill', *Human Resource Development Quarterly*, vol. 16, no. 2, pp. 179–84.

Simpson, J. (2010) 'In what ways does coaching contribute to effective leadership development?', *International Journal of Evidence Based Coaching and Mentoring*, Special Issue, vol. 4, pp. 114–33.

Thomas, K.W. and Kilman, R.H. (1978) 'Comparison of four instruments measuring conflict behavior', *Psychological Reports*, vol. 42, pp. 1139–45.

Truijen, K.J.P. and van Woerkom, M. (2008) 'The pitfalls of collegial coaching', *Journal of Workplace Learning*, vol. 20, no. 5, pp. 316–26.

Watkins, M. (2003) *The First 90 Days: Critical success strategies for new leaders at all levels*, Boston, Mass., Harvard Business School Press.

Whitmore, J. (2002) *Coaching for Performance* (3rd edition), London, Nicholas Brealey Publishing.

Whitmore, J. (2009) *Coaching for Performance* (4th edition), London, Nicholas Brealey Publishing.

Whitmore, J. (2008) 'Live and learn', *Coaching at Work*, vol. 3, no. 6, pp. 28–31.

Wong, K.-F. (2003) 'Empowerment as a panacea for poverty – old wine in new bottles? Reflections on the World Bank's conception of power', *Progress in Development Studies*, vol. 3, no. 4, pp. 307–22.

Part 2

Part 2 Leading, managing, caring in context

Joan Simons and Sara MacKian

Introduction

Part 1 of this book considered what it means to be a manager or a leader in practice, and what demands are placed on them in terms of understanding the identities, relationships and needs of the people they work with. Having considered these very personal and practical demands in Part 1, Part 2 moves on to explore the wider *context* within which care takes place and the implications of this for leadership and management. For while the daily demands of managing staff and leading teams in practice are uppermost in the mind of any manager, they must also ensure they have a clear overview of the wider context in which those individuals and teams work.

This second part of the book explores how managers or leaders can create a caring environment while ensuring safe, ethical and quality outcomes for both their staff and service users.

Part 2 covers the following two areas.

Chapters 11–15 look at what is involved in **creating the caring environment**. Chapter 11 begins by exploring the physical environment in which care takes place, and how an understanding of the relationship between place, identity, power and wellbeing can help a manager develop a more informed approach to managing the spaces in which care is delivered. Drawing on insight from human geography on therapeutic landscapes, Helen Lomax suggests that both leadership and management have a role to play in creating a caring environment. As well as inhabiting distinctive spatial environments, all organisations have unique cultures which influence 'the way things are done around here'. Therefore, in Chapter 12 Richard Hester, Anita Rogers and Martin Robb explore how organisational structure and culture influence the working relationships within any workplace.

Increasingly, patients and service users are also expected to take an active role in shaping the care environment. In Chapter 13, Liz Tilley and Rebecca Jones draw on the growing body of literature within health and social care on the importance of listening to, and working with, patients and service users. In so doing, they highlight both the challenges engendered by working in partnership with service users, while also critically exploring some practical and managerial solutions to these issues.

This drive to increase participation reflects a broader political imperative to make services more responsive to the needs of users. Chapter 14 therefore moves on to look at this wider political landscape and its influence on health and social care management. Michelle Gander shows how this can place conflicting demands on managers. Economy, efficiency and effectiveness may be the mantra of 'new public management', but managers are dealing with vulnerable people who have complex needs and not just the 'bottom line'. Therefore, the chapter stresses the importance of ethics as part of a continuing public service tradition.

Picking up on this theme of the vulnerable nature of many service users, in Chapter 15 Jeanette Copperman and Hilary Brown provide a clear pathway for managers through the complex minefield of safeguarding. They highlight how ineffective, distanced, collusive, or even abusive, managements have repeatedly been identified as contributory factors in a range of cases where safeguarding has failed vulnerable adults and children. Exploring the possible causes of this, Copperman and Brown suggest that an open and supportive organisational culture, together with strong leadership, are key to promoting protection for vulnerable service users.

Having considered in the previous five chapters the wider context in which managers and leaders operate, together with the vulnerability of many of the people who use health and social care services, Chapters 16–20 look at **leading for ethical and quality care** and encourage you to explore the *ethical and legal requirements* of good leadership and management. In Chapter 16, Richard Hester and Anita Rogers begin by suggesting that ethics and morals are fundamental to health and social care practice, yet the proliferation of guidance, regulatory standards and codes of practice is not always conducive to developing sound ethical practice in an already complex field. They suggest that a morally active manager should be aware of regulations and guidance, but can also draw on their own core values in order to act in an ethically principled way.

Given this complexity, in Chapter 17 Joan Simons explores how risk is an inevitable feature of health and social care; showing how mistakes and challenges are often a feature of structural failings, rather than a case of individual bad practice. Simons describes practical ways in which managers can create a culture of safety, rather than a culture of blame, and explores how to deal with complaints in a way which ensures that lessons are learned and the quality of services is improved.

Developing the theme of providing quality services, Chapter 18, by Liz Tilley, Jan Walmsley and Rebecca Jones, explores the key questions facing managers tasked with delivering quality care. They begin by considering the origins of 'quality' in health and social care, outlining key events (failures in quality) and policies which initiated a shift from professionally led definitions of quality to increasing involvement from external regulators and the wider public. This chapter considers the variety of data that managers might use to assess quality, and explores the key role of leadership in creating a culture where delivering quality becomes the responsibility of *all* staff.

Having considered the organisational and policy context in which managers operate, Chapter 19 reflects on the complex legal frameworks that govern the provision of health and social care services. Understanding the authority of the law and the statutory responsibilities and procedures of their organisation is a key requirement of any manager. However, Rod Earle explores how law is also about the individuals and cultures which enact it. He concludes that legislation does not make decisions; it simply sets the parameters and provides the framework within which leaders, managers and practitioners make decisions.

In the concluding chapter, Sara MacKian explores the challenging context facing the managers and leaders of the future. This final chapter of the book suggests that developing a sustainable strategy for management involves an ongoing process of actively understanding not only your own strengths and weaknesses, passion and vision, but also these elements within the people you work with. MacKian provides practical ways of thinking about how you can enhance your own leadership and management journey.

The chapters in Part 2 continue to introduce key tools which will help you to develop a finely tuned sense of judgement about the *context* you are working within, and to support you in providing quality outcomes for service users. The authors' aims as you complete this book are that you will have gained an understanding of the core principles of leadership and management, rooted in the foundations of the four basic building blocks of the **fully rounded caring manager**, and that you will feel confident in your ability to use and apply your new knowledge and insight in a variety of contexts on your leadership journey.

Chapter 11 Exploring the caring environment

Helen Lomax

11.1 Introduction

Figure 11.1 The layout of a care home's day room influences how residents use the space

> Hospitals, like all buildings, are both shaped by people and capable of shaping occupants' behaviours and feelings … They are complex places that are simultaneously physical, social and symbolic environments.
>
> (Adams et al., 2010, p. 659)

The starting point for this chapter is that, for managers in health and social care, *space matters*. The materiality of buildings – their design, décor, smells and sounds – and the feelings they evoke in the people who are cared for and work in them, can promote positive caring and learning relationships. Conversely, if poorly managed, such spaces can diminish the caring experience in ways which impact negatively on the wellbeing of both staff and service users. This chapter focuses on the 'geographies' of the caring environment. It draws on developments within organisational psychology and human geography on the therapeutic potential of environments (Ulrich, 2001) and growing

'Geographies' means the way in which people and objects are arranged in relation to each other.

evidence about the ways in which the material and social properties of space shape learning and caring.

The physical factors which affect the wellbeing of practitioners, and hence their sense of agency, include workplaces that enable social contact with a wide range of colleagues, and have spaces where they can have private conversations, not only to exchange information but also to share decision making and seek advice (Eraut, 2006).

The emphasis in this chapter on the caring environment and its management is framed by the concept of 'affordances' (Gibson, 1979). This offers a valuable approach for exploring how environments shape the actions of the people who use them while also recognising the potential (or agency) of people to shape their use. As Gibson (1979) and Varlander (2012) argue, the qualities of an object or an environment (for example, chairs organised around the edge of a day room) 'afford' certain actions or ways of being in a space. This, in turn, produces particular kinds of identities: for example, passive disengagement rather than shared activity and belonging. It is important to note that this does not preclude other ways of being in these spaces; some people (service users and staff) will adapt spaces to suit their needs, actively challenging the organisation of the care environment to suit their own purposes (for example, clustering chairs in small groups in order to promote social interaction). However, because institutional spaces are suffused with differences of status and power (Foucault, 1994; Wong, 2003), it makes certain 'default' actions which maintain (rather than challenge) the customary use of space more likely.

As this chapter explores, the notion that 'space matters' (Andrews and Moon, 2005), and that seemingly small changes can produce significant benefits for patients and staff, offers enormous scope for managers and leaders in health and social care to influence the environment in a positive way.

A second framework which has considerable potential for exploring the capacity of managers to positively enhance the caring environment is Michael Eraut's important work on 'learning affordances', in which he suggests workplaces need to be organised and managed in a way which supports learning (Eraut, 2006). His development of Gibson's concept of affordances elaborated the way in which health and social care environments may afford (or not) possibilities for exchanging information, decision making, coaching and teaching and the important role of the manager in this regard. This includes managing the workplace so that physical spaces and working arrangements are organised in order to maximise these opportunities. The notion that environments afford particular experiences is important for managers and leaders seeking to manage environments and lead for quality.

Drawing on the four building blocks of the **fully rounded caring manager**, this chapter explores the following core questions.

- What is meant by 'the caring environment'?
- How can managers and leaders work with staff and service users to create a caring environment?
- How can differences in power and status be overcome to manage the caring environment for the benefit of service users and staff?
- Which leadership styles can most effectively support the delivery of a caring environment?

11.2 Environment matters

The suggestion that the built environment shapes people's capacity to work effectively, learn, heal, rest and engage in healthful activities is gaining increasing importance in the literature on health and social science. Seminal work in health geography has explored the ways in which the design of healthcare environments conveys who is welcome in which spaces, how they are expected to conduct themselves, and even how they should feel (Gieryn, 2002). Kearns and Barnett (1999) propose that these messages are encoded in the design and décor of institutional spaces. For example, whether chairs are organised in rows or clustered together in small groups; whether they are upholstered in soft, comfortable textiles or hard plastic; whether floors are covered in carpet and the choice of lighting (strip or 'soft'); these factors subtly convey how the space should be used by whom, when and for how long. For instance, floor coverings might at first seem of minimal relevance to the health and social care manager, but research suggests that carpet is better suited for elderly patients who walk more efficiently (taking longer steps and at greater speed) and feel more secure on carpet than on hard surfaces (Wilmott, 1986). While Ulrich (2001) reports that family and friends make longer visits to rehabilitation patients when the rooms are carpeted, findings which he suggests support the view that carpet in patients' rooms and waiting areas might promote improved patient outcomes by heightening social support from visitors.

The potential for the caring environment to promote wellbeing has gained increasing attention over the last 20 years, with more studies exploring the impact of the built environment on health. Much of this research has been in health and social care, examining the impact of specific environmental factors such as the design and layout of spaces;

whether spaces enable the occupants to experience the 'natural' world (sunlight and plants); and the impact of colour and texture (on walls, furniture and floor coverings). This work is beginning to provide important evidence for the ways in which the physical environment can aid recovery, reduce anxiety, limit the use of analgesia and reduce the length of stay for hospital patients (Ulrich, 2001; Dijkstra et al., 2006). Growing awareness of the importance of the physical properties of buildings is informing the ways in which health and social care spaces are designed, constituting a departure from the minimalist and functional designs typical of the mid to late 20th century and their replacement with distinctive, postmodern designs. For example, the Starship Hospital for children in Auckland, New Zealand, was designed to maximise therapeutic potential; curves, pastel colours, artwork and wool carpeting replace straight lines, hard white surfaces and vinyl (Kearns and Barnett, 1999). There are numerous examples in the UK too. Maggie's Centre in Nottingham (Figure 11.2) is one of 14 centres providing support for people affected by cancer, care which is inspired by the Centre's 'non-institutional nature-inspired design ... sheltered by trees ... a harmony of light and space', according to architect Piers Gough (2013).

Figure 11.2 Maggie's Centre in Nottingham is 'sheltered by trees ... a harmony of light and space' (Gough, 2013)

Looking at Figures 11.1 and 11.2, how do you think you would feel in each of these spaces, and why?

The idea that hospital spaces can be designed to maximise therapeutic potential underpins the design of several new flagship children's hospitals, including Liverpool's Alder Hey Hospital in the Park (under construction at the time of writing) and the Evelina Children's Hospital in London. Key to their design and planning is the idea, inspired by Roger Ulrich (2001; Ulrich et al., 2010), of the therapeutic importance of nature and its impact on healing (Wilson, 1984). This can be seen in the choice of materials which evoke and/or expose patients to nature (for example, with views of the natural environment) and designs which maximise natural lighting, both of which are beneficial for recovery and wellbeing (Diette et al., 2003; Walch et al., 2005; Nguyen et al., 2010). These studies are enormously helpful for managers thinking about how they might improve therapeutic outcomes for patients and service users.

While these are examples of state-of-the art health architecture, the evidence base is derived from empirical work involving often quite simple (and cost-effective) modifications to patients' environments. For example, Ulrich's study of post-operative pain (2001) showed how a tree view reduced post-operative stay; while a Swedish hospital is reporting significant reductions in children's anxiety during painful procedures when they are carried out in rooms decorated with animal themes (Simons, 2012). Nguyen et al. (2010) report similar reductions in children's pain and anxiety when music is introduced in the care environment. However, despite the evidence base supporting the therapeutic benefit of small modifications to the caring environment, it is easy to overlook them in practice. This is illustrated in the following case study, in which Jill describes her mother's experience of end-of-life care in a purpose-built hospice.

Case study 11.1: A good space to die?

The care my mother experienced was brilliant in so many respects. The staff were kind and we were made very welcome. Mum was kept comfortable in a light and airy room which we were encouraged to make hers, bringing in pictures and items from home. However, one thing which I found quite upsetting at the time was the way in which, although there was a beautiful view of the park just outside Mum's window, her bed was turned away from it. It took what felt like an age to get staff to agree to turn it to face the window – the problem seemed to be to do with staff needing access to both sides of the bed, the location of the plug sockets, and the way in which the other furniture was designed to fit into the space.

The bed was eventually moved, but it was quite stressful having to ask. I was at a low ebb anyway, and other family members didn't want me to 'make a fuss' in case it made things difficult for Mum. But I felt it was important that Mum should be able to enjoy her last days with a view of the trees, which thankfully, after we spoke to the staff, she did.

Jill's experience shows the important ways in which spaces shape patients' experiences, the small modifications which can make significant differences to service users and their families; and the ways in which staff may, in unintentional ways, hamper the affordances offered by state-of-the-art spaces (in the case study, by locating beds in ways which maximise the care of patients' bodies but curtail their psychosocial and therapeutic potential). This shows how important it is when designing care spaces for liaison between all parties – from the architect and the electrician to managers and staff – to ensure the environment is functional to deliver technology-assisted care while simultaneously supporting optimum therapeutic value.

Which would you prioritise in organising a caring environment – ease of working practices or patients' preferences? And why?

The **Plan–Do–Study–Act (PDSA) tool** might help you to consider a small-scale change to the care environment, assessing its impact on staff and service users.

11.3 People make places

> [P]eople make spaces, but spaces may be used to make people: both by constraining them and by offering them opportunities in the performance and construction of identity …
>
> (Halford and Leonard, 2003, p. 202)

As explored in the previous section, health geographers and environmental psychologists have increasingly focused on the therapeutic potential afforded by the caring environment. These developments provide evidence for the therapeutic potential of the tangible physical properties of care spaces, which suggests the ways in which buildings shape people. A second important and related area of study has been to consider how people themselves assign meanings to places, emphasising the significant ways in which spaces are invested with symbolic meanings which afford particular relationships that can enhance or inhibit their therapeutic potential (Street and Coleman, 2012).

This section draws on the concept of *symbolic meaning* (Kearns and Barnett, 1999) which elaborates how the meaning of spaces can be both fixed and fluid, depending on people's personal biography and experience. The concept of symbolic meaning is helpful for thinking about how care spaces afford different meanings for different people (patients, family members and staff) and how meanings can become contested between groups. This has important implications for the leader and manager in health and social care.

Health geographers are increasingly interested in the ways in which 'smellscapes' and 'soundscapes' can evoke strong feelings about place. Can you recall the sounds and smells associated with a particular place and the feelings they evoked for you?

A fascinating example, which has generated important insights from historians and health and social care researchers, is the symbolic meaning of the hospital bed. At first sight, its meaning may appear transparent and of little consequence: an object for lying and sleeping on, designed to optimise staff access to the patient's body. However, it is these very affordances (lying down, sitting up, eating, sleeping, birthing, dying) and the spatial practices they engender (being monitored, observed and examined, cared for and loved) which constitute it as a 'contested object' (Adams et al., 2010). This can be illustrated with reference to sociological research on the hospital bed as a space for birthing.

'Spatial practices' means how people organise their bodies and other people's bodies within spaces.

For example, Fannin (2003, p. 517) explored the ways in which the transformation of delivery rooms into more 'homelike' birthing spaces (through the introduction of rocking chairs, textiles, pastel paint and upholstered headboards) has rendered them as 'doubled spaces'. As she describes, this transformation has been criticised by some feminists who see it as an appropriation of the symbolic meanings of home and a camouflage for the continuing medical control of birth. Others have suggested it is one of the means by which midwives have wrested control of childbirth from obstetricians, the normality of which is suggested in the homelike quality of the soft furnishings and décor.

'Doubled spaces' bear the signs of both the domestic and the technical environment.

The significance of the hospital bed and the spatial practices it affords is further suggested in research on the maternal posture in labour. Gupta and Nikodem (2000) observe that the majority of pregnant women in western societies deliver in a dorsal, semi-recumbent or lithotomy position (the woman lying on her back on the delivery bed), enabling practitioners to observe and monitor the baby more easily. They and other researchers suggest this perspective is grounded in a western view in which birth is perceived primarily in terms of the activity of the uterus and the acts of the attendants, rather than those of the woman giving birth (Arney, 1982). An alternative, and more empowering, perspective is that women should be supported to be active participants in their care and treated with respect as individuals (Green, 2012). This suggests a different sort of birthing environment. It is clear, therefore, that maternity spaces, through their design and décor, convey particular meanings about how the space should be used; whether the birthing woman is active or passive; the sorts of pain relief she might use; and even the meaning of birth itself (Figure 11.3).

For an interesting discussion about the meaning of patients' clothing in care spaces, see Topo and Iltanen-Tähkävuori (2010) and the response by Twigg (2010).

'The decorations and permanent fixtures in a place … tend to fix a kind of spell over it; even when a customary performance is not being given in it' (Goffman, 1969, p. 126). Do you agree?

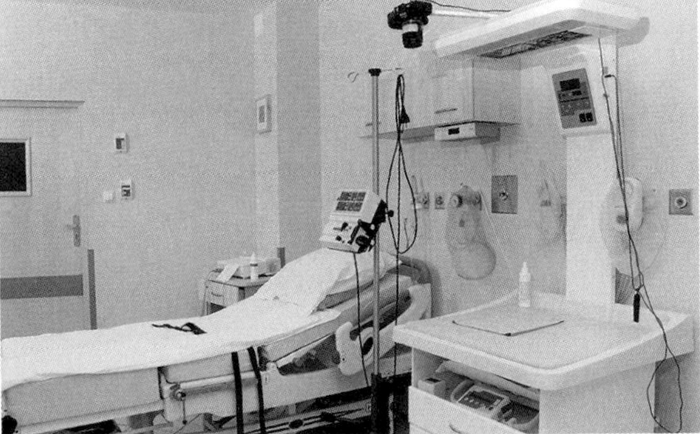

Figure 11.3 Subtle changes to an environment can convey very different messages about how a space should be used and the sort of care you might experience in it

'[T]he environment has the potential to strengthen the individual's inner powers, or alternatively, it can disempower the individual' (Topo and Iltanen-Tähkävuori, 2010, p. 1682). Can you think of some examples of this?

11.4 Making and managing therapeutic spaces

> Without such anchoring of ourselves in things … we are, literally, lost.
>
> (Young, 1997, p. 151)

So far, this chapter has explored the ways in which spaces have therapeutic potential; the contested meaning of space; and the suggestion that spatial practices can reinforce power differences between carers and those they manage and care for. This section brings these themes together to consider the ways in which the **fully rounded caring manager** can work with service users and staff to enhance the caring environment. It draws on the concept of 'emotional geographies' which emphasises the importance of both **personal awareness** and **team awareness** when managing the care environment.

'Emotional geographies' means how people feel *in* and *about* places.

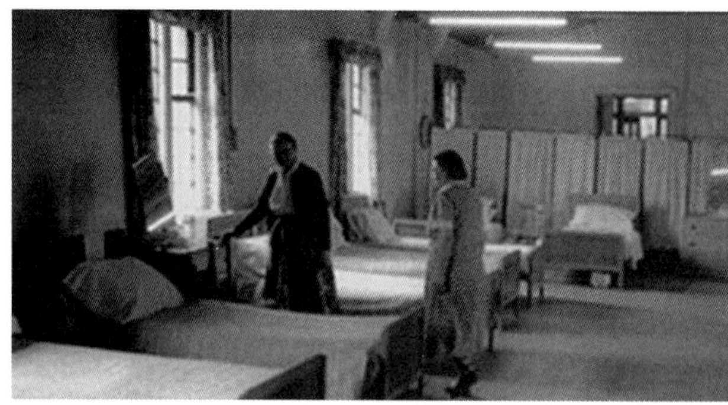

Figure 11.4 A residential care home for women (Townsend, 1962) in which 'There are no signs of personal possessions … There is no privacy' (Johnson et al., 2013)

Figure 11.4 is from the influential work of Peter Townsend (1962) on residential care homes. It suggests that transitions to residential care can present fundamental challenges to an individual's spatial and emotional geographies (Davidson and Milligan, 2004; Milligan, 2005). This is because transitions, whether through illness, ageing or the associated changes in living arrangements, can disrupt a person's sense of identity and belonging. This point is made by the geographer Ann Varley (2008), who asserts the importance of the 'material markers' (possessions and everyday spatial regimes) which anchor people to place and help to maintain a coherent sense of self. Examples might include the daily walk to the shops, encompassing familiar sights, sounds and social connections, but they can also comprise the personal possessions which signify these routines and relationships. As Johnson et al. (2013) suggest, in their discussion of Townsend's image, a move to residential care can disrupt these important markers when 'There are no signs of personal possessions … There is no privacy'.

Figure 11.5 A room in a modern residential home (Johnson et al., 2013)

As the more recent image in Figure 11.5 shows, most contemporary residential homes have actively embraced developments in gerontology and social work. They encourage residents to personalise spaces in ways which recognise the importance of personal possessions as symbols and reminders of self, acknowledging that people are rooted in place and space (Wiles et al., 2009). Residents no longer share bedrooms, and spaces are decorated and personalised to give a homelike feel – although, as the authors note, this homeliness is tempered by the commode and hospital-style bed tray (Rolph et al., 2009). The importance of connection to the external environment is also considered; in Figure 11.5, the small window overlooks the grounds of the home. However, as Torrington (2011) and others have found, even with careful management, transitions to residential care involve fundamental adjustments to the ways in which people connect with their living environments and, through this, a sense of who they are. It is not simply that the familiar living spaces are replaced with new and unfamiliar ones but, rather, that transitions to residential care redefine people's spatial routines in which activities which once happened in private locations, and at times of the individual's choosing, now take place according to an institutional regime. As Torrington (2011) describes, all the activities of daily living – pottering in the house or garden, listening to music, singing, watching television and reading – take place within an organisation framework, necessitating the negotiation of new geographies and relationships. This can be difficult for some residents who may be unable or unwilling to establish new geographies; for example, they may be wary of the consequences of challenging possession of a particular spot in the day room or uncertain about their welcome in the staff-managed kitchen.

These tensions, about how space is used and by whom, are exemplified in the next case study. Here Claire, a resident of Hilltop, a home for elderly people, describes her experience of transition to residential care and particular difficulties in using the garden. As the case study explores, Claire's understandings of the meaning and use of the garden are different from that envisaged by Rose, the care home manager; a difference which unsettles Claire and challenges her sense of identity.

Case study 11.2: Therapeutic landscapes

Claire (a resident of Hilltop): 'It's not that I'm unhappy here but … I used to be a keen gardener. It's something I've always loved. Derek and I had a wonderful garden. At one time we grew most of our own vegetables and fruit. We even kept a few chickens – the children loved them. After Derek died, I couldn't manage it all on my own but I still made sure I kept the front nice. Right up until I moved here, I was doing my own window boxes and a stroll in the garden with a cup of tea would often turn into an afternoon's weeding. Now that I'm here, while of course I can go into the garden and walk around, it's not the same. I don't feel like I can touch the plants – they're not mine, they're somebody else's.'

Rose (the manager of Hilltop): 'One of the things we're very proud of here at Hilltop is our beautiful garden. We're quite fortunate to be located in the grounds of the old Manse with gardens that date back to the 18th century – but they take some looking after! We're very fortunate in that we've been able to employ a gardener who's doing a fantastic job of keeping the grounds in good order, so that our residents have all the advantages of a beautiful, tranquil space without any of the hard work! We've also made some improvements recently, installing a new sensory garden which we encouraged residents to choose the plants for.'

Recalling Wong's concept of 'power-over' (see Chapter 1), Claire's experience of the garden might suggest an imbalance of power between service users and staff. Do you agree?

As Claire's experience suggests, transitions to residential care can reconfigure relationships with the living environment in ways which necessitate a fundamental shift in identity. Claire no longer describes herself as 'a gardener' but someone who 'used to be a keen gardener'. This is because, even though the care home she lives in has a garden which is ostensibly for residents' use, unspoken and perhaps spoken rules about the ways in which it can be used (geographies of ownership) mean that Claire cannot mobilise an important source of pleasure, identity and wellbeing (Ulrich, 2001; Tse, 2010).

Claire's experience contrasts noticeably with how Rose, the manager, envisages the garden as affording new possibilities and benefits for residents. She describes with pride the handsome formal gardens and the new sensory area that she has had installed. She is pleased too with the contract she has secured with a gardener who, she feels, is doing a fantastic job of keeping the garden in order so that, as she sees it, residents can 'have all the advantages of a beautiful, tranquil space without any of the hard work!'

The contrasting meanings of the garden can be further understood in the context of Thomas Gieryn's theorisation of environments as spaces which take on, and are given, meanings beyond those envisaged by their creators and which symbolise power (Gieryn, 2002). In the case study, the physical properties of the garden – its seating, formal planting and walkways – convey it as a space for passive enjoyment, closing down the possibilities for other uses such as gardening. This is further evidenced in Rose's views on whether residents might take a more active role in the planning and maintenance of the garden. Rose is unequivocal in her view that residents should be encouraged to choose plants. However, the suggestion that they might be involved in the practicalities of gardening is viewed with anxiety about the safety of some of the more vulnerable residents and concerns about organisational liability should residents injure themselves. Furthermore, as she explains, she simply does not have the time or resources to manage an additional activity.

What sort of leadership style is Rose exhibiting in the management of the care home environment?

Rose's concerns about how she can best use the inevitably limited resources available to maintain a safe, secure environment for residents are recognisable characteristics of a managerialist approach. In this, concerns with efficiency (residents' safety and managerial accountability for resource allocation) override the impacts on service users and staff. According to the leadership grid developed by Blake and Adams McCanse (1991), Rose's management style reflects a 'matriarchal/patriarchal' approach to leadership. Such a leader emphasises efficiency and results; and, while they also show a high concern for people, they do not integrate the two, preferring to minimise the impact of 'human elements'. Such a manager is unlikely to

Torrington (2011) notes the inverse relationship between safety and wellbeing: the Design in Care Environments (DICE) study demonstrates an inverse relationship between environments with high safety scores and quality of life.

work distributively with others in order to consider the ways she can achieve organisational priorities (residents' safety) while balancing the human elements of the service. As Northouse (2010, p. 75) explains, this type of manager is sometimes referred to as a 'benevolent dictator'; that is, someone who 'acts graciously but does so for the purpose of goal accomplishment [and] treats people as if they were dissociated from the task'.

However, note that the matriarchal/patriarchal leader is not uncaring. Rose's rationale indicates her concern for the safety of those she is responsible for, concerns which are grounded in the economic and political demands of contemporary health and social care. Numerous well-publicised scandals concerning the safety of residential care homes suggest increasing unease about the wellbeing of vulnerable adults in institutional spaces, and a corresponding rise in the regulation of residential and nursing homes in the UK. As Chapter 19 explores, managers are legally and morally accountable for providing safe, secure environments for service users and staff. There are also legitimate concerns about the spiralling cost of residential social care borne by the state and by individuals and their families and the ways in which this necessarily limits the care that can be delivered. However, the consequences of Rose's management style are that it limits the possibilities for *working with* residents and staff to creatively imagine the garden space and its potential for transforming care. An aversion to taking risks and an overemphasis on efficiency and safety may deprive staff and service users of an important role in decision making and the possibilities of transforming the caring environment to make it more therapeutic.

In contrast, the next case study illustrates how a transformational model of leadership which recognises the importance of the care environment can empower both staff and service users. The case study draws on Bronwyn's experiences of managing Dan y Coed, a residential home for elderly people in Wales. Like Hilltop, Dan y Coed is a typical converted residential building located, like many such properties, in a suburban area of town. What is not ordinary, however, is Bronwyn's leadership style. A transformational leader, Bronwyn understands the significance of the care environment, its impact on wellbeing, and her responsibilities as a manager to promote opportunities for social connectivity and learning through effective leadership (Eraut, 2006).

Case study 11.3: Transforming 'islands of the old'

Bronwyn and her team work hard to enhance the experience of residents. This includes challenging the common perception of care homes as being divorced from the neighbouring community. As she says, 'other care homes seem to isolate themselves behind closed doors'. In contrast, Bronwyn and her staff actively seek out opportunities to integrate with the local community. This includes involving young people from the neighbouring community in holiday and other celebrations and, led by some of the residents and in partnership with a local school, Welsh conversation classes.

As Bronwyn explains, involving the community in this way is a 'win–win' situation. The young people acquire experience and develop relationships with older people, while furthering their understanding of their language and cultural heritage. While for residents, she describes the benefits of passing on cultural knowledge and maintaining links with the younger generation, and the important pleasures of social interaction and connection. As she says, 'the Welsh classes are an important source of enjoyment, helping maintain intergenerational connections which are a routine and taken-for-granted feature of community life but one which can become lost to the residents of care homes.'

As the case study shows, Bronwyn and her staff believe strongly in the residential home as a place 'where you come to live' – a philosophy which they enact through carefully planned activities designed to reinforce connections and learning opportunities. Framed by a distributed style of leadership (The King's Fund, 2011), these opportunities are strengthened by the devolution of responsibility to those residents, staff and community members who have the expertise and enthusiasm to lead them. A final benefit of Bronwyn's approach is the way in which her understanding of the spatial geographies of the built environment enables her to maximise wellbeing despite the limitations afforded by the physical structure of the care home. As she explains, it would be 'very easy to close up shop and become this self-contained building where nobody knows what's going on'. And indeed, the architecture of most care homes lends itself to such practice. However, Bronwyn works hard at creating a sense of community, both within the care home itself and through strengthening the links between the care home and its neighbours. As she argues, this is crucial to quality of life, a view which is supported by a growing evidence base on the importance for wellbeing of social relationships and opportunities for continued social engagement (Bartley, 2012).

11.5 Leading for the caring environment

> The true test of a servant-leader is this: Do those around the servant-leader become wiser, freer, more autonomous, healthier, and better able themselves to become servants? Will the least privileged of society be benefited or at least not further deprived?
>
> (Greenleaf, 2007, p. i)

A manager who shows **contextual awareness** understands the importance of the care environment and enacting this understanding in practice. A manager who shows **team awareness** recognises the importance of relationships for achieving goals.

Case study 11.3 explored how a leadership style predicated on **team awareness**, which sought to enhance and develop relationships among residents, family and friends, illustrates what can be achieved by a manager with a strong **contextual awareness**. In taking a wider spatial approach (one which sees care as everyone's business and the care home as part of the wider community landscape), Bronwyn is fostering important connections with the community, sustaining the geographies of belonging, and nurturing the creative talents and leadership skills of staff and residents. The next case study develops these ideas further, to explore the ways in which managers can reconfigure spatial geographies within stigmatised and poorer communities in order to build social capital and enhance reputational geographies (Parker and Karner, 2011).

Case study 11.4: Transforming spaces – building community capital

Ewan is a community development manager for a city council in an economically disadvantaged neighbourhood in a large city. He manages a community centre and a small team of staff and volunteers. An experienced manager, he thinks carefully about the spaces in which care is delivered and the ways in which these can be mobilised to enhance community wellbeing. Ewan's approach is evidence-based. He uses his local knowledge, based on time spent getting to know residents and observing the atmosphere in and around the neighbourhood. He is committed and passionate, with a good understanding of the wider context: a neighbourhood characterised by high levels of income-poverty and ill health, but more particularly a neighbourhood which is stigmatised locally as a 'failed estate'. He could, as he explains, 'close the doors, create a space away from prying eyes'. However, Ewan is a values-based leader, prepared to take risks and challenge others by embracing opportunities for learning and social connectivity.

An example of one such opportunity occurred when Ewan was approached by an artist to work with local people on an arts installation on the history and contemporary meaning of neighbourhood spaces. Ewan saw the potential of this project immediately. His local knowledge meant that he was aware that the neighbourhood park was an underused and contested space, prone to vandalism and often empty. As one elderly resident explained, 'the broken glass and mess make it a no-go area for youngsters'. With this in mind, Ewan listened to the artist's plans to work participatively with young people and adults, seeing its potential to enhance community engagement and positively impact on wellbeing.

Ewan's hunch was correct. Supported by the city gallery, the artist was able to work creatively with children to explore their experiences, while child-led interviews with older residents documented the history and personal relevance of neighbourhood space, enabling important intergenerational connections. These activities and the creative outputs they generated were then displayed in the gallery and community centre, communicating positive messages about the neighbourhood and its residents in ways which positively transformed both their sense of themselves (a 'community' with an interesting history and some potentially great green spaces) and the perceptions of others about the area. More particularly, the visual evidence that the young people assembled about the ways in which the park might support health and wellbeing and what could be done to maximise this was vital data that residents, supported by Ewan, could use to lobby the council for improvements.

Finally, the young people participating in the project also benefited. They learned new skills (such as photography, project management and public speaking) and gained confidence; an important outcome in a neighbourhood where educational achievement, youth employment and child wellbeing are among the lowest in the UK.

What leadership approach did Ewan take to support residents to use their neighbourhood spaces?

'Community capital' is the economic and human resources (skills, trust, sense of belonging, friendship and learning networks) that a community has at its disposal which can positively enhance community life.

Ewan recognised that, in itself, an arts project would not solve the problem of chronic underinvestment, the legacy of unemployment and its impact on this community and its environment. He was also aware that there is no 'quick fix' to these issues. Instead, he looked around for ways in which he could work positively with residents and others in order to build *community capital*. In doing so, Ewan exemplified elements of the **fully rounded caring manager** who understands the wider context within which they are working. In Ewan's case, this meant understanding the social, political and economic contexts of people's lives, recognising that any solutions need to address the underlying causes (Bartley, 2012) and mobilising existing resources through a distributed model of leadership. His decision to work with the community artist in order to build social capital (Parr, 2007) is characteristic of such an approach. By devolving responsibility in this way, Ewan ensured that others (residents, centre staff, etc.) were given opportunities to develop their skills and, importantly, their own leadership potential (Burns, 1978).

Moreover, Ewan's **contextual awareness** encompasses an understanding of the therapeutic potential of environments. The cosy interior of the community centre (carpeted and with a central large wooden table, smaller tables and armchairs) signals that this is a homely space where residents are welcome to pop in for a cup of tea, knit, read, seek advice or use the computers. In the warmer months, this includes setting out chairs and tables on the pavement and residents planting spring bulbs and summer bedding. The use of external space in this way is practical (the popularity of the community centre means the extra seating is much needed) but it also reflects an understanding of the symbolic meaning of space.

Figure 11.6 Transforming spaces? The community centre decorated for Halloween by the residents

As Figure 11.6 shows, the community centre is regularly decorated for celebrations, holidays and other events. As Ewan explained, this is about more than giving young people the opportunity to engage in 'fun arts activities'; it is about positively transforming a potentially stigmatising space (a place where people, often in desperate circumstances, turn for help) in a neighbourhood which has a historically negative reputation. To achieve this, Ewan draws on the symbolic potential of material objects (art, plants and furniture) as a way of promoting positive representations of the neighbourhood space and to confront the negative perceptions of those who 'sit in judgement of this community'.

In this way, Ewan's approach exemplifies many elements of the **fully rounded caring manager**. This includes a strong sense of the importance of the material and felt contexts in which services are delivered, but also a sound understanding of the importance of relationships for achieving goals. As the case study exemplifies, Ewan is a team player, who nurtures the skills of the people he works with in order to lead the aspirations of those he serves. In so doing, Ewan exemplifies elements of a servant leader who is 'attentive to the concerns of those whom they are working for … tak[ing] care of them and nurtur[ing] them' (Northouse, 2010, pp. 384, 385).

Reflect on the different approaches of Rose and Ewan. Which do you identify with more, and why?

11.6 Conclusion

This chapter explored the important ways in which environments matter. Drawing on theoretical developments and evidence from human geography and organisational psychology, it considered the ways in which health and social care environments can shape the experiences of people who are cared for and who deliver care. This included a consideration of the ways in which the material and felt experience of place can have therapeutic benefits, including improved recovery, heightened social support, reduced pain, and enhanced wellbeing. Drawing on the concept of 'affordances', the chapter considered the idea that places make people, and that people themselves shape places in ways which can positively enhance care and improve outcomes.

The malleability of environments has enormous potential for managers seeking to lead for quality; this chapter explored how the therapeutic environment, even in the seemingly ordinary and the most challenging circumstances, can be mobilised for the benefit of service users and staff. Examples of innovative practice in health and social care illustrate how, through a distributed model of leadership, managers can work positively with staff, service users and others in order to provide the best possible care for the people they serve.

Key points

- How people relate to health and social care environments, their design, and the feelings they evoke are important factors in the experiences of those who deliver and receive services.
- The potential for the care environment to promote health and wellbeing is evidenced by a growing number of studies exploring the impact of the built environment on measures of pain, recovery time and length of stay.
- The ways in which spaces are mobilised can enhance or diminish the therapeutic potential of the caring environment. Managers need to be aware that spaces have symbolic meaning and a life and significance beyond that imagined by their creators.

- An understanding of the importance of the material and felt contexts in which services are delivered and a strong sense of **team awareness** – which recognises the importance of relationships and the ways in which people themselves make places – are critical for realising the therapeutic potential of the caring environment.
- A distributed model of leadership, which encompasses the principles of transformational and servant leadership, can enable managers to positively enhance the therapeutic environment and lead for quality.

References

Adams, A., Theodore, D., Goldenberg, E., McLaren, C. and McKeever, P. (2010) 'Kids in the atrium: comparing architectural intentions and children's experiences in a pediatric hospital lobby', *Social Science & Medicine*, vol. 70, pp. 658–67.

Andrews, G. and Moon, G. (2005) 'Space, place and the evidence base. Part 1: An introduction to health geography', *Worldviews on Evidence-Based Nursing*, Second quarter, pp. 55–62.

Arney, W. (1982) *Power and the Profession of Obstetrics*, Chicago, The University of Chicago Press.

Bartley, M. (2012) *Life Gets under Your Skin*, published by the UCL Research Department of Epidemiology and Public Health on behalf of the ESRC International Centre for Lifecourse Studies in Society and Health (2008–2017 RES-596-28-0001), London, UCL.

Blake, R. and Adams McCanse, A. (1991) *The Leadership Grid*, Houston, Tex., Gulf Publishing Company.

Burns, J.M. (1978) *Leadership*, New York, Harper & Row.

Davidson, J. and Milligan, C. (2004) 'Embodying emotion, sensing space: introducing emotional geographies', *Social and Cultural Geography*, vol. 5, no. 4, pp. 523–32.

Diette, G.B., Lechtzin, N., Haponik, E., Devrotes, A. and Rubin, H.R. (2003) 'Distraction therapy with nature sights and sounds reduces pain during flexible bronchoscopy: a complementary approach to routine analgesia', *Chest*, vol. 123, pp. 941–8.

Dijkstra, K., Pieterse, M. and Pruyn, A. (2006) 'Physical environmental stimuli that turn healthcare facilities into healing environments through psychologically mediated effects: systematic review', *Journal of Advanced Nursing*, vol. 56, no. 2, pp. 166–81.

Eraut, M. (2006) Editorial: 'Learning contexts', *Learning in Health and Social Care*, vol. 5, no. 1, pp. 1–8.

Fannin, M. (2003) 'Domesticating birth in the hospital: "family-centred" birth and the emergence of "homelike" birthing rooms', *Antipode*, vol. 35, no. 3, pp. 513–35.

Foucault, M. (1994) *The Birth of the Clinic*, New York, Vintage.

Gibson, J.J. (1979) *The Ecological Approach to Visual Perception*, Boston, Mass., Houghton-Mifflin.

Gieryn, T. (2002) 'What buildings do', *Theory and Society*, vol. 31, pp. 35–74.

Goffman, I. (1969) *The Presentation of Self in Everyday Life*, Harmondsworth, Penguin.

Gough, P. (2013) 'Maggie's Centre' [Online], www.maggiescentres.org/centres/nottingham/introduction.html (Accessed 21 January 2013).

Green, J.M. (2012) 'Integrating women's views into maternity care research and practice', *Birth. Issues in Perinatal Care*, vol. 39, no. 4, pp. 291–5.

Greenleaf, R. (2007) 'The servant-leader', *The International Journal of Servant-Leadership*, vol. 3, no. 1, p. i.

Gupta, J.K. and Nikodem, C. (2000) 'Maternal posture in labour', *European Journal of Obstetrics and Gynaecology and Reproductive Biology*, vol. 92, no. 2, pp. 273–7.

Halford, S. and Leonard, P. (2003) 'Space and place in the construction and performance of gendered nursing identities', *Journal of Advanced Nursing*, vol. 42, no. 4, pp. 201–8.

Johnson, J., Rolph, S. and Smith, R. (2013) *The Last Refuge Revisited* [Online], www.open.ac.uk/hsc/research/research-projects/the-last-refuge-revisited/the-last-refuge-revisited.php (Accessed 22 January 2013).

Kearns, R. and Barnett, J.R. (1999) 'To boldly go? Place, metaphor and the marketing of Auckland's Starship Hospital', *Environment and Planning D: Society and Space*, vol. 17, pp. 201–26.

Milligan, C. (2005) 'From home to "home": situating emotions within the care-giving experience', *Environment and Planning*, vol. 37, pp. 2105–20.

Nguyen, T.N., Nilsson, S., Hellström, A.L. and Bengtson, A. (2010) 'Music therapy to reduce pain and anxiety in children with cancer undergoing lumbar puncture: a randomized clinical trial', *Journal of Pediatric Oncology Nursing*, vol. 27, no. 3, pp. 146–55.

Northouse, P.G. (2010) *Leadership: Theory and Practice* (5th edition), London, Sage.

Parker, D. and Karner, C. (2011) 'Remembering the Alum Rock Road: reputational geographies and spatial biographies', *Midland History*, vol. 36, no. 2, pp. 292–309.

Parr, H. (2007) *The Arts and Mental Health: Creativity and inclusion*, London, ESRC.

Rolph, S., Johnson, J. and Smith, R. (2009) 'Using photography to understand change and continuity in the history of residential care for older people', *International Journal of Social Research Methodology*, vol. 12, no. 5, pp. 421–39.

Simons, J. (2012) 'Where pain management is good it is almost invisible', *An Appreciative Enquiry of International Practice in the Management of Children's Pain*, London, Florence Nightingale Foundation.

Street, A. and Coleman, S. (2012) 'Introduction: real and imagined spaces', *Space and Culture*, vol. 15, no. 1, pp. 4–17.

The King's Fund (2011) *The Future of Leadership and Management in the NHS: No more heroes*, London, The King's Fund.

Topo, P. and Iltanen-Tähkävuori, S. (2010) 'Scripting patienthood with patient clothing', *Social Science & Medicine*, vol. 70, pp. 1682–9.

Torrington, J. (2011) 'The design of supportive living settings for people with dementia', KTEQUAL Conference, University of Sheffield, 27 January.

Townsend, P. (1962) *The Last Refuge: A survey of residential institutions and homes for the aged in England and Wales*, London, Routledge.

Tse, M.Y.T. (2010) 'Therapeutic effects of an indoor gardening programme for older people living in nursing homes', *Journal of Clinical Nursing*, vol. 19, no. 7–8, pp. 949–58.

Twigg, J. (2010) 'Welfare embodied: the materiality of hospital dress: a commentary on Topo and Iltanen-Tähkävuori', *Social Science & Medicine*, vol. 70, pp. 1690–2.

Ulrich, R.S. (2001) *Effects of Healthcare Environmental Design on Medical Outcomes*, Tex., International Academy for Leadership and Health.

Ulrich, R.S., Berry, L.L., Quan, X. and Parish, J.T. (2010) 'A conceptual framework for health environments', *Research and Design Journal*, vol. 4, no. 1, pp. 95–114.

Varlander, S. (2012) 'Individual flexibility in the workplace: a spatial perspective', *Journal of Applied Behavioural Science*, vol. 48, no. 1, pp. 33–61.

Varley, A. (2008) 'A place like this? Stories of dementia, home, and the self', *Environment and Planning D: Society and Space*, vol. 26, pp. 47–67.

Walch, J.M., Rabin, B.S., Day, R., Williams, J.N., Choi, K. and Kang, J.D. (2005) 'The effect of sunlight on postoperative analgesic medication use: a prospective study of patients undergoing spinal surgery', *Psychosomatic Medicine*, vol. 67, pp. 156–63.

Wiles, J., Allen, R., Palmer, A., Hayman, K., Keeling, S. and Kerse, N. (2009) 'Older people and their social spaces: a study of well-being and attachment to place in Aotearoa New Zealand', *Social Science & Medicine*, vol. 4, pp. 664–71.

Wilmott, M. (1986) 'The effect of a vinyl floor surface and carpeted floor surface upon walking in elderly hospital inpatients', *Age and Aging*, vol. 15, pp. 119–20.

Wilson, E.O. (1984) *Biophilia*, Cambridge, Mass., Harvard University Press.

Wong, K.-F. (2003) 'Empowerment as a panacea for poverty – old wine in new bottles? Reflections on the World Bank's conception of power', *Progress in Development Studies*, vol. 3, no. 4, pp. 307–22.

Young, I.M. (1997) *Intersecting Voices: dilemmas of gender – political philosophy and policy*, Princeton, NJ, Princeton University Press.

Chapter 12 Making sense of organisational culture

Richard Hester, Anita Rogers and Martin Robb

12.1 Introduction

Figure 12.1 Handle with care

> 'Ruling the country is like cooking a small fish' – Lao Tsu (Chinese philosopher, 6th century BC)
>
> (Quoted in Feng and English, 2011)

It is important to managers in health and social care to make sense of organisations and their 'cultures' because the organisation provides a context for everything that managers do. Managers and leaders within organisations need to understand how organisations work and how they can affect the behaviour of people as well as the effectiveness of the organisation.

As the quotation above suggests, 'ruling' – or, as we might say today, 'managing' – a large organisation needs to be done very carefully in the same way you might approach cooking a small fish or baking a fine muffin (Figure 12.1). The tiniest error can sometimes lead to disastrous consequences.

This chapter explores several ideas about organisational culture, including the important roles that *structure* and *power* play. In doing so, it addresses the following core questions.

- What is the significance of both organisational structure and culture to the way managers work?
- How is leadership manifested within particular organisational cultures?
- What is the dynamic relationship between power, culture and the people in organisations?

12.2 What is an organisation and why is it important?

An organisation can be defined as a social arrangement – a way of arranging a set of people and resources together to achieve certain goals.

The system that results will have both formal ways of doing things (structure and rules) and informal ways of acting and behaving (culture). This system is experienced as a living, dynamic and interactive thing which, in turn, is shaped by its relationship to external factors such as other organisations, the clientele, law, social policy and public opinion (Seden, 2003, p. 108).

Structure

The structure of an organisation can be defined as the internal rules and processes that enable the organisation to work: the formal system of 'task and reporting relationships' that controls, coordinates and motivates employees so they can work together to achieve the organisation's goals. This is at the heart of the manager's day-to-day role.

Since the early 20th century, people have attempted to identify the best organisational structure for the particular goals of the workplace (Taylor, 1911). Based on some ground-breaking experiments in the 1930s (Mayo, 1933), much work focused on the importance of good human relationships which can achieve an environment where motivated workers produce better outcomes. More recent studies have recognised the complexity of organisational structures, acknowledging that behaviours are shaped as much by the structures of an organisation as by the personalities (and relationships) within them (for example, Mintzberg, 1981, 1994; Kakabadse et al., 1988; Brody, 1993; Handy, 1993, 1999; Morgan, 1997).

Which is most influential in your experience of management – the structure of organisations or the personalities within them?

Organisations in health and social care

Within the context of health and social care, it is perhaps worth pausing to look at a term that is often associated with large public sector organisations – *bureaucracy*. Often used in a derogatory way, bureaucracy can mean very different things, depending on the context in which it is used. For example, in Chapter 1 it is coupled with 'box ticking'. It is often expressed as a kind of frustration that things are stuck or immovable. In this chapter, the term is used to mean a particular way in which some organisational structures and processes are set up.

The term 'bureaucracy' was perhaps most famously used by the German sociologist and economist Max Weber (1864–1920) back in the early 20th century (Figure 12.2). Weber was not a fan of bureaucracies as he believed they could not deal with power or change effectively but instead deadened innovation. It helped, however, that he identified several characteristics of bureaucracies which are still useful today in making sense of organisations in health and social care (see Box 12.1).

Box 12.1: Characteristics of bureaucracy (based on Weber, 1922)

Figure 12.2 Max Weber was critical of the rules, duties and control inherent in bureaucracies

1 Fixed and official jurisdictional areas are ordered by rules, i.e. laws and administrative regulations.
2 'Lower offices' are supervised by the higher ones in a hierarchy and levels of graded authority.
3 Management is based on official documents.
4 The officials have thorough and expert training.
5 The organisation requires the full-time work of the official.
6 Management follows rules.

Can you think of any examples of organisations that are run like this? What are the benefits?

Traditionally, organisations in health and social care have been based on this bureaucratic model of a *hierarchical,* organisational structure. Each post carries specific responsibilities and the person occupying it should have relevant skills. Despite Weber's concerns, bureaucracies are not necessarily bad news. They have many advantages, as well as difficulties. Clear rules and procedures help the people who implement them and attempt to make processes visibly fair. This is of fundamental importance in the current era which demands transparency in public services.

Nevertheless, there are limitations to the bureaucratic model in health and social care, for example as identified by Coulshed and Mullender (2001, pp. 30–31).

- It is best suited to routine, stable and unchanging tasks – the focus in health and social care on people inevitably means unpredictability and a need for flexibility.
- The question of professional autonomy – for instance, for health care professionals and social workers – means some workers expect to have the authority to make specialised and complex decisions. In the tensions between professional autonomy and bureaucratic processes, managers are often equated with bureaucracy and there is a pervasive concern that managerialism supersedes local expertise by imposing centralised control.
- There are competing stakeholders beyond the immediate employing organisation – including professional bodies and organisations, employers' organisations, partner organisations, service users and carers.
- The increasing diversity of tasks and service users requires greater complexity in the shape of the organisation. Sometimes workers are placed in integrated teams – for example, in health care trusts or youth offending teams – creating complex managerial supervision and accountability.

What would more autonomy for professionals mean in the absence of bureaucracy?

In health and social care, the size of organisations ranges from a very small care home to large local authorities. In general, social services departments, benefits agencies, hospitals, youth offending teams, national voluntary agencies, and many other organisations involved in health and social care, use variously modified forms of a bureaucratic model. The shape is pyramidal, with the head person at the top, middle managers in between, and front-line managers and staff at the bottom. The bigger the organisation gets, the taller the pyramid becomes, with increasing distance between the decision makers and those who have to implement the decisions. (The role of 'distance' is discussed in terms of its impact on ethical issues in Chapter 15.) In addition, the middle layer of management has become increasingly costly, leading to a public perception of excessive management, which is why some of the reorganisations of the early 21st century attempted to cut out the layers of middle managers (Figure 12.3).

Figure 12.3 An excess of management?

However, there is an increasing array of different types of organisational structures that do not conform to a bureaucratic model, or that have little 'pockets of activity' that are differently organised. For instance, is a residential care home, where the residents need to feel 'at home', best conceptualised as a bureaucracy, or do the residents form part of the organisation, perhaps organising some of the functions themselves? A larger organisation, which is responsible for its management, may well be a bureaucracy but a registered manager may operate a different kind of structure within the home. In the voluntary sector, there are organisational types that are very different from mainstream models: in some contexts, 'managers' as such might not even exist.

Collaborative or collective ways of working may lack visible managers or rotate the management roles, for instance in women's refuges or organisations run by service users. This can cause difficulties for outsiders looking for a point of liaison and influence, but it may have many advantages for the staff or service users who may feel more informed and empowered. A non-hierarchical organisation still needs to have ways of organising to make decisions, and to coordinate and allocate activities, but it may involve more people or a more diverse cross-section of people in these managerial processes.

The bureaucratic structure usually contains mechanisms to challenge decisions but these may seem so complex that workers lose confidence in their effectiveness. There may be consultation with workers but little organisational flexibility to incorporate their views. This may result in an informal network of consensus between workers and clients which can subvert or side-step formal procedures and replace them with informal ones.

The following case study introduces two workers and the manager of a youth offending team. We shall return to this case study throughout the chapter.

Case study 12.1: Antonio, Michelle and their manager, Maxwell

Antonio and Michelle work in a youth offending team (YOT), bringing together workers from several agencies such as the police, the probation service and children's services. The team is led by Maxwell, a local authority manager. Antonio, one of the YOT workers, is a police officer, and Michelle is a children's social worker.

The latest missive from the Youth Justice Board was a new procedure to inform the assessment of young people who are referred to the team by the court. While Michelle was happy to adapt her practice, Antonio found the change in direction irritating and unnecessary. Over time, Antonio persuaded Michelle and other colleagues to develop a procedure based on the new policy but with significant omissions that were not altogether in line with published policy.

In a seminal work, Lipsky (1980) describes social workers in large public agencies as 'street-level bureaucrats' because often they make flexible decisions in practice that are not in line with published policy:

> At best, street-level bureaucrats invent benign modes of mass processing that more or less permit them to deal with the public fairly, appropriately, and successfully. At worst, they give in to favoritism, stereotyping and routinizing – all of which serve private or agency purposes.
>
> (Lipsky, 1980, p. xii)

However, since this seminal work was published, counterarguments have developed. For example, Wastell et al. (2010) suggest that:

> Lipsky (1980: 201) saw [street-level bureaucrats] as idealistically motivated to help services users. Others have seen professionals as actuated mainly by self-interest … and the experience of the last 20 years has seen increased attempts to control professional practice. There may be something to this argument, but there are legitimate grounds for anxiety that the imposition of bureaucratic control may have gone too far and may already have become seriously counterproductive.
>
> (Wastell et al., 2010, p. 318)

Are rules made for breaking? Can you think of any advantages of the team following Antonio's 'slightly modified' approach to assessment?

It is important to remember that implementation is critical here. Rules do not equate with outcomes. People get in the way. As a manager or leader, it is important to think about *how* you and your staff implement the rules, address the targets, and thus shape the performance of your organisation.

Figure 12.4 summarises six structures that may currently be used in health and social care organisations.

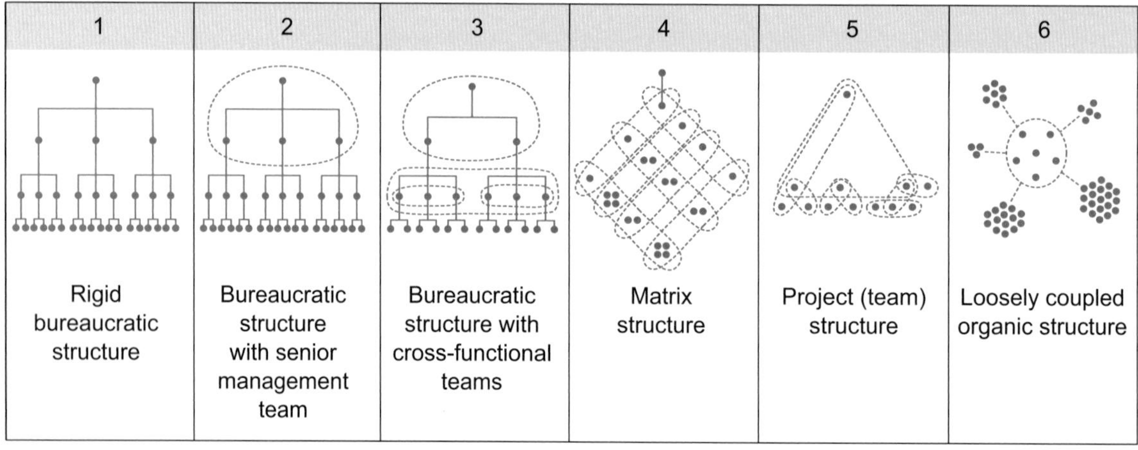

Figure 12.4 Types of organisational structure (Huczynski and Buchanan, 2001, p. 504)

Which of the diagrams in Figure 12.4 most accurately illustrates your organisation, or one you are familiar with? What are the advantages and disadvantages of this structure?

Of course, structure is not the whole story. People matter too. As suggested above, people can, and do, mediate within organisational structures. That is why it is important to examine the role of organisational culture in order to make sense of how organisations function in practice.

12.3 Organisational culture: the answer to everything and nothing

> The report cites a 'fundamental breach of NHS values' in which targets were prioritised above everything else. There is pressure to deliver more for less and in a culture obsessed with targets, managers, fearful of reprisals should targets be missed, are likely to cut corners.
>
> (Spellman, 2010)

What is culture?

As the quotation above suggests, shortcomings in care provision are often attributed to a 'culture' of failure or low expectations. Services may be 'taken to task' for fostering a 'blame culture' and a 'no blame' or 'learning' culture may be encouraged in its place. More widely, the fears expressed about a 'litigation culture' spreading across the Atlantic and taking root in the National Health Service in the UK seem to have been well founded (Adams, 2012).

'Culture' is characterised as something deeply engrained and all-pervasive in an organisation. On the negative side, it is often seen as a serious obstacle to change; while, more positively, paying attention to issues of culture is regarded as an essential component of any change process. Wide-ranging cultural change is often seen as vital if organisational change is to be 'real' and lasting.

Is culture always something that needs 'changing'? That is, is it *always* problematic?

Culture and organisations

According to van den Berg and Wilderom (2004, p. 570), 'Organisational culture is defined as shared perceptions of organisational work practices within organisational units'. Social psychologist Diane Watson (1996) described how the notion of organisational culture had become a significant feature of managerial and organisational discourse since the 1980s, and she traced this to specific developments at a societal level. As managers and business leaders looked for new ways to be successful in increasingly competitive environments, and as public bodies also began to be exposed to the harsh winds of competition, attention focused on the ways in which the shared values of an organisation could be harnessed for business ends.

Watson points to the popularity of writings by management consultants, such as Peters and Waterman's immensely successful book *In Search of Excellence* (1982), which suggests that 'excellence' is about having a strong organisational culture and a sense of shared values. In Watson's words:

> People in such 'strong culture' organizations, it is claimed, do not need to be closely supervised by managers, directed by rule books and procedure manuals, or monitored by tight control and surveillance systems. People do what is beneficial to the organization as a whole and they do it, not because they are told to, but *because they want to.*
>
> (Watson, 1996, p. 271)

What impediments might there be to such a strong organisational culture?

Watson points out that, as with the definition of culture more generally, what different people actually mean by the term 'organisational culture' varies enormously. However, she quotes a useful summary by Ott (1989) of some of the characteristics of organisational culture as expressed by a wide range of writers on the subject:

- Organisational culture is the culture that exists in an organisation, something like a societal culture.
- It is made up of such things as values, beliefs, assumptions, perceptions, behavioural norms, artefacts and patterns of behaviour.
- It is a socially constructed, unseen and unobservable force behind organisational activities.
- It is a social energy that moves organisation members to act.
- It is a unifying theme that provides meaning, direction, and mobilisation for organisation members.
- It functions as an organisational control mechanism, informally approving or prohibiting behaviours.

(Based on Ott, 1989, p. 50, quoted in Watson, 1996, p. 272)

Clearly, the notion of organisations having a shared culture in this sense depends on seeing them as distinct social entities, sharing a collective life that transcends the individual attitudes and practices of the individuals who are part of it, as well as the formal rules and regulations that are meant to define it. Writers on culture, whether at a societal or an organisational level, argue that the importance of culture lies in its capacity to give meaning and coherence to the life of a social unit (Figure 12.5).

Figure 12.5 A coherent team is important in any unit

Shared practices and collective values can be seen as the glue that holds a group together and enables it to carry out its shared goals and tasks. The implication is that a strong, shared culture leads to a flourishing and successful community; whereas a weak or divided culture undermines the achievement of collective aims. Equally, of course, a strong, negative culture can have detrimental effects (see Chapter 15 for more about this in relation to defence against anxiety).

How does evidence-based practice fit with a culture of ritualised practice?

Over time, people who belong to particular groups or communities develop shared ways of doing and thinking about things. Similarly, the members of organisations – including health and social care organisations – develop habitual routines and rituals for 'getting the job done'. They also develop a shared sense of the *meaning* of their joint activity, which entails the development and maintenance of *shared values.* These shared ways of acting, talking and thinking become embedded in the life of the organisation, whether at a formal level in mission statements, procedures and guidelines, or at a more informal level as 'the way we do things around here'.

Certainly, the individual members of an organisation contribute to developing the culture of the unit. However, the culture of an organisation, like the culture of an ethnic or a national group, also has the capacity to shape the actions and behaviours of individuals. Culture provides the template for individual and collective action. When you join an organisation or a team, you need to fit in with or adapt to the culture of that unit in order to 'get on'. New members are socialised to fit in with the cultural norms of the group they join.

What would you imagine is the culture of a typical youth offending team? Do you think Antonio and Michelle would 'buy in' to the same culture or are there major potential conflicts associated with their different professions of policing and social work?

Organisational culture can exist at different levels within health and social care. It is possible to talk about either the culture of the sector as a whole or the culture of a particular organisation within it. At the local level, the distinctive culture of a social work department, a primary care practice, or a residential care home can be identified. It may also be possible to identify a distinctive set of routines and values in an individual team or a professional group *within* an organisation.

SWOT analysis can be used to reflect on the strengths and weaknesses of an organisation's culture. Which aspects of your organisation's culture (or one that is familiar to you) are positive and which are negative? What opportunities and threats arise as a result of this?

Rather like identity, organisational culture can be seen as *relational*: that is, it is defined in relation to, or even in opposition to, other groups with different ways of doing and thinking about things. For example, if you are in social work or social care, you might think you share values and ways of doing things that are very different from those in the health service. In a youth offending team, the culture of Antonio, the seconded police officer, may be significantly different from that of the specialist accommodation worker or the drugs specialist. For example, would Antonio and the accommodation worker understand drug misuse, or homelessness, differently?

However, as you will see later, we should not make too much of this idea of cultures being 'boxed off' from each other. Most people identify with more than one 'culture': perhaps the general culture of the service as well as their own local team culture. Cultures need to be seen, therefore, as dynamic processes and not as fixed and static.

Components of organisational culture: the cultural web

Gerry Johnson and his colleagues (2005), in developing work dating from 1992, proposed a 'cultural web' as a relatively straightforward approach to analysing organisational culture (Figure 12.6).

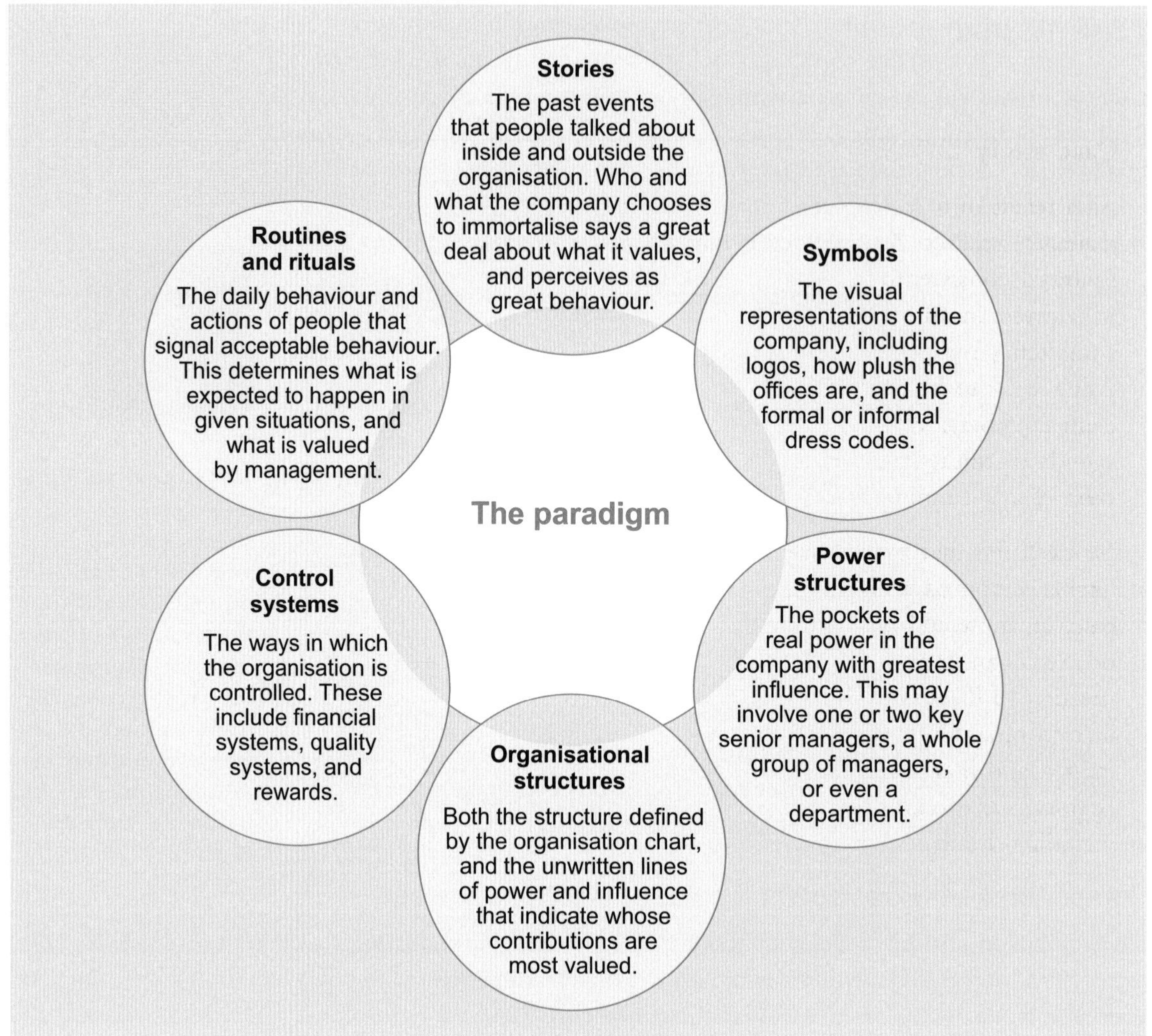

Figure 12.6 A tangled cultural web? (Based on Johnson et al., 2005)

They suggest that the culture of an organisation can be understood through the elements in this diagram. A manager can gain necessary knowledge and power by analysing these aspects of an organisation and coming to terms with how it works. Power, within this web, can be seen as the manager's lever for leading, for setting the tone and for creating improvement cultures.

12.4 A critical view of organisational culture

Case study 12.2: Whose culture?

As a result of a recent assessment audit, Maxwell (the YOT manager) realised that the assessment procedures were not being followed consistently by the team. The challenge for Maxwell was to address, in an open and supportive way, the need for a consistency of approach without alienating the rest of the team. He didn't want to be accused of excluding the views of any of the team members, as the importance of 'inclusivity' had been on the agenda of the team meeting almost every fortnight, so tempers were clearly running high.

Maxwell felt that by 'pro-social modelling' (see Box 12.2) his 'inclusive approach' (a method the staff use with the young people), he would be able to reinforce inclusivity as a key feature of the organisational culture. On that basis he called a special team meeting to discuss assessment and think about how to fully incorporate all members of the team. He made sure everyone was invited and that an agenda was sent well in advance. He used every opportunity to encourage participation in the team meeting, including 'brainstorming', small groups and other exercises.

Box 12.2: What is pro-social modelling?

> The term pro-social modelling in its most limited sense refers to the way in which probation officers, or others who work with involuntary clients, model pro-social values and behaviours in their interactions with clients ... The term pro-social practice or pro-social model is also often used by practitioners to describe a still broader approach to the supervision of offenders which includes collaborative problem solving and role clarification.
>
> (Trotter, 2009, p. 142)

One approach to analysing organisational culture reflects the definition of culture as a distinctive, shared 'way of life'. In this definition, the patterns of talk and behaviour in a group or community are seen as expressing its collective values. As mentioned earlier, this broad approach to the study of culture is now widely accepted in academic circles and in everyday thinking. However, this understanding of culture has also been criticised by people working within a critical social perspective, which emphasises issues of knowledge, power, difference, language and embodiment, as these will influence how individuals fare in relation to particular cultural norms. Cultural studies since the 1980s, influenced by the work of Marxist writers such as Antonio Gramsci (1971) and post-structuralist thinkers such as Michel Foucault (1970), have criticised earlier approaches for viewing culture as a monolithic, homogeneous characteristic. Instead, writers such as Stuart Hall (1981) have proposed a view of culture as a site for negotiating meanings through dialogue and discourse.

So, what are the key features of this more critical view of culture, and what are the implications for an exploration of the culture of health and social care organisations? And how might this help in understanding the case of Antonio, Michelle and Maxwell in a different way?

A critical view of culture sees it as reflecting power relationships within a group, a community or an organisation, an approach influenced by the idea of 'hegemony' (Gramsci, 1971). Broadly speaking, different sets of ideas that reflect differing social interests are constantly struggling for supremacy in any society. In other words, culture can be seen as a terrain – a battleground, in some instances – in which competing interest groups struggle for dominance. The dominant values and practices in any society or community tend to be those of the groups with most power. In an organisational context, the 'dominant' culture may be that of the most powerful level in the hierarchy (that is, management or key stakeholders), or a powerful professional group, or even a particular gender or ethnic group. However, Foucault's work is a reminder that power operates at all levels and the struggle for dominance is ongoing (see also Wong, 2003, in Chapter 1).

Case study 12.3: Leadership style and culture

After the team meeting called by Maxwell, Antonio and Michelle went to the local wine bar and were joined by two other members of the team who regularly socialise with them. Eventually, the discussion got on to Maxwell's leadership style. While they had all enjoyed some of the creative exercises, and acknowledged that he talked a lot about democratic processes and inclusion, they felt the actual process of consultation seemed to stop at the point where team members disagreed with Maxwell. Although Antonio was supportive of Maxwell as team leader, he was very critical of what he saw as double standards.

What interests are competing in the case study? Would an understanding of the fully rounded caring manager (see Chapter 1) help in understanding where some of the tensions originate?

Culture as an active, interactive and dynamic process

As already noted, a critical approach resists the notion that culture is a fixed essence or something that people simply have to accept and fit in with. Mumby (1994) argues that an organisation does not *have* a culture; it *is* a culture. Taking a critical view, culture is actively created by the members of a group, even if they do it in the context of the power relationships described above. Culture is made and remade on a daily basis, during people's everyday actions in the group. In the case study, the sense that culture is specifically the product of interactions between people is particularly relevant. Mumby emphasises culture as active 'sense-making' by groups of individuals, and he goes as far as claiming that 'communication is culture' (Mumby, 1994, p. 12).

This turns the accepted notion of culture as 'a way of life' on its head. Instead of seeing people's everyday interactions as a reflection of an existing set of values, a critical approach sees culture being constantly created and re-created through communication – and specifically through language. According to this view, the ways in which people talk – the kinds of language and terminology used, the stories that circulate in the group – *are at the heart of organisational culture.* This echoes the emphasis on discourse and narrative described in Chapter 6. Writing on organisational culture, Bate (1984, p. 48) asserts that language is 'the main symbolic offering of culture'; while Barley, also working in the same field, claims that 'organisations are speech communities sharing socially-constructed systems of meaning' (1983, p. 393) (both cited in Brooks and MacDonald, 2000). This sits more easily within the definition of culture as having a shared identity.

Thus a critical social perspective views organisational culture as:

- *Diverse* – an organisation may have more than one culture, and different values and practices may compete with each other.
- *Reproducing relationships of power* – the dominant culture tends to reflect the interest of powerful groups in the organisation, but the struggle for dominance is ongoing.
- *Active, interactive and dynamic* – culture is made and remade in every encounter.

Images of organisational cultures – the use of metaphor

Figure 12.7 An example of an organisational metaphor

Some of the managers involved in producing this book were asked what metaphor they would use to describe their organisation. One suggested a polar bear (Figure 12.7); another suggested Mary Poppins. The polar bear metaphor could have meant the organisation was white and fluffy on first appearance but with sharp claws and teeth! In fact, it was meant to convey that the organisation could withstand a very harsh environment. You may have your own view on what the Mary Poppins metaphor conveys.

What metaphor would you use to describe the culture of an organisation you are familiar with?

Metaphors are helpful in allowing us to make conceptual links. Morgan (1997) suggested several ways of making sense of organisational design and how it can interact with 'culture', using a series of metaphors to do so. Metaphor, he says, stretches the imagination to aid understanding. The metaphor of the organisation as a machine, with a system of interlocking parts, is a common one. Another image is of the organisation as an organism: a living thing that can be born, grow, decline and die. This metaphor brings out the importance of adapting to the environment and reflects Mumby's (1994) notion of a culture being made and remade.

More disturbing metaphors are those of the organisation as a psychic prison, like Weber's 'Iron Cage' (Weber, 1922), or an instrument of domination where workers are trapped, disempowered or limited by the organisational culture.

The suggestions of Morgan (1997) can help managers think creatively about organisational shapes and functions and their impact on the human experience. While the use of metaphors gained popularity in the 1980s and 1990s, some authors have argued that metaphors cannot be easily translated into measurable components and thus can only give an incomplete and, in extreme cases, a misleading understanding (Reed, 1990; Alvesson, 1993).

Is the advantage of using a metaphor to describe the culture of an organisation outweighed by its limitations?

12.5 Leadership within organisational culture

A manager's relationship with organisational structure is positional: that is, their authority comes from the terms of their employment. However, a manager's relationship with organisational culture might be much more personal and influential. For example, a new manager may discover that there is already a positive culture that guarantees a good start; or they may find there is a culture in place which will undermine even their best intentions. Therefore, it is important that managers work to create and model a positive organisational culture.

In some settings, such as day centres, this openness and dialogue will include the full participation of service users. The failure to promote a positive culture can contribute to a climate where abuse is possible. Peace (2000) reviews the nature of institutional abuse and suggests some points for managers to consider that would contribute to a climate of openness and awareness in care environments (see Box 12.3).

Box 12.3: Points for practice

- Has your agency or service developed policies and procedures to protect vulnerable service users from abuse?
- Has your staff team examined the way you work and how you would define abuse in your setting?
- If you work in an institutional setting, would you call all areas of practice acceptable? Are there any that are unacceptable? What can you do about this?
- Do staff support and help each other in their day-to-day work? Can you learn from one another's experiences? Do you have systems of appraisal and staff development?
- Is there a system for recording information on abusive practice?
- Some of the people you care for may be at risk of abuse from other residents or patients. Do you know how to intervene to safeguard those who find themselves at risk?

(Based on Peace, 2000, p. 32)

Note that Peace uses 'structural' devices to ensure a correct climate and culture; that is, she suggests putting in place systems and processes to provide ongoing 'checks and balances' that guide a regular review of anticipated trouble spots. You might have noticed (or perhaps will notice) that this idea of checks and balances overlaps with several other chapters in this book: for example, exploring environments (Chapter 11), professional development (Chapter 9) or safeguarding (Chapter 15). However, the manager also has to facilitate a culture that will support the effective use of such checks and balances. In 1993, Brody stressed that managers set the tone in their organisations through the way they lead – and, of course, the same is true for leaders of all descriptions. This is just as true today. Setting the tone can be done in front-line managing too, even when the manager's power over structures, policies and procedures is limited. Indeed, everyone can contribute to setting the tone, which can be seen as a core principle of effective leadership.

More recently, in 2005, the NHS Institute for Innovation and Improvement produced a guide entitled *Building and Nurturing an Improvement Culture*. This defined some of the negative cultures that have existed within the sector, such as blame cultures, 'macho' cultures and cultures of secrecy. Cultures that do not promote improvement may be characterised by slow and unclear decision-making processes, not sharing information, accepting inefficient systems, keeping your head down, and doing the minimum. The guide suggests that the characteristics of 'improvement cultures' are as follows.

- Patient or service-user centredness
- Belief in human potential
- Encouragement of improvement and innovation
- Recognition of the value of learning
- Effective teamworking
- Communication
- Honesty and trust

(Based on NHS IfII, 2005, pp. 12–13)

Such characteristics can be very powerful, particularly when used together with structural devices such as those suggested by Peace.

Power and influence

> The formal structure of the workplace shapes a manager's roles, tasks and responsibilities towards others. It defines their territory or sphere of influence. In particular, it defines their legitimate authority and power.
>
> (Seden, 2003, p. 122)

As discussed in Chapter 1, power can be 'negative, destructive or repressive', but equally it may be 'productive and generative' (Wong, 2003, p. 311).

If you want to explore this idea further, see Chapter 10 on developing a coaching style of management.

The language of *empowerment* has pervaded health and social care for several years and generally means the transfer of power from an advantaged group to a more disadvantaged one, or the development of 'power-from-within' (see Chapter 1) among those who are usually seen to have little power. Managers have to acknowledge that they do have powers – generally more than their staff or service users – and the onus is on them to behave in ways that are empowering for others (Seden, 2003). However, someone standing up as a leader can also mobilise power even if they do not hold it positionally as a manager.

Conger and Kanungo (1998) developed a set of strategies that leaders and managers can rely on to empower others. They include having a shared vision, attempting to remove organisational conditions of powerlessness, and developing a sense of self-efficacy through role modelling, risk taking, persuasion and helping in goal attainment.

If such strategies are not part of the existing organisational culture, part of a caring manager's role is to promote them. They can exercise the power of role and position to do so, as they probably have some control over human and physical resources. Box 12.4 describes seven *levers of power,* at least a few of which a front-line manager can draw on.

Box 12.4: The seven levers of power

1 *Reward power:* The ability to influence the rewards others have, from bonus payments, to holidays and the opportunity to work at home occasionally.
2 *Coercive power:* The authority to hire, fire and discipline others.
3 *Legitimate power:* The authority to appraise, supervise and organise workload.
4 *Personal power:* The power gained by personal characteristics, including personality, ethnicity, age, gender and socio-economic group.
5 *Expert power:* Power gained from the acquisition of skills, knowledge, and professional qualifications.
6 *Information power:* Possessing information and deciding to what extent to share or disclose this.
7 *Connection power:* Making contacts and building networks through meetings, conferences, partnerships, support groups and unions.

(Based on Kakabadse et al., 1988, pp. 215–25)

In the case study, which lever of power could Maxwell have drawn on to improve the situation for his staff?

Maxwell felt he needed to control the situation as a manager, which was in conflict with his belief in inclusivity and transformational leadership. He realised that the way the new policy had been introduced to the team influenced their reaction to the need to change their practice. In hindsight, he accepted that he should have pointed out the benefits of the change to the team before trying to implement it. Perhaps he failed to draw on the right levers of power. Managers like Maxwell can, of course, also be on the receiving end of the power and authority of senior managers, management committees, commissioning agencies or inspectorial bodies. This can make their position feel ambiguous and uncertain; how they might manage that is explored further in Chapter 20.

12.6 Conclusion

This chapter considered the significance of organisational structures and cultures to the way in which you might carry out your everyday work responsibilities. It is difficult to do justice to the huge literature on organisational structure and culture, so seminal organisational theories were selected as a broad means of understanding the ways in which organisations function. Understanding organisational culture is, of course, a key part of this understanding. As you saw, a discussion of power and influence underlines how managers can attempt to guide practices and improve services.

So what about the muffins and the fish mentioned in the Introduction to this chapter? If organisational structures are sometimes mind-boggling in their complexity, even more so are the complex, informal power relationships and 'ecologies' that exist between human beings. As ecologists remind us all the time, making small changes can have a major impact – both positive and negative – on the way in which organisations and the people within them behave. Massive, rapid and thoughtless organisational change often ends in disaster 'ruling the empire'.

Therefore, change, however big or small, should always be made with great care and attention to detail. Leaders and managers need to be equipped with the knowledge of how organisations work – the cultures at play – and, more importantly, to think about how they might work better and their role in achieving that.

Key points

- An understanding of both organisational structure and organisational culture is important for managers working within health and social care.
- Organisational structure and culture can influence relationships within organisations.
- Bureaucracies have valuable characteristics as well as being inhibitors of change and effectiveness.
- An appreciation of power is necessary in understanding the operation of culture within organisations.
- Metaphors can be helpful in making sense of organisational cultures but, equally, they need to be used carefully as they can also be misleading.
- The manager's role is to use their understanding of both structure and culture to lead organisations in creative and supportive ways.

References

Adams, S. (2012) 'Fear of litigation "stopping hospitals admitting mistakes"', *Daily Telegraph*, 2 October [Online]. Available at www.telegraph.co.uk/health/healthnews/9579901/Fear-of-litigation-stopping-hospitals-admitting-mistakes.html (Accessed 14 January 2013).

Alvesson, M. (1993) *Cultural Perspectives on Organisations*, Cambridge, Cambridge University Press.

Barley, S.R. (1983) 'Semantics and the study of occupational and organizational cultures', *Administrative Science Quarterly*, vol. 28, pp. 393–413.

Bate, S.P. (1984) 'The impact of organizational culture on approaches to organizational problem-solving', *Organizational Studies*, vol. 5, no. 1, pp. 43–66.

Brody, R. (1993) *Effectively Managing Human Service Organisations,* London, Sage.

Brooks, I. and MacDonald, S. (2000) '"Doing life"': gender relations in a night nursing sub-culture,' *Gender, Work and Organisations*, vol. 7, no. 4, pp. 200–21.

Conger, J. and Kanungo, R. (1998) *Charismatic Leadership in Organizations*, Thousand Oaks, Calif., Sage.

Coulshed, V. and Mullender, A. (2001) *Management in Social Work* (2nd edition), Buckingham, Palgrave.

Feng, G.-F. and English, J. (2011) *Tao Te Ching by Lao Tsu: A translation by Jane English and Gia-fu Feng* (3rd edition), New York, Vintage.

Foucault, M. (1970) *The Order of Things: An archaeology of the human sciences*, London, Tavistock.

Gramsci, A. (1971) *Selections from the Prison Notebooks*, London, Lawrence and Wishart.

Hall, S. (1981) 'Notes on deconstructing the popular', in Samuel, R. (ed.) *People's History and Socialist Theory*, London, Routledge, pp. 227–40.

Handy, C. (1993, 1999) *Understanding Organisations* (4th edition, revised 4th edition), Harmondsworth, Penguin.

Huczynski, A. and Buchanan, D.A. (2001) *Organizational Behaviour: An introductory text* (4th edition), Harlow, Pearson Education Limited.

Johnson, G., Scholes, K. and Whittington, R. (2005) *Exploring Corporate Strategy: Text and Cases* (7th edition), Harlow, FT/Prentice Hall.

Kakabadse, A., Ludlow, R. and Vinnicombe, C. (1988) *Working in Organisations*, Harmondsworth, Penguin.

Lipsky, M. (1980) *Street Level Bureaucracy,* New York, Russell Sage Foundation.

Mayo, E. (1933) *The Human Problems of an Industrialised Civilisation*, New York, Macmillan.

Mintzberg, H. (1981) 'Organisation design: fashion or fit?', *Harvard Business Review,* January/February, pp. 103–16.

Mintzberg, H. (1994) *The Rise and Fall of Strategic Planning*, London, Prentice Hall.

Morgan, G. (1997) *Images of Organisation*, London, Sage.

Mumby, D.K. (1994) *Communication and Power in Organizations: Discourse, Ideology and Domination*, Norwood, NJ, Ablex Publishing Corporation.

NHS Institute for Innovation and Improvement (NHS IfII) (2005) *Building and Nurturing an Improvement Culture: Personal and organisational development. Improvement Leaders' Guide*, Coventry, NHS IfII.

Ott, J.S. (1989) *The Organizational Culture Perspective*, Pacific Grove, Calif., Brooks/Cole.

Peace, S.M. (2000) 'Residential care for adults', *Research Matters,* October 2000–April 2001, pp. 30–2.

Peters, T.J. and Waterman, R.H. (1982) *In Search of Excellence*, New York, Harper & Row.

Reed, M. (1990) 'From paradigms to images: the paradigm warrior turns post-modern guru', *Personnel Review,* vol. 19, no. 3, pp. 35–40.

Seden, J. (2003) 'Managers and their organisations', in Henderson, J. and Atkinson, D. (eds) *Managing Care in Context*, London, Routledge (K303 Set Book).

Spellman, R. (2010) 'Mid Staffs: NHS culture is to blame', Letters, *The Guardian*, 26 February. Available online at www.guardian.co.uk/society/2010/feb/26/midstaffs-nhs-culture-to-blame/print (Accessed 23 September 2012).

Taylor, F.W. (1911) *Principles of Scientific Management*, New York, Harper.

Trotter, C. (2009) 'Pro-social modelling', *European Journal of Probation*, vol. 1, no. 2, pp. 142–52.

Van den Berg, P.T. and Wilderom, C.P.M. (2004) 'Defining, measuring, and comparing organisational cultures', *Applied Psychology: An International Review,* vol. 53, no. 4, pp. 570–84.

Wastell, D., White, S., Broadhurst, K., Peckover, S. and Pithouse, A. (2010) 'Children's services in the iron cage of performance management: street-level bureaucracy and the spectre of Švejkism', *International Journal of Social Welfare*, vol. 19, pp. 310–20.

Watson, D. (1996) 'Individuals and institutions: the case of work and employment', in Wetherell, M. (ed.) *Identities, Groups and Social Issues*, London, Sage/The Open University, pp. 239–82 (D317 Reader).

Weber, M. (1922) *Wirtschaft und Gesellschaft*, Part III, Chapter 6, pp. 650–78.

Wong, K.-F. (2003) 'Empowerment as a panacea for poverty – old wine in new bottles? Reflections on the World Bank's conception of power', *Progress in Development Studies*, vol. 3, no. 4, pp. 307–22.

Chapter 13 Involving service users and carers

Liz Tilley and Rebecca L. Jones

13.1 Introduction

"Of course, the first rule of effective management is active participation."

Figure 13.1 The first rule of effective management

The involvement of the public in how services are designed and delivered has become a policy priority in recent years (Newman, 2001; Jupp, 2008; Beresford et al., 2011). It has particular resonance in health and social care, where specific groups of people have campaigned hard for greater involvement in decisions that affect their health and social care arrangements. This is a highly significant – but contested – area of practice. It also has direct implications for leaders and managers who are tasked with organising and facilitating involvement across a variety of care contexts.

In the past few years, a wealth of material has been produced about the theory and practice of involving service users (for example, GSCC, 2007), including training materials about how best to do so (Figure 13.1). This covers involvement in health and social care decisions and the design of individual care packages and assessments; involvement in groups or committees to influence local service provision; and involvement at a national level with respect to policy development. Members of the public have been involved in health and social care within the wider context of an increase in consumerism and a renewed focus on 'localism', community engagement and quality improvement through increased accountability (Allen et al., 2012).

Involvement is frequently posited as a 'good thing', something that managers can and ought to be doing. But *why* is involvement so important, and *how* can managers facilitate it in a way which moves beyond tokenistic approaches that leave people feeling frustrated and disengaged? If involvement can take place across different contexts and for different purposes, what methods of involvement are most suitable and who should be involved? Some commentators have suggested that involvement precipitated by people 'in authority' will inevitably (if inadvertently) become a mechanism for legitimising decisions that have already been made, thus reproducing (and sometimes further entrenching) power imbalances between those 'in charge' and those receiving services (Hodge, 2005). However, this view has been countered by researchers who are keen to explore creative ways in which providers and users of services can collaborate to produce 'new collectivities' between officials and citizens, leading to sometimes small, but nevertheless positive, change (Barnes et al., 2004; Jupp, 2008).

This chapter argues that, for involvement to occur in meaningful and transformative ways, it requires a cultural shift in attitudes, supported by managers who display a genuine commitment to participation for political and moral reasons, as well as recognising the ways in which involvement can contribute to service improvement. Managers' leadership skills are crucial in conveying to people the imperatives and rationale for involvement. Therefore, involvement is a key example of where managers can learn and develop from a sound understanding of leadership skills and theory – which is also a key theme of this book.

In the context of this chapter, the terms 'people who use services' and 'service users' refer to both people who receive health and social care services and their informal carers, such as family members.

Drawing on theoretical approaches and the findings from a variety of research projects, this chapter addresses the following core questions.

- Why is it important for health and social care managers to involve people who use services in their work?
- When and how should service users be involved?
- What are the opportunities and challenges for managers to involve other people in health and social care?
- What role can leadership play in supporting involvement?

13.2 Making the case for involvement

Before reading any further, think of as many reasons as you can why managers might want to involve service users in the design and delivery of their services.

There are different ways of approaching the question 'Why involve service users?' One argument is that professionals and service users often have conflicting views about what is important in the delivery of services, and may value different indicators of 'quality' (McIver, 2006; Beresford et al., 2011). For example, while professionals may value particular practical or clinical outcomes, users may highlight that how they *felt* about the care interaction was just as important as what resulted from it (Entwistle et al., 2008). Another key reason for involving people in decisions about their care is that the emerging evidence suggests that it may also lead to an improvement in outcomes (Lorig et al., 1999, quoted in McIver, 2006). The self-management of chronic disease is one such example. As McIver argues, an important role for managers is ensuring that clinicians provide good quality information in order to support patients to participate in decision making in an informed way. Involving service users in planning and developing services can also lead to the creation of more innovative and responsive services, the production of more accessible forms of information for people, the development of more favourable views of service users by staff, and a willingness by organisations to be more transparent (Crawford et al., 2002, quoted in McIver, 2006; Hind, 2011).

For individuals to be genuinely supported to participate in decisions about their care, a service context is required in which the views, perspectives and experiences of service users are respected (Horwath et al., 2012; Hughes, 2012). Managers have an opportunity to lead on and champion the kind of shift in attitudes that may be necessary to make this happen. Service users can be involved at an individual and a service level, despite a culture that is dominated by a systems perspective. Such examples are, however, quite rare. Meaningful involvement is more likely when a manager is in place who champions an approach in which service users are listened to, and where their views are sensitively and carefully incorporated into the development of services.

Think about a time you witnessed service user involvement in a health or social care service. What role do you think the managers involved played and how effectively did they deploy leadership skills?

The origins of involvement in health and social care

Listening to people who use health and social care services has been on the policy agenda for many years now, but it emerged as a distinct priority in care services in the 1970s. In the UK in 1974, Community Health Councils (CHCs) were founded. These were local bodies set up to represent the interests of local people to NHS managers. This was perhaps the first notable attempt to make care services accountable at a local level and to encourage the public's participation in the development of services. In the 1970s, this was viewed as a radical idea, an innovative method for improving services. Dr David Owen, then Minister for Health, wrote:

Looking back now, do you think that is how CHCs are remembered? How might current participation initiatives be seen in 40 years' time?

> The decision to establish community health councils will probably be looked back on by social historians as the most significant aspect of the whole of the NHS Reorganisation Act 1973. For the first time there exists a strong consumer body to both criticize and champion the NHS.
>
> (Owen, 1976, quoted in Hogg, 2007, p. 130)

In the 1970s, CHCs were envisaged as a mechanism for addressing the continued health and welfare inequalities across the UK and the patchy implementation of national policies at local level that resulted in poor outcomes for particular groups of people. Professionals (especially doctors) were viewed by government as a stumbling block to change; it was contended that CHCs would provide a new platform from which the public could hold them to account and challenge the entrenched power of clinicians in service development. CHCs remained in place for nearly 30 years.

Since the 1970s, the context in which people are engaged in discussions about public services has shifted significantly. This reflects a wider trend towards 'participatory governance' (Hickey and Mohan, 2004), in which members of the public are encouraged to join decision-making bodies, respond to consultations, and volunteer in their local community. This area of practice gained considerable attention under the New Labour government (1997–2010) and the Coalition government that followed (Allen et al., 2012). For example, the statutory duty to involve and consult was heralded under Section 11 of the Health and Social Care Act 2001. This was followed by several policy documents that aimed to strengthen a culture of involvement, often linked to wider discourses about giving the public a greater say in shaping public services (Home Office/ODPM, 2005; DH, 2006, 2010; Scottish Executive, 2007). Participation is also a fundamental principle underpinning policy frameworks for children and young people, and is a key focus of the UN Convention on the Rights of the Child, ratified by the UK government in 1991 (Leverett, 2008).

Newman (2001) argues that, in the UK, such developments were promoted by central government to put pressure on local service providers to be more effective and efficient, but also because they were seen to have an 'educative' value for those who participated. Indeed, many people who have participated in decisions about services value the experience and want to see it further strengthened, despite acknowledging the challenges and frustrations (Beresford et al., 2011). However, the involvement of service users in health and social care has also been influenced by a neo-liberal market model of public services, in which patients, carers and users of social care are reframed as 'consumers'. The assumption underpinning this model is that people can, should and *want to* take greater individual responsibility for the care they receive. This idea is more hotly contested (Horwath et al., 2012), as discussed next.

Two approaches to involvement

Beresford and Croft (2003) argue that there have been two main approaches to participation in recent years: the 'consumerist/managerialist' and the 'democratic/citizenship' approach, which both have significantly different objectives and philosophical roots. The consumerist/managerialist approach treats people as 'consumers' or 'customers' and frames involvement in terms of drawing on consumers' experiences to help improve the efficiency and effectiveness of an organisation. This type of involvement tends to be reactive rather than proactive; it focuses on feedback on existing services, rather than helping to design new ones. For many managers in practice, this view of involvement has a strong appeal because it presents an opportunity to support other areas of responsibility, such as service improvement. However, as Beresford and Croft point out, there are ambiguities in this approach, with its focus on consumer rights and choice 'co-existing with the imperatives of profitability and the market economy' (2003, p. 22). This approach risks excluding the voices of 'hard-to-reach' groups and frames involvement *from the perspective of services.* A common critique of this model of participation is that while such interventions may look like attempts to involve people in decision-making processes, 'the reality may be rather the desire to generate consensus around an already agreed agenda' (Jupp, 2008, p. 332).

The quotations below are from a research project which explored the views of probation officers and offenders regarding the process of involvement and engagement in sentence planning. Probation officers were clear that the systems they had in place to engage offenders in creating a sentence plan did not support genuine involvement, and were more about satisfying senior managers and inspectors:

> [I]t is all about targets which don't have anything to do with the actual job.
>
> (Hughes, 2012, p. 57)

When asked about their 'involvement in sentence planning', two service users commented:

> I think she wrote something down on paper, which I just signed.
>
> That phrase means absolutely nothing to me.
>
> (Hughes, 2012, p. 60)

On the other hand, the 'democratic/citizenship' approach to participation has developed out of grassroots initiatives by service users themselves (Beresford and Croft, 2003; see Figure 13.2). This 'democratic' model of involvement emphasises people's rights and entitlements as *citizens* (as opposed to 'consumers'). This, they argue, was borne out of the radical campaigning movements among disabled people, mental health 'survivors', and other users of health and social care services, who view involvement as a means to fight oppression and to promote citizenship. This model of participation is about liberation and the redistribution of power and, as such, its proponents assume that people who use services must be engaged in service design and development from the earliest possible stage. Drawing on the work of Priestly (1999), Beresford and Croft (2003, p. 23) argue:

> This model is concerned with bringing about direct change in people's lives, through *collective* as well as individual action, by enabling people to have more say over what happens to them.

Figure 13.2 Participation can allow a diverse range of people to influence the services they use

How useful do you think these two models of participation are for managers? What questions do they raise about power and leadership?

While government policy frequently appears to blur the boundaries of these two approaches, suggesting that people embody identities as consumers and citizens simultaneously and unproblematically, this view has been challenged in the literature. Researchers suggest that participation frequently happens within contexts that limit the scope for empowerment by reproducing normative boundaries around what constitutes appropriate behaviour in meetings. That is, 'shutting down' discussions or comments which are seen as overtly 'challenging' or veer beyond a set agenda (Hodge, 2005; Tilley, 2007), or which act to subtly incorporate people into particular points of view, rather than empowering them to express their own experiences or opinions (Brin Hyatt, 1997). Participation has also been critiqued by people who have been involved in participation activities and have left the process feeling disaffected, disempowered and even exploited:

Drawing on Wong's web of power from Chapter 1, you can see that the model of involvement used by managers can have important implications for how power is distributed, and to whom.

> I get frustrated ... For the last two or three years, I've gone to meetings and meetings and they've said this, that and the other – and nothing's seemed to materialise. (Carer/relative)
>
> (Beresford et al., 2011, p. 329)

This does not mean that more formal forms of engagement cannot work, or are not valued by people. Indeed, important changes have been effected in organisations by inviting service users on to boards and other committees, and involving them in the institutional structures and discussions (see Box 13.1).

Box 13.1: Reviewing Scottish health services for people with learning disabilities

In 2004–2005, NHS Quality Improvement Scotland (QIS) reviewed health services for children and adults with learning disabilities in Scotland. People with learning disabilities and their carers were involved as members of the review teams, supported by two leading voluntary organisations.

People were involved in a variety of ways, including meetings and interviews with healthcare staff and other stakeholders, visits to health services, and evaluating NHS Boards' self-assessment documents. People with learning disabilities were also involved in team meetings that took place through the review process, and they received training and preparation beforehand. They were paid for their work, as were all other reviewers. People with learning disabilities and their carers were seen as 'experts' in understanding the experiences of health care from a patient's perspective.

> The process of including people with learning disabilities as reviewers was not straightforward and required plenty of time and resources, alongside the commitment of senior managers who led on the review of services, and those managers whose services were being reviewed. However, everyone involved commented that the process was useful and enjoyable. Involving people impacted on staff, who began to view service users' experience and expertise in new ways; gave confidence to the reviewers; and improved the quality of the reports that followed.
>
> (Based on Campbell and Martin, 2010)

It is clear from the example in Box 13.1 of successful service user involvement not only that it requires planning, resources and commitment but also that it has positive outcomes. Effective methods of involvement are discussed further later in this chapter. The next section discusses two different ways of conceptualising service user involvement in the design and delivery of care services.

13.3 Envisaging involvement: ladders and mosaics

There is a growing recognition that involving people in one-off consultation events, distanced from wider decision-making processes, offers limited scope for really understanding people's experiences (Shephard and Treseder, 2002, quoted in Leverett, 2008). This view was first voiced by Sherry Arnstein, writing in 1969 about citizen involvement. She conceptualised her analysis into a 'ladder of participation', which became a powerful tool for managers in the subsequent decades who were grappling with how best to involve people. The ladder (Figure 13.3) indicates a progression of engagement activity, and clearly privileges citizen control above informing or consulting.

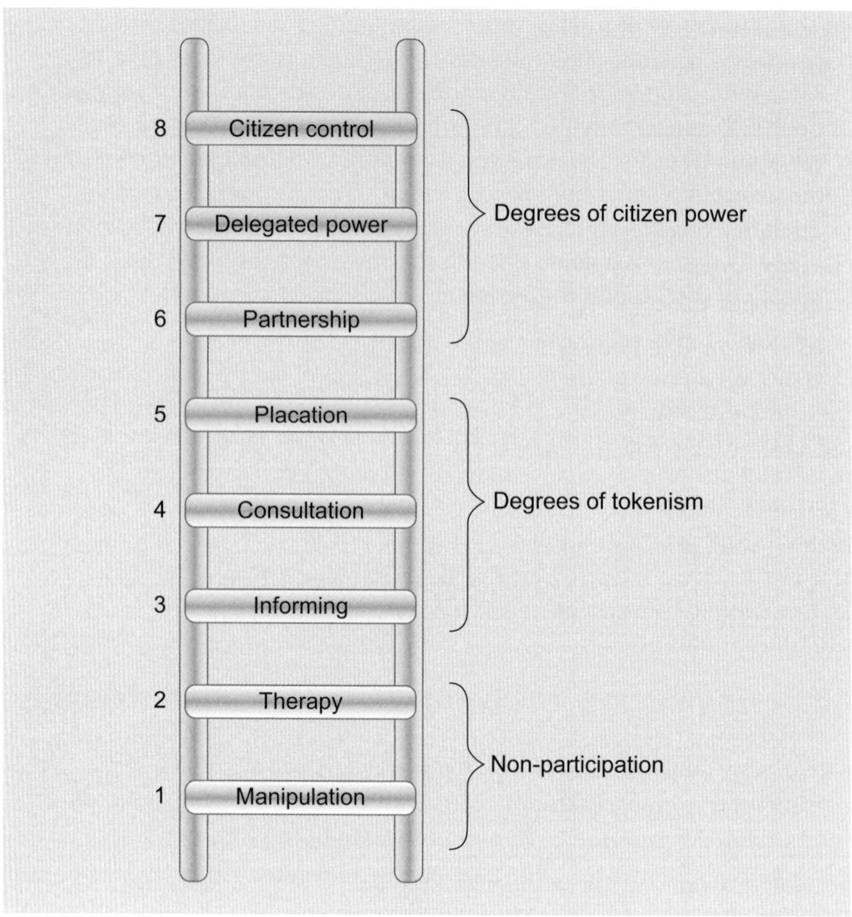

Figure 13.3 The ladder of participation (Arnstein, 1969)

Arnstein's ladder has been criticised for assuming everybody *wants to be* actively engaged. Do you think this is a fair assumption to make?

Arnstein's model has been adapted subsequently for different contexts, most notably by Roger Hart, who produced a version of the ladder specifically relating to children and young people (Hart, 1992).

Recalling the example of the review of health services for people with learning disabilities in Scotland (Box 13.1), you could see it as an example of rung 6 or rung 7 on the ladder. People with learning disabilities and their carers, and the voluntary agencies they worked with, had some delegated power and could be said to be working in partnership with statutory services. Alternatively, it could be argued that this example was more like rung 5 'placation' or even rung 4 'consultation': service users' participation was limited to the particular area of reviewing the quality of services.

They did not have the power to control other aspects of the service and their capacity to act on their findings was limited.

As Leverett (2008) argues, while the ladder metaphor is useful for drawing attention to practices which look like involvement but, on closer inspection, turn out to be instances of manipulation or placation, its tendency to categorise participation hierarchically is problematic. Not everyone wants to participate, and some service users may find the involvement process highly challenging, for several complex psychological and social reasons (Horwath et al., 2012). Managers need to create a culture in which people can be involved in ways that are appropriate for them, rather than privileging only those who are willing and able to take full 'citizen control'.

Ultimately, the idea of a ladder of participation seems difficult to reconcile with what actually happens in practice. In many ways, it presents a false expectation of what managers should be trying to achieve within services and sets up everyone to fail. Tritter and McCallum (2006) instead propose the analogy of a mosaic (Figure 13.4).

> A completed mosaic creates a picture that is the product of the complex and dynamic relationship between individual and groups of tiles. Tiles of different colours and shapes are essential to creating a complete picture, which without systematic integration reveals only chaos. This analogy captures interactions between individual users, their communities, voluntary organisations and the healthcare system on which successful user involvement depends. The importance of user involvement is the engagement of diverse users and health professionals as co-producers. The mosaic illustrates the relationship between horizontal and vertical accountability and enables user involvement to be mapped and monitored.
>
> Building a successful user involvement system requires connecting with diverse individuals and groups at local, organisational, and national levels.
>
> (Tritter and McCallum, 2006, p. 165)

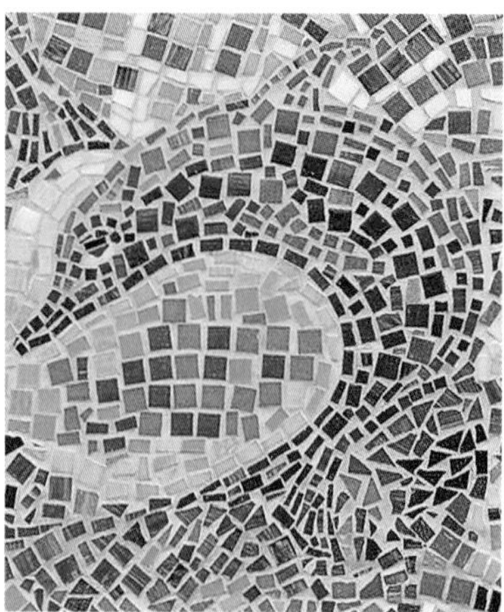

Figure 13.4 Participation is like a mosaic

So, in the example in Box 13.1, people with learning disabilities might be represented by the larger square pieces within the dolphin shape in Figure 13.4. Their families might be represented by the smaller pieces making up the dolphin. The voluntary organisations, the various parts of the healthcare service and Quality Improvement Scotland (QIS) might be imagined as the background pieces, with their more hierarchical relationships and structures reflected in how this part of the mosaic is more strongly horizontal and vertical. All of the pieces have different roles to play and there is no assumption that some forms of involvement are more important than others.

Thinking about involvement as a mosaic highlights the importance of valuing different forms of knowledge. This is not about prioritising one person's or one group's perspective and expertise above the other; it is about reflecting carefully on how different experiences and standpoints can be incorporated in ways that lead to new solutions. The mosaic metaphor is also useful because it suggests that power is not there to be taken from one, to be given to another, as implied by Arnstein's ladder. Rather, the implication is that power is *distributed*, albeit unevenly, between different stakeholders.

Recalling Wong's web of power in Chapter 1, what type(s) of power do you think are required to promote the idea of involvement as a 'mosaic'? How can managers use power to facilitate involvement?

The next section explores some of the specific challenges facing managers who want to listen to people and incorporate their views.

13.4 The challenges and dilemmas of involvement for managers

Thinking about involvement as a mosaic suggests paying attention to the small-scale and everyday activities as well as the formal consultations and meetings; that is, the cement holding the pieces of the mosaic together (see Box 13.2).

Box 13.2: Everyday forms of participation

Eleanor Jupp (2008) studied participation in two housing estates in Stoke-on-Trent, England. She found that while 'official' forms of participation, such as special neighbourhood meetings, were often experienced by residents as disempowering and unhelpful, more everyday and ordinary forms of participation were common and had significant benefits. For example, residents worked with local authority staff to set up a youth forum which improved relationships between older and younger people. People conceptualised participation as 'helping out' rather than the more formal 'participating' or 'volunteering'.

Jupp argues for the importance of settings where people feel 'at home' and 'comfortable'. She also argues that managers in service-led participation initiatives can learn from the experiences of grassroots community-led networks in terms of thinking through the forms of engagement that people respond well to. Another example is growing a community garden which brings together people from that community (Figure 13.5).

Figure 13.5 Community gardens such as this one can involve people in local service delivery

As a manager, how could you enable 'everyday' and 'comfortable' kinds of activity to facilitate people's participation?

However, sometimes more formal forms of participation are also useful or necessary, as part of the mosaic of involvement. What role, then, can managers play in ensuring these more formal forms of participation are effective and fulfil their potential?

Involving people more formally

Leaders and managers in health and social care may have both an obligation and an aspiration to involve people formally in developing services. This is particularly challenging if those people are considered 'vulnerable' or 'at risk'. Participation is often restricted to those groups of people who are perceived to engage more easily and readily in the involvement process (Hill et al., 2004). However, as Horwath and colleagues argue in the context of young people:

> This means that young people who may already be marginalized because of age, ability and personal circumstance are further disadvantaged by being deprived of opportunities to influence policy and practice, even though their experiences indicate that they may not be happy with these policies and the way they inform practice.
>
> (Horwath et al., 2012, p. 155)

The same is likely to be true in services for disabled and older people, for people whose first language is not English, and for people with particularly complex healthcare conditions. So what can managers do to address this potentially vicious circle?

Horwath et al. (2012) explored the promotion of participation among young people who have experienced violence. They met young people in four European countries (including the UK) who had experienced domestic violence, racial harassment, forced marriage, and war. The purpose of their research was to produce training materials to assist practitioners, managers and policy makers to ensure young people with such experiences were involved more effectively in policy design.

Their research was influenced by the work of Shier (2010), who argues that participation often needs to be a long-term process that promotes personal development and is underpinned by a belief in people's inherent capabilities and knowledge. Shier also contends that professionals should be aware that those people being involved might be leaders within the context of their own communities and should be supported to speak on behalf of themselves and their communities where possible.

'The process of participation, especially of socially excluded, marginalized and vulnerable children and young people, may be as important as the outcomes of participation since it empowers them to address their situations' (Horwath et al., 2012, p. 156).

After meeting with groups of young people across Europe, Horwath and colleagues concluded that four key factors influenced their experience of participation. These four factors relate to the four building blocks of the **fully rounded caring manager** which again demonstrates their importance (see Box 13.3).

Box 13.3: The process of participation

Context

The level and scale of participation can and should vary, depending on what managers and policy makers are trying to achieve. This may also be affected by the laws and policies on participation in relation to particular projects. The quality of the involvement process depends on how willing managers are to engage with people, and the extent to which they are prepared to be challenged, or even embarrassed, by people's views (**contextual awareness**).

The facilitator

The person assigned to work with people in the participatory process is crucial to the experience. This may be a manager, or somebody appointed by the manager. Effective engagement highly depends on the beliefs, values and attitudes of the person or people leading the involvement process. A successful facilitator is someone who: can support people to be involved, without patronising them; does not use stereotypes; can adapt their style to suit the needs of the group; enables people to speak freely; and ensures everyone feels 'safe' to speak up (**personal awareness**).

Past experiences of those being involved

Some people may enter the participatory process with low self-esteem and little confidence, and a concern that they lack the necessary knowledge. Others may instinctively distrust or be intimidated by people in a position of 'authority'. These people need additional time and support to develop their trust of those in power, and to develop the skills and resources to enable them to address their anxieties and participate fully (**goal awareness**).

Group dynamics

Participation sometimes requires people to come together in groups. While there can be many advantages to this approach, managers must also be mindful of the difficulties it can present to some individuals. Everyone involved must feel safe and that their contribution is valued, and facilitators need to ensure that each person's needs are met. The group mix (in terms of age, gender, ethnicity, sexuality, ability, etc.) may also impact on people's experience of the process, so managers and facilitators need to explore this carefully and consider the ways in which diversity may influence how people can get involved (**team awareness**).

Managers and leaders must be prepared to face their own anxieties about what might emerge from the participatory process, and to keep an open mind. Horwath et al. (2012) conclude their research by posing several questions designed to assist managers with supporting better involvement practice (see Box 13.4). It is useful for managers to bear these questions in mind when they start a more formal type of involvement initiative.

Box 13.4: Key questions to ask when promoting better involvement in practice

1 How do we view participation and the role of people in participatory activities?
2 To what extent does the socio-legal context in which we are operating promote participation?
3 What does my service really want to achieve through this participatory activity?
4 What are the inhibitors and promoters that will affect the level of participation we can strive for?
5 Are there any physical, time and resource constraints affecting what we can achieve?
6 How will we identify people? What are the implications of this process for the group composition and people's individual needs?
7 Who should be involved?
8 What approach will be taken to reconcile differing perspectives?

(Based on Horwath et al., 2012, pp. 160–1)

Which tool in the toolkit could help you answer the questions in Box 13.4?

Whose voice?

The following case study, from Learmonth et al. (2008), concerns a CHC member who had recently retired and was active within local voluntary groups.

Case study 13.1: Being ordinary?

> She had joined a health authority task group that was reviewing local maternity services, a group which had made a number of controversial proposals and was attracting a lot of press interest. Problems were mounting such that there was a need to convene an urgent meeting, and, as CHC chief officer, I was asked to coordinate her attendance. Although I told her of the circumstances surrounding the need to meet urgently, she was unavailable on the first date proposed because, she said, she was having her hair done; the second, because she had promised to look after her grandchildren; the third, because she was meeting up with friends to go shopping in town. In the event, the meeting went ahead without her. Now, it is important to stress that we are not implying any criticism of her actions. As an unpaid volunteer, we are hardly surprised that she decided to privilege her personal priorities over her CHC work.
>
> (Learmonth et al., 2008, pp. 111–12)

Learmonth and colleagues wrote about the 'Catch-22' situation facing public involvement in health care. They argue that patient representatives are not only required to be 'ordinary', in order to recover and represent the views of the wider public in ways that services cannot, they are also expected to conduct themselves in much the same way as healthcare professionals. For example, it is assumed that participants will be knowledgeable about health care, prepared and able to dedicate significant time to the role, and be accepted as 'equals' around the meeting table.

Learmonth and colleagues wonder to what extent these 'ordinary' and 'extraordinary' characteristics can be reconciled in practice. They argue that 'ordinariness' may make it difficult – if not impossible – for people to make a genuine contribution to decision making:

> [O]rdinary people are the very individuals that managers and health-care professionals seem to have been socialized *not* to take seriously and furthermore, for health managers, the political costs of ignoring ordinary people's views is generally negligible.
>
> (Learmonth et al., 2008, p. 111)

One notable challenge for managers, therefore, is deciding *who* to involve and *how*. This raises the question of representativeness; that is, who can be deemed valid and reliable to represent others. It also raises issues about effectiveness; in other words, which service users offer the greatest return after their participation. Learmonth et al. (2008) argue that a key problem therefore is the performance management of involvement. While this may appear to stand in tension with the principles of participation that were outlined above (Shier, 2010), it may be a genuine cause for concern among managers with only a limited amount of time and resources for specific involvement activities, who must demonstrate value for money, accountability and transparency. But the danger is that service users are unintentionally drawn into institutional frameworks that seek to control their behaviour and contribution, and bring them in line with existing agendas (Learmonth et al., 2008). This tension is at the very heart of the participatory process. It can only be reconciled by strong leadership and a genuine commitment to engage people *on their own terms*. This is explored further next.

Gauging the impact of involvement

Learmonth et al. (2008) suggest that, in the past, involvement was too dominated by manager-led targets, with opportunities missed for service users to take a more leading role in setting the agenda. However, service users have made it clear that they also want to know what happens after making their contribution. One of their chief complaints is that involvement can sometimes feel 'tokenistic' and not 'real'. A key frustration expressed by service users is that, too often, they are not informed about or involved in discussions regarding the *impact* of their participation (Beresford et al., 2011), although they also welcome openness about the wider constraints and are realistic about budgetary and other concerns (Connelly and Seden, 2003).

Rather than gauging the effectiveness and impact of involvement from a managerially defined perspective, Learmonth et al. (2008) suggest that people are given time and space to develop their own agendas, even if these initially seem idiosyncratic, or 'wrong'. But this is not the easy road; it requires managers to draw on key leadership skills, such as creating a vision for meaningful engagement, and communicating their vision with passion (see Chapter 3). It also requires managers and leaders to recognise and facilitate the leadership capacity of service users themselves. By enabling people to pose the questions and negotiate the method of involvement, managers are supporting their potential to become leaders in their own communities, using distributed and transformational leadership to develop 'power-from-within' among the participants (Wong, 2003).

However, another important task for managers is to demonstrate that involvement is more than just 'a good thing'; a focus on the four building blocks of a **fully rounded caring manager** can be helpful here. Particularly in periods of financial constraint, all decisions concerning resources and staff time need to be explained and justified (**contextual awareness**). Managers need to provide evidence to senior leaders and staff that involvement is a genuinely worthwhile activity for everyone (**team awareness**). Of course, it helps if there is a senior leader in the organisation who is actively championing involvement (GSCC, 2012). But this will not always be the case and, in such scenarios, front-line managers need to become the championing leaders, exemplifying confidence and a belief in the importance of involvement (**personal awareness**). They also need to keep focused on the task at hand and *why* it is needed (**goal awareness**).

How can managers better assess the impact of involvement?

Recent research on the impact of involvement shows that, when practised well, it benefits service users, staff and services (Campbell and Martin, 2010; Hind, 2011; Horwath et al., 2012). Involvement can increase participants' self-confidence and self-belief, build capacity for leadership among service users, and improve people's skills. It can also help to reduce inequalities between service users and professionals and shift the balance of power between those who deliver services and those who receive them. Involvement can support staff to change their attitudes towards service users, and increase trust between different groups of people. It can, crucially, also have an impact on the quality of services, making them more sensitive and responsive to service users' needs (McIver, 2006). But, even if you fully support participation through strong leadership skills, how do you know whether the participatory process has been effective, and has met its objectives?

There are various ways in which managers can collect evidence to measure the impact of involvement. Feedback surveys are often used (McIver, 2006), but some contexts may require a more nuanced approach. For example, you may need to have interviews or hold meetings with key stakeholders to ascertain people's experience of the process, and what might have changed as a result. You may want to invite an independent individual or organisation to evaluate the activities that have taken place, to explore what worked and what could have been done differently (GSCC, 2012). Each context will require a tailored approach and a manager's role is, partly, to consider how best to measure the impact of involvement in their own setting, and which mechanisms can be used to feed this information back to the relevant stakeholders.

It is also very important that the manager leading involvement has the opportunity to analyse and reflect on the processes and procedures they use and adjust them as necessary. A tool that can help facilitate reflection on the impact of particular initiatives is the **Plan–Do–Study–Act (PDSA) tool**. This enables a manager to analyse and reflect on various stages of a process to increase the likelihood of success, making small changes in response to the findings.

Wherever possible, managers should also ensure they give feedback to people who gave up their time to participate in the process. The impact of this, in terms of building trust and confidence in the service and improving relations between practitioners and service users, should not be underestimated.

13.5 Conclusion

This chapter explored how and why involvement has become such an important issue in the policy and practice of social care. It should be on the agenda of every manager and leader. However, involving people in the delivery of services is a complex and contested undertaking.

The notion of 'participation' is ill defined and has too often relied on traditional methods of consultation, excluding the harder-to-reach groups.

This chapter also showed that, while the notion of a ladder of participation can be helpful in asking whether service user involvement is tokenistic, conceptualising participation as a mosaic may be a more helpful way of thinking about participation in everyday practice. When conducted sensitively and robustly, research suggests that involving people who use services can have a beneficial impact on individuals, practitioners and services. But it requires time, resources and commitment. Perhaps most importantly, involvement works best when it is championed by transformational leaders within services who are open to the challenges it poses, and the ways in which involvement can shift power relations between services and the people who use them.

Through the process of involvement, managers often face a multitude of perspectives and points of view among different staff and service users, and will need to find ways to reconcile these. This is not an easy undertaking but managers should not seek a homogeneous response. Meaningful involvement starts from a willingness by managers to accept and welcome a diversity of perspectives. It is only by engaging with a variety of points of view that services can be challenged and, ultimately, improved.

Key points

- The involvement of service users is relevant to managers across a range of health and social care settings, and is a key factor in improving services.
- Conceptualising participation as a mosaic may be helpful and can ensure that both formal and less formal forms of involvement are equally valued.

- Managers must be mindful of who they involve and how, and be prepared to adopt innovative and nuanced approaches, particularly for those in 'hard-to-reach' groups.
- Involvement is more likely to be meaningful when a manager with strong leadership skills champions the involvement of service users in a wide range of activities and processes.
- An important part of the process of involvement is reflecting on what has been achieved and how things might be done differently in future.

References

Allen, P., Townsend, J., Dempster, P., Wright, J., Hutchings, A. and Keen, J. (2012) 'Organizational form as a mechanism to involve staff, public and users in public services: a study of the governance of NHS Foundation Trusts', *Social Policy and Administration*, vol. 46, no. 3, pp. 239–57.

Arnstein, S.R. (1969) 'A ladder of citizen participation', *Journal of the American Institute of Planners*, vol. 35, pp. 216–24.

Barnes, M., Newman, J. and Sullivan, H. (2004) 'The micro-politics of deliberation: case studies in public participation', *Contemporary Politics*, vol. 10, no. 2, pp. 93–110.

Beresford, P. and Croft, S. (2003) 'Involving service users in management: citizenship, access and support', in Reynolds, J., Henderson, J., Seden, J., Charlesworth, J. and Bullman, A. (eds) *The Managing Care Reader*, London, Routledge/The Open University, pp. 21–8 (K303 Reader).

Beresford, P., Fleming, J., Glynn, M., Bewley, C., Croft, S., Branfield, F. and Postle, K. (2011) *Supporting People: Towards a person-centred approach*, Bristol, The Policy Press.

Brin Hyatt, S. (1997) 'Poverty in a "post-welfare" landscape: tenant management policies, self-governance and the democratisation of knowledge in Great Britain', in Shore, C. and Wright, S. (eds) *The Anthropology of Policy: Critical perspectives on governance and power*, London, Routledge, pp. 217–38.

Campbell, M. and Martin, M. (2010) 'Reducing health inequalities in Scotland: the involvement of people with learning disabilities as national health service reviewers', *British Journal of Learning Disabilities*, vol. 38, pp. 49–58.

Connelly, N. and Seden, J. (2003) 'What service users say about managers; the implications for services,' in Henderson, J. and Atkinson, D. (eds) *Managing Care in Context*, London, Routledge/The Open University, pp. 27–48 (K303 Set Book).

Crawford, M.J., Rutter, D., Manley, C., Weaver, T., Bhui, K., Fulop, N. and Tyrer, P. (2002) 'Systematic review of involving patients in the planning and development of healthcare', *British Medical Journal*, vol. 325, pp. 1263–5.

Department of Health (DH) (2006) *A Stronger Local Voice: A framework for creating a stronger local voice in the development of health and social care services*, London, DH.

Department of Health (DH) (2010) *Liberating the NHS: Local democratic legitimacy in health*, London, DH.

Entwistle, V., Calnan, M. and Dieppe, P. (2008) 'Consumer involvement in setting the health services research agenda: persistent questions of value', *Journal of Health Services Research & Policy*, vol. 13, Supplement 3, pp. 76–81.

General Social Care Council (GSCC) (2007) *Eight Principles for Involving Service Users and Carers*, London, GSCC.

General Social Care Council (GSCC) (2012) *Report on Involving People Who Use Services and Their Carers in the Work of the General Social Care Council 2001–2012*, London, GSCC.

Hart, R. (1992) *Children's Participation: From tokenism to citizenship*, Florence, UNICEF International Child Development Centre.

Hickey, S. and Mohan, G. (eds) (2004) *Participation: From Tyranny to Transformation*, London, Zed Press.

Hill, M., Davis, J., Prout, A. and Tisdall, K. (2004) 'Moving the participation agenda forward', *Children and Society*, vol. 18, pp. 77–96.

Hind, A. (2011) 'The drugs, the NHS, recovery and me', *Advances in Dual Diagnosis*, vol. 4, no. 2, pp. 84–90.

Hodge, S. (2005) 'Participation, discourse and power: a case study in service user involvement', *Critical Social Policy*, vol. 25, no. 2, pp. 164–79.

Hogg, C.N.L. (2007) 'Patient and public involvement: what next for the NHS?', *Health Expectations*, vol. 10, pp. 129–38.

Home Office/ODPM (2005) *Citizen Engagement and Public Services: Why neighbourhoods matter*, London, Office of the Deputy Prime Minister.

Horwath, J., Kalyva, E. and Spyru, S. (2012) '"I want my experiences to make a difference": promoting participation in policy-making and service development by young people who have experienced violence', *Children and Youth Services Review*, vol. 34, pp. 155–62.

Hughes, W. (2012) 'Promoting offender engagement and compliance in sentence planning: practitioner and service user perspectives in Hertfordshire', *Probation Journal*, vol. 59, no. 1, pp. 49–65.

Jupp, E. (2008) 'The feeling of participation: everyday spaces and urban change', *Geoforum*, vol. 39, pp. 331–43.

Learmonth, M., Martin, G.P. and Warwick, P. (2008) 'Ordinary and effective: the Catch-22 in managing the public voice in health care?', *Health Expectations*, vol. 12, pp. 106–15.

Leverett, S. (2008) 'Children's participation', in Foley, P. and Leverett, S. (eds) *Connecting with Children: Developing working relationships*, Bristol, The Policy Press, pp. 161–203.

Lorig, K.R., Sobel, D.S., Stewart, A.L., Brown, B.W., Bandura, A. and Ritter, P. (1999) 'Evidence suggesting that a chronic disease self-management programme can improve health status while reducing hospitalisation: a randomised trial', *Medical Care*, vol. 37, no. 1, pp. 5–14.

McIver, S. (2006) 'User perspectives and user involvement', in Walshe, K. and Smith, J. (eds) *Healthcare Management*, Maidenhead, Open University Press, pp. 435–53.

Newman, J. (2001) *Modernising Governance: New Labour policy and society*, London, Sage.

Owen, D. (1976) *In Sickness and in Health: The politics of medicine*, London, Quartet Books.

Priestly, M. (1999) *Disability Politics and Community Care*, London, JKP.

Scottish Executive (2007) *Better Health, Better Care: Action Plan*, Edinburgh, The Scottish Government.

Shephard, C. and Treseder, P. (2002*) Participation: Spice it up! Practical tools for engaging children and young people in planning and consultation*, Cardiff, Achub y Plant/Save the Children.

Shier, H. (2010) '"Pathways to participation" revisited', in Percy-Smith, B. and Thomas, N. (eds) *A Handbook of Children and Young People's Participation: Perspectives from theory and practice*, London, Routledge, pp. 215–29.

Tilley, E. (2007) 'Advocacy for people with learning difficulties: the role of two organisations', unpublished PhD thesis, Milton Keynes, The Open University.

Tritter, J.Q. and McCallum, A. (2006) 'The snakes and ladders of user involvement: moving beyond Arnstein', *Health Policy* , vol. 76, pp. 156–68.

Wong, K.-F. (2003) 'Empowerment as a panacea for poverty – old wine in new bottles? Reflections on the World Bank's conception of power, *Progress in Development Studies*, vol. 3, no. 4, pp. 307–22.

Chapter 14 Understanding changing approaches to management

Michelle Gander

14.1 Introduction

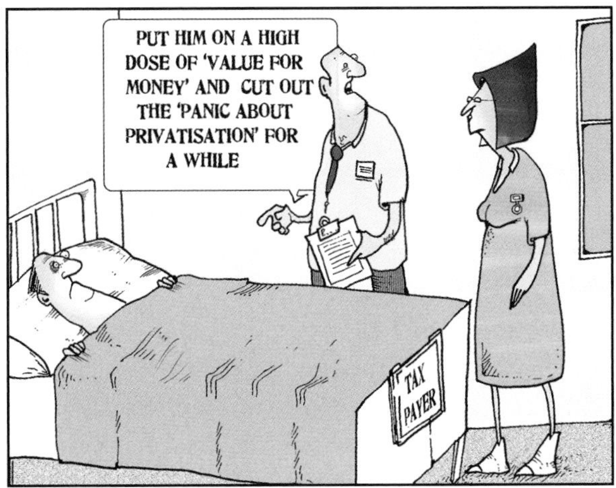

Figure 14.1 What drives management decisions?

> Organization doesn't really accomplish anything. Plans don't accomplish anything, either. Theories of management don't much matter. Endeavors succeed or fail because of the people involved. Only by attracting the best people will you accomplish great deeds.
>
> (Colin Powell, US Secretary of State)

Being a manager and a leader in health and social care requires multiple management skills such as managing change, carrying out staff appraisals, and supporting staff through stressful situations. It also involves strong leadership in creating a caring environment which supports service users and their relatives in the most effective way.

Earlier chapters discuss how all of these skills contribute towards the four basic building blocks of the **fully rounded caring manager**: **personal awareness, goal awareness, team awareness** and **contextual awareness**. This chapter focuses specifically on one aspect of the fourth building block – the broader **contextual awareness** a leader or manager must cultivate; that is, an awareness of the policy drivers and rationale which shape the environment in which they and their organisations operate. Managers not only have to be able to balance the everyday requirements of their organisation and team, using their leadership and interpersonal skills; they also have to understand why other demands are being made of them. These demands include cutting costs, doing more with fewer resources, and getting 'value for money'. All of these demands require skills such as managing budgets and risk, contract management, making purchasing decisions and, above all, understanding the *context* of why these demands are being made (Figure 14.1).

The sheer size of organisations such as the National Health Service (NHS) means that what seems like a small change can be very costly: for example, an average increase of 1 per cent in staff pay would add around £400–500 million to NHS expenditure (The King's Fund, 2012). The concern might then be that patients' care would worsen because of efforts to reduce costs elsewhere. There is a real need, therefore, for managers in health and social care to be able to both work efficiently with their teams and protect the quality of the service they deliver.

Working in the health or social care sector means that many people work within the public sector as part of the welfare state, although not exclusively, and that work is affected by the changes to social policy that governments make. As you may know – either through direct experience working in these sectors or just from your knowledge of current politics – rhetoric around the welfare state is highly politicised and, to manage and lead within health and social care, managers need to understand the context of care work. Even for people working in private-sector provision, their organisations still operate within this general area, so a good understanding of it is still relevant.

This knowledge is built from an understanding of the history of the welfare state described in Chapter 1 and an awareness of the ideas that have led to the prevailing approach of *new public management* (NPM) and the practice of *managerialism* within the public sector. By starting to understand the rationale behind NPM, and its impacts, it will improve our understanding of the conflicting demands made on managers and the role they play in ensuring the sustainability of the NHS and social care services. So, this chapter explores the following core questions.

- What are 'new public management' and 'managerialism' and how does understanding these frameworks support managers in their everyday role?
- Why is there so much emphasis on business management tasks – such as budgeting, cutting costs and managing staff – in a sector that is meant to be all about caring?
- What difference has increasing efficiency in the health and social care sector made to the role of managers?

14.2 Management in the welfare state

As earlier chapters show, the idea of a welfare state is arguably one of the longest-lasting in British history. The starting premise was that the state would guarantee full male employment; that it would provide for people affected by sickness, disability, unemployment, old age or the death of a spouse; that there would be equal and free access to health and education at the point of use; and that the state would both finance and deliver these services (Lowe, 2005). However, even at the time of inception, there was concern that public monopolies not open to competition could not operate successfully and that smaller competing public organisations were needed. From 1940 to 1970, there were significant and continuous equalisations of income across the UK with increased life expectancies and higher educational attainment and social mobility (Glennerster, 1995). But, by the 1950s and 1960s, concerns were growing about the sustainability of the system which had contributed to those advances, and the question of how to finance this huge public welfare enterprise became a key political issue (Field, 2010).

From the 1980s, the trend of equalising wealth was reversed through policy changes implemented by the Conservative government. These were partly in response to the slowing economy in the 1970s but also a result of the ideological spread of monetarism and central government moving back to a more neo-liberalist idea of government. A new political agenda emerged, focused on marketisation, competition, individualisation and home ownership and the concentration of public spending on people most in need. The ultimate impact of the changing emphasis of economic policy was a move back to societal divisions resembling the pre-welfare state of the 1930s (Lowe, 2005).

By 1988, financial constraints began to have an effect and the resources available to fund services per head of population declined. The impact of this in health and social care was long waiting lists and organisations running out of money before the end of the financial year. Dissatisfaction with state services was growing, and the Conservatives looked to the private sector which they believed delivered a better model for service provision.

The New Right thinking of the 1980s, of which the Prime Minister, Margaret Thatcher, was a key proponent, advocated a laissez-faire approach to state intervention, promoting the dismantling of the welfare state and the privatisation of nationalised industries.

The New Labour government in 1997 introduced what was labelled 'the third way', revising the typical social democracy model to include the concept of economic efficiency. This explicitly removed the idea of 'equality of outcome' from social policy and replaced it with the idea of 'equality of opportunity'. This reflected Labour's growing interest in 'social inclusion', leading to the development of the Social Inclusion Unit in 1997, acknowledging the contribution of structural causes to poverty. However, alongside this emphasis on social justice, there continued a New Right critique of government based on the idea that the welfare state created as many problems as it solved (Lowe, 2005).

A structural deficit occurs from a long-term fundamental imbalance in government receipts and expenditures. Deficits are financed by borrowing and, if a country's ratio of debt to gross domestic product (GDP) gets too high, investors can have a crisis of confidence, leading to a reduction in a country's ability to borrow finance at a low rate of interest.

This brief overview of the politics of the welfare state shows that the drive behind the highly debated Health and Social Care Bill 2010–12 had similarities to many previous governments' concerns about monolithic state organisations delivering welfare. With unemployment rising to 2.51 million at October 2012, and predicted to peak at 2.85 million in 2013, the current economic climate is as significant as that in the late 1970s. This rate of unemployment is an indicator of the state of the economy and when the Conservative–Liberal Democrat Coalition government came to power in 2010, it immediately put measures in place to cut the structural deficit by reducing public sector spending with an expectation that the private sector would step in and create jobs. However, by 2012, statistics seemed to suggest otherwise and, with the UK entering a 'double-dip recession' (O'Connor, 2012), it seemed clear that, without any new policies to encourage growth in the private sector, the public sector would continue to be susceptible to cuts in funding. Therefore, managers and leaders are expected to manage services with fewer resources per capita but without any decrease in the expected quality of provision.

Managers and professionals in service

> I love working with the clinicians and, on an individual level, we get on great. But I get really annoyed with this constant 'them-and-us' syndrome that seems to exist when we talk about each other as a group. I'm here for the patients just as much as they are and I'd like to see the doctors doing all the admin that it takes to

> run this place – ensuring all the managers are reporting on their performance indicators, managing the budgets, reporting on the finances each month. Sometimes, though, you'd think we made all this stuff up just to annoy them!
>
> (Jane, hospital administrator, personal communication)

Some of the images portrayed of staff working in health and social care assume a clear distinction between practitioner–professionals and managers, suggesting that the work they do is philosophically different and their relationships are therefore strained or combative. It is assumed that managers are committed to running bureaucracies, to finding financial efficiencies, and to establishing and applying rules; while practitioner–professionals are committed to providing expert services and advice for their service users (Table 14.1). This is the somewhat clichéd picture of bureaucratic–professional order (Clarke and Newman, 1997), which assumes that each culture is distinctive in terms of not only the work they do but also their language, values and relationships.

Table 14.1 Activity contradictions (based on Flynn, 1999)

Role activity	Manager	Professional
Source of legitimacy	Hierarchical authority	Expertise
Goals or objectives	Efficiency	Effectiveness
Mode of control	Compliance	Trust
Service users	Corporate	Individuals
Reference group	Bureaucratic sponsors	Professional peers
Regulation	Hierarchical	Self-regulation

How relevant do you think these distinctions are in health and social care practice today?

Although there is rarely such a clear distinction in reality, the assumptions behind this model do influence working relationships and are therefore worth exploring further. It suggests practitioner–professionals work in a world of complexity, uncertainty and ambiguity and have the autonomy to exercise professional judgement in the best interests of their service users, including having considerable discretion in using resources. Their claims to autonomy and status result from their expert knowledge and skills, and their actions are seen as based on a trust relationship with service users. They are seen as having power over other people in the organisation, as well as considerable personal power, meaning they can mobilise change. In contrast, this model suggests that managers claim their privileges based on institutionalised hierarchical authority with their primary objective being efficiency. They are agents of the organisation rather than of individual service users; their power base is often through control in the form of policies and regulations; they are subject to corporate control; and they are accountable to their managers in turn.

In fact, such boundaries are more likely to be blurred. For example, the manager is often also in practice, or the practitioner also has management responsibilities, their common goal being to ensure high quality outcomes for service users. Therefore, working practices rarely fall completely into the ideal types outlined in Table 14.1. The changing nature of career pathways in the health and social care professions means there is much more cross-over as practitioner–professionals move into positions where their primary responsibility is managing the operational work of other professionals and of the allied resources (Causer and Exworthy, 1999). For example, in the NHS, general management was established in 1983 as an outcome of the Griffiths Report (1983) which weakened the autonomy of medical and nursing practitioner–professionals. Although this process eroded the role and number of nurse managers, at the same time, it led to an increase in management in the role of ward sisters – renamed ward managers.

In social work, the role has also been increasingly redefined, stressing the importance of managerial activities. Care managers are now charged with assessing service users' needs, and ensuring these are met through the package of services purchased, as well as being accountable for ensuring that the resources available are rationed to guarantee enough budget remains to the end of the year (Causer and Exworthy, 1999).

An unintended consequence of creating management routes for practitioner–professionals is that it led to vertical segregation within organisations (see Box 14.1).

Box 14.1: The glass escalator effect

Of the people employed on lower grades within the NHS, 53 per cent are women, yet only 28 per cent of consultants are female (Deech, 2009). Simpson (2004) suggests that men in female-dominated occupations benefit from their minority status: a 'glass escalator' helps them move more quickly into roles which are inherently seen as 'masculine' (for example, away from front-line services) and they are 'pushed' up the hierarchy (Williams, 1992). This is certainly true in the NHS, where men hold more senior posts and take less time to reach them (6.9 years compared with 11.4 years for women). So the unintentional outcome of blurring the manager–practitioner career route is the concentration of men in senior positions. As suggested in Chapter 1, this is not productive from a management perspective, as extensive research has revealed how a management team with a heterogeneous view is far more productive for businesses than a homogeneous team (Brown, 2002).

The next section explores the changing approaches to public sector management and how this has shaped people's experiences of managing and leading within health and social care.

14.3 Changing management contexts

> I know it sounds clichéd but I became a nurse because I wanted to help people, wanted to make a difference – and there were nurses in my family who, for all of its difficulties, loved the job. Nursing was what I always wanted to do from since when I can remember. But never did I want to manage other people or wrangle with budget forecasts and make decisions between not overspending my temporary staff budget or hiring an agency nurse!
>
> (Satvinder, ward sister, personal communication)

The wider political context in which managers operate has changed considerably over the years (Figure 14.2). Before the 1980s and the spread of neo-liberalism, people who entered public service were considered to be serving society and most entered to make a contribution to the public good. Staff were either expert practitioner–professionals or administrators who carried out public administration.

However, there is little agreement on what this 'traditional' public administration model was, and it is hotly debated in public policy circles (see, for example, Lynn, 2001). For instance, it has been argued that public administration is 'neutral, hostile to discretion and to citizen involvement, uninvolved in policy, parochial, and narrowly focused on efficiency' (Denhardt and Denhardt, 2000, quoted in Lynn, 2001, p. 146). But it has also been described as 'a traditional, progressive-era set of doctrines of good administration, emphasising orderly hierarchies, depoliticized bureaucracies, and the elimination of duplication or overlap' (Hood, 1996, p. 268).

Managerialism is the theory that any organisation – from hospitals and social work departments, to advertising agencies and coffee shops – can be run in the same way using generic management skills.

Perhaps not surprisingly, given this lack of agreement over precisely what public administration might entail, there have since been numerous attempts to modify the role of management within public services. After the Conservative government was elected in 1979, 'managerialism' was introduced into the public sector, with leaders from the private sector hired to replace the 'passive bureaucratic administrator'. The result was a move from an emphasis on service efficiency to a focus on financial efficiency. This was arguably the tipping point from the 'public service tradition' to 'new public management' (NPM). Just as there is no clear agreement on what public service administration was, there is no clear agreement on what NPM is. However, it can be 'handy shorthand' for 'a way of reorganizing public sector bodies to bring their management, reporting and accounting approaches closer to ... business methods' (Dunleavy and Hood, 1994, p. 16). Critics have seen it as imposing a market-based ideology on public sector organisations.

NPM has also been seen as a framework to modernise and increase the effectiveness of the public sector by importing corporate management tools to achieve cost benefits without negative impacts on quality outcomes. Foster and Wilding (2000) suggest that NPM has led to practitioners being more accountable to taxpayers and service users for what they do. At the same time, they express concern that NPM can destroy positive aspects of professionalism: the ability to do high-quality work and provide individualised services for patients or service users. There has been considerable and ongoing criticism of the attempt to bring public management into line with private management. For example, Stewart and Walsh (1992) argue that 'in adopting a private sector language there is a danger that organizations in the public domain will neglect the values inherent in that domain' (quoted in Boyne et al., 1999, p. 407).

Ferlie and his colleagues (1996) suggested that, by 1996, there were at least four distinguishing models of NPM that represented a move away from traditional public administration:

1 The Efficiency Drive
2 Downsizing and Decentralization
3 In Search of Excellence
4 Public Service Orientation.

The following year, in 1997, the newly elected Labour government began to introduce its modernisation agenda which, some commentators suggested, heralded a move away from NPM. However, other commentators suggested that this was still NPM but in another guise (Clarke and Newman, 1997). Many aspects of NPM (for example, financial efficiency, value for money and human resource management) have continued through its different guises. More recently, the growing emphasis on network governance could be seen as simply the current 'flavour' of an ongoing NPM agenda (Figure 14.2).

What do you think are the benefits and the drawbacks of introducing business approaches to managing health and social care?

In the 1980s, public sector organisations were required to 'do more with less', and one of the biggest changes to social policy at that time was the creation of quasi-markets through the purchaser–provider split (see Box 14.2).

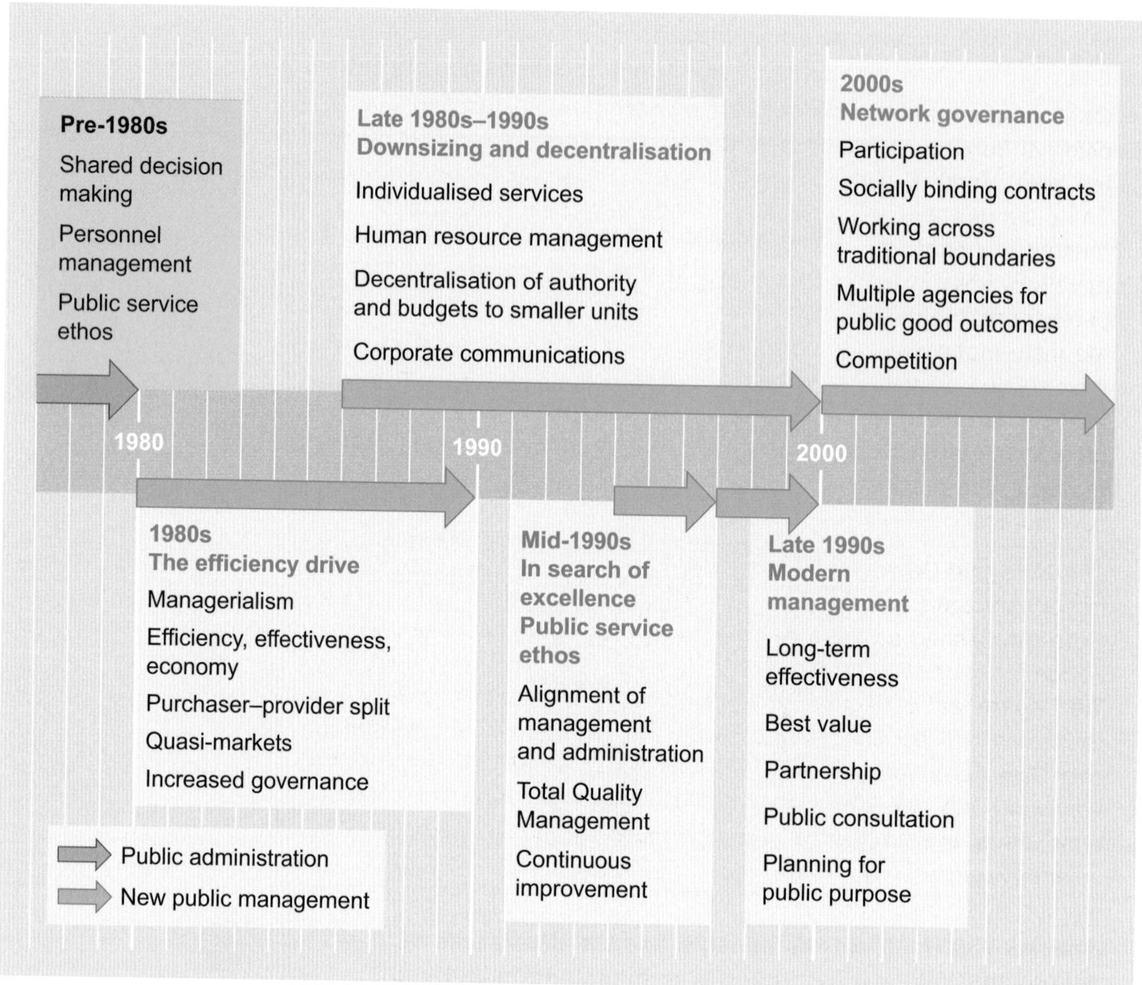

Figure 14.2 Time line of the evolution of NPM

Box 14.2: Competition and quasi-markets

Quasi-markets have features that make them both similar to and different from conventional markets. Central to the quasi-market is the distinction between the roles of the purchaser and the provider. The purchaser (for example, the social services or social work authority) is publicly funded. Provider units are drawn from statutory, private or voluntary sectors, and compete for contracts from purchasers. In conventional markets, profit and financial targets are the main motivation. Although providers compete in quasi-markets, their service delivery objectives may take precedence over meeting financial targets. The 1980s was also the time of a wide-ranging programme of privatisation and many public service organisations moved to the private or voluntary sector, for example those running care homes.

The NHS and Community Care Act 1990 promoted the development of self-managed units in the health service. Consequently, hospitals were established as autonomous, self-managing trusts. They were no longer under the authority of local government but answerable to the Department of Health. This department continued to allocate resources and set performance targets but managers had discretion over their operation. There was a move away from standardised services – the 'one size fits all' attitude – to more varied approaches to meet individual requirements better. However, if voluntary sector or private agencies fail to meet their targets, the result may be redundancies or closure of the agency. Management then becomes more complex with the span of control resting over multiple agencies to deliver outcomes to service users.

Although competition and quasi-markets became important in the 1980s, this is still a key topic with the publication of the *Open Public Services* White Paper in 2011, allowing for every public service (except national security, front-line policing and the judiciary) to be opened up to providers from both the private and voluntary sectors to 'deliver better services for less money'. However, in practice, small or voluntary sector organisations struggle to compete against large corporate organisations, thereby limiting full and diverse competition.

Since the introduction of NPM, there has been an increasing emphasis on audit and control, public sector workers being 'measured' in various ways against external benchmarks. At the heart of such measurements is the desire to improve the efficiency and effectiveness of service provision, which is considered next.

14.4 The 'three Es': economy, efficiency, effectiveness

A significant change from the 1980s onwards was the emphasis on financial management and 'value for money'. The public sector was seen as wasteful and underperforming and the main changes at this time were increased financial control with efficiency, effectiveness and economy taking centre stage. Audit functions emerged to provide government with a greater oversight of finances and management. It was argued that to manage service delivery effectively, managers must know how well they are performing, and typically performance was deemed to be measurable through the 'three Es': **E**conomy, **E**fficiency and **E**ffectiveness (see Box 14.3).

Box 14.3: What is the cost of good nutrition?

'82,192 uneaten hospital meals thrown in the bin every day … 67% of hospital staff unhappy to eat the food they serve to patients' (Campaign for Better Hospital Food, 2012)

Economy measures the costs of inputs to the organisation and the costs related to transforming those inputs into service delivery. Cost management is critical as up to 70 per cent of organisational total costs are related to service delivery. Significant economy measures have been taken over hospital food, managers driving down costs by outsourcing and reducing the amount spent on the raw ingredients. Economy is a simple equation of actual costs not exceeding planned costs and reducing actual costs wherever possible. However, might it be a false economy if that cheaper food ends up in the bin?

Efficiency measures how well an organisation uses its resources – the productivity. *Productivity* is measured as the ratio of the cost of the output (sales of the services delivered) to the cost of the inputs (staff, energy and raw materials). This ratio can be improved by increasing the productivity, that is increasing outputs while keeping the inputs constant, or by keeping the output constant and reducing the input. Efficiency measures are somewhat limited as they focus on whether people are busy rather than on the quality of the output being delivered. It can even lead to a lower-quality service: for example, producing more hospital meals with fewer ingredients but of lower nutritional value.

Effectiveness is a measure of how well an organisation does what it said it was going to do, and how well the services delivered meet the needs of people using them. Of course, measuring this is much more difficult as it means measuring levels of satisfaction and identifying the correct measure to add value. Organisations often use external benchmarking to provide measures of effectiveness against similar organisations, such as mortality or readmission rates in neighbouring hospitals. For example, even though hospital food may be more expensive, it might be more *effective* to provide nutritious meals which patients want to eat, rather than very cheap ones which end up in the bin.

The example of hospital food helps in understanding the intricacies of trying to balance the 'three Es'. A report in 2011 found that more than two-thirds of people took their own food into hospital and many thousands became malnourished during their hospital stay (Soil Association, 2011). This does not suggest the effective management of food policy in these hospitals. However, as Case study 14.1 shows, being efficient and effective does not necessarily involve increasing costs overall.

Case study 14.1: Reconciling efficiency and sustainability

There is a primary emphasis on public sector bodies achieving efficiency savings in their procurement purchasing. One region in England took an innovative approach to this, focusing on sustainability and the role it may play in supporting 'value for money' and a more effective service in hospital food provision.

> Since 2001 the National Health Service in Cornwall has pioneered an innovative approach to buying and cooking food for its three flagship hospitals: the Royal Cornwall Hospital, St Michael's and the West of Cornwall Hospital ... There have been major changes in the food served ... These include the introduction of a local, clotted-cream ice cream which is higher in calories and less likely to melt before patients eat it. The new ice cream has proved very popular, and has cut the amount spent on expensive, powdered drink supplements previously given to elderly patients to maintain their calorie intake. ... The Cornwall Food Programme has achieved all this without increasing costs – and within the Royal Cornwall Hospital's food budget of £2.50 per patient per day.
>
> (Russell, 2007, pp. 7, 8)

14.5 Beyond the 'three Es': governance, people and ethics

As well as introducing more financial management since the 1980s, successive governments have also wanted to ensure an increased oversight of public sector organisations, and a more robust approach to people management. This section explores these two factors before moving on to ask what the emphasis on the 'three Es' may have overlooked when it comes to management and leadership in health and social care.

Governance

Part of the increased oversight of public sector organisations has involved a move to new corporate governance structures based on a Board of Director model, the organisation being run by a Chief Executive Officer (CEO). This move tried to reduce the power of professionals which, it was argued, had a poor reputation of being elitist, and uncaring to their service users. It was also an attempt to devolve power and responsibility to the local level.

According to the Independent Commission on Good Governance in Public Services (OPM/CIPFA, 2004) the function of governance is to 'ensure that an organisation ... fulfils its overall purpose, achieves its intended outcomes and operates in an effective, efficient and ethical manner. This principle should guide all governance activity.' Organisational governance covers all aspects of management, including how the organisation operates, the relationships between the main stakeholders, and the organisational goals. Some of the key principles of good governance are that everyone in the organisation should know their role, how it supports the organisation's goals, and their responsibilities. They should be open, honest and transparent in decision making, engaging with staff and other stakeholders openly and honestly, and carrying out robust risk management processes.

To understand why governance is considered so important, it is helpful to look at what happens when governance goes wrong (Case study 14.2). In 2006, the District Auditor concluded that, because of failures in corporate governance, University Hospital North Staffordshire NHS Trust was responsible for its deteriorating financial position, leading to a forecast deficit position of £15.5 million in 2005/06.

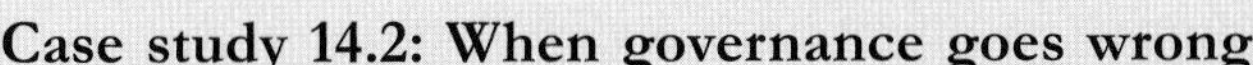

Case study 14.2: When governance goes wrong

The District Auditor's report found the following:

- The Trust did not operate appropriate governance arrangements to enable it to achieve its statutory duty to break even. The Trust Board did not review or approve a budget for 2005/06 until December 2005 and there was a lack of adequate challenge and scrutiny by the Board of financial assumptions.

- The Trust failed to take account of the local primary care trusts' (PCTs) financial position and commissioning intentions which sought to reduce activity with the Trust. Consequently the initial income budget was overstated by £9 million …
- There was a failure to adequately report and manage serious cashflow problems. This came to a head in August 2005 when only 4% of creditors were paid within 30 days.

(Audit Commission, 2006)

Failures such as this may lead to an increase in private companies taking over the running of hospitals such as, for example, Circle being granted a 10-year licence to run Hinchingbrooke Hospital in Huntingdon, Cambridgeshire, after the hospital accrued a £40 million debt. The debt was partially incurred as a result of customer choice (originally introduced to drive up standards), with local patients and general practitioners not favouring this hospital, leading to a fall in income as patients were referred elsewhere. However, despite initial reports of successfully turning the hospital around, the latest figures on patient satisfaction tell a different story, and the newspaper headlines have gone from 'Turned around by Circle in 6 months' (Adams, 2012) to 'It's a pain: first privately-run NHS hospital falls 19 places in health league table in five months' (Gregory, 2012). This suggests the solutions offered by private management may not be as simple as some people might have hoped.

In the quotation at the start of this chapter, Colin Powell suggests people rather than management theories lead to success or failure. How might such a view contribute to understanding what happened at the hospital in North Staffordshire or Hinchingbrooke?

People management

The people management role of a manager in health and social care is key to the recruitment and retention of their staff. It also has the potential to develop their teams to be effective through personal and professional development practices (see Chapters 9 and 10). Before the

1980s, people management in organisations, and especially in the public sector, was done by personnel departments. Personnel management up to this point had four characteristics:

1 a paternalistic approach
2 standardisation of practice
3 collectivised industrial relations
4 standards for staff training and equality and diversity.

As a result of the drive for the 'three Es' in public sector management, these conventional themes have weakened and 'personnel management' gave way to *human resource management* (HRM) (Boyne et al., 1999). This is understood to ensure that the right staff are recruited, they are managed effectively for the good of the organisation, and they are encouraged to stay with the organisation (Figure 14.3).

Figure 14.3 Good practice in HRM?

As with many of the other changes introduced to public sector management since the 1980s, HRM was imported from the private sector. It stresses performance-based rewards for staff; a reduction in the costs of employment; empowerment of organisations to take strategic decisions in the HRM field; increased flexibility in order to respond to customer demands; increased individualisation of the employment relationship; and decentralisation (Truss, 2008). Central to this is the notion that HR functions should move away from simply administrative and people support roles, to become more strategically involved in the organisation than had been the case (Table 14.2).

Table 14.2 Differences between personnel and human resource management

Personnel management	Human resource management
Emphasis on collectivity	Emphasis on individuals
Associated with trade unionism	Associated with capabilities, performance and outcomes
Centralisation of HR responsibility	Devolution of responsibility for managing people
Operationally orientated	Operates at strategic and operational levels

Unlike personnel management, HRM:

> is not driven by concepts of fairness, the welfare needs of employees and the need to maintain good relations with the unions. It is driven by the demands of those leading public organizations for effective job performance, high quality of output, service to customers and value for money.
>
> (Farnham and Horton, 1996, quoted in Boyne et al., 1999, p. 410)

Such drives can result in a devolution of power to increase the flexibility of decision making among those closest to the decisions being taken. However, it has also signalled a move away from standardised employment practices and a reduction in capacity for collective wage bargaining.

According to Wong's web of power (see Chapter 1), what sorts of power did employees have under the old-style personnel management compared with HRM approaches?

Despite the introduction of private sector HRM ideas into the public sector, evidence suggests that differences in HRM practice between public and private organisations are significant (Boyne et al., 1999; Truss, 2008). Truss (2008) suggests that the old 'personnel' style of management still exists and that the new HRM type has been 'grafted on' to create something new for the public sector.

It seems that some of the older good practice – relating to, for example, staff training and development, equal opportunities and national pay bargaining – continues to coexist with the newer more strategic and performance management-related aspects of private sector HRM.

None the less, with all the emphasis on economy, efficiency and effectiveness, some critics began to express concern that the management of health and social care was forgetting about the quality of processes and outcomes for service users. From the 1990s, therefore, several quality initiatives began to emerge, such as *total quality management* (TQM), and a quality agenda became central to health and social care delivery. By 2008, Lord Darzi's Report, *High Quality Care for All*, was suggesting that quality should be the organising principle of the NHS. In some sense, a focus on quality helps to move questions of economy, efficiency and effectiveness towards solutions which might better serve end users as well as organisational needs, thereby avoiding some of the problems associated with a focus on just the 'three Es'.

TQM is an integrative model of management designed to continuously improve the quality of service delivery, by ensuring that all staff within an organisation own responsibility for the quality of processes. In many ways, TQM works very well with distributed leadership, where all members of staff take responsibility for working towards their unit's goals.

Consequences for leadership and management: a 'fourth E'?

The move from the more traditional public service to a managerialist environment has had significant consequences for the management and leadership of public sector organisations. The drive for efficiency of scale requires harnessing the energy of all levels of staff, not just the senior management team. Distributed leadership has therefore become particularly important (see Chapter 3, Section 3.5), as it promotes leadership engagement throughout an organisation so that all levels of staff are working towards the organisation's goals. However, the goals of health and social care organisations are often very different from those of private organisations, which is perhaps why problems such as those at Hinchingbrooke Hospital arise. The difficulty in slotting private sector business models wholesale into the public sector therefore suggests that perhaps a 'fourth E' is required in our understanding of the wider context of public sector management: *ethics*.

Ethics

Some writers have questioned whether too much identification with private sector styles of management has undermined public integrity (for example, Kolthoff et al., 2007). There have been many reports in the media about what happens when people's ethical behaviour in a caring environment does not match that which society expects. For example, there have been cases of patients being forcefully restrained, or

'[F]ears are often expressed that exposing managers to the private sector values might cause them to lose their integrity' (Kolthoff et al., 2007, p. 415).

not given basic nursing care, the physical and sexual abuse of vulnerable adults, patients leaving care dehydrated and malnourished; the list goes on. Chapter 16 describes how many workers in this sector feel 'stuck' in unsatisfactory, often unethical, working conditions; however, they are often unwilling to 'rock the boat' because of the possible consequences. This suggests that, in addition to taking measures to enforce economy, efficiency and effectiveness, guidelines are needed for how to manage integrity in an NPM environment (Kolthoff et al., 2007).

Frederickson (1999) suggested that managers in public sector organisations were inherently more ethical than those in the profit-based private sector. However, there is evidence to suggest this is now diminishing among younger employees (Lyons et al., 2006). Therefore, a key leadership role in the future will probably be a reinvigoration of the idea of public service, emphasising integrity and an ethical approach to management. This will ensure that not only are health and social care institutions run according to the 'three Es' but also that the 'fourth E' of ethics is an integral part of organisational culture. For example, in the case of the Cornish hospitals, while acknowledging the three Es, they arguably also took an *ethical* approach to managing their patients' food and nutrition.

While NPM is more concerned with a results-based than an ethics-based approach to management, there have been increasing calls for a more ethically driven management approach within health and social care in response to high-profile failings in the sector. Whether it was played out in reality or not, the notion of justice and integrity has always been implicit in public administration but not in free-market or even quasi-market frameworks. Feedback from service users suggests that, for them, a core measure of the quality of their care is whether they are treated with respect and dignity (Department of Health, 2010). While managers have to respond to and cater for the 'three Es' of NPM demands, therefore, they must also ensure they do so while considering the ethical dimensions to their management and leadership practice.

What impact would working towards the four Es have on your role as a manager?

14.6 Conclusion

> I range from being a practitioner, a practice teacher, a manager of people, a manager of budgets, a manager of services, a manager of complaints and being responsible for attitudes in the department as well.
>
> (Jo, voluntary sector manager, personal communication)

This chapter looked at the shifting complexity of working in the public sector – a sector which continually changes, driven by the ideology of the government of the day. It described the emergence of NPM – a theoretical framework and approach to management which, since the 1980s, has overhauled the way health and social care is organised and managed. In particular, you saw how a shift from public service administration to NPM began to blur the boundaries and role distinctions between general managers and practitioner–managers. The chapter then explored some of the impact of this on leaders and managers as they attempt to negotiate tensions between professionals, service users, other staff, senior management and external requirements.

While NPM emphasises the 'three Es' of economy, efficiency and effectiveness, this chapter stressed the important role of ethical behaviour in the effective running of public services. When this fundamental part of leadership and management in health and social care is absent, the quality of experience is diminished for service users and it can undermine any efficiencies previously gained. Managers today, arguably, walk a fine line between being responsible to senior management (and, ultimately, the government) for the efficient and effective use of resources, and an ethical duty to provide a service that cares for its users as much as the finances, in a sustainable and ethical way.

Key points

- In health and social care, all staff work in the context of a highly politicised landscape.
- Managers and practitioners require an understanding and empathy of each other's roles to ensure that the outcomes for both service users and the organisation are satisfied.
- Since the 1980s, the context of management in the public sector has moved from one of public administration to an approach based on managerialism and new public management (NPM).
- Managerialist approaches continue to be highly relevant in the public sector today but they should be combined with the public service tradition of public good to ensure appropriate management in a public context.
- Managing integrity and managing *with* integrity are signs of strong leadership in health and social care.
- To ensure quality outcomes for service users, a 'fourth E' – ethical management – should be added to the 'three Es' of NPM (economy, efficiency, effectiveness).

References

Adams, S. (2012) 'Hinchingbrooke hospital turned round by Circle in 6 months', *The Telegraph*, 1 August [Online]. Available at www.telegraph.co.uk/health/healthnews/9443682/Hinchingbrooke-hospital-turned-around-by-Circle-in-six-months.html (Accessed 29 January 2013).

Audit Commission (2006) 'Failures in governance arrangements at University Hospital North Staffordshire NHS Trust', Press release, 24 April [Online]. Available at www.audit-commission.gov.uk/pressoffice/pressreleases/Pages/failuresingovernancearrangementsatuniversityhospitalnorthstaffordshirenhstrust.aspx (Accessed 16 March 2012).

Boyne, G., Jenkins, G. and Poole, M. (1999) 'Human resource management in the public and private sectors: an empirical comparison', *Public Administration*, vol. 77, no. 2, pp. 407–20.

Brown, W.A. (2002) 'Inclusive governance practices in nonprofit organizations and implications for practice', *Nonprofit Management and Leadership*, vol. 12, no. 4, pp. 369–85.

Campaign for Better Hospital Food (2012) 'Enough is enough' [Online]. Available at www.sustainweb.org/hospitalfood/ (Accessed 12 October 2012).

Causer, G. and Exworthy, M. (1999) 'Professionals as managers across the public sector', in Exworthy, M. and Halford, S. (eds) *Professionals and the New Managerialism in the Public Sector*, Maidenhead, Open University Press, pp. 83–101.

Clarke, J. and Newman, J. (1997) *The Managerial State: Power, politics and ideology in the remaking of social welfare*, London, Sage Publications.

Darzi, Lord A. (2008) *High Quality Care for All*, London, The Stationery Office.

Deech, Baroness R. (2009) *Women Doctors: Making a difference*, London, Department of Health.

Denhardt, R.B. and Denhardt, J.V. (2000) 'The new public service: serving rather than steering', *Public Administration Review*, vol. 60, no. 6, pp. 549–59.

Dunleavy, P. and Hood, C. (1994) 'From old public administration to new public management', *Public Money & Management*, vol. 14, no. 3, pp. 9–16.

Department of Health (2010) *Essence of Care*, London, The Stationery Office.

Farnham, D. and Horton, S. (1996) *Managing People in the Public Services*, London, Macmillan.

Ferlie, E., Ashburner, L., Fitzgerald, L. and Pettigrew, A. (1996) *The New Public Management in Action*, Oxford, Oxford University Press.

Field, F. (2010) *The Welfare State – Never Ending Reform* [Online]. Available at www.bbc.co.uk/history/british/modern/thatcherism_01.shtml (Accessed 14 January 2013).

Flynn, R. (1999) 'Managerialism, professionalism and quasi-markets', in Exworthy, M. and Halford, S. (eds) *Professionals and the New Managerialism in the Public Sector*, Maidenhead, Open University Press, pp. 18–36.

Foster, P. and Wilding, P. (2000) 'Whither welfare professionalism?', *Social Policy and Administration*, vol. 34, no. 2, pp. 143–59.

Frederickson, H.G. (1999) 'Ethics and the new managerialism', *Public Administration and Management: An Interactive Journal*, vol. 4, no. 2, pp. 299–324.

Glennerster, H. (1995) *British Social Policy Since 1945*, Oxford, Blackwell Publishers.

Gregory, A. (2012) 'It's a pain: first privately-run NHS hospital falls 19 places in health league table in five months', *The Mirror News*, 6 October [Online]. Available at www.mirror.co.uk/news/uk-news/hinchingbrooke-hospital-first-privately-run-nhs-1363151 (Accessed 29 January 2013).

Griffiths Report (1983) *NHS Management Inquiry Report*, London, DHSS.

HM Government (2011) *Open Public Services* (White Paper), Cm 8145, London, The Stationery Office.

Hood, C. (1996) 'Exploring variations in public management reform of the 1980s', in Bekke, H.A., Perry, J.L. and Toonen, T.A. (eds) *Civil Service Systems in Comparative Perspective*, Bloomington, Ind., Indiana University Press, pp. 268–87.

Kolthoff, E., Huberts, L. and van den Heuvel, H. (2007) 'The ethics of new public management: is integrity at stake?', *Public Administration Quarterly*, vol. 30, no. 4, pp. 399–439.

Lowe, R. (2005) *The Welfare State in Britain Since 1945*, Basingstoke, Palgrave Macmillan.

Lynn, L.E., Jr (2001) 'The myth of the bureaucratic paradigm: what traditional public administration really stood for', *Public Administration Review*, vol. 61, no. 2, pp. 144–60.

Lyons, S.T., Duxbury, L.E. and Higgins, C.A. (2006) 'A comparison of the values and commitment of private sector, public sector, and parapublic sector employees', *Public Administration Review*, vol. 66, no. 4, pp. 605–18.

O'Connor, S. (2012) 'GDP data confirm UK double-dip recession', *The Financial Times* [Online]. Available at www.ft.com/cms/s/0/08be8858-c104-11e1-853f-00144feabdc0.html#axzz1zplDxSFr (Accessed 6 July 2012).

OPM/CIPFA (2004) *The Independent Commission on Good Governance in Public Services*, London, OPM and CIPFA.

Russell, C. (2007) 'Executive summary', *A Fresh Approach to Hospital Food*, Bristol, Soil Association.

Simpson, R. (2004) 'Masculinity at work: the experiences of men in female dominated occupations', *Work, Employment & Society*, vol. 18, no. 2, pp. 349–68.

Soil Association (2011) *First Aid for Hospital Food*, Bristol, Soil Association.

Stewart, J. and Walsh, K. (1992) 'Change in the management of public services', *Public Administration*, vol. 70, no. 4, pp. 499–518.

The King's Fund (2012) 'How is the NHS performing?', *Quarterly Monitoring Report* [Online]. Available at www.kingsfund.org.uk/quarterlyreport (Accessed 15 October 2012).

Truss, C. (2008) 'Continuity and change: the role of the HR function in the modern public sector', *Public Administration* , vol. 86, no. 4, pp. 1071–88.

Williams, C.L. (1992) 'The glass escalator: hidden advantages for men in the "female" professions', *Social Problems*, vol. 39, no. 3, pp. 253–67.

Chapter 15 Managing safeguarding across health and social care

Jeanette Copperman and Hilary Brown

15.1 Introduction

Figure 15.1 'Lying is done with words, and also with silence' (Rich, 1977)

Safeguarding arouses strong emotions, uncertainty and anxieties. For example, you may have a strong reaction to Figure 15.1. It shows the former television presenter Jimmy Savile and the then 14-year-old singer Coleen Nolan on *Top of the Pops* in 1979. Coleen subsequently described how uncomfortable and intimidated she felt as a young person being 'intimately cuddled' yet not feeling able to 'make a fuss' (Nolan, 2012). Of course, with the benefit of hindsight, we may now think differently about what we are seeing, but millions of people saw this image and, while it might have made some uncomfortable, no one saw a reason to take action or question what might have been hidden in the silence.

Safeguarding issues are a core responsibility of all staff in any organisation dealing with potentially vulnerable people. It is therefore a fundamental part of everyday practice across health and social care. This chapter explores the role of managers in protecting children and adults at risk from abuse or neglect and why this is such a complex area of their work. For some managers, safeguarding makes up as little as 5 per cent of their workload while others manage teams whose main focus is safeguarding. Whether tackling occasional cases or managing safeguarding specialists, the task requires intuition and judgement as well as adherence to policy and procedures in circumstances that may be fraught and sometimes even threatening.

This chapter tries to unpack the role of management and leadership in containing the anxiety that safeguarding cases arouse. The chapter explores the psychological mechanisms that support the 'not seeing' of abuse and the silencing of victims, as well as the professional and statutory frameworks that are put in place to help managers frame what is happening and respond appropriately.

You may believe that institutions which exist explicitly to care for vulnerable people provide a safe environment where abuse should not and cannot take place. However, it is a sad fact that predatory people often target children and vulnerable adults specifically in those organisations which are meant to protect them (DH, 2004). It is frequently hard to 'see' such grooming and abuse occurring and difficult to accuse someone when all there is to go on is a hunch that something is not quite right. Yet, while some managers might choose to ignore such concerns and hunches, others lead decisively, using their intuition and judgement, and taking a proactive stance (see Box 15.1).

Chapter 2 shows how being proactive can increase vigilance, improve collaboration and help people express their voice. As you read this chapter, reflect on the importance of proactive management for safeguarding.

Box 15.1: An example of safeguarding leadership

Roger Jones is a former member of the Board of Governors at BBC Wales (1997–2002) and Chairman of the UK charity Children in Need. He allowed himself to see the risk of predatory people and took the decisive step to ban Jimmy Savile as part of the charity's enhanced child protection policies, despite there being no public accusations against Savile at the time (BBC News, 2012). For Jones, his position of authority included acting on his intuition and taking a strong – even unpopular – stance as a leader responsible for potentially vulnerable children and young people. Analysing Roger Jones's actions according to Wong's web of power (see Chapter 1), he clearly demonstrated 'power-from-within' as a decisive leader, but he also used 'power-with' other people in the charity to achieve 'power-over' potential abusers.

Despite clear safeguarding systems being in place for everyone to follow, critical management decisions and sound situational leadership play an extremely important role when there is a need to act decisively and with urgency. With this in mind, this chapter explores the following core questions.

- What is safeguarding and why is it so challenging?
- How do abuse, vulnerability and risk interact?
- How can effective management and leadership in health and social care contribute to the protection of vulnerable adults and children?
- What role should management and leadership play in a multi-agency and an interprofessional protection system?

15.2 What is safeguarding and why is it so difficult to manage?

The term 'safeguarding' was introduced under the Labour administration of 1997–2010 as an attempt to broaden 'child protection' to include multi-agency support for families in need, rather than simply concentrating on investigating incidents of abuse once something bad had happened (Parton, 2011). Safeguarding is about a general vigilance towards ensuring safety, as well as the formal safeguarding system. It includes the small acts carried out each day, at work and at home – as parents, carers, practitioners and managers – to keep ourselves, our clients and our loved ones safe. It also includes the formal professional processes of sharing information, making referrals and contributing to assessment and investigation.

The term 'safeguarding' is used here to encompass two meanings: first, the careful attention needed to ensure a person's safety and wellbeing that is everyone's business; and, second, the formal system through which concerns are reported and investigated.

In the four nations of the UK, a broad spectrum of concerns are covered by safeguarding guidance, from physical and sexual abuse to neglect and discrimination (see DH, 2000; National Assembly for Wales, 2000; DHSSPSNI, 2006; Scottish Government, 2007). The types of abuse covered by such guidance may be deliberate or unintended, one-off events or cumulative breaches of a person's privacy or rights. It may often be easier to define and identify abuse than neglect; and both can take place in families, institutions and neighbourhoods, or within the confines of a relationship between just two people.

Given this diverse range, a crucial point in terms of safeguarding is the decision around when intervention should take place. The standards for assessing the threshold for intervention change over time. For example, in the UK, the physical punishment of a child used to be seen as an adult's right rather than an act of abuse, while elder abuse and intimate partner violence have only recently become matters of state and public concern (Brown and Seden, 2003; Grant, 2012). It is difficult then to define 'risk' or 'abuse' precisely, as reference points will vary over time, across different professions or agencies and in different contexts.

The picture is complicated by the sheer diversity of safeguarding concerns (see Box 15.2).

Box 15.2: Types of abuse

Abuse and neglect among older people in the UK

The UK prevalence study for older people (O'Keefe et al., 2007) suggested that 4 per cent of people aged 66 or over are neglected or abused each year, often by someone they would hope to trust. In these cases, 51 per cent of perpetrators were partners, 49 per cent were family members, 13 per cent were care workers and 5 per cent were close friends. (Note that some people reported abuse from more than one person.)

Neglect was the most frequent type of abuse, followed by financial, psychological, physical and then sexual abuse. And 6 per cent of the abused people reported two different types of abuse.

Children at risk

Children in families experiencing multiple disadvantages such as poverty and mental health issues, or where there is domestic violence and/or alcohol or substance misuse, are much more likely to be at risk than others (Cleaver et al., 2011). In 2009, child protection registrations had risen to 37,900 in England: of these registrations, 45 per cent were for neglect, 25 per cent for emotional abuse, 15 per cent for physical abuse and non-accidental injury, and 6 per cent for sexual abuse (Parton and Berridge, 2011). Most child and adult abuse takes place within the context of the family or close relationships.

Institutional abuse

In the wake of the exposure by the BBC's *Panorama* programme of abuse at Winterbourne View, and the failure to take notice of the concerns of families and former workers (Flynn, 2012), the regulator (the Care Quality Commission) made unannounced inspections. They found that nearly half of the learning disability hospitals and care homes inspected in England did not meet required standards, indicating poor management and practice which can allow abusive cultures to develop.

The difficulties of facing up to abuse

There are always going to be inherent dilemmas in health and social care work. Regarding children, there is the enduring tension between intervening to protect them from significant harm, while balancing the rights of parents to the privacy of family life. When working with vulnerable adults, there is always a dilemma about respecting individual autonomy and positive risk taking while assessing capacity in a nuanced way to promote a person's wellbeing.

The high profile, and often oversimplified, media portrayal of complex situations adds to the pressures of making difficult decisions in frequently uncertain circumstances. For example, the death of Peter Connelly in London in 2007 resulted in a high-profile media campaign and generated widespread public outrage:

> On November 11, 2008, two men were convicted of causing or allowing the death of 17-month-old Baby Peter, including his stepfather. The baby's mother had already pleaded guilty to the charge. During the trial, the court heard that Baby Peter had been used as a 'punch bag' and that his mother had deceived and manipulated professionals with lies and on one occasion had smeared him with chocolate to hide his bruises. There had been over 60 contacts with the family from a variety of health and social care professionals, and he was pronounced dead just 48 hours after a hospital doctor failed to identify that he had a broken spine. He was the subject of a child protection plan with Haringey local authority in London – the local authority that had been at the center of failures to protect Victoria Climbié in 2003.
>
> (Parton and Berridge, 2011, p. 79)

If practitioners feel they are being scrutinised rather than helped, they can become defensive; and filling in the necessary paperwork can then seem to take over from building meaningful relationships with service users. Managing such anxiety is therefore a central part of overseeing the safeguarding process.

Peter's story makes painful and overwhelming reading. What kind of emotions does reading about Peter and other stories like his evoke for you?

The Laming Report (2009) after Peter Connelly's death drew attention to the challenges of the practice context his social workers were operating in, including low morale, poor supervision and heavy caseloads. Spurred on by media scrutiny, the government commissioned the Munro Review of children's social care services to make recommendations to address these weaknesses. The review strongly criticised the narrowly prescriptive, oversimplified and heavily bureaucratised practices set out for practitioners and managers which they argued took time away from face-to-face work and the task of building relationships with families (Munro, 2011). The review highlighted some of the difficulties in balancing the need to make safeguarding procedures and practices robust and at the same time take account of the uncertainties and human dimensions of the work. Munro highlighted the management of anxiety as one key component of good practice and argued that while it is not possible to eliminate risk completely, it is possible to create organisations which support strategies to *minimise* those risks.

Among other things, therefore, managing safeguarding is about the management of often overwhelming feelings in the managers themselves and in the practitioners they manage; these can include fear and feelings of being intimidated, duped or overly drawn in. This chapter therefore stresses the contention of Parton (2006) that, to safeguard effectively, we have to *embrace* anxiety and uncertainty. The next section explores how good leadership can interrupt self-protective psychological and organisational defences to help practitioners 'do the right thing', even when it is painful and uncomfortable to do so. This will be illustrated through an unfolding case study of a manager in a young people's sexual health centre.

15.3 Managing the safeguarding process

Serious case reviews for children are carried out by Local Safeguarding Children Boards (LSCBs) in England and Wales for every case where abuse or neglect is known or suspected, and a child either dies or is seriously harmed, and there are concerns about how organisations or professionals worked together to safeguard that child.

One of the main sources of understanding about how to pick up early warning signs or investigate abusive practices has been the succession of formal inquiries and serious case reviews. Through these, the following common factors have emerged in both child and adult services.

- *The importance of a supportive organisational culture:* giving workers manageable caseloads is extremely important, as is management's ability to listen to the concerns of front-line practitioners.
- *The multi-agency nature of protection:* interprofessional collaboration and communication are essential to effective safeguarding – no single agency has the whole picture.
- *Historical awareness:* it is important to be alert to patterns of abuse and not treat each incident as a one-off discrete occurrence.

- *Fully operating safeguarding policies and procedures:* it is fundamental for each workplace to have appropriate safeguarding strategies and induction in place and that ongoing training is used to maintain a clear focus on safeguarding. There must be a designated lead to whom staff members can report suspected abuse or neglect.
- *Keep the service user in focus:* practitioners must be supported to keep the child or vulnerable adult and their family or carers (if they are not implicated in the abuse) at the centre of practice, keeping them informed and involved as much as possible.
- *The importance of taking action:* make decisions and do not procrastinate in the face of ambiguity.

Of particular relevance here is the finding that ineffective, distanced, collusive or even abusive managements have been identified as contributory factors in a range of child and adult cases (Laming, 2003, 2009; Flynn, 2012). The problem is often not that there is insufficient information, because usually several agencies have information on their records, but rather, unless something (a referral, or a visible injury or a constellation of concerns) propels that information into a multi-agency process, these pieces of the jigsaw are never assembled. When the question 'Who knew?' is asked, the answer is usually 'Everyone and no one'.

From a manager's perspective, these common factors echo the importance of the four building blocks of a **fully rounded caring manager**:

- **goal awareness** – protecting vulnerable people
- **personal awareness** – training, knowing your limitations, strong leadership
- **team awareness** – working in partnership and listening to colleagues across agency boundaries
- **contextual awareness** – knowing the wider context and history of each situation.

Suitably equipped, the caring manager has a mandate to intervene.

The manager's mandate to intervene

England, Wales, Northern Ireland and Scotland each has separate guidance setting out the duties and responsibilities of organisations to keep children safe, but they agree that a child is anyone who has not yet reached their 18th birthday and this provides managers with a clear mandate. The situation is less clear cut with adults because not all 'vulnerable' adults are at risk of 'abuse' and not all 'abused people' are 'vulnerable'. Many adults who use health or social care services can manage their own safety and access necessary services and potential sources of help if they are victimised. However, children and some vulnerable adults often do not have the capacity to make decisions in circumstances of risk, abuse or exploitation, nor can they act to remove themselves from potentially harmful situations (Flynn, 2007); they need agencies to act decisively on their behalf. Therefore, vulnerability

> is not usually caused by a single factor such as youth, frailty, disability or mental illness: it is much more likely to occur at the intersection of these factors with other forms of social disadvantage and to be complicated by insensitive or discriminatory service provision.
>
> (Brown and Seden, 2003, p. 231)

Case study 15.1: Managing intervention

Angie, a manager in a sexual health advice centre for young people, is concerned about two girls, aged 16 and 17, who dropped in at the clinic. They have been loud and provocative with the young male receptionist and no one is keen to work with them.

Angie assigns them to an experienced practitioner, Jenny. It emerges that the girls are both truanting from school and being brought to the clinic by two older men who buy them things and who they call their 'boyfriends'. The girls appear to be having unprotected sex with several different men. Although they insist they are okay and enjoy the 'parties' and the presents, Jenny is increasingly concerned about possible sexual exploitation. She is torn between the need to involve other agencies and maintaining the girls' trust, which is causing her considerable anxiety. Angie is concerned about Jenny's wellbeing as well as the risks to the young women involved.

Never ignore a safeguarding concern – if you are not sure what to do, contact the safeguarding lead in your agency or the relevant local social care team.

In this case study, Angie has to balance the agency's duty to report suspected abuse with supporting Jenny to ensure the girls remain engaged with the service. It is Angie's role to supervise Jenny, help her piece together a picture, liaise with other agencies and decide with them whether an appropriate threshold has been overstepped. Frequently, as in this case, a decision has to be made before the facts are clear.

How should Angie manage this situation? How might she draw on the four building blocks of the caring manager to consider her next steps?

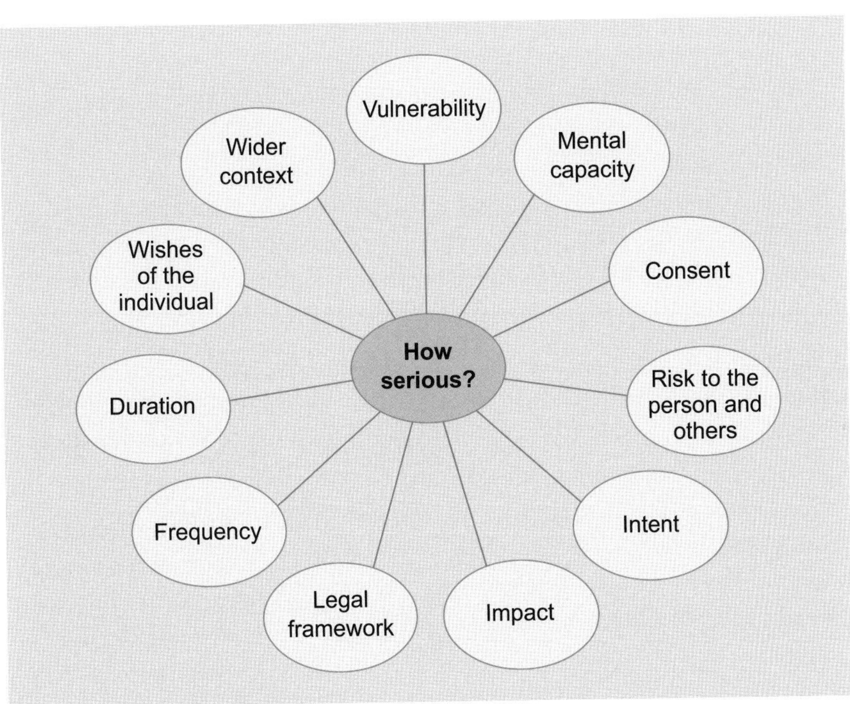

Figure 15.2 Assessing seriousness in adult safeguarding (based on Hughes, 2006, in Gaylard, 2008, p. 15)

As Figure 15.2 shows, there are several – often conflicting – factors which Angie and Jenny need to consider. Angie is concerned about the girls' wellbeing but also respects Jenny's worry that, if they act too soon, the girls could disappear from sight and become exposed to greater risk.

It is easy to forget that young people who challenge can still be vulnerable underneath, and that their defiance may mask a history of abuse and neglect (Figure 15.3).

Case study 15.2: Managing intervention (continued)

Angie telephoned her agency's child protection lead at headquarters, plus her local contacts in children's social care and the police, to discuss what to do. The social worker asked for more information and initially said that, as the girls were 16 and 17, it would be hard to prioritise the case, as children's social care was so overwhelmed.

Angie asked Jenny to find out more about the girls' home backgrounds. One of them lived in a children's home, the other was unhappy at home and stayed away as much as possible. This raised the agency's level of concern and Angie supported Jenny to discuss the agency's concerns with the girls. This was a fraught decision.

As Angie persisted with other agencies, more information about what was happening in the local area began to emerge. The police knew the local children's home; they had been called several times when girls went missing at night; they also knew that pimps were operating in the area. There was a previous allegation against some men but the Crown Prosecution Service did not pursue the case as they decided the girl in that case was not a credible witness.

Safeguarding a vulnerable child overrides confidentiality yet, given the girls' ages, this was an uncomfortable situation for Angie and Jenny as they risked losing their trust. Several agencies were now involved and the girls could legitimately feel confidentiality had been breached. Angie and Jenny believed they were doing the right thing, but it was hard, especially as children's social services had been reluctant to get involved and Angie remained concerned for Jenny in coping with her feelings of betraying the girls' trust, although it was necessary. This worry was compounded by the fact that the counsellors within the agency who used to provide support on difficult cases had recently been cut back.

Figure 15.3 Is it always easy to spot vulnerability?

What can a manager do to support practitioners both during and after a safeguarding alert?

As Angie and Jenny's experience shows, even when practitioners know they are acting in the best interests of the people they care for, acting on concerns over safeguarding issues opens up a complex emotional terrain, one in which it is often crucial to gain a multi-agency perspective.

Managing the multi-agency network

As you saw in the examples of Baby Peter and Angie, often in cases of abuse or neglect no single agency has the whole picture and it is the manager's task to piece together a picture with the practitioner across a range of agencies.

There are different ways of coordinating this, depending on the context, and in each of the four nations of the UK, arrangements are in place to manage interagency working around safeguarding. For example, in England and Wales, the social care service has the lead responsibility for coordinating the protection network for both adults and children, and partnership working is managed through Safeguarding Children and

Safeguarding Adults Boards. The importance of clear leadership and effective management to coordinate such multi-agency networks cannot be overstressed (see Box 15.3). The first stage is to clarify concerns, often through a case conference. The information and evidence gathered here have to serve three different ends:

- To establish matters of fact.
- To find out what needs the person has for immediate and long-term protection, treatment or support.
- To decide what action should and can be taken against a perpetrator and what other agencies should be involved.

(Based on Brown and Seden, 2003)

Box 15.3: Managing relationships in adult protection

Manthorpe et al. (2010) found that managers in adult safeguarding roles see building good relationships with their counterparts in other agencies and an understanding of each other's roles as key. Their research showed that effective managers resolved difficulties informally among networks as well as in formal meetings and developed information-sharing protocols which had joint agency ownership.

As the case study of the two young women shows, it can be difficult to fully and openly involve the person who is the focus of intervention as a partner in the process, and sometimes confidentiality has to be broken. Difficult as this initial meeting may be to coordinate and manage, it is important to remember that the case conference is not an end-point, but rather the start of a process for putting in place active safeguarding strategies, longer-term counselling, and support or protection. If long-term plans are made, the responsibility is too often left with social services, other agencies defining their role only in terms of initial assessment or investigation. Distributed leadership, where each agency takes responsibility for achieving its goal while communicating with each other, can help to keep all agencies more proactively and cohesively involved. This may require a focus on organisational culture, which is considered in the next section.

15.4 Promoting a safeguarding culture

Figure 15.4 The psychoanalyst Isabel Menzies Lyth (1917–2008)

> In child protection, a key responsibility of leaders is to manage the anxiety that the work generates.
>
> (Munro, 2011, p. 107)

As you have seen, a central message to emerge from serious case reviews and inquiries is the importance of supporting workers throughout and beyond the process of safeguarding. This has been written into formal processes across health and social care. For example, standards for employers and a supervision framework have been recommended to improve front-line social work practice with children (DCSF, 2010), and safeguarding training is now a routine part of training in health trusts for all staff. However, Ferguson (2011) and other writers suggest there is a need to dig below the organisational surface to understand the barriers to good safeguarding practice that may persist beneath formal processes and procedures. It is not enough to exhort people to do better when what might be stopping them is an overarching anxiety about getting it wrong.

The psychoanalyst Isabel Menzies Lyth (Figure 15.4) applied psychoanalytical ideas to understanding the conscious and unconscious processes at work in health and social care institutions (see also Chapter 6). She found that, in the face of human suffering, organisations develop mechanisms for defending against the anxieties inherent in such work. She pointed to the way in which hospitals encourage nurses to maintain an emotional detachment from patients by breaking down the work into small compartments, and privileging tasks over relationships.

Organisational defences such as these can stop people being able to talk about the pain they experience in doing their work and can permeate the whole way an organisation functions (Menzies Lyth, 1990).

Ferguson (2011) suggests that a supportive organisational culture where managers pay attention to what workers actually do and where uncomfortable feelings can be voiced is integral to safeguarding. Without this, even well-intentioned practitioners become emotionally distanced and start seeing vulnerable adults and children as 'cases' rather than 'people'. Ferguson argues that this emotional detachment is part of what happened to Peter Connelly. He highlights the fact that Peter was seen in the three days before his death by a social worker on a home visit, a paediatrician who did not examine him for injuries, and his doctor who described him as being in a 'sorry state' but did not touch him. It is certain that the child had serious injuries while in the presence of these three professionals, yet: 'The painful truth is that no one touched Peter. He was an object of disgust' (Ferguson, 2011, p. 100).

Denial and bystanding

Ferguson (2011) argues that 'denial and bystanding' can emerge as defences against anxiety, people actively 'looking away' when confronted with situations which appear utterly hopeless and incomprehensible (Cohen, 2001). This is illustrated by the five hospital nurses who, having observed Victoria Climbié's injuries in July 1999 while she was taking a bath, failed to note their concerns formally. The obstacles which exist between information and action (Cohen, 2001) help to explain how well-intentioned and experienced nurses failed to act in the face of evidence of marks and injuries on Victoria. It is one thing to know about something, quite another to act on it (Ferguson, 2011). This echoes almost all the inquiries that are referred to in this chapter and it is the job of managers to ensure their workers stay alert in ways that do not burden them to the point of inaction.

The painful nature of unbearable feelings and an unconscious desire to repress them might go some way to explaining the inaction of health and social care staff and management in such situations. The risks of this happening are much greater in organisations that do not actively work to acknowledge and support workers with their feelings.

In the case study, one of the anxieties Angie had to manage for herself and Jenny was the fear that the girls would disappear once other agencies became involved. The culture of regular supervision within the agency had been weakened with the loss of counsellors, putting at risk the resilience of the workers engaging in very stressful situations. It would have been easy for Angie to actively 'look away', in the same way social services initially tried to do.

It is an ordinary impulse to recoil from difficult, unloved children or adults almost without being aware that we have done so. In addition to having a supportive organisational culture, therefore, staying engaged and keeping the vulnerable individual in clear view means developing strong professional and **personal awareness**. Ferguson (2011) argues that, to do this, people need opportunities to explore their often uncomfortable feelings and reactions with someone else outside the situation, through sensitive supervision.

What might the unspoken anxieties have been in Angie's workplace? Did you spot any defences which stopped people confronting their difficult feelings?

Effective supervision

Ruch (2011) suggests that effective support structures and supervision can help to create 'emotionally informed thinking spaces' which can make the unbearable bearable. Yet sadly, supervision can be the first task to be dropped from crowded diaries (see Chapter 9 for more on this), and the culture of an organisation might view supervision as a luxury rather than as integral to safe practice. Workers in low-status employment, such as care assistants in care homes or children's homes, often do not receive the sort of supervision that might help them reflect on complex situations. Regular and good quality supervision within the context of a trusting relationship where uncomfortable feelings can be voiced can radically alter how a situation is viewed and how a practitioner responds in the face of upsetting and alarming experiences.

As a manager, making time for your own reflection is also crucial so that staff can see you operating from a position of integrity and congruence.

Effective supervision can also help to uncover and explore biases which may prevent action being taken. Munro (2008) suggests that once people have formed a picture of a person or situation, they have a strong tendency to 'cling' to that belief and then often 'overgeneralise' from specific pieces of evidence. Exploring assumptions, bias and emotions is a complicated aspect of supervising anyone involved in safeguarding. Emotion can be a useful source of intelligence about a situation (see Chapter 2) but it is hard for people to be objective about their own thinking and emotions. The 'rule of optimism' – whereby practitioners are likely to put the most positive spin on situations – has also been identified as a potential bias in safeguarding (Dingwall et al., 1995). Supervisors like Angie should, therefore, help to create a culture in which challenging a decision is seen not as a personal criticism but as an intellectual task that is 'morally necessary' to ensure the best standards of care for service users (Munro, 2008).

Where would you go for support to explore difficult experiences and emotions? Are there ways to boost that support?

15.5 Leading with integrity and resilience

Case study 15.3: Managing intervention (continued)

In a supervision session with Jenny, Angie learned that before she joined the agency, another practitioner, Jeff, had worked with the girls but they had behaved inappropriately with him, making sexual advances. He decided that it wasn't worth putting a lot of energy into them and they could look after themselves. Jenny felt that this had influenced the general feeling towards the girls, including why the young receptionist, Bryn, was so reluctant to deal with them. Jenny and Angie didn't know, but Bryn had his suspicions that the girls were vulnerable because he had seen them in local bars drinking with much older men, but had taken his lead from Jeff and preferred to steer clear of the whole issue. After all, he was 'just the receptionist'; surely they were old enough to look after themselves if what he saw in the bars was anything to go by. He just didn't want to get involved!

As you have seen, managers can play a role in promoting safe practice by promoting a culture within which uncomfortable and difficult feelings can be voiced. Using their leadership skills, they can also demonstrate a clear commitment to supporting staff and service users, however tough the situation is. For example, Angie supported Jenny but, with her heavy work commitments, it was unlikely she would have uncovered Bryn's true feelings about the young women very easily. Evidence shows that there are commonly such pockets of informal information that are not turned into more formal concerns or complaints. Often this is the result of protection strategies used to 'depersonalise' the situation and 'withdraw' from it (Hughes and Pengelly, 1997).

In Angie's case, Jeff's personal unease with the girls' behaviour towards him made him step back from his professional awareness of their vulnerability. Instead of seeing their emergent sexuality being taken advantage of, he started mistrusting and blaming them. The second strategy, of withdrawal behind the lines, often involves retreating to the 'primary task' and applying it rigidly, as Bryn did: 'I'm just the receptionist'. You also saw this in operation with the initial response of the children's social services, their priority being 'children' rather than young people over the age of consent. Such strategies can have serious implications for interagency collaboration. Therefore, a manager needs to be aware of these processes in operation, as well as attentive to information that is emerging from a range of sometimes conflicting sources.

How might Angie have supported Bryn to stay engaged with these difficult young people without having to feel vulnerable himself?

Good leaders manage safety

Jeff and Bryn had felt uncomfortable and, while they may not have been at risk of physical harm themselves, if their concerns were not managed effectively, it might have stopped them performing their roles effectively. Braithwaite (2012) notes that little attention has been paid – in either national or local safeguarding policies – to the issue of risk to staff and not just to vulnerable client groups. Fear often triggers avoidant behaviour and it is little wonder that young, inexperienced, often female, health and social care workers baulk at visiting homes where they may feel threatened or intimidated.

In England and Wales, 9.4 per cent of social workers and probation officers have reported being assaulted at work, and 9.5 per cent have been threatened, compared with an average of 1.2 per cent for all occupational groups (Littlechild, 2005). Healthcare staff are also affected by violence: 55,993 physical assaults against NHS staff were reported in England in 2007/08. One-third of lone community-based nurses have reported being assaulted or harassed while at work (BBC News, 2007; NHSBSA, 2009). Findings from the British Crime Survey on risk of violence at work indicated that health and associate health professionals were among the most at-risk occupations (HSE, 2012); while a survey in 2010 of social workers and managers revealed that one-third had been physically assaulted and 90 per cent had been verbally abused while on duty (Community Care, 2010).

Despite a lone-working policy in the NHS (NHSBSA, 2009), two-thirds of lone-working nurses said that their employers did not always know their whereabouts and almost three-quarters did not always receive all the information they needed about the risks associated with a home visit (BBC News, 2007).

Other research has shown that, although physical violence is usually reported to management, there is serious underreporting of verbal threats and abuse and that this can have a cumulative effect on practitioners' wellbeing over time (Littlechild, 2005). Many of the social workers in Littlechild's study were reluctant to report verbal threats and abuse because they were so commonplace. Even service users who were frightening were still perceived as vulnerable and this sort of risk was seen as part of the job of working with 'difficult' people. However, despite the fact that many health and social care sector staff routinely absorb such risks, it still takes its toll, which managers should remain aware of.

Under health and safety legislation, safety at work is the joint responsibility of the organisation and the individual but it is often the line manager who holds responsibility on behalf of the organisation for ensuring 'safe working'. With good supports and explicit risk management in place, it is possible to support workers even in situations of high risk. Recognition by senior management of the demands placed on staff, and an acknowledgement that arrangements should be in place to ensure effective staff support for all, develops 'environmental resilience' at the organisational level. This approach has made a difference even in the most extreme settings. For example, applied in the most disturbed prisoner programme in HM Prison Service, the benefits appeared to include improved morale, well-functioning teams, and a calm and ordered atmosphere (Clarke, 2008).

The place of whistleblowing

When adequate supervision and support are *not* in place, individuals can end up having to negotiate anxiety and uncertainty on their own, sometimes through whistleblowing. In the case study, Jenny was lucky that Angie supported her in exploring her concerns. However, there is not always someone to support a practitioner in this way, especially when abuse appears to be happening at an institutional level (see Box 15.4).

Box 15.4: Whistleblowing

Margaret Haywood was initially struck off the nursing register for going under cover in a BBC *Panorama* television programme to expose poor patient care on an elderly people's ward. She said:

> I did voice my concerns through my immediate line manager and I also went to my ward manager but nothing was really taken on board.
>
> (BBC News, 2009)

Crucially, she received the support of her professional association – the Royal College of Nursing – with her appeal and was later reinstated. She explained her motivation as follows:

> I was convinced that it was the right thing to do. I had reported the issues and nothing had been done. I felt I owed it to the people on the ward.
>
> (The Guardian, 2009)

As a whistleblower, Margaret Haywood had to step outside her organisation to be heard; she demonstrated courage and resilience as a leader in standing up for what she believed in. However, sometimes it is possible to take a moral stand *within* the organisation, as evidenced by the case of Roger Jones (see Box 15.1).

He used the advantage of his positional authority, together with clear situational leadership, to exert his power within BBC Wales and Children in Need to voice his concerns. Box 15.5 describes the protection available for whistleblowers like Margaret Haywood.

Box 15.5: Protection for whistleblowers

Professional whistleblowers are protected by the Public Interest Disclosure at Work Act 1999 and can be bound by their own codes of professional conduct if they belong to one of the professions with a duty to report unsafe practice (see also Chapter 19). However, as whistleblowers can face marginalisation and even dismissal, it is important to get advice from organisations such as Public Concern at Work if you ever consider whistleblowing.

15.6 Conclusion

Every day, children and vulnerable adults are kept safe by the actions of practitioners and their managers. Policies and formal procedures alone will not secure a safe outcome for vulnerable service users and patients unless managers make thoughtful decisions, support the practitioners involved, and work with the different agencies implicated. This will depend on their ability to grasp the issues, pick out what is salient in a host of complex and conflicting information, be clear about the thresholds for intervention, have a clear understanding of different types of risk, and be able to make a critical analysis of the needs of everyone involved. Frequently, it also requires the conviction of a determined leader acting on what they believe to be the best interests of the people they work with and care for.

Some writers have argued that effective safeguarding requires a larger social policy infrastructure and resources to underpin it (Reece and Stein, 2012). However, in the meantime, managers need to keep an eye on the needs of vulnerable individuals and groups, and support their staff as they go about this crucial, yet emotionally challenging, aspect of their work. Therefore, it is helpful for managers working in safeguarding to be mindful of the four building blocks of the **fully rounded caring manager**: **personal awareness** and **team awareness** enable a manager to recognise the impact that stressful work has on both them and their team physically and emotionally, as well as the need for effective support; **goal awareness** and **contextual awareness** require a manager to keep sight of the aim everyone is working towards while being conscious of the challenging environment in which they strive to reach that goal.

Key points

- Safeguarding covers a whole spectrum of risk management from everyday mistreatments and boundary violations to serious cases of abuse and neglect.
- Managers can draw on legislation, regulation and guidance in effective safeguarding, but when and how to act is always a matter of judgement, informed by experience, research and clear thinking.
- Ineffective, distanced, collusive or even abusive management has repeatedly been identified as a contributory factor in a range of cases where safeguarding has failed vulnerable adults and children.
- Usually, no single agency has the whole picture; contributing to and managing multi-agency communication is therefore an important aspect of protecting vulnerable people.
- An open and supportive organisational culture and regular supervision that encourages workers to share their anxieties are key to promoting protection for vulnerable service users and patients.

References

BBC News (2007) 'Lone nurses "at risk of attack"', 8 July [Online], http://news.bbc.co.uk/1/hi/health/6276680.stm (Accessed 17 July 2012).

BBC News (2009) 'Calls for whistle-blower review', 16 April [Online], http://news.bbc.co.uk/go/pr/fr/-/1/hi/england/sussex/8003228.stm (Accessed 23 January 2013).

BBC News (2012) 'Jimmy Savile: Children in Need had ban – Sir Roger Jones', 29 October [Online], www.bbc.co.uk/news/uk-wales-20120302 (Accessed 10 November 2012).

Braithwaite, R. (2012) *Guide to Working in Fear – How to work and practise when you feel frightened* [Online], www.ccinform.co.uk/articles (Accessed 15 June 2012).

Brown, H. and Seden, J. (2003) 'Managing to protect', in Seden, J. and Reynolds, J. (eds) *Managing Care in Practice*, Milton Keynes, London, Routledge/ The Open University, pp. 219–48 (K303 Set Book).

Clarke, J. (2008) 'Promoting professional resilience', in Calder, M.C. (ed.) *Contemporary Risk Assessment in Safeguarding Children*, Lyme Regis, Russell House Publishing.

Cleaver, H., Unell, I. and Aldgate, J. (2011) *Children's Needs – Parenting Capacity. Child abuse: parental mental illness, learning disability, substance misuse and domestic violence* (2nd edition), London, The Stationery Office. Available online at www.education.gov.uk (Accessed 3 October 2012).

Cohen, S. (2001) *States of Denial: Knowing about Atrocities and Suffering*, Cambridge, Polity Press.

Community Care (2010) 'Social workers subject to abuse, threats and violence?', 5 May [Online], www.communitycare.co.uk/social-workers-subject-to-abuse-threat (Accessed 21 July 2012).

Department for Children, Schools and Families (DCSF) (2010) *Working Together to Safeguard Children*, London, The Stationery Office.

Department of Health (DH) (2000) *No Secrets: guidance on developing and implementing multi-agency policies and procedures to protect vulnerable adults from abuse*, London, The Stationery Office.

Department of Health (DH) (2004) *Committee of Inquiry – Independent investigation into how the NHS handled allegations about the conduct of Clifford Ayling*, London, The Stationery Office.

Department of Health, Social Services and Public Safety Northern Ireland (DHSSPSNI) (2006) *Safeguarding Vulnerable Adults: regional adult protection policy and procedure guidance*, Ballymena, Social Services Directorate.

Dingwall, R., Eekalaar, J. and Murray, T. (1995) *The Protection of Children: State intervention and family life* (2nd edition), Oxford, Blackwell.

Ferguson, H. (2011) *Child Protection Practice*, Basingstoke, Palgrave Macmillan.

Flynn, M. (2007) *The Murder of Steven Hoskin: A Serious Case Review* [Online], Cornwall Adult Protection Committee, www.cornwall.gov.uk (Accessed 22 October 2012).

Flynn, M. (2012) *South Gloucestershire Safeguarding Adults Board: Winterbourne View Hospital* [Online], http://hosted.southglos.gov.uk/wv/report.pdf (Accessed 2 October 2012).

Gaylard, D. (2008) 'Policy to practice', in Mantell, A. and Scragg, T. (eds) *Safeguarding Adults in Social Work*, Exeter, Learning Matters, pp. 9–30.

Grant, G. (2012) 'Safeguarding vulnerable adults over the life course', in Katz, J., Peace, S. and Spurr, S. (eds) *Adult Lives: A life course perspective*, Bristol, The Policy Press/The Open University, pp. 230–41 (K319 Set Book).

Guardian (2009) 'Nurse struck off for secret filming of hospital for BBC's Panorama', 17 April [Online], www.guardian.co.uk (Accessed 24 January 2013).

Health and Safety Executive (HSE) (2012) *Violence at Work: Violence at work statistics from the 2010/11 British Crime Survey and RIDDOR* [Online], www.hse.gov.uk/statistics/ (Accessed 15 January 2013).

Hughes, J. (2006) *Chairing Multiagency Adult Protection Meetings*, Isle of Wight, Making Connections, Training and Consultancy.

Hughes, L. and Pengelly, P. (1997) *Staff Supervision in a Turbulent Environment*, London, Jessica Kingsley.

Laming, Lord H. (2003) *Victoria Climbié Inquiry Report*, London, The Stationery Office.

Laming, Lord H. (2009) *The Protection of Children in England: A Progress Report*, London, The Stationery Office.

Littlechild, B. (2005) 'The stresses arising from violence, threats and aggression against child protection social workers', *Journal of Social Work*, vol. 5, pp. 61–82.

Manthorpe, J., Hussein, S. and Penhale, B. (2010) 'Managing relations in adult protection: a qualitative study of the views of social services managers in England and Wales', *Journal of Social Work Practice*, vol. 24, no. 4, pp. 363–76.

Menzies Lyth, I.E.P. (1990) 'A psychoanalytical perspective on social institutions', in Trist, E. and Murray, H. (eds) *The Social Engagement of Social Science, Volume 1: The socio-psychological perspective*, London, Free Association Books.

Munro, E. (2008) 'Improving reasoning in supervision', *Social Work Now*, no. 40, August, pp. 3–10.

Munro, E. (2011) *The Munro Review of Child Protection: Final Report – a child-centred system*, London, The Stationery Office. Available online at www.education.gov.uk/munroreview (Accessed 21 July 2012).

National Assembly for Wales (2000) *In Safe Hands: implementing adult protection procedures in Wales*, Cardiff, National Assembly for Wales.

NHSBSA (2009) *Not Alone: A guide for the better protection of lone workers in the NHS* [Online], www.nhsbsa.nhs.uk/Documents/Security Management (Accessed 21 July 2012).

Nolan, C. (2012) 'I didn't make a fuss ... no one did back then', *The Mirror*, 1 October [Online], www.mirror.co.uk/news/uk-news/coleen-nolan-on-sir-jimmy-savile-1353195 (Accessed 14 January 2013).

O'Keefe, M., Hills, A., Doyle, M., McCreadie, C., Scholes, S., Constantine, R., Tinker, A., Manthorpe, J., Biggs, S. and Erens, B. (2007) *UK Study of the Abuse and Neglect of Older People: Prevalence survey report*, London, Comic Relief and Department of Health.

Parton, N. (2006) *Safeguarding Childhood: Early intervention and surveillance in a late modern society*, Basingstoke, Palgrave Macmillan.

Parton, N. (2011) 'Child protection and safeguarding in England: changing and competing conceptions of risk and their implications for social work', *British Journal of Social Work*, vol. 41, pp. 854–75.

Parton, N. and Berridge, D. (2011) 'Child protection in England', in Gilbert, N., Parton, N. and Skivenes, M. (eds) *Child Protection Systems: International trends and orientations*, Oxford, Oxford University Press, pp. 60–88.

Reece, G. and Stein, M. (2012) 'Older children and the child protection system', in Blyth, M. and Solomon, E. (eds) *Effective Safeguarding for Children and Young People*, Bristol, The Policy Press.

Rich, A. (1977) *Women and Honor: Some notes on lying*, Pittsburgh, Penn., Motheroot Press. Available online at www.goodreads.com/quotes/257040-lying-is-done-with-words-and-also-with-silence (Accessed 8 April 2013).

Ruch, G. (2011) 'Where have all the feelings gone? Developing reflective and relationship-based management in child-care social work', *British Journal of Social Work*, 5 October, pp. 1–18.

Scottish Government (2007) *Adult Support and Protection (Scotland) Act*, Edinburgh, The Stationery Office.

Chapter 16 Morals and ethics in leadership and management

Richard Hester and Anita Rogers

16.1 Introduction

Figure 16.1 Are you morally active?

> Unsurprisingly the effect of people living longer has been to put the social care system under greater strain. Concerns have been raised about the quality of services people have been receiving. A report last year by the Equality and Human Rights Commission described cases of people being left in bed for 17 hours or more between care visits and a failure to wash people regularly. But those are the 'lucky' ones who get help at all.
>
> (BBC News, 2012a)

> Barclays chief executive Bob Diamond resigned this morning with immediate effect over the rate-fixing scandal at the bank ... The bank's chairman, Marcus Agius, who had yesterday announced his own departure from the bank, will instead stay on and become full-time chairman, tasked with leading the search for a new chief executive.
>
> (The Week, 2012)

The two very disparate situations described above, at face value, have little in common. The first is just one example of several scandals that have been exposed within the health and social care sector. The other is an example set in the context of the tensions caused by the disparity in pay between the very wealthy people in our society and everyone else. There is a slight irony here with Figure 16.1. It was Benjamin Franklin (1706–1790), smiling enigmatically on the US$100 bill, who once said, 'Sell not virtue to purchase wealth, nor liberty to purchase power'. This is probably as good a place as any to start a discussion on ethics and morality.

The common thread, of course, is that both opening quotations raise ethical and moral issues, not dissimilar to those that a manager or leader faces in their everyday work in health and social care.

'The world today seems to be conspiring against trust … the patterns and routines we invest with the authority to guide our lives all too often fail to repay trust's devotion' (Bauman, 2008, p. 64).

Zygmunt Bauman's book on *Postmodern Ethics* (1993) suggests that the conditions in which we experience contemporary life make it more important than ever that we, as individuals, act on ethical standpoints through 'moral impulse' rather than be guided by 'the rule book'. He argues that moral and ethical issues must be dealt with at a personal level – face to face, one to one – in a way that is both unconditional and infinite, beyond any rational weighing up of an imaginary ledger of 'rights' and 'wrongs'. This seems like quite a tall order but it is by no means a new idea (Figure 16.2).

In Charles Dickens's novel *Great Expectations* (1861), when Philip Pirrip wraps up a piece of pork pie for Abel Magwitch, a starving convict, he does it through a moral impulse, not because he is frightened or thinks it will change his life.

Figure 16.2 Moral impulse?

If we need to engage with morality in a new, proactive way – although not everyone agrees (see, for example, Ten Bos, 1997) – then it poses a challenge to leaders and managers in the health and social care professions to make sure that, through their position of authority, they can act in a moral and ethical way in order to avoid yet another exposé of uncaring nurses or thoughtless care assistants. Furthermore, it is their responsibility to see that their colleagues, who are often staff accountable to them, understand why it is important to fully grasp the moral and ethical context they work in, and to think of ethical issues as part of their everyday work–life experience.

To help your understanding of morals and ethics, this chapter looks at several ethical frameworks which underpin what Bauman (2008) describes as 'normative regulation'. It also examines a few definitions of words such as 'moral', 'ethical', 'values' and, importantly, 'need', which may impact on the way in which you as a manager carry out your responsibilities. This then leads to the idea of the *morally active manager* (Husband, 1995). It is suggested this is more important than ever as a concept for leaders and managers in health and social care, in addressing some of the crises that we will, no doubt, continue to encounter in the future.

This chapter addresses the following core questions.

- How should we consider the claim that the practice of health and social care is a moral and ethical enterprise?
- How might we examine some ethical dilemmas in everyday practice?
- What is required for a manager in health and social care to be morally active?

16.2 Competing frameworks

The journey starts with a review of two of the main ways of moral reasoning suggested by moral philosophers in the European tradition – deontology and utilitarianism. Then there is a short review of the most commonly encountered ethical theories that will help managers and leaders in health and social care settings. From there begins the exploration of how leaders and managers can reflect and act on the ethical issues that inform everyday practice in health and social care.

This chapter considers *morals* to be the guiding principles for everyday life and *ethics* to be the manual that we may refer to in order to judge 'what to do'.

'Deontology' comes from the Greek word *deon*, meaning duty or law. It is often associated with 'non-consequentialism'; that is, a focus on *intention* rather than *outcome*.

Deontology

Theories of deontology are of special relevance to health and social care workers. The concept of deontology suggests that our moral conduct should be guided by *universally* recognisable rules and regulations which it is our duty to obey. In other words, we should do that which we ought to do because it is the right thing to do and it is our duty to do it. That is, we should conduct ourselves in such an ethical manner as to reflect other more universal principles of conduct than merely concern for the consequences of our actions.

Many of the professional codes of conduct are based on ethical principles embedded in the moral theories of deontology: for example, the *Nursing and Midwifery Council Professional Code of Conduct*, which is binding for all UK-registered nurses; the *Medical Research Council Code for Researchers*; and *The British Association of Social Work Code of Ethics*.

The German philosopher Immanuel Kant (Figure 16.3) is perhaps best known for the moral theory of deontology. To explain it, he developed three 'categorical imperatives' (see Box 16.1).

Box 16.1: Kant's categorical imperatives

Figure 16.3 Immanuel Kant (1724–1804)

Kant developed these imperatives in order to direct and inform the 'moral agent' along specific lines of arguments and judgements:

- Act only according to that maxim by which you can also will that it would become a universal law.

> - Act in such a way that you always treat humanity, whether in your own person or in the person of any other, never simply as a means, but always at the same time as an end.
> - Act as though you were, through your maxims, a law-making member of a kingdom of ends.

Basically, according to this theory, when we consider our moral actions, we should be capable of following universal moral principles, which we are happy to follow and happy for other people to follow, in order to demonstrate respect towards others and the duty that we owe to them.

According to this view, what moral or ethical failings may have caused the situations reported in the opening quotations?

One well-known framework within the Kantian tradition is the 'four principles approach' developed by Beauchamp and Childress (2008):

1 Respect for autonomy: that is, the moral obligation to respect the autonomy of each individual and to treat people as 'ends' in themselves rather than just 'means to ends'.

2 Beneficence: that is, doing good.

3 Non-maleficence: that is, not doing harm, as emphasised in the Hippocratic Oath.

4 Justice: that is, the moral obligation to deal fairly in the face of competing claims.

(Based on Dawson and Butler, 2003, p. 240)

'In a pure and holy way, I will guard my life and my art and science' (part of the Hippocratic Oath).

However, there are several problems with such a principles-based approach. One is the problem of *interpretation*. For example, what does 'doing good' mean in a particular circumstance? Second, as Bauman said, moral responsibility should not depend on a rational calculation. Third, and perhaps the most well-known critique of a deontological position, is the scenario of a terrorist who knows the location of a bomb that will kill thousands of people. Is it right to suspend your ethical standpoint about that one individual, and force them to tell you the location of the bomb (by torture if necessary) for the benefit of the thousands who will die?

Clearly, interpretation is difficult and, perhaps not surprisingly, not all sets of principles are the same. For example, in social work, the 'four stocks of ethical practice' (Clark, 2000) – respect, justice, citizenship and discipline – include the notion of community, which is absent from the four principles approach. Ann Gallagher (2011), a nursing ethicist, applies a 'four-quadrant approach' to the ethical issue of restraint. She tells Cora's story (see the case study below), and analyses it using the four-quadrant principles of *medical indications*, *quality of life*, *patient preferences* and *contextual features*.

Case study 16.1: Cora's story

Cora Jamison recently moved from her home to a nursing home. She has a diagnosis of dementia and is becoming increasingly frail. She wanders continuously around the home and repeatedly goes to the front door and says she wants to go home. One of the staff tells her: 'You cannot go home today. It's Sunday and there is no transport.' Mrs Jamison accepts this and continues to wander from room to room.

Staff discuss how to manage Mrs Jamison. Her husband is particularly anxious that she remains safe; he tells staff when she was at home he had to ensure doors were locked and she had a table fixed on her chair to prevent her from getting up so she could rest. He suggests staff might use a tracking device that will sound an alarm if she attempts to leave the home.

(Gallagher, 2011, p. 19)

Mrs Jamison's case suggests psychological and technological restraints, which are far removed from the emphasis on autonomy in Beauchamp and Childress's four principles approach. Using the four-quadrant approach raises several questions (Gallagher, 2011, p. 20).

- What are her capabilities? What are the goals for her care? What other interventions might be considered? *(Medical indications)*
- What distress is Mrs Jamison experiencing? Will the tracking device be a cost or a benefit to the quality of her life? *(Quality of life)*

- What does Mrs Jamison want? Does she have the capacity to express her preferences? *(Patient preferences)*
- What are the family, legal, religious or cultural issues that must be considered? *(Contextual features)*

There are no easy answers to these questions and a compromise may be inevitable to maintain Mrs Jamison's safety.

As you can see from Cora's story, making an ethical and moral decision about an intervention in the life of another person, whichever framework or set of principles is used, requires a manager and their staff to exercise reflective vigilance. The four quadrants highlight Mrs Jamison's needs and capacities as an individual within the context of her immediate social relationships. What is less of a consideration in this case is the balance between need and resources and that, in itself, can lead to an altogether different way of looking at ethical issues.

As a counterargument to such principled approaches, the idea of utilitarianism is examined next.

Utilitarianism

Utilitarianism is a form of ethical reasoning which primarily concerns the *end result* of our actions. It suggests, when deciding on a particular moral activity, consideration should be given to the amount of good and public welfare that will be increased through our actions, rather than our intentions to act morally.

Perhaps the greatest exponent of this form of ethical reasoning was the British philosopher John Stuart Mill (1806–1873). Based on the work of the social reformer Jeremy Bentham (1748–1832), Mill suggested that what people desire most from life is happiness and contentment and thus most of our actions should be geared towards attaining and promoting this goal. However, Mill's interpretation of the moral philosophy of utilitarianism ultimately differed significantly from Bentham's original ideas. For Mill, a moral act was considered good if it promoted the happiness and wellbeing of *the majority* of the people. Inbuilt into this theory, however, was a conscious recognition that some individuals might 'lose out' and that the wishes of a minority of individuals may well be overruled or disregarded for the 'greater good' of the whole community. Utilitarianism thus rejects *personal* bias, thereby avoiding the problems associated with a multitude of possible principles and the subsequent clashes between them (Brykczynska and Simons, 2011).

As Brykczynska and Simons (2011, pp. 27–28) suggest:

> Accordingly, it could be argued that the shortened working hours for health-care workers legislated by the European Union is a utilitarian solution to individual preferences (and work practices). Overall, more good will be accomplished if patients are treated by rested and healthy carers than if they are looked after by dangerously exhausted staff. Thus, even if we personally wanted to and were prepared to work extra hours in the day or week, this approach might not be in the long-term interest of our patients and the majority of other health-care staff. In such a case, we should be prepared to put aside our personal preferences … and accept those decisions which promote the common good for the majority …

This theory can be applied to the case of Cora.

Case study 16.2: Cora's story (continued)

Before moving to the care home, the sticking point for Cora was her pet goldfish to which she had become emotionally attached. The goldfish was one of the few objects, or indeed living things, with which Cora still had a relationship. It was clear that the rules of the residential home categorically stated that no pets were allowed. At one point, the move to the care home was in jeopardy due to the impasse.

Eventually, the management team agreed to allow an exception to be made for Mrs Jamison so that she could keep her goldfish. Her husband was struck by all the fuss that was made over what seemed to him to be a very small issue and one that was clearly in the interests of both Cora and the staff looking after her.

Can you think of any utilitarian arguments that would either justify this decision or preclude it?

As far as Mr Jamison was concerned, Cora *needed* to have her pet goldfish with her, and he could see no reason why this should be prevented. Yet the care home had to follow protocol and consider the potential impact on other residents as well. For Cora, abstract issues of the 'greater good' would seem somewhat redundant here. There are, of course, many other frameworks informing moral reasoning and ethical decision making, and perhaps one of the most pervasive in health and social care is the idea that everyone has certain 'needs' and 'rights' which can provide a practical framework for action. Yet, in a sector where resources are rarely in abundance, one of the primary questions we have to consider first is 'What constitutes "need"?'

The concept of need

In the context of health and social care, need is often the pivot around which decisions are made about individuals. However, when decisions have to be made that weigh one need against others, it is never straightforward or obvious. Need drives the development of services and the allocation of resources. Yet the concept of need is subject to interpretation and is therefore not unproblematic. The rest of this section addresses the following questions.

What does someone need to live an autonomous, fully participative life?

- What is need?
- Who defines it?
- How is the balance of need and resource resolved?

An *objective* view of need distinguishes between 'needs' and 'desires'. Unlike desires, if needs are not satisfied, serious harm of some objective kind will result (Feinberg, 1973, 1984, 1986). Needs in the objective view are related to certain biological, psychological and socially necessary components to human agency, health and wellbeing, such as those in the famous 'hierarchy of needs' identified by the American psychologist Abraham Maslow (1908–1970) (see Maslow, 1970).

In this sense, needs can be independent of people's knowledge of them. For example, even before the action of the hormone insulin was understood, and artificial forms of it were available, people with diabetes still needed insulin (Doyal and Gough, 1991). However, while some basic needs which can be objectively identified – such as the need for water and food – might be assumed to be taken for granted in health and social care practice, sometimes even these are not met.

For instance, in 2011, more than 150 National Health Service patients in England and Wales either starved to death or died from dehydration in hospital, according to the Office for National Statistics (Osborne, 2012).

As an alternative to an objective view, a *constructivist* view of need suggests that many needs depend on the prevailing social conditions; in other words, they are socially constructed. Needs in this context are recognised as such only if they are considered legitimate by a particular society. The society in which you live therefore influences what is recognised as a need. People living in poverty, for example, often live in need of the basics of life. However, poverty in the UK is calculated in different ways, depending on whether it is considered as 'relative' or 'absolute' poverty. Absolute poverty is the state of severe deprivation of basic human needs, whereas relative poverty is being below some relative income threshold, where this threshold differs for each society or country. For example, someone considered to be in relative poverty in the UK would be considered wealthy in another, less affluent country.

The use of relativity as a concept to measure poverty can be unhelpful, as described graphically in this report from 2012:

> A fall in income throughout society in tough economic times has meant that thousands of families have been lifted above the poverty line without their circumstances changing at all.
>
> The number of children living in poverty in the UK fell by 300,000 last year as household incomes dropped, official figures have revealed.
>
> (BBC News, 2012b)

In such situations, semantic distinctions between 'objective' and 'socially constructed' needs do not explain to struggling families that, in relative terms, they are now 'better off'. Nor does it explain what happened to the patients whose basic human needs were not met and who died from dehydration or starvation in hospital.

So why is it that even basic needs are sometimes unfulfilled? Given the range of ethical frameworks and moral codes to follow, why do crises like those reported in the opening quotation still occur? To help answer this question, the next section explores the nature of *organisational socialisation*, the issue of *proximity in decision making* and the phenomenon of *organisational terrorism*. It looks at the roles they play in creating individual and systemic flaws in the moral fabric of services in health and social care.

16.3 Weak links in the moral chain

The weakest link?

Art Wolfe is an American ethicist who, in a seminal paper on business ethics published in 1991, addressed how things can go so wrong in organisations whose central purpose is to protect and enhance the human condition. He noted that, in large organisations, individuals become associated with their role rather than their personal identity, and are 'shuffled like playing cards' for organisational ends. Wolfe suggested there is a danger of 'moral conditioning' of individuals in large organisations, where they are left unable to resist authority even when they know it is wrong. The power of the organisation is such that they fail to see themselves as separate moral agents. (Chapter 12 also explores the power of organisational culture.)

'In our large institutions, we do what the man in charge says and let our individual consciences slip away' (Wolfe, 1991, p. 425).

In addition, Wolfe argued that large institutions introduce the problem of proximity, that is the physical and emotional distance from the decision maker to the final recipient of the impact of that decision:

> The decision makers are, I assume, reasonable, humane, sensitive individuals, yet by the time their decision reaches its destination, the impact is often tragic.
>
> (Wolfe, 1991, p. 427)

Wolfe suggested that, when we act individually our whole range of sensing abilities, including our conscience, is involved, and we see and feel the impact of our actions. But this proximity is lost in large institutions (see Box 16.2).

Box 16.2: Negative influences on care

There is an example of how well-meaning individual behaviours can be influenced by the organisation in which people work in the independent inquiry into care provided by Mid Staffordshire NHS Foundation Trust (2010). A significantly higher death rate than was expected between 2005 and 2009 triggered the inquiry, which found numerous people had 'appalling experiences' due to'systemic failings'.

The report recognised a lack of management and leadership:

> It is difficult to believe that lapses on the scale that was evidenced could have occurred if there had been an adequately implemented system of nursing and ward management.
>
> I got no sense that the nurses had any protection whatsoever … they were not supported …
>
> (Consultant's testimony)

A previous patient also recognised that the situation nurses found themselves in could not have been easy for them:

> I cannot believe that supposedly fully trained nurses with vocation, care and compassion gain any satisfaction from such an abysmal situation.
>
> (Patient's testimony)

It was recognised that 'many staff, during the period under investigation, did express concerns about the standard of care being provided. The tragedy was that they were ignored.'

People are 'socialised', often very quickly, into fulfilling the expectations of the organisation they work in. The very famous Stanford University prison experiments illustrate this with shocking results

(Zimbardo, 1972). Volunteers were assigned the role of either prison guard or prisoner. Within six days the experiment had to be abandoned as the volunteers had assumed the roles of abusive prison guard and victimised prisoner, respectively. Several 'prisoners' even had breakdowns.

This is important because most people are members of particular communities – be they professional, political or cultural. As such, they are conditioned to see, experience and interpret things in a certain way. We are also subject to prevailing social paradigms, such as capitalism, which shape the meaning we give to any circumstance (Wolfe, 1991). Rogers (2009) explored the extent to which those involved in health and social care are collectively caught in this particular paradigm. Many employees, regardless of a fundamental commitment to doing a good job, feel 'stuck' in unsatisfactory working conditions. Perhaps they disagree with the latest policy that has 'come down' from central government, and which they must now implement. However, they are cautious or unwilling to 'rock the boat' for fear of repercussions, as they have 'jobs to keep and mortgages to pay'. There is a real tension here between the commitment to 'do a good job' and the uncertain prospects of capitalism in crisis.

The report of the Mid Staffordshire NHS Foundation Trust inquiry identified real fear among staff, which probably prevented them taking constructive action to improve patient care, as follows.

- There was an atmosphere of fear of adverse repercussions. Several staff witnesses described a forceful style of management (perceived by some as bullying) which was used occasionally.
- The high priority placed on meeting targets generated a fear that failure to meet them could lead to dismissal.
- Understaffing was a constant problem and staff even expressed fear about losing their registration because of the unsafe care delivered as a result.

Typically, people make one of four responses to such 'organisational terrorism' (Caldwell and Canuto-Carranco, 2010): exit, voice, neglect or loyalty. Of these four, voice is the ethical choice and, while this action requires courage and risk taking, examples abound where individuals or groups decide to challenge unethical behaviour (see Box 16.3).

Box 16.3: Responding to organisational terrorism

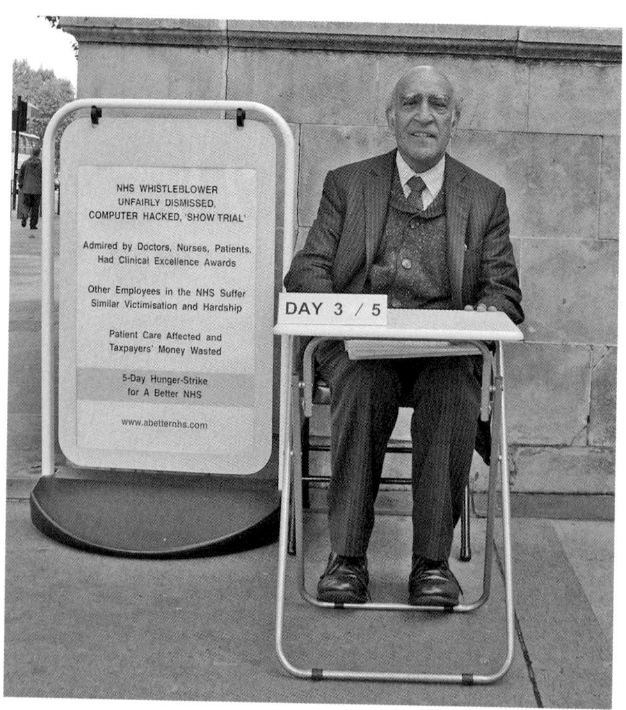

Figure 16.4 The consequences of speaking out

Dr Narinder Kapur, a leading neuropsychologist, was dismissed from his post in 2010, allegedly as a result of 'whistleblowing'. He spoke out against the use of underqualified and unsupervised staff, which he said was putting patients at risk. In October 2012, he staged a five-day hunger strike outside the Department of Health's head office to protest against the treatment of whistleblowers in the health service (Figure 16.4).

Speaking at the start of his hunger strike, Dr Kapur said he drew on inspiration from Gandhi and his faith: 'I am fortunate that God has given me the strength, knowledge, experience, determination, resources and good health to be able to make a protest in this way.'

(Based on Webb, 2012)

What issues would you stand up for, and why?

16.4 What can be done? Introducing the morally active manager

While many moral and ethical choices may focus directly on the immediate circumstance of the service user, others will call upon the manager to take a more organisational or political view and, on many occasions, will require the manager to take a stand, possibly involving discomfort and personal risk. This section explores a range of ethical choices and actions that a manager in health and social care may face at the interface between workers, service users, the organisation and society. Ethical choices and dilemmas often involve a clash of major belief systems or values and this is also explored.

The ethic of justice and the ethic of care

There is a growing interest now in the 'ethics of care' – approaching ethics from a feminist and an environmental perspective. This is in contrast to the 'ethics of justice' which has long dominated the thinking of moral philosophers and the conduct of organisations.
Lawrence Kohlberg (1963), a Harvard psychologist, explored this in his seminal studies in the mid-20th century which posed the famous 'Heinz dilemma' (see Box 16.4).

Box 16.4: Heinz steals the drug

In Europe, a woman was near death from a special kind of cancer. There was one drug that the doctors thought might save her. It was a form of radium that a druggist in the same town had recently discovered. The drug was expensive to make, but the druggist was charging ten times what the drug cost him to make. He paid $200 for the radium and charged $2,000 for a small dose of the drug.

The sick woman's husband, Heinz, went to everyone he knew to borrow the money, but he could only get together about $1,000 which is half of what it cost. He told the druggist that his wife was dying and asked him to sell it cheaper or let him pay later.

> But the druggist said: 'No, I discovered the drug and I'm going to make money from it.' So Heinz got desperate and broke into the man's store to steal the drug for his wife. Should the husband have done that?
>
> (Kohlberg, 1963, p. 19)

From the responses given to this dilemma, Kohlberg identified six stages of moral development from the *pre-conventional,* through *conventional* to *post-conventional.* In the first pre-conventional stage, an individual's actions are governed by obedience and fear of punishment; in other words, self-interest and rote behaviour. Moving up the moral reasoning hierarchy, at the conventional level, an individual is concerned with the impact on relationships and conformity in order to maintain social order. At the highest level of moral development, according to Kohlberg's scheme, an individual's behaviour becomes more concerned with abstract and internalised principles of justice and universal human rights.

Kohlberg's conception of justice follows that of the philosophers Immanuel Kant (see Box 16.1) and John Rawls (1921–2002), as well as great moral leaders such as Mahatma Gandhi (1869–1948) and Martin Luther King, Jr (1929–1968). According to them, the principles of justice require us to treat the claims of all parties in an impartial manner, respecting the basic dignity of all people as individuals. The principles of justice are therefore universal, they apply to all, and can guide us towards decisions based on an equal respect for all. Consequently, the answer to Heinz's dilemma would be not to break into the drugstore.

However, Carol Gilligan, one of Kohlberg's students, noticed that women rarely achieved the highest standards of morality according to Kohlberg's hierarchy. In her studies, she identified a different kind of ethic – an 'ethic of care' (Gilligan, 1982). In contrast to Kohlberg's 'ethic of justice', which is based on a system of morality resting on claims of universality, an 'ethic of care' proposes a morality that grows from a recognition that people are embedded in webs of social relationships. Yiannis Gabriel identifies one of the implications of an ethic of care:

> Care is attending to the needs of others to whom we feel close and for whom we are prepared or expected to take responsibility … A fundamental aspect of the ethics of care is that those close to us and in direct contact with us are experienced as entitled to more care and attention than those distant and unknown.
>
> (Gabriel, 2008, p. 177)

Immediacy, context, interconnectedness and particularity are all hallmarks of an ethic of care. The ethic of care emphasises the personalised bond and is less concerned with the principle of universal equality. Therefore, in Heinz's case, the answer to the dilemma might be to think of his wife's claims for life to be superior to the pharmacist's need for intellectual copyright and income.

> Those who conscientiously care for others are not seeking primarily to further their own *individual* interests; their interests are intertwined with the persons they care for. Neither are they acting for the sake of *all others* or *humanity in general*; they seek instead to preserve or promote an actual human relation between themselves and *particular others*.
>
> (Held, 2006, p. 12, quoted in Gabriel, 2008, p. 178)

How well do you think large care institutions can support an ethic of care?

The clash of these two ethics – an ethic of justice and an ethic of care – accounts for many ethical dilemmas in health and social care. Gabriel (2008) describes the following case of a junior doctor in a gynaecology department.

> A pregnant woman came in through A&E [Accident and Emergency]. She was having problems with her pregnancy. I asked the registrar what to do. They decided that the best thing to do was get the woman scanned to find the problem. However, being a night shift there were no porters to be seen and the scanning units

> were closed. I felt the anxious woman could not stay in A&E surrounded by drunks and druggies as it was inappropriate. Instead of calling for porters, which would have taken time, I and the registrar moved the pregnant lady to the maternity ward ourselves where we opened up a scanning unit to find out what was wrong with the lady's pregnancy. I was proud of the leadership that I had received from my registrar; not every registrar would have done this but he solved the problem and delivered good patient care in the process. The problems were resolved within an hour with only skeletal night staff.
>
> (Gabriel, 2008, p. 180)

The individualised care this patient received at the expense of the anonymous 'drunks and druggies' illustrates the ethic of care prevailing over the ethic of justice. One line of moral thought focuses on logic, justice and social organisation, the other on interpersonal relationships. Reconciling the two ethics, or knowing which should prevail at any given moment, requires an internal ethical system to guide decisions, and an organisation which recognises and supports a climate of ethics. This is one of the fundamental tasks of the morally active manager or leader.

Becoming a morally active manager in health and social care

As mentioned at the beginning of this chapter, the term 'morally active manager' resonates with the notion of Bauman (1993) of a person's impulse or capacity to act morally from within, as opposed to acting in response to externally imposed ethical frameworks. Husband (1995) explored this in relation to social work but it is relevant to any management role within health and social care (Dawson and Butler, 2003).

True freedom for an individual is not freedom *from* others but freedom *with* others, in the context of social obligations within a network of relationships.

To be morally active, suggests Husband, is to be reflective in everyday practice, taking personal responsibility for decisions and the consequences that flow from them. It requires an understanding of the range of ethical frameworks that guide practice and sometimes compete with each other. It means considering what makes things go so badly wrong, in spite of a burgeoning interest in ethics and a proliferation of ethical codes of conduct and guidelines that both guide and confine practice.

Such a level of awareness suggests that being morally active means making ethical choices through the development of an internal moral compass (Dawson and Butler, 2003). This requires a sometimes painful challenge to cherished values, a vigilant pursuit of unconscious assumptions, and often uncomfortable confrontation with the existing situation. However, not everyone wants to expose themselves in such a way. With the proliferation of codes, guidance, rules and regulations, it might be tempting to substitute those as a moral compass instead, rather than having to make difficult ethical decisions alone. Sometimes the difficulty in taking a morally active position therefore means people end up being 'jobsworths' instead, relying on the codes and 'the letter of the law' to avoid having to make difficult judgements themselves. Or, as in the case of staff at the Mid Staffordshire NHS Foundation Trust, they were afraid to object too loudly as they feared the consequences for them personally.

Clearly, delivering health or social care is rarely straightforward, and how to *be* a 'moral' manager within that complexity is contested terrain. One of the complications of health and social care management in the 21st century is that different professions are working together, each with their own values, ways of working, and ethical traditions. Some professions which once held considerable 'moral authority' no longer do, while many people engaged in the work of health and social care do not belong to a traditional profession at all. The *commodification* of the health and social care workforce, the emergence of the knowledgeable consumer, a growing awareness of diversity, and the promotion of 'evidence-based practice', have all had an impact on the sorts of issues a morally active manager may confront (Dawson and Butler, 2003).

A manager therefore faces several questions and issues, from the global to the local level, which do not always have easy answers. For example, the individual versus the common good; the balance of need versus resource; the nature of need; the fundamental rights that require protection; and, finally, to what extent should the state or an agency intervene? Therefore, two key questions which might help to guide a manager's ethical and moral considerations in any given situation are:

- Whose needs are being served? (Figure 16.5)
- What assumptions, values and cultural norms might be guiding my behaviour?

Recall the report of the Mid Staffordshire NHS Foundation Trust inquiry. How might a morally active manager have used these two questions to lead change in response to that report?

'The meeting's at 10. I'll send you a copy of the agenda, the hidden agenda and your personal agenda.'

Figure 16.5 *Cui bono*?

Asking such questions takes a morally active manager into the sphere of leadership, as the answers may provide triggers to leading a situation or an organisation in a new direction. There has been much discussion in the world of health and social care in recent years about the importance of 'transformational' leadership (see Chapter 3). This type of leadership, which inspires other people to look beyond self-interest in order to serve the collective good, seems an appropriate form of leadership to consider in relation to the morally active manager. Indeed, Turner and colleagues (2002) found a correlation between transformational leaders and complex moral reasoning. These leaders drew on sophisticated conceptualisations of interpersonal situations and considered a wide range of solutions and behavioural options; they went beyond applying 'the letter of the law'. This form of leadership is guided by several factors which can be linked to the four building blocks of the **fully rounded caring manager** (Table 16.1).

Table 16.1 Guiding moral leadership (based on Dawson and Butler, 2003, p. 254)

Building block	**Leadership factors**
Personal awareness	*Self-awareness:* developing a growing awareness of your own strengths and limitations, governing assumptions and consequent behaviours. *Values:* being aware of your values and how to stay true to them.
Team awareness	*Sensitivity:* being sensitive to other people and the environment. *Values:* being aware of other people's values and how they may differ from yours.
Goal awareness	*Practice wisdom:* knowledge and experience of good practice in health and social care and how to support it in other people. *Reflexivity:* having the capacity to reflect on practice experience and to learn from it to always strive for the best outcomes.
Contextual awareness	*Sensitivity:* being sensitive to the environment. *Appreciation of risks:* daring to take risks and being prepared to accept responsibility.

16.5 Conclusion

'Being a morally active manager is not necessarily going to be the route to popularity but it should be a means of ensuring that individual managers can defend their own actions, which will come from critical reflection on the decision to be made' (Dawson and Butler, 2003, p. 256).

The moral and ethical issues encountered in health and social care are complex and multilayered. While there are various ethical codes designed to guide conduct, they often highlight different principles that can lead to contradictions and complications in practice. For the front-line manager or leader, this clash of codes can create additional confusion in making ethical and moral decisions. While meeting needs is perhaps considered as one of the most fundamental tasks of health and social care managers, the debate surrounding definitions of need and how to balance need with resource is highly contested, meaning additional layers of ethical decision making have to be put in place. In addition to this, fundamental belief systems, underpinned for example by an ethic of care or an ethic of justice, can be in tension in any given circumstance.

As you have seen throughout this chapter, social, organisational and political factors play important roles in the ethical, moral and service violations that, sadly, appear to be a regular feature of health and social care provision. You have seen how such issues as proximity, organisational socialisation, self-interest and 'organisational terrorism' can conspire against even the most well-intentioned care providers.

Nevertheless, there is considerable theoretical and practical clarity about how best to support service users, colleagues and the community in achieving the fundamental goal of any intervention: to promote, with dignity and respect, an individual's full functioning and active participation as a citizen. Being a vigilant and morally active manager, who is not afraid to lead others through this difficult terrain, requires the ongoing development of self-awareness, reflexivity, individual conscience, mercy, compassion, valour and courage. This may be a tall order, but it is one which is worth pursuing.

Returning to the opening quotation about patients being left unattended for 17 hours, how can things be done differently? Perhaps by going beyond the ethics of practice laid out in guidelines and frameworks, to being mindful of how people have struggled with these dilemmas in the past, developing a critical engagement with your own morals, ethics and passion to combat that which we know is wrong.

Key points

- Ethics and morals are important in health and social care practice because very often the focus of care is vulnerable people whose needs and rights can easily be ignored.
- There is a proliferation of guidance, guidelines, regulatory standards and codes in health and social care which is not always conducive to developing sound ethical practice in an already complex field.
- Increasing regulation and bureaucracy can lead to risk avoidance and defensive practice. Organisational culture is thus a key component to developing an organisational context for ethical behaviour.

- While an ethic of justice in part underpins the idea of universal health and social care provision, an ethic of care should be central to the everyday role of the morally active manager.
- The morally active manager is aware of regulations and guidance but, in addition, can draw on principles and values in order to act in an ethically principled way.

References

Bauman, Z. (1993) *Postmodern Ethics,* Oxford, Blackwell.

Bauman, Z. (2008) *Does Ethics Have a Chance in a World of Consumers?,* Cambridge, Mass., Harvard University Press.

BBC News (2012a) 'Analysis: Why social care has to change', 10 July [Online]. Available at www.bbc.co.uk/news/health-13889758 (Accessed 14 January 2013).

BBC News (2012b) 'Child poverty down as household income drops', 14 June [Online]. Available at www.bbc.co.uk/news/uk-18436795 (Accessed 12 October 2012).

Beauchamp, T.L. and Childress, J.F. (2008) *Principles of Biomedical Ethics* (5th edition), New York, Oxford University Press.

Brykczynska, G. and Simons, J. (2011) *Ethical and Philosophical Aspects of Nursing Children and Young People*, Oxford, Wiley Blackwell.

Caldwell, C. and Canuto-Carranco, M. (2010) 'Organizational terrorism and moral choices – exercising voice when the leader is the problem', *Journal of Business Ethics*, vol. 97, pp. 159–71.

Clark, C. (2000) *Social Work Ethics*, Basingstoke, Macmillan.

Dawson, A. and Butler, I. (2003) 'The morally active manager', in Henderson, J. and Atkinson, D. (eds) *Managing Care in Context*, London, Routledge/The Open University, pp. 237–56 (K303 Set Book).

Doyal, L. and Gough, I. (1991) *A Theory of Human Need*, Basingstoke, Macmillan.

Feinberg, J. (1973) *Social Philosophy*, London, Prentice Hall.

Feinberg, J. (1984) *Harm to Others*, Oxford, Oxford University Press.

Feinberg, J. (1986) *Harm to Self*, Oxford, Oxford University Press.

Gabriel, Y. (2008) 'Latte capitalism and late capitalism: reflections on fantasy and care as part of the service triangle', in MacDonald, C. and Korczynski, M. (eds) *Service Work: Critical perspectives*, London, Routledge, pp. 175–90.

Gallagher, A. (2011) 'Ethical issues in patient restraint', *Nursing Times*, vol. 107, no. 9, pp. 18–20.

Gilligan, C. (1982) *In a Different Voice: Psychological theory and women's development,* Cambridge, Mass., Harvard University Press.

Held, V. (2006) *The Ethics of Care: Personal, political, and global*, Oxford, Oxford University Press.

Husband, C. (1995) 'The morally active practitioner and the ethics of anti-racist social work', in Hugman, R. and Smith, D. (eds) *Ethical Issues in Social Work*, London, Routledge, pp. 84–104.

Kohlberg, L. (1963) 'The development of children's orientations toward a moral order. I. Sequence in the development of moral thought', *Vita Humana*, vol. 6, pp. 11–33.

Maslow, A. (1970) *Motivation and Personality* (2nd edition), New York, Harper and Row.

Mid Staffordshire NHS Foundation Trust Inquiry (2010) *Independent Inquiry into Care Provided by Mid Staffordshire NHS Foundation Trust January 2005–March 2009 Volume I*, London, The Stationery Office.

Osborne, H. (2012) 'NHS: 150 patients die from starvation and dehydration on wards', *International Business Times* [Online]. Available at www.ibtimes.co.uk (Accessed 9 October 2012).

Rogers, A. (2009) 'Organizational reconfiguration in health care: a life and death struggle', *Organisational & Social Dynamics*, vol. 9, no. 2, pp. 225–48.

Ten Bos, R. (1997) 'Essay: business ethics and Bauman ethics', *Organisation Studies*, vol. 18, pp. 997–1014.

Turner, N., Barling, J., Epitropaki, O., Butcher, V. and Milner, C. (2002) 'Transformational leadership and moral reasoning', *Journal of Applied Psychology*, vol. 87, no. 2, pp. 304–11.

Webb, S. (2012) 'Brain doctor unfairly sacked stages hunger strike in protest at treatment of whistleblowers in the NHS', *Daily Mail*, 2 October [Online]. Available at www.dailymail.co.uk/news/article-2211703/Brain-doctor-unfairly-sacked-stages-hunger-strike-protest-treatment-whistleblowers-NHS.html (Accessed 14 January 2013).

The Week (2012) 'Bob Diamond quits Barclays but Marcus Agius will stay', *The Week* [Online]. Available at www.theweek.co.uk/city/barclays-scandal/47751/bob-diamond-quits-barclays-marcus-agius-will-stay (Accessed 5 July 2012).

Wolfe, A. (1991) 'Reflections on business ethics: What is it? What causes it? And, what should a course in business ethics include?', *Business Ethics Quarterly*, vol. 1, no. 4, pp. 409–39.

Zimbardo, P. (1972) *The Psychology of Imprisonment: Privation, power and pathology*, Stanford, Calif., Stanford University.

Chapter 17 Managing challenges

Joan Simons

17.1 Introduction

Figure 17.1 Finding solutions to problems

> The ultimate measure of a man is not where he stands in moments of comfort and convenience, but where he stands at times of challenge and controversy.
>
> (Martin Luther King, Jr, 1963, p. 79)

Managers working in health and social care today are expected to do more with less, and to be more efficient as well as more humane and ethical (Hatch and Cunliffe, 2006). Since 2006, the economic environment has worsened, making the challenges that leaders and managers face even harder. Such demands can easily lead to tension, conflict and challenges: for example, from an angry service user to a difficult member of staff, an increase in complaints, or a rise in accidents on a unit. Whatever the challenges are, managers are expected to know what to do and how to deal with each one in a way that will not only help to solve the problem but also involve ensuring it will not arise again (Figure 17.1).

This chapter addresses several challenging issues, to help your understanding of how and why challenging situations arise. It also explores strategies that can be used to deal with them, as well as the steps that can be taken to prevent or reduce their reoccurrence. The chapter focuses specifically on two of the four building blocks of a **fully rounded caring manager** – **team awareness** and **contextual awareness** –and addresses the following core questions.

- What challenges might a manager or leader in health and social care have to deal with and how can the promotion of a safety culture be effective in reducing them?
- How can conflict be managed?
- How can a manager in health and social care promote good practice as well as handle complaints?
- How can using risk assessment and risk management strategies reduce or prevent complaints?

17.2 Leadership and promoting a safety culture

Figure 17.2 Managing safety requires strong leadership

In 2006, the Healthcare Commission reported on the findings of an investigation into the many deaths at Stoke Mandeville Hospital in Buckinghamshire resulting from two outbreaks of *Clostridium difficile* infection. This is a highly infectious bacterium which causes severe diarrhoea. Between October 2003 and June 2005 there were two outbreaks of *C. difficile*, leading to 36 deaths, the majority of these patients acquiring the infection in hospital. The infection control team tried unsuccessfully, during both outbreaks, to gain a dedicated area for patients with *C. difficile*. The senior managers of the Hospital Trust did not support this move and were reluctant to implement the advice of both the infection control team and the local health protection unit. Box 17.1 shows the Healthcare Commission's conclusion.

Box 17.1: Extract from the Stoke Mandeville inquiry report

We conclude that the first hospital-wide outbreak was a consequence of a poor environment for caring for patients, poor practice in the control of infection, lack of facilities to isolate patients and insufficient priority being given to the control of infection by senior managers.

[...]

At the most senior level of management, there was a lack of effective leadership, accountability and support for the control of infection. The director of infection prevention and control had not persuaded the board to give sufficient priority to the control of infection in general and to the control of *C. difficile* in particular.

The achievement of the Government's targets was seen as more important than the management of the clinical risk inherent in the outbreaks of *C. difficile*. This was a significant failing.

This report includes many examples of the advice of the infection control team being overridden, even at the height of the second outbreak. Some of the required changes were implemented after the first outbreak, while others of perhaps greater importance were not. The most significant lesson – the importance of rapid isolation – was not acted upon.

[...]

> Staff portrayed the executive team as a closely knit inner circle and considered their style of management to be oppressive and intolerant of failure. ... The Healthcare Commission considered that the approach of the trust's leadership to the investigation was defensive.
>
> (Healthcare Commission, 2006, pp. 5, 6–7)

Quality relationships based on fairness and empathy play a pivotal role in creating positive safety climates and work environments (Squires et al., 2010).

This report is just one example of where poor care has resulted in unnecessary patient deaths. The report quite clearly identifies system failures that contributed to an increased number of deaths of elderly patients as a result of a hospital-acquired infection. There is a clear link here between leadership and safety outcomes (Figure 17.2).

Another example of a report of preventable deaths of vulnerable service users is the case of a fatal fire in 2004 at Rosepark Care Home in Lanarkshire, in which 14 elderly residents died. The report of the Fatal Accidents and Sudden Deaths Inquiry (Sheriffdom of South Strathclyde, Dumfries and Galloway, 2011) found that some residents might have been saved if the fire service had been called sooner. Management did not properly appreciate its role and responsibilities in relation to issues of fire safety. The policy at the home meant that, on hearing a fire alarm, a member of staff had to locate the fire before calling the fire brigade. This meant a delay of nine minutes (see Box 17.2).

Box 17.2: Extract from the Rosepark Care Home Inquiry report

> [The] deficiencies in the management of fire safety at Rosepark contributed to the deaths in that a number of key circumstances would have been quite different if there had been an adequate system of fire safety management ... None of the staff on duty on the night of the fire had been trained in the use of fire extinguishers.
>
> [...]
>
> The way the staff responded on the night of 31 January 2004 was just what might be expected of staff who had not received adequate fire training and who had, by reason of exposure to

> false alarms, become complacent. Had the staff been properly trained in a matter consonant with the task that would face them in that emergency situation, they would have behaved quite differently and that, either on its own, or in conjunction with other changes which would have been put in place had the system of fire safety management not been defective, would have avoided some or all of the deaths.
>
> (Sheriffdom of South Strathclyde, Dumfries and Galloway, 2011, para. DS3.2)

Both of the above cases seem to show that lives were lost as a result of a sequence of events which, in hindsight, should have been avoided. The culture in any health and social care service can significantly influence the actions and reactions of staff. The rest of this section explores the consequences of a 'blame culture', and then contrasts this with the benefits of a 'safety culture'.

Approaches to attributing error

There are two approaches to attributing error in the study of safety.

1 The traditional approach that focuses on human error and tends to attribute blame to individuals – this is known as a 'blame culture'. Historically, this has been the predominant culture in health and social care and medicine.

2 The systems approach, which focuses on the chain of events leading to an adverse incident. This is used in the aviation industry.

To distance an individual's unsafe acts from institutional responsibility might appear to be in the interests of managers. However, this not only victimises the individual, it also hinders the development of safer delivery of care (Reason, 2002). It would not have solved the problems in either of the cases above. Leape and Berwick (2000) suggest that nursing uses a culture of blame in an attempt to achieve good performance, because error is regarded as someone's fault, caused by a lack of sufficient attention. Such an approach tries to use blame to achieve good performance but, instead, leads to a fear of recrimination when an incident occurs, which in turn can lead to incidents being underreported (Sprinks, 2012). Moumtzoglou (2010) found that nurses gave five reasons for not reporting an adverse incident:

1 Fear of the press
2 Fear of the regulatory body
3 Difficulty in handling adverse events
4 Needing the confidence to bring it up
5 Fear of complaints from patients.

The list suggests that the individual is not at fault; it is the system in which they work. To help understand the systems approach, Reason (2002) developed the Swiss cheese model (Figure 17.3). Slices of Swiss cheese with various holes in them represent an organisation's layers of defence against error. The holes in defence mechanisms due to activity failures (things that go wrong at the front line) and latent failures (the conditions that allow things to go wrong in the first place) are always changing. When the holes in defences line up, adverse incidents will occur, as in the two cases described above.

Figure 17.3 The Swiss cheese model (Reason, 2002)

To achieve a whole-systems approach to managing care safely, there has to be an understanding of how individual practice connects with organisational objectives (Simmons, 2006). This means that all staff should contribute to the development of the organisation's capacity to review and improve services. In the two outbreaks of *C. difficile* described above, there was a clear disconnection between the front-line staff who were delivering care and the senior management team whose objectives were focused on cost cutting.

Who had the most power at Stoke Mandeville – the infection control nurses or senior management? If the roles had been reversed, would the infection have been isolated sooner?

Focusing on error and the person involved isolates the incident from the system in which the individual is working. At Stoke Mandeville, the spread of *C. difficile* could have been reduced by hand washing; however, the nurses reported they were too overwhelmed by their workload to wash their hands carefully. This situation was the result of not having enough staff on duty to deliver care effectively because of the financial constraints imposed by the system in which they were working.

Can you see how the holes in the slices of cheese fell into alignment at Stoke Mandeville, resulting in the serious incident occurring?

A study of the link between leadership and safety outcomes in hospitals found that, among 200 health professionals, quality relationships based on fairness and empathy play a pivotal role in creating positive safety climates and work environments (Squires et al., 2010). Managers should, therefore, aim to develop high-quality relationships through effective leadership practices and good **team awareness**.

Parnes and colleagues (2007) studied what they termed the 'error cascade' – whereby a series of events leads to an adverse incident – and how this can be prevented. They found that simple attentiveness, vigilance and perseverance often stopped an error cascade. In the case of the fire at Rosepark Care Home, there were several opportunities for individuals to stop the error cascade, such as calling the fire brigade more promptly and not waiting until the fire was located, or doors were being closed to prevent its spread. In this way, these actions could have shifted a slice of cheese in the Swiss cheese model and prevented the error cascade from continuing.

Errors can occur through the simplest oversight, such as not passing on an important message, or assuming someone else has done it.

By focusing on the characteristics that prevent an error cascade, a 'culture of safety' may be cultivated which potentially increases the likelihood of:

- the chance discovery of events
- corrective action even in the absence of protocols.

Errors detected by chance can lead to system changes in an environment that promotes safety. However, prevention of error at the unit and individual level depends on the staff's ability to identify and analyse errors and adverse events as they occur, and to learn from them. In order to have the skill to identify errors, all staff must have the necessary level of competence. At the organisational level, efficient personnel management is required to cope with unexpected situations at all times. In the case of the *C. difficile* outbreak, the response of senior management meant it neither reacted appropriately to the calls from the infection control team to close a ward and isolate sick patients, nor provided much-needed extra staff to deal with the outbreak effectively and stop the error cascade.

Clearly, it is not possible to prevent all the errors that may occur in the delivery of health and social care. However, by developing a culture that empowers staff and service users alike to ask questions and act on the cues of an error, a safety culture can develop and errors will be significantly reduced.

Reflecting on the findings of the Healthcare Commission (see Box 17.1), it appears, in hindsight, to be obvious what went wrong at Stoke Mandeville Hospital. But it is also necessary to explore further why senior management did not support the requests of the infection control nurses. Adair's model of action leadership (described in Chapter 3) can help here, in considering why there was not the necessary alignment between the goals of senior management and the goals of practitioners.

Adair's model requires balance between the individual, the team they work in and the goal they are working towards. In considering what was out of alignment resulting in the spread of *C. difficile*, clearly senior management and front-line practitioners were not working towards the same goal. The practitioners were trying to keep the patients in their care safe, by reducing the spread of infection, which required the isolation of infected individuals and enough staff to do this. On the other hand, the senior team was working towards the goal of achieving Trust status, which required cost savings and ran contrary to closing a ward or employing more staff. The goals of the two groups could be said to be in opposition, as one required saving money and the other required spending it. This very clear conflict of interest was created by the structural arrangement within the Trust, the strategic management being at odds with the operational management.

Stoke Mandeville Hospital Trust seemed to have an autocratic style of leadership. What difference could distributed leadership (see Chapter 3) have made to the situation?

Promoting safety: lessons from aviation

Many comparisons have been made between the delivery of health and social care and the aviation industry (Ottewill, 2003; Singh et al., 2006). They suggest that safety is a higher priority in aviation, from which the health and social care system could learn how to promote safety and prevent adverse incidents.

In the 1980s, the aviation industry had to deal with several unexpected accidents. The investigations revealed, surprisingly, that many serious accidents were occurring in well-serviced aircraft. The cause was often what Mann (2004) calls 'the human factor' – the natural propensity for human beings to make mistakes. The findings indicated that, although the aircraft were in good working order, and the pilots were well qualified to do their jobs, it was how they managed situations that led to accidents. As a result, the airline industry recognised that having cutting-edge technical ability in their pilots and crew was not enough. They needed to focus on both the technical training and the human factor, as each was vital.

Mann (2004, p. 12) showed that mistakes were caused by flight crews being subject to:

- fatigue, stress or an overload of work
- cognitive errors
- errors of individual or team judgement such as poor decision making
- ineffective communication, often relating to personal style.

As a result, the following principles are now used to promote good working relationships between aviation crew members.

- Focus on the situation, issue or behaviour, not on the person.
- Maintain the self-confidence and self-esteem of others.
- Maintain constructive relationships with your employers, peers and managers.
- Take initiative to make things better.
- Lead by example.

(Mann, 2004, p. 12)

Team awareness is an important element in promoting a safety culture.

By promoting good relationships, especially between senior managers and front-line staff, making group decisions can be facilitated more readily. The principles of good relationships are listed in Box 17.3.

Box 17.3: Principles of good relationships (Mann, 2004, p. 13)

- Approach tasks on the basis of facts; don't argue merely to support your own preconceptions.
- Don't change your mind simply to avoid conflict.
- View differences of opinion as supporting effective decision making rather than a hindrance to successful outcomes.
- If you are the [leader or manager], be aware that, if you state your opinion from the outset, other team members may not want to contradict you even if they suspect you are wrong.
- Encourage team members to express their views and doubts at any stage.
- The reasons behind decisions should always be explained to all team members.

Does a sense of powerlessness in front-line staff contribute to an error cascade occurring?

To summarise, technical skills and knowledge are not enough to promote a safety culture; effective team decision making is also vital. Recalling the case studies of the *C. difficile* outbreaks and the fire at the care home, both units had appropriately qualified staff to carry out their roles. However, in the case of the hospital, the infection control team was unsupported in their decision making by senior management and, in the case of the care home, repeated false alarms led to a level of complacency among the staff. In both situations, cultural factors impeded the development of a protective safety culture.

Developing a safety culture is challenging and time consuming. The **GROW tool** and the **goal-setting tool** can be used to define what you are trying to achieve and to develop a strategy to achieve your goal.

Having focused on two negative examples of dealing with challenges in health and social care, it is also important to recognise that learning from positive examples can be very effective. This is explored in the next section.

17.3 Learning from positive experience: the role of appreciative inquiry

The following case study is a good example of how a simple initiative made a real difference to patients' experience.

Case study 17.1: The Red Water Jug Scheme

Figure 17.4 Red water jugs are a success in hospitals

The Ward 17 nursing team at Milton Keynes Hospital NHS Foundation Trust won the prestigious 'Nursing Team of the Year' award at the Nursing Times Awards in 2009 for their innovative Red Water Jug Scheme.

Two health care assistants – Sue Dearlove and Marie Turney – had the simple idea of the red water jug (Figure 17.4) to help ensure that patients are adequately hydrated. Adequate hydration, as well as good nutrition, is essential for good health and for a patient's recovery but, according to national NHS figures, many people are already dehydrated when admitted to hospital. The red water jug is a simple way of ensuring that patients get help when they need it, to prevent dehydration and to promote recovery. Those with red water jugs by their beds are identified as needing extra help or support, and at risk of dehydration if that help is not forthcoming.

The visual cue of the red water jug identifies patients who require help with their fluid intake, and the scheme has been commended both nationally and internationally. The red water jug is a powerful reminder to staff to react in a particular way – that is, to attend to that patient's hydration needs.

The Red Water Jug Scheme is an example of something that worked well being recognised and celebrated and then implemented more widely. This initiative has been promoted nationally and taken up by several areas caring for elderly service users and patients who need help with maintaining their hydration. Some areas have also incorporated a red tray system for people who need help with eating meals. This is an example of learning from something that has gone well. *Appreciative inquiry* is a systematic way of promoting this sort of learning (see Box 17.4).

Box 17.4: Learning through appreciative inquiry

The four stages of appreciative inquiry are:

1 Discover
2 Dream
3 Design
4 Deliver.

Appreciative inquiry begins with all the diverse individuals who claim an interest appreciating, or valuing, the best of what already exists (discover), then envisioning what might be (dream). The process continues with discussion about what should be (design). Then those parties can, collectively, work to make their vision become what is (deliver), sometimes through apparently relatively minor but collective changes in behaviour (Cooperrider et al., 2008).

By using appreciative inquiry, knowledge can be gained from examples of good practice so that they can be replicated and extended to other areas, as with the Red Water Jug Scheme.

People often learn from mistakes. What difference do you think learning from success can make at both the individual and the team level?

17.4 Dealing with conflict and complaints

So far, this chapter has focused on how ineffective leadership can lead to disastrous consequences, and the need for a safety culture to prevent such incidences reoccurring. In contrast, it has also considered how to learn from and repeat good practice. Another challenge a manager is likely to encounter is *conflict*, either between staff or between staff and service users.

Managing conflict

This topic can be considered with the help of another case study, as follows.

Case study 17.2: James and Geraint

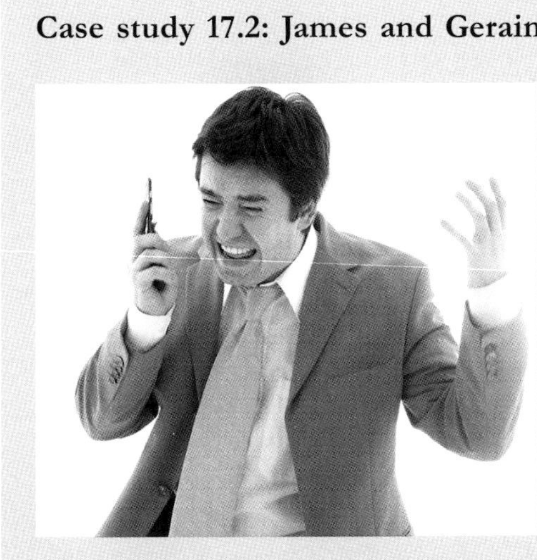

Figure 17.5

James worked as a manager at a day centre for service users with learning disabilities. The most popular weekly activity was a music session run by a renowned local musician called Geraint. Most service users were transported to the day centre for these sessions in a minibus with a few more people arriving by private transport. One morning, as James was setting up for the music session, he got a mobile phone call from the minibus driver to say that the minibus, which was full, couldn't make it to the day centre as a fallen tree was blocking the route.

James had to think on his feet and made arrangements for the service users to be returned home, rather than sit, possibly for hours, trying to make their way to the day centre. Then James realised he had to cancel the music session as there would not be the required minimum number of participants. James rang and explained to the three people who had planned to attend by private transport. Then he rang Geraint, the musician who led the week session, to explain that the session had to be cancelled. On hearing this, Geraint was furious. He shouted down the phone: 'Who do you think you are cancelling *my* session?' James calmly explained the series of events but Geraint continued to shout down the phone, and then abruptly hung up.

So, what was going on between the day centre manager and the musician? What could James have done differently? By his actions, he managed to stop the possibility of an error cascade (see Section 17.2). He demonstrated the necessary characteristics – attentiveness, vigilance and perseverance – in what he knew would be the face of adversity. He realised that if the session was not cancelled, and the minibus driver persisted in trying to reach the day centre, the vulnerable passengers would experience long delays, leading to anxiety and distress. By ensuring they were returned home safely, without delay, he managed to stop potentially serious errors occurring.

However, clearly, the eminent musician was not used to having his session cancelled. But James would not have being doing his job if he had not raised his concerns about the service users sitting in the minibus for several hours. Although the phone call to the musician was a very stressful encounter, James felt he had done the right thing in handling the situation.

How could James have avoided the conflict with Geraint? Was he too hasty in cancelling the session?

You can see from this case that conflict can occur in the workplace in an unexpected way. Recognising conflict, or the stress and tension that often precede conflict, is a necessary skill to develop as a manager. Dealing effectively with situations rapidly can defuse conflict and make it more manageable. In conflicts, a person's behaviour is usually characterised by one of two extremes:

- *assertiveness* – that is, they attempt to satisfy their own concerns

or

- *cooperativeness* – that is, they attempt to satisfy the other person's concerns.

These two extremes of behaviour can be used to define five approaches to dealing with conflict suggested by Thomas and Kilman (1978) (see Box 17.5).

Box 17.5: Approaches to dealing with conflict

1. *Competing* is a style in which a person advocates their own needs over the needs of others. It relies on an aggressive style of communication, a low regard for future relationships, and the exercise of coercive power *over* other people.
2. *Accommodating*, also known as smoothing, is the opposite of competing. People using this style yield their needs to those of others, trying to be diplomatic and cooperative, and developing power *with* others.
3. *Avoiding* is a common response to the negative perception of conflict – hoping that, without dealing with the issue, it will go away. But, generally, all that happens is that feelings are pent up, views remain unexpressed, and the conflict festers until it becomes too big to ignore.
4. *Compromising* is an approach to conflict in which people gain and give in a series of trade-offs. While satisfactory, compromise is generally not satisfying.

> 5 *Collaborating* is the pooling of individual needs and goals towards a common goal. Often called 'win–win problem-solving', collaboration requires assertive communication and cooperation in order to achieve a better solution than each individual could have achieved alone.
>
> (Based on Thomas and Kilman, 1978)

By understanding each of Thomas and Kilman's styles and its consequences, people can adjust their behaviour in various situations, as follows.

1 By using a 'competing' style, an individual might force others to accept their solution, but this acceptance may be accompanied by fear and resentment.
2 By 'accommodating', the relationship may proceed smoothly, but may build up feelings of frustration because an individual's needs are not being met.
3 By 'avoiding' all discussion of the conflict, both parties may remain oblivious to the real underlying issues and concerns, only to have to deal with them in the future, which may culminate in a formal complaint.
4 By 'compromising', an individual may feel fine about the outcome, but still harbour resentment in the future.
5 By 'collaborating', an individual may not gain a better solution than a compromise might have yielded, but they will probably feel better about their chances for future understanding and good working relationships.

In the case of James and Geraint, the conflict was not resolved, and James probably harboured feelings of resentment towards Geraint for his unreasonable and aggressive behaviour during their phone call.

Applying Thomas and Kilman's model of conflict to the exchange between James and Geraint, how else do you think the phone call could have been handled?

Dealing with complaints

Every year the NHS delivers 380 million treatments, which result in 95,000 complaints (Mayor, 2007). To put these figures in perspective, one complaint is received for approximately every 400 treatments delivered. In adult social care in England, complaints rose from 1052 in 2009/10 to 1820 in 2010/11, an increase of 73 per cent in one year (Local Government Ombudsman, 2011). However, it must be acknowledged that these figures only include those individuals who submitted complaints. Many more may be unhappy with the care delivered but are not prepared to go through what could be perceived as the bureaucratic and daunting process of submitting a formal complaint. Anna Walker, Chief Executive of the Healthcare Commission, suggests that 'complaints represent raw feelings and should be listened to and learnt from. At the centre of each one is an individual who may have genuinely suffered, as a result of perhaps not what went wrong, but how they were dealt with' (Healthcare Commission, 2007, p. 2).

The Social Care Institute for Excellence (SCIE) provides a guide for individuals who want to make a complaint about community care (Independent Age, 2013). The guide contains information on the Health and Care Professions Council Code of Practice for social workers, so that a complainant can identify whether they feel that their social worker was not working within their professional code. Guides such as this attempt to make submitting a complaint less daunting for service users, but they can make dealing with complaints harder for professionals and managers.

Managers in health and social care are responsible for dealing with complaints that come to their unit. The golden rule when dealing with complaints is that the purpose is to settle a grievance as quickly as possible. Whiteley (2010) provides a step-by-step guide on responding to complaints (see Box 17.6.)

Whiteley (2010) suggests that apologies are important and should be given, but they are *not* an admission of liability.

Box 17.6: Overview of the complaints process (based on Whiteley, 2010)

Step 1
• **Accept the complaint** • **Analyse and define the complaint**
When a complaint has been received, it is necessary first to accept the complaint that is being made. Then it is important to identify the scope of the complaint; in other words, establish what the focus is and who is involved, speak to the complainant and identify why they have made the complaint and what outcomes they want from the complaint system.
Step 2
• **Plan an investigation and investigate the complaint** • **Gather, analyse and evaluate information**
The approach here must address the needs of the individual complaint, and therefore will differ for every complaint. A clear plan will set out the methods to be used to tackle the problem identified. Interviews with managers can ascertain what should have happened and, if there was a failing, whether it was caused by individuals failing to do what they should have done, or because the necessary support, supervision, policies or procedures were not in place. Once the necessary information has been collected, a judgement can be made about the basis of the complaint.
Step 3
• **Make a decision**
Having gathered and evaluated the information, a decision can be made. Three issues need to be considered: 1 Has there been a fault of some kind? If the answer is yes, what was the effect and what action needs to be taken now? 2 If there has been a fault, it is necessary to acknowledge this and say sorry to the complainant. 3 If action needs to be taken, it is necessary to draw up a plan of action to include what will be done, who will do it and when it will happen.

Step 4
• **Communicate the decision**
The individual dealing with the complaint will at this point communicate the decisions made to the complainant. The response letter will be proportionate to the nature and complexity of the complaint, and can range from one or two pages to a comprehensive report. All responses to the complaint should include: • a summary of the complaint • the steps taken in response to it • what has been considered • the decisions taken with explanations • what will happen now • what the complainant can do if they are not happy with the outcome. This letter needs to be written with skill to ensure that the complainant understands the gravity with which their complaint has been dealt with. Complainants are less likely to challenge a decision if they can understand why it has been reached and accept the reasoning behind it.

Through this process, a manager taking a systems approach, as opposed to an individual approach, will probably not only get information that meets the requirements for dealing with that complaint but also get an insight into how to improve the service in their unit, so that further complaints can be avoided.

Knowing that health and social care work involves challenges in the form of accidents and incidents, there must be both policies and procedures in place to assess the likelihood of adverse events happening and processes to reduce or minimise their occurrence – that is, the manager must be *risk aware.*

17.5 Risk assessment and management

Figure 17.6 Mind the gap!

Working in health and social care, there are many hazards that are recognised and need to be avoided (Figure 17.6). The final section of this chapter focuses on an adverse incident that occurs regularly in both health and social care, presenting challenges for staff and service users alike. Falls are common in both hospitals and care homes, where rates vary from 3 to 13 falls per 1000 bed days. In UK care homes, residents fall two to six times a year (Dickson and Woodward, 2000), while UK hospitals reported 221,000 falls in the year 2011/12 (NHS: The Information Centre, 2012) with 1 to 2 per cent of falls in elderly people resulting in a hip fracture (Masud and Morris, 2001; Healy and Oliver, 2006).

As a result of this widespread problem, it is recognised that patients need to be assessed for their risk of falling, and several risk assessment tools have been developed (Poe et al., 2005; Bucher et al., 2007). Oliver and colleagues (2006) reviewed 92 published papers on interventions to prevent falls in hospitals and care homes and found that a single intervention – using a hip protector – was helpful in care homes. However, in hospitals a multi-intervention approach was necessary, including assessing individuals for cognitive impairment or dementia, reviewing their medication, and the use of personal alarms.

Milisen and colleagues (2009), in a feasibility study on using a Fall Prevention Practice guideline, found that it took about half an hour. Most doctors, nurses, occupational therapists and physiotherapists felt that fall prevention was important but there was a lack of agreement about how to integrate the guideline with practice. The main obstacles were a lack of both time and cooperation among healthcare workers.

It appears, therefore, that the risk of falls is well recognised and fall prevention strategies are available. You might think then that fall prevention is an accepted and integrated part of practice. However, the study by Milisen et al. (2009) shows that it is not enough to have information or even a practice guide; the practice guide needs to be implemented and to be given a priority among many other competing priorities. Managers can make a difference to this situation by demonstrating to their staff that an issue such as fall prevention is fundamental to the delivery of care and that the safety of patients or service users is essential. In this way, managers have the opportunity to prioritise accident prevention and create a culture of safety among the practitioners being managed, so that they work together to prevent accidents such as falls occurring, and do not think they are 'too busy' to do so.

How does risk management relate to promoting a safety culture, as discussed earlier in this chapter?

Returning to Adair's leadership model (see Chapter 3), leadership is particularly relevant here. Adair (2002) suggests that, as a team, there needs to be a well-articulated sense of common purpose, so that everyone is working towards the same goal. By working together, the team brings synergy to any task, as long as there is effective communication and each individual member is clear about their own responsibility. Effective leadership – which ensures a balance between task, team and individuals – has the potential to create and maintain a culture of safety where vulnerable service users receive the best quality care.

It is important for managers or leaders to recognise that, in trying to promote a culture of safety, they have the power to do so. Formal authority is only one source of power in organisations; other sources include personal characteristics, expertise, coercion, control of scarce or critical resources (budgets, staff), and opportunity (access to powerful people) (Gaventa, 2003). Furthermore, the influential French philosopher Michel Foucault (1994) suggested that the power of interactions does not belong to an individual or a group of individuals but, rather, is a force in itself. This stance is developed in Wong's web of power (see Chapter 1), which conveys clearly the relational aspects of power and is worth bearing in mind when managing risks and challenges.

While a culture based on individual blame might assume the power to prevent problems lies in having power *over* someone, what you have seen in this chapter is that, in practice, developing 'power-*with*' and 'power-*from-within*' is often the basis of many positive examples of risk management, effective teamwork and conflict resolution. An understanding of power informed by such awareness therefore creates the possibility of forming more equitable relationships which recognise and acknowledge the complex operation of power *between* people.

As a manager, or an aspiring manager, in health or social care, how do your relationships with your team or senior colleagues influence your perception of power?

17.6 Conclusion

This chapter began with two cases of a disaster in health and social care which could have been prevented. Sadly, such mistakes are not uncommon; however, they *are* avoidable, and this chapter explored how a leader or manager might try to avoid such mistakes in the first place. In doing so, this chapter focused on the challenges that a manager in health and social care may encounter, and how the promotion of a safety culture can influence practice by avoiding a focus on individuals, and developing a systems approach to dealing with adverse incidents. This can be further enhanced by implementing an approach that both highlights and celebrates good care.

Even in well-managed areas of practice, managers have to deal with issues such as conflict or complaints. This chapter outlined the options for dealing with conflict and a step-by-step method of acknowledging and resolving complaints.

The final issue of risk management demonstrated the need for effective leadership by articulating to care workers the priority of promoting a culture of safety. As a manager or leader, the approach taken to managing errors and challenges is influenced by working relationships. Underpinning all relationships is the issue of power, which can be seen as a positive productive force to be used in your role as a manager when dealing with and managing the unavoidable challenges encountered in health and social care.

Key points

- Challenges in health and social care are frequently created by systems, not individuals.
- A culture of blame can lead to cover-ups and denials, leading to even bigger problems, whereas developing a safety culture helps to prevent errors occurring.
- People learn from successes as well as mistakes, so celebrating success is one way to promote a culture of safety.
- Risk is an inevitable feature of health and social care, therefore sound management practice and strong leadership should be in place to assess, manage and minimise risk.
- Dealing with complaints is part of the manager's role. A structured approach can help prevent reoccurrences.
- Identifying where power lies, and recognising its influence, can increase a manager's effectiveness in dealing with conflict and promoting safety.

References

Adair, J. (2002) *Effective Strategic Leadership*, London, Macmillan.

Bucher, G.M., Szczerba, P. and Curtin, P. (2007) 'A comprehensive fall prevention program for assessment, interventions and referrals', *Home Health Care Nurse*, vol. 25, no. 3, pp. 174–83.

Cooperrider, D., Whitney, D. and Stavros, J.M. (2008) *Appreciative Inquiry Handbook: for leaders of change* (2nd edition), Brunswick, OH, Crown Custom Publishing Inc.

Dickson, B, and Woodward, M. (2000) *Accident Prevention in the Elderly in Nursing Homes*, Second year report, Newcastle, Gateshead, South Tyneside, Sunderland and Northumberland Registration and Inspection Areas for Care Homes.

Foucault, M. (1994) *Power. Essential Works of Foucault 1954–1984* (ed. Faubion, J.D.), London, Penguin Books.

Gaventa, J. (2003) *Power after Lukes: A review of the literature*, Brighton, Institute of Development Studies.

Hatch, M.J. and Cunliffe, A.L. (2006) *Organization Theory: Modern, symbolic, and postmodern perspectives* (2nd edition), Oxford, Oxford University Press.

Healthcare Commission (2006) *Investigation into Outbreaks of* Clostridium difficile *at Stoke Mandeville Hospital, Buckinghamshire Hospitals NHS Trust*, London, Healthcare Commission.

Healthcare Commission (2007) 'Watchdog urges NHS to learn from "raw feelings of patients" in report on 16,000 complaints', Press release [Online], www.healthcarecommission.org.uk (Accessed 14 June 2012).

Healy, E. and Oliver, D. (2006) 'Prevention falls and injury in hospitals. The evidence for interventions', *Health Care Risk Report*, June, pp. 12–17.

Independent Age (2013) Guide 18 'Complaints about community care and NHS services in England' [Online], www.independentage.org/advice/guides-and-factsheets/all-guides-and-factsheets.aspx (Accessed 25 February 2013).

King, M.L., Jr (1963) *Strength to Love*, Philadelphia, Pa., Fortress Press.

Leape, L.L. and Berwick, D.M. (2000) 'Safe health care: are we up to it?', *British Medical Journal*, vol. 320, pp. 725–6.

Local Government Ombudsman (2011) *Annual Report* [Online], www.lgo.org.uk/publications/annual-report/ (Accessed 15 June 2012).

Mann, C. (2004) 'Safety culture?', *Nursing Management*, vol. 11, no. 7, pp. 10–13.

Mayor, S. (2007) 'Care of dying patients and safety dominate commission's report on NHS complaints', *British Medical Journal*, vol. 334, p. 278.

Masud T. and Morris R.O. (2001) 'Epidemiology of falls' *Age and Ageing*, suppl. 4, pp.3–7.

Milisen, K., Annelies, G. and Dejaeger, A. (2009) 'Use of a Fall Prevention Practice guideline for community-dwelling older persons at risk for falling: a feasibility study', *Gerontology*, vol. 55, pp. 169–78.

Moumtzoglou, A. (2010) 'Factors impeding nurses from reporting adverse events', *Journal of Nursing Management*, vol. 18, pp. 542–7.

NHS: The Information Centre (2012) *Hospital Episode Statistics: Admitted Patient Care 2011–12*, HES Online, www.hesonline.nhs.uk/Ease/servlet/ContentServer?siteID=1937&categoryID=193 (Accessed 25 February 2013).

Nursing Team of the Year Award (2009) *The Red Jug Scheme* [Online]. Available at: http://miltonkeynes.com/milton-keynes-hospital-nurses-win-major-national-award.html (Accessed 6 January 2011).

Oliver, D., Connelly, J.B., Victor, C.R., Shaw, F.E., Whitehead, A., Genc, Y., Vanoli, A., Martin, F.C. and Gosney, M.A. (2006) 'Strategies to prevent falls and fractures in hospitals and care homes and effect of cognitive impairment: systematic review and meta analysis', *British Medical Journal*, vol. 334, no. 7584, pp. 82–5.

Ottewill, M. (2003) 'The current approach to human error and blame in the NHS', *British Journal of Nursing*, vol. 12, no. 15, pp. 919–24.

Parnes, B., Fernald, D., Quintela, J., Araya-Guerra, R., Westfall, J., Harris, D. and Pace, W. (2007) 'Stopping the error cascade: a report on ameliorators from the ASIPS collaborative', *Quality and Safety in Health Care*, vol. 16, pp. 12–16.

Poe, S.S., Cvach, M.M., Gartrell, D.G., Radzik, B.R. and Joy, T. (2005) 'An evidence-based approach to fall risk assessment, prevention, and management: lessons learnt', *Journal of Nursing Care Quality*, vol. 20, no. 2, pp. 107–16.

Reason, J. (2002) 'Human error: models and management', *British Medical Journal*, vol. 320, pp. 768–70.

Sheriffdom of South Strathclyde, Dumfries and Galloway (2011) 'Determination by Sheriff Principal Brian A. Lockhart in respect of the Inquiry into deaths at Rosepark Care Home' [Online], www. scotcourts.gov.uk/opinions/2011FAI18.pdf (Accessed 19 May 2011).

Simmons, L (2006) *Social Care Governance: A practice workbook*, London, Social Care Institute for Excellence.

Singh, H., Petersen, L.A. and Thomas, E.J. (2006) 'Understanding diagnostic errors in medicine: a lesson from aviation', *Quality and Safety in Health Care*, vol. 15, no. 3, pp. 159–64.

Sprinks, J. (2012) 'Eradicating NHS blame culture will improve safety, nurses argue', *Nursing Standard*, vol. 26, no. 35, p. 10.

Squires, M., Tourangeau, A., Spence Laschinger, H.K. and Doran, D. (2010) 'The link between leadership and safety outcomes in hospitals', *Journal of Nursing Management*, vol. 18, pp. 914–25.

Thomas, K.W. and Kilman, R.H. (1978) 'Comparison of four instruments measuring conflict behavior', *Psychological Reports*, vol. 42, pp. 1139–45.

Whiteley, P. (2010) 'An integrated approach to dealing with complaints in the workplace', *Nursing Management*, vol. 17, no. 8, pp. 28–31.

Chapter 18 Quality in health and social care

Liz Tilley, Jan Walmsley and Rebecca L. Jones

18.1 Introduction

Figure 18.1 What does 'good quality' care look like?

> 'Everyone has two jobs: improving care as well as providing care' (Sven-Olaf Karlsson, formerly Chief Executive Officer of Jönköping County Council, Sweden).
>
> (Quoted in The King's Fund, 2011, p. 14)

All of us – at some point in our lives – will require health or social care services. In that situation, what kind of care would we want and expect; how would we recognise good quality care; and how might we – and other people – identify scope for improvement?

Quality management has become a key feature of health and social care policy (Figure 18.1). If you are a manager, you will be aware of the pressure to deliver 'quality' services. As a patient, service user, carer or member of the public, you will be aware of news stories concerning 'failing' services, and government ambitions to drive quality through regulatory frameworks, professional standards, efficiency, information and service user choice. You will also have your own views about what constitutes quality care and there is an extensive and very influential literature dedicated to it (for example, Donabedian, 2003; Tierney, 2006). And still quality remains a nebulous concept. While it should be at the centre of *all* health and social care practice, 'quality' is a word that frequently causes people's eyes to glaze over.

And yet, ask most practitioners and managers why they work in health and social care, and the response is often 'to make a difference' or 'to improve people's quality of life'. Everyone recognises that quality matters. Valerie Iles (2011) advocates moving services from caring *for* people to caring *about* them, if they are to bring about the improvements in quality which have proved challenging to get right (see also Chapter 1). She argues that this shift requires commitment and leadership from both managers and professionals. Managers *and* practitioners must find ways to bring about the small-scale everyday improvements that collectively result in better health and social care systems.

The concept of quality is both elusive and contested. Recent definitions of quality in health and social care include:

- 'clinically effective, personal and safe' (Department of Health, 2008, pp. 8–9)
- 'effective … efficient … accessible … acceptable/patient centred … equitable … safe' (World Health Organization, 2006, pp. 9–10)
- 'What is quality? … whether the service does what it says it does … whether the service does what people want and need it to do … whether people are getting what they paid for' (People First Dorset, 2012).

A key role for managers is to listen to and reconcile these multiple perspectives on quality. This chapter will therefore explore the following core questions.

- Why does a focus on quality matter?
- What is quality and who defines it?
- How can quality be identified, implemented and measured?

18.2 The importance of focusing on quality

> There is a good deal of evidence available as to what constitutes good care, and good commissioning. Our findings from this inspection programme show that there remains a significant shortfall between policy and practice.
>
> (Dame Jo Williams, Chair of CQC, 2012, p. 4)

The aim of services should not be to provide care that is just 'good enough'. They should endeavour to provide *really* good care; care that we would expect for ourselves and for our friends and family. This includes care that is safe, effective and most likely to have beneficial effects for service users. But a focus on quality also has important implications for working environments and relationships. For example, aspiring to provide quality care can support staff motivation and development (Martin and Henderson, 2005), while care that is poorly organised drives out employees who cannot work in an environment where they cannot do a good job (Cavendish, 2011).

Clearly, quality matters, therefore, to both service users and staff, and there have been many initiatives to change the behaviour of professionals and to improve the quality and efficiency of care. Success has been mixed and quality improvement remains central to policy and practice debates (Doran et al., 2011; Iles, 2011). But where did this focus on policy come from; and why does it continue to preoccupy us?

Quality in health and social care was historically defined by professionals, who were 'experts' in their particular field (Walker et al., 2003). This came under attack from the 1980s as several factors – social, political and economic – came together. Successive scandals, particularly about child protection and residential care, raised concerns among both politicians and the public that policy guidance was not being translated into practice. In the context of hospital care, the publication of the Kennedy Report in 2001 identified numerous failings that had led to one-third of children receiving 'less than adequate care' at the Bristol Royal Infirmary (BRI), with fatal consequences for many of them (Figure 18.2). The report highlighted that:

- Care arrangements at the BRI were unsafe; and the state of buildings and equipment and lack of staff training had the potential to cause actual harm.

- There was no requirement for hospital consultants to update their skills; they worked without supervision or appraisal. Their high status meant they were accountable to no one.
- Managers found it difficult to bring about change when faced with resistance from clinicians.
- There were no published standards of care; staff, patients and the public were not clear what to expect from the service.
- While information about mortality rates (and other data) was available, this information could not be accessed by the public.
- There was no systematic mechanism for monitoring the clinical performance of professionals or the hospital.

(Based on Kennedy, 2001)

Figure 18.2 Poor quality management and leadership had fatal consequences at Bristol Royal Infirmary in the 1990s

The problems at BRI only came to light when an anaesthetist 'blew the whistle' because managers were consistently failing to act on the problems. Afterwards, he could only get a job in Australia.

The Kennedy Report drew attention to the ways in which parts of the health service were shrouded in a professional 'mystique' that meant members of the public were effectively in the dark. It highlighted why a vigilant approach to quality is so important, flagging the need to examine the ways in which particular processes lead to particular outcomes. It also explored the relationships between key stakeholders (such as clinicians and managers), concluding that a breakdown in communication between different individuals and groups had led to the dire consequences.

However, the report states explicitly that it 'is not an account of bad people. Nor is it an account of people who did not care, nor of people who wilfully harmed patients' (Kennedy, 2001, Synopsis). Rather, it is an account of well-meaning people who lacked insight and benchmarks about how their practice compared with that of others, operating in a system with structural flaws and a tragic lack of leadership.

In what ways might the four building blocks of a fully rounded caring manager have pre-empted, or even prevented, the poor quality care described in the Kennedy Report?

Such high-profile failures brought quality into sharp relief from the 1980s, and undermined previously held assumptions that professionals were solely responsible for quality. Øvretveit (1997) argued that the consequences of the drive for quality involved managers in a bid for power over the processes that influenced service quality within European healthcare systems. Since the 1980s, tensions between professional and managerialist approaches to quality have resurfaced time and again, suggesting that questions of who 'owns' quality continue to distort the debate and distract attention from improving care in practice (Iles, 2011).

Quality and resources

A particularly tricky issue arises when providing high-quality services demands more resources. Sometimes, quality improvements can be achieved without greater resources, but this is not always so, as the following case study demonstrates.

Case study 18.1: The Flexible Response Service – luxury or quality?

Members of the integrated health and social services learning disability team in Westminster, London, were aware that some people could not access day service provision because of their challenging behaviour. Service providers agreed that a more personalised service was needed, with much closer working between clinicians and other staff. This led to the Flexible Response Service (FRS). By working intensively with individuals, the service was able to make services more accessible to people with learning disabilities who had challenging behaviour.

A particular feature of the service was that clinical staff were involved in providing direct personal support to service users, as well as offering more traditional clinical support.

(Based on Carnaby et al., 2011)

The authors of the article about this service report:

> While there has been a largely positive reception for the FRS … the service is highly resource intensive. There has been criticism that using clinical staff to provide direct support is a 'luxury' or a 'waste' of 'expertise'. These minority views have been heard and understood as a part of a perspective that advocates consultancy and guidance giving as a model of clinical input. While consultation has its place, the relative success of the FRS has demonstrated the need to enable support workers to become more highly skilled by clinicians working alongside, modelling, reflecting and empowering them to develop sophisticated strategies and approaches.
>
> (Carnaby et al., 2011, p. 44)

Do you think it is a 'luxury' for people with complex needs to be supported by staff with specialist clinical skills?

Quality particularly comes to the fore in times of budget reductions, when it is no longer possible to address problems by increasing spending on staffing and new services. This was the case in the 1980s, as it has been more recently with recessionary pressures hitting the public purse. The emphasis then shifts to improving services through greater efficiency and cost-effectiveness (see also Chapter 14). It is argued that improving quality leads to a reduction in costs, while poor quality almost always costs more in the long run (Martin and Henderson, 2001; Iles, 2006). However, the mantra that 'good quality costs less' is perhaps unsurprisingly touted in periods of economic constraint, whereas in boom times we are told that greater investment leads to better services! The 'efficiency savings' required in health and social care services in the UK since 2011 led to government programmes and circulars emphasising the importance of achieving 'value for money'. The rhetoric was that quality *can* be achieved for less, although the evidence does not always support this position.

While the jury is still out on the question of whether and when quality care costs more or less, everyone agrees that service users benefit if their requirements are better met; although at what level they should be met remains contested, as the FRS case study shows. And while there are many such examples of good practice, it is important to acknowledge that too many people are still not receiving quality care (CQC, 2012). This point is reiterated in Valerie Iles's book *Why Reforming the NHS Doesn't Work: The importance of understanding* how *good people offer bad care*. She was writing in 2011 in the wake of further scandals in learning disability services, hospital scandals such as Maidstone and Tunbridge Wells and Mid-Staffordshire, and child protection crises, including that of Peter Connelly (Baby P) in 2007 in Haringey, London. Iles argues that inadequate care prevails in many quarters, despite numerous well-meaning managers, professionals and front-line practitioners, and despite sustained investment under the New Labour government (1997–2010).

Questions about quality therefore continue to be highly pertinent and relevant in the management and leadership of health and social care. The next section explores different perspectives on how quality can be improved, and considers the manager's role in reconciling these diverse approaches.

18.3 Perspectives on quality

Case study 18.2: Whose views should managers take into account?

Sadiq: Following my letter of complaint about the care I received in hospital, I was told that the consultant was outstanding in his field and the treatment he gave would be the best in the region. I didn't care. He was still rude and arrogant and had failed to diagnose my problem!

> *Lucy:* I had been warned about my local maternity service by friends who had felt let down by their experiences. Also, there are poor statistics relating to medical interventions there. But my antenatal care painted a very different picture ... caring and compassionate practitioners who were always willing to talk and answer our questions. It left me feeling very confused. Was this a bad service or not?

The cases of Sadiq and Lucy show that ideas about what quality looks like vary depending on who you consult. Managers and leaders must take account of a diverse range of perspectives on quality, both to meet statutory and organisational demands and to ensure that key stakeholders 'own' understandings of good quality care. Therefore, this section explores perspectives on quality framed by professionals, regulatory regimes and service users.

Professional approaches to quality

Events in the 1980s and 1990s resulted in a shift in how quality was defined and measured. Consequently, professionals no longer dominate the quality agenda, although quality cannot be achieved without their leadership and commitment. As discussed in Chapter 14, 'professional' approaches, including approaches to quality, tend to be characterised by:

- a focus on the relationship between practitioner and service user without taking account of resource constraints
- quality and competence assessed by peers from the same profession (if at all)
- primary loyalty and accountability to the professional body and not to the employer.

The advantage of this approach is that professionals feel they 'own' quality standards, rather than them being imposed; but sometimes, as shown by the Kennedy Report into the Bristol Royal Infirmary, this can become a cosy relationship in which professional incompetence is not challenged. In this classic professional approach to quality, there is no systematic external scrutiny or guarantee that individual professionals are indeed practising competently and according to the latest evidence (Walker et al., 2003). However, that does not mean there is no merit in professional approaches to quality. A focus on what is best for individual patients, rather than resource constraints, can be a useful counterbalance to other pressures on services. Loyalty to a professional body, rather than to an employer, can help staff to 'whistleblow' when poor practice is institutionalised, as happened at the BRI. Peer review of competence and quality can therefore complement review by outsiders, but such professional approaches to quality are most beneficial when they are teamed with other approaches.

Managerialist approaches to quality

Figure 18.3 Managerialist approaches to care?

Since the 1980s, 'managerialist' approaches to improving the quality of care (Figure 18.3) have been advocated by successive governments (see Chapter 14). 'Quality' was the concept used to legitimise shifts in the way health and social care was structured, managed and delivered. However, quality was also the tool used to effect these changes. The government's White Paper *Caring for People: Community Care in the Next Decade and Beyond* (DHSS, 1989) identified for the first time in the personal social services the notion of quality control as a way of achieving a high standard of care (James, 1992).

Managerialist approaches continue in this century. Their central tenets are that quality can be improved by:

- efficiency
- choice
- competition
- innovation.

Effective leaders include quality as part of their vision for service delivery, achieved through distributed leadership, where all team members have the goal of ensuring quality processes *and* end results.

There have been fierce debates regarding the appropriateness of these approaches for health and social care (Beresford et al., 2011). Iles

(2011) argues that, while the principles themselves may not be inherently problematic, regarding them as *ends* rather than *means* has distorted priorities and outcomes. This occurs because the principles are relatively easy to turn into targets and results can then be shown in publicly available league tables. However, meeting a particular efficiency target, for example, does not necessarily mean quality care has been delivered or experienced (as shown in the next case study).

Case study 18.3: Paula

Paula is 84 years old and has been offered a personal budget by her local council. The council congratulates itself on having met its target of getting more older people on to personal budgets: a key policy priority, as this demonstrates that people have more 'choice and control'.

Currently, Paula lives alone at home and has reduced mobility after a hip replacement two years ago that led to further health problems. She also has early-onset dementia although she can still make some decisions. She is in regular contact with her son, but he lives in a different town, and has health problems too, meaning he cannot be as involved in the decisions regarding Paula's care as he was when she had her hip operation.

Paula had been receiving advocacy from a local group but they are closing down following efficiency savings initiated by the council which had retendered services previously provided by three local voluntary organisations (awarding the contract to a large national provider). Local knowledge and contacts were lost during the transition to the new service, and Paula no longer has an advocate.

The council informed Paula that she could use her personal budget to purchase services at home, or to attend day services, or use the money in other 'innovative' ways. She had no idea what this meant in practice. Paula just wants to know that she can get up, get washed and dressed, and eat a good meal. She feels anxious about travelling and going to new places, but she enjoys talking to people. She's not even sure she wants to live in her own home any more as she's worried about coping. But she's been told by the social worker that independent living is a good thing and that everything will be done to keep her there.

From the local council's perspective, quality has been achieved in Paula's case. Service users are offered more choice and control (tick!); competition in advocacy has led to a 'leaner' service with lower overheads (tick!); innovation has been delivered through offering personal budgets (tick!); and more people have been enabled to live independently – a key social care target (tick!). However, it looks different from Paula's perspective. She was left to make decisions without support and information and consequently felt anxious and uncertain, if not actually unsafe.

This does not mean that elements of choice and control, efficiency, innovation and competition cannot support an improvement in the quality of health and social care. Members of the disability movement campaigned hard for the right to choose how they spend the funds they are entitled to. And there are numerous success stories of people who have received personal budgets and are finally getting services that support them to flourish. But these principles are not sufficient.

How might an emphasis on goal awareness and contextual awareness support a manager in ensuring the right outcomes for service users such as Paula?

Amartya Sen (2002) encourages us to question whether choice supports or impairs our freedom. Barry Schwartz (2004) argues that while *some* choice is good, *more choice* is not necessarily *better*. Valerie Iles (2011) suggests that, in defining quality through choice, the responsibility for quality inadvertently shifts from service providers and commissioners on to the shoulders of patients and service users. She describes an occasion when a Director of Commissioning at a local hospital surgical unit responded to a Medical Director's concern about quality of care by suggesting that it was no longer a commissioning concern as patients could choose to go elsewhere. Iles writes:

> If we think carefully about this instance we might suggest that, for a choice of this sort to be meaningful, patients would need to know enough about the quality of different services to be able to make an initial choice, understand and afford the consequences of that choice (e.g. increased travelling time for themselves and their families) and be able to change their choice midway through their experience if they find it unsatisfactory. Furthermore that they fully understand all the consequences of that choice – for example that they may be unable to access local physiotherapy services on discharge but have to travel to those attached to the hospital they chose instead.
>
> (Iles, 2011, pp. 54–55)

Offering people a choice does not – in itself – lead to better care. It can be a method of helping to *achieve* better care, but it depends on processes, skills and practitioner–service user interactions that make the choice meaningful. It requires managers to keep their **goal awareness** focused on providing not just choice but also quality care from the perspective of the service user or patient; this means it is essential to have a wider **contextual awareness**, beyond institutional targets.

'[Q]uality support is therefore not about the services and buildings that people can "slot in" to, but the ways in which staff working with an individual identify likes and dislikes, sensory needs and communication abilities and use this knowledge to build a lifestyle with the person and his or her network that promotes citizenship' (Carnaby et al., 2011, p. 40).

Likewise, all managers will be aware of the drive to implement more 'efficient' ways of working as another indicator of quality. Recall the Flexible Response Service in Case study 18.1. The authors suggested that the service could arguably make efficiency savings by reducing the skill mix in the team and losing clinical expertise. This would certainly reduce costs, and possibly save time by reducing paperwork and meetings. But can it be guaranteed that such savings would deliver the person-centred care that is the central goal of the service? Or would it leave users, as in Paula's case, confused and feeling vulnerable?

Regulation and performance indicators

In the UK, successive governments have developed and strengthened the regulatory framework in health and social care. While there is not space here to discuss in detail the variety of regulatory mechanisms available (nor the range of agencies and frameworks), they are clearly significant to managers in health and social care.

Anyone who has worked in a service organisation understands the pressures associated with quality inspections and performance management, and the implications of being judged as failing. There is pressure to adopt a compliance-based approach, assuming most providers are happy to comply with a view to improving quality. Walshe (2002) suggests that, in practice, many regulators may adapt their approach in the light of the situation at hand, taking a more sympathetic attitude to a manager and a service that is open about its shortcomings.

The external regulatory pressures facing managers in health and social care change frequently but show no sign of diminishing. Managers must meet the requirements without compromising the overall quality and safety of their service. In Paula's case, she was informed by her social worker that independent living is a 'good thing' and, clearly, for people who value independent living, it *is* good. However, Paula's needs mean that independent living is causing her anxiety, and probably a lack of sleep, leading inevitably to a deterioration in her health and a reduced quality of life. The danger in applying a quality initiative such as independent living without an accurate assessment of an individual's needs is that it can actually do more harm than good. By focusing solely on regulatory requirements, managers run the risk of focusing on 'what can be seen to be done', rather than improving what actually *needs* to be done. It is a difficult balancing act.

The literature on practice highlights the usefulness of performance indicators, optimistically asserting that they provide genuine verification of improvements in quality (Freeman, 2006). The academic literature on performance management systems is more sceptical, arguing that too many problems remain with validity, reliability and perverse incentives (Figure 18.4). For example, in 2004, a target was introduced that 98 per cent of patients attending accident and emergency (A&E) services in English acute hospitals should wait less than four hours to be treated. Hospitals which met the targets were rewarded with significant new sums of money. While this might sound like a sensible way of measuring and incentivising an important aspect of quality (timeliness), some staff argued that, in practice, it led to a wide variety of behaviours which actually *undermined* quality. These included: discharging patients before they were fully assessed or stabilised; admitting patients to wards unnecessarily or to inappropriate wards; 'admitting' patients to A&E rather than to a ward (Health Policy and Economic Research Unit, 2005). Management strategies had been effective in meeting performance indicator targets, but at what cost to the quality of care?

Figure 18.4 Is money always an effective incentive to improve quality?

'[N]ot all kinds of information are amenable to being collected or codified and the digital revolution has, to date, succeeded in privileging only the data that can. The audit culture that it has spawned thus measures only some of the things we may deem important, and it is worth looking at some of the less beneficial features of this culture' (Iles, 2011, p. 19).

One problem with performance indicators is they may not capture information that is crucial to the *experience* of service users, for example pain management. When services are paid on the basis of their results (which comes to mean how well they meet the performance indicators), there is a danger that managers are encouraged to focus most of their efforts on the aspects of the service that are being measured by the indicators. As a result, aspects of the service that cannot be measured so easily can become deprioritised. Even when particular activities are incentivised by payments, as in the report by Doran et al. (2011), while quality of care initially improved for incentivised activities, it quickly plateaued. More worryingly, after three years, quality of care for non-incentivised activities fell significantly.

So, not all that counts can be counted and not all that can be counted counts. This is reflected in the comments made by managers in a research project on implementing person-centred approaches, for example:

> One of our biggest problems in dealing with the top coming down is performance indicators which have been set by the government and that's what's leading the service. And that's nothing to do with what individuals want – a person-centred approach. Again, we're encouraged to do reviews and assessments and things, hit targets, deadlines and things, which in our work don't necessarily apply.
>
> (Beresford et al., 2011, p. 193)

So, while managers must be prepared to measure and record data about their service, they must also examine this data critically and sensitively, so that it does not inadvertently distort practice.

Service user perspectives

So far, this chapter has focused on quality as defined and measured by professionals, policy makers and regulators. You may be wondering where is the voice of service users, patients, carers and the wider public in this debate. Although it is hard to define quality, it is possible to tease out what it means in practice. Just as people know a poor-quality service when they see and experience it, equally they can recognise a high-quality one from first-hand experience. This first-hand experience, according to some commentators, is what determines quality (Beresford et al., 2011). From a manager's perspective, quality derives from knowing who uses your service, understanding what they would like from you, and being able to respond appropriately to their requirements (Martin and Henderson, 2001).

There has, therefore, been a drive to put service user outcomes at the centre of quality. This has a long history in social care through, for example, action research projects and the formal involvement of service users in quality assurance mechanisms. More recently, healthcare strategies across the UK have also begun to pay much closer attention to involving patients in defining what quality looks like, and how it can be measured (see also Chapter 13). One prominent example of an attempt to systematically measure patient satisfaction with quality is the Patient Reported Outcome Measures (PROMS).

Introduced in England by the Department of Health in 2009, PROMS is a system for measuring the outcomes of a range of simple surgical procedures (knee and hip replacements, and hernia and varicose vein operations) by asking patients questions about their health in five dimensions, pre-surgery and post-surgery:

- mobility
- self-care (e.g. washing and dressing)
- usual activities (e.g. work, study, housework, family or leisure activities)
- pain or discomfort
- anxiety or depression.

What patients report is quantified into a five-digit number string describing their health state, called the EQ-5D 'health profile'. In August 2011, it was proposed to link payments to hospitals to data generated in this way, to link quality to payment (HSJ, 2011). However, this was resisted by the British Orthopaedic Association, representing the doctors who perform the operations, on the grounds that it may lead to hospitals denying these operations to people with co-morbidities (other serious health problems) because they were least likely to see significant benefit (HSJ, 2011). In effect, they were arguing that, in this instance, using patients' reports of quality would lead to perverse incentives to treat only the patients who were most likely to report that their experience had been high quality!

Emphasising service users' perspectives on quality raises numerous dilemmas for managers and leaders, but they need not feel overwhelmed or disempowered. As Chapter 13 shows, there are various approaches available to gather service users' perspectives. And, while there are challenges involved in defining quality with reference to the views of service users, such as the thorny issues of which service users are heard, this is arguably the reason for services.

Which approach to quality resonates most with you, and why – the professional, the managerialist or the service user perspective? Can you see the benefits and advantages of the approaches you would not naturally use?

Managers must reconcile the different perspectives on quality explored here, and often this must be achieved within the context of wider constraints. This calls for strong leadership alongside competent management skills. Martin and Henderson (2001) suggest it is useful for managers to bear in mind the following points.

- Put the patient or service user first as a way of cutting through competing requirements.
- Remember that organisations are designed to cope with populations, but patients and service users are individuals.
- Facilitate good communication by being open about differences and difficulties.

The next section explores implementing quality services, and assessing whether quality objectives are being met. It also explores how effective managers can identify and tackle dilemmas inherent in delivering a 'quality' service.

18.4 Implementing and measuring quality

Quality can only be improved if you know your starting point, and have ideas and processes to make a change, and a method to monitor its success. This is a key role for managers. 'Systems' thinking is therefore imperative for managers seeking to deliver quality care. All too often, one change made within a service can later have unintended (and unwelcome) consequences.

This is the thinking behind the **Plan–Do–Study–Act (PDSA)** model, which is widely used in health and social care. Using PDSA highlights the importance of linking *processes* to *outcomes*, helping managers to understand cause and effect, by promoting a continuous (incremental) approach to quality improvement. Small changes are introduced and assessed for their impact, as opposed to a major systems change. This approach requires teams to work together and benefits from an environment which supports shared leadership. It also involves a good understanding of how to measure outcomes.

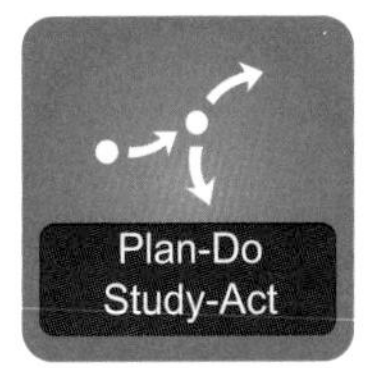

Outcomes and standards in health and social care

This chapter has already discussed a major limitation of the 'audit culture' – that it does not take into account 'soft' indicators that are not easily codified and counted. And yet, managers do need to know whether their service is delivering (Martin et al., 2010). Measuring the work done by a service can also demonstrate progress, and there has been an increasing focus on using outcomes and standards to help measure whether a service is doing well. Nocon and Qureshi (1996, p. 7) defined an outcome as 'the impact, effect or consequence of a service or policy' (quoted in Pinnock and Dimmock, 2003, p. 258). However, outcomes are also used to define what people want to see happen in the future. The word 'outcome' is regularly used as a shorthand for objectives that set out 'desired' or 'hoped-for' results (Martin and Kettner, 1996); that is, results that someone hopes to achieve through a care plan, a service plan, an interagency strategy or even a national policy.

A focus on measuring outcomes requires the involvement of service users, advocates and carers in deciding what is important. A care service might have an outcome which declares that 'people are involved in decisions that affect their lives'. One agreed measure of progress might be attendance at user-group meetings. If attendance is poor, managers need to ask why and explore how to implement change. Commissioning an external organisation to review these meetings could help to do this. Such a review might show that users see attending personal reviews and having an effective voice there as more important than group meetings. This might necessitate a change to the outcome, to one based on satisfaction with reviews.

Once a set of outcomes has been agreed, how can managers go about achieving them? Martin and Henderson (2001) argue that outcomes must be broken down into standards that are:

- measurable
- attainable
- real indicators of quality (not just numbers)
- clear and unambiguous
- consistent with the service aims and values
- set in conjunction with the people who will be asked to achieve them.

(For more details, see Martin and Henderson, 2001, pp. 194–5.)

'[O]ften people's involvement with [health and] social care services does not have a tidy beginning, middle and end and … in some cases their contact with the service may extend over a lifetime' (Pinnock and Dimmock, 2003, p. 277).

If the standards that managers set do not meet these criteria, there is a risk that staff will not understand precisely what is required, and will not know whether they have achieved what is expected. Managers must also recognise that, while some standards are relatively easy to identify and monitor (such as the number of people attending an activity each week), other standards are more complex (such as the extent to which people really enjoy and benefit from the activity). Managers must also use their judgement and expertise to decide *when* is the best time to measure (and thus evaluate) outcomes. While it might sometimes feel intuitive and practical to evaluate an outcome at the point of completion, people's interactions with health and social care services are not always this straightforward.

Understanding 'what made the difference' is a major difficulty in the study of outcomes (Dickinson, 2008). This is another reason why the **PDSA tool** can be so powerful; it gives managers an opportunity to distinguish between cause and effect, and to track the results that lead from the introduction of very specific processes and interventions.

The importance of leadership in implementing quality

This chapter stresses that *both* management *and* leadership are required to achieve quality services. As argued in Chapter 1, the same four building blocks are needed for *both* **fully rounded caring managers** *and* **leaders**. **Personal**, **team**, **goal** and **contextual awareness** all support the sustainability of high-quality *caring* services. The King's Fund Commission Report on the NHS (2011) acknowledges that there is considerable overlap between leaders and managers – they are deeply entwined and mutually dependent. The Commission argues that there are, however, distinctive areas of practice and that, while good management is about 'getting the job done', leadership is required to motivate people to be fully engaged. It is this full engagement of staff that leads to true quality in services.

However, this is not about 'heroic' leadership but, rather, an environment in which leadership that is 'shared, distributed and adaptive' (The King's Fund, 2011, p. 28) is highly valued (see Chapter 3). People in formal leadership positions need to recognise other people's expertise and vision as well as developing their own skills and education (Figure 18.5). In the NHS, this must involve supporting the leadership of both clinicians and non-clinical managers. Emerging international evidence on leadership and quality improvement suggests that there is a clear relationship between the two. For example, research into the performance of 1300 hospitals in the UK showed that those which invested more in leadership, management and effective succession planning produced higher quality patient care and productivity (Dorgan et al., 2010).

Figure 18.5 Leaders are always learning

The distributed model of leadership for quality improvement that is advocated by the King's Fund Commission is supported by Professor Kim Turnbull James of Cranfield Business School. Acknowledging the challenges involved in encouraging all practitioners and managers to become leaders, she argues:

> Leadership must be exercised across shifts 24/7 and reach to every individual: good practice can be destroyed by one person who fails to see themselves as able to exercise leadership, as required to promote organisational change, or who leaves something undone or unsaid because someone else is supposed to be in charge.
>
> (Turnbull James, quoted in The King's Fund, 2011, p. 19)

How far do you think this recommendation is tenable? Are you persuaded that this is the key to quality? How might this vision be supported in practice?

The Report's findings relate to the NHS but are just as relevant to social care. The Commission argues that leadership cannot be restricted to particular individuals or even institutions or organisations. It is not viable for leadership to be situated in *either* health *or* social care. What is needed is leadership of care *systems*; leadership *across* the care pathway, and engagement with stakeholders and processes in health, social care, housing, education and youth services:

> Leadership development must not focus purely on technical competencies, but on the ability to create climates in which individuals can themselves act to improve services and care. Staff at all levels need to be given the skills to have the courage to challenge poor practice.
>
> (The King's Fund, 2011, p. 21)

It seems effective leadership is considered essential to harness everyone's efforts to achieve good quality care.

18.5 Conclusion

This chapter emphasised that delivering services that people can trust, and that staff can be proud of, is central to the manager's role; and that distributed leadership is an essential part of this. This is not just about 'getting the job done'; it demonstrates a deep commitment to continually making things *better*. Quality services are not static, and must respond to the needs of the people who use them. This requires managers to lead by example, emphasising the importance of quality, and supporting all members of staff to deliver it. It is about reconciling multiple, sometimes conflicting, perspectives and it involves balancing budgets and regulatory pressures against the views of practitioners and service users. It requires managers to set standards for their service; put processes in place to make changes; and then monitor those changes. Managers need to be alert to the links between what they do (processes) and what happens (outcomes), and to act accordingly. Performance indicators, standards and systems for evaluation are integral to this picture but, on their own, they are not enough and can sometimes even have a negative impact on quality.

As effective leaders, managers must champion *excellent* services and communicate this vision to other stakeholders. This is never easy, and it is made more challenging in periods of significant change and resource constraint. However, a key role for managers is to ensure that the delivery of quality services remains a priority for everyone. Achieving this demands leadership at all levels, as quality is *everybody's* responsibility.

Key points

- Many service users continue to receive care that they, or others, consider is poor. Therefore, the question of quality is a priority for leaders and managers.
- The definition of 'quality' requires exploration from multiple perspectives.
- While managers naturally tend to focus on managerialist approaches to quality, it is important that they also take account of service user and professional approaches.
- Delivering quality services means delivering services that are continually (if gradually) improving. Tools such as the PDSA model can help to achieve this.

- Systems are required to set standards, implement processes to meet these standards, monitor progress, and respond accordingly.
- Individual commitment and distributed leadership can make a huge difference to the quality of care provision.

References

Beresford, P., Fleming, J., Glynn, M., Bewley, C., Croft, S., Branfield, F. and Postle, K. (2011) *Supporting People: Towards a person-centred approach*, Bristol, The Policy Press.

Carnaby, S., Roberts, B., Lang, J. and Nielsen, P. (2011) 'A flexible response: person-centred support and social inclusion for people with learning disabilities and challenging behaviour', *British Journal of Learning Disabilities*, vol. 39, pp. 39–45.

Cavendish, C. (2011) 'The floodgates open as angry nurses and relatives speak out to The Times', *The Times*, 27 September, p. 13.

Care Quality Commission (CQC) (2012) *Learning Disability Services Inspection Programme: National overview* , CQC, Newcastle upon Tyne. Available online at www.cqc.org.uk/sites/default/files/media/documents/cqc_ld_review_national_overview.pdf (Accessed 12 March 2013).

Department of Health (DH) (2008) *High Quality Care for All: NHS next stage review final report*, London, DH.

Department of Health (DH) (2009) *Patient Reported Outcome Measures (PROMS): Standards*, London, DH.

Department of Health and Social Security (DHSS) (1989) *Caring for People: community care in the next decade and beyond*, London, HMSO.

Dickinson, H. (2008) *Evaluating Outcomes in Health and Social Care*, Bristol, The Policy Press.

Donabedian, A. (2003) *An Introduction to Quality Assurance in Health Care*, New York, Oxford University Press.

Doran, T., Kontopantelis, E., Valderas, J., Campbell, S., Roland, M., Salisbury, C. and Reeves, D. (2011) 'Effect of financial incentives on incentivised and non-incentivised clinical activities: longitudinal analysis of data from the UK Quality and Outcomes Framework', *British Medical Journal*, vol. 342, p. D3590.

Dorgan, S., Layton, D., Bloo, N., Homke, R., Sadun, R. and van Reenen, J. (2010) *Management in Healthcare: Why good practice really matters*, Report by McKinsey & Co. and the Centre for Economic Performance [Online], http://cep.lse.ac.uk/textonly/_new/research/productivity/management/PDF/Management_in_Healthcare_Report.pdf (Accessed 27 April 2011).

Freeman, T. (2006) 'Performance measurement and performance', inWalshe, K. and Smith, J. (eds) *Healthcare Management*, Maidenhead, Open University Press, pp. 300–20.

Health Policy and Economic Research Unit (2005) *BMA Survey of A&E Waiting Times*, London, British Medical Association.

Health Service Journal (HSJ) (2011) 'Medics resist plan to link pay to PROMs', 30 August [Online], www.hsj.co.uk/exclusive-medics-resist-plan-to-attach-pay-to-proms/5034323.article (Accessed 28 February 2013).

Iles, V. (2006) *Really Managing Health Care* (2nd edition), Maidenhead, Open University Press.

Iles, V. (2011) *Why Reforming the NHS Doesn't Work: The importance of understanding how good people offer bad care* [Online], www.reallylearning.com/Free_Resources/Really_Managing_Healthcare/why-reforming-nhs-book.html (Accessed 5 October 2011).

James, A. (1992) 'Quality and its social construction by managers in care service organizations', in Kelly, D. and Warr, B. (eds) *Quality Counts: Achieving quality in social care services*, London, Whiting and Birch/SCA CoPublication.

Kennedy, I. (Chair) (2001) *The Report of the Public Inquiry into Children's Heart Surgery at the Bristol Royal Infirmary 1984–1995. Learning from Bristol*, Cm 5207(1), London, The Stationery Office. Available online at www.bristol-inquiry.org.uk/final_report/rpt_print.htm (Accessed 27 April 2011).

Martin, L. and Kettner, P. (1996) *Measuring the Performance of Human Service Programs*, Thousand Oaks, Calif., Sage Publications.

Martin, V. and Henderson, E. (2001) *Managing in Health and Social Care*, London, Routledge/The Open University (B630 Set Book).

Martin, V., Charlesworth, J. and Henderson, E. (2010) *Managing in Health and Social Care* (2nd edition), Abingdon, Routledge.

Nocon, A. and Qureshi, H. (1996) *Outcomes of Community Care for Users and Carers*, Buckingham, Open University Press.

Øvretveit, J. (1997) 'A comparison of hospital quality programmes: lessons for other services', *International Journal of Service Industry Management*, vol. 8, no. 3, pp. 220–35.

People First Dorset (2012) *The Days of Our Lives: a People First quality checker's report about the Ferndown Bungalow* [Online], http://peoplefirstdorset.org.uk/site/wp-content/uploads/2012/04/ferndown.pdf (Accessed 14 December 2012).

Pinnock, M. and Dimmock, B. (2003) 'Managing for outcomes', in Henderson, J. and Atkinson, D. (eds) *Managing Care in Context*, London, Routledge/The Open University, pp. 257–82 (K303 Set Book).

Schwartz, B. (2004) *The Paradox of Choice: Why more is less*, New York, HarperCollins.

Sen, A. (2002) *Rationality and Freedom*, Harvard, Mass., Harvard Belknap Press.

The King's Fund (2011) *Report from the King's Fund Commission on Leadership and Management in the NHS: No more heroes*, London, The King's Fund. Available online at www.kingsfund.org.uk/publications/future-leadership-and-management-nhs (Accessed 28 February 2013).

Tierney, A. (2006) 'Quality relevance impact', *Journal of Advanced Nursing*, vol. 53, no. 1, pp. 6–8.

Walker, S., Murray, B. and Atkinson, D. (2003) 'Quality matters', in Henderson, J. and Atkinson, D. (eds) *Managing Care in Context*, London, Routledge/The Open University, pp. 159–84 (K303 Set Book).

Walshe, K. (2002) 'The rise of regulation in the NHS', *British Medical Journal*, vol. 324, pp. 967–70.

World Health Organization (2006) *Quality of Care: A process for making strategic choices in health systems*, Geneva, WHO.

Chapter 19 Law, leadership and management

Rod Earle (with acknowledgement to Ann McDonald and Jeanette Henderson)

19.1 Introduction

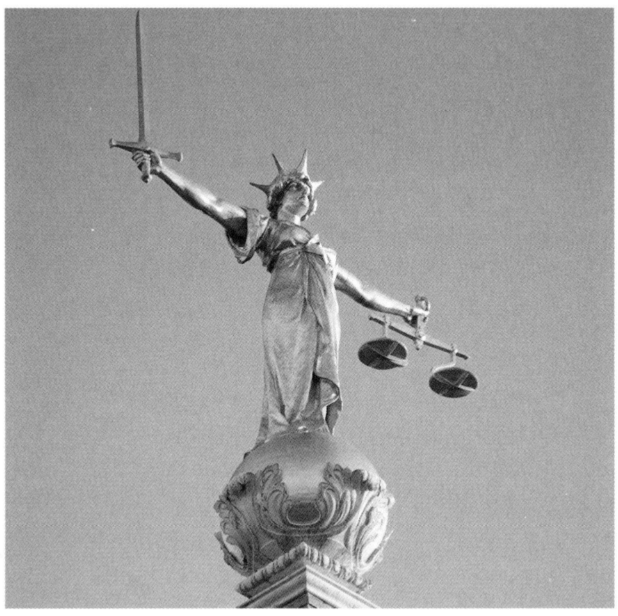

Figure 19.1 'Be you never so high, the law is above you.' (Sir Thomas Fuller, 18th-century lawyer)

The job of a manager is commonly imbued with ideas about power, hierarchy and authority (Wajcman, 1998). These are also features of law. As Figure 19.1 suggests, law is 'high and mighty' – it stands above us. Of course, it would be simplistic to think that either law or management could be reduced to this image, and most of this book is dedicated to demonstrating this. However, this chapter focuses on law and how it works in the context of practice in health and social care.

This chapter develops the building block **contextual awareness** introduced in Chapter 1. This involves some appreciation of quite complex legal frameworks. This chapter will examine the way in which general frameworks of law help to structure management practice and create opportunities to demonstrate leadership. In looking at these frameworks, law is characterised as a *dynamic* process rather than static rules set in stone. The idea of law explored here is that it is a continuous articulation, combining personal practice and social procedure, belief and aspiration, and is subject to review and revision rather than blind obedience. Legislation does not make decisions: it simply sets the parameters and provides the framework within which leaders, managers and practitioners make decisions. In this characterisation, the law does not just sit above you; it runs through you.

This chapter addresses the following core questions.

- How does the law operate in the workplace in relation to leadership and management?
- What are the legal frameworks for health and social care provision?
- What dilemmas, tensions and conflicts are front-line managers in health and social care likely to encounter with legal issues?
- How does knowledge of the law and legal frameworks give managers in health and social care leadership opportunities?

19.2 The background and context of law

There is some obvious correspondence between the job of management and the way the law works. Management, like law, is often concerned with decision taking and rule making. Law is frequently seen as impersonal and abstract: something 'out there' to be obeyed. Law has great authority, enormous power and somehow 'sits above people'. Perhaps that is also a common experience of (or even aspiration for) some managers, but it is not the model endorsed in this book.

The words at the start of this chapter – 'Be you never so high, the law is above you' – were used in 1977 by a famous English Law Lord, Lord Denning. He used them in a controversial Appeal Court ruling against the Labour Attorney General, the highest legal authority in the land and a member of the government. The Attorney General had refused to allow a legal action against the plans of the Post Office Workers Union to boycott all communications with the apartheid regime in South Africa. The Union was extending solidarity action to the black South African liberation movement, led by the African National Congress and its imprisoned leader, Nelson Mandela. However, the Union found itself facing a legal challenge from an activist who wanted the courts to rule against its plans. The Labour Attorney General refused him permission to take his case to court, and the Court of Appeal then overruled the Attorney General in a dramatic ruling in which Lord Denning quoted those words of the 18th-century lawyer Sir Thomas Fuller, on the ultimate reach of law's power. Denning's view was that no one should be refused access to a hearing through the courts and, in refusing the activist, the Attorney General had acted in a manner that was 'ultra vires' – meaning beyond his powers.

As with most issues of this kind, complex and intricate points of law were argued over at great length, but the case is also interesting, now, for the way it reveals wider relationships between law and norms, power and authority, the individual and the state. This story of law is all about history, politics and struggles. The apartheid regime in South Africa, and the formal institutionalisation of racism that it represented, have now been dismantled but, back then and there, it was the norm. It was legitimate because it was established in law and to oppose it was a crime in South Africa and pretty unpopular here in the UK in the 1970s. The law may seem to be 'above the fray' but, as history tends to reveal, it is rarely as neutral as it seems.

Figure 19.2 Dieu et mon droit – 'God and my right' – is the motto on the royal coat of arms. It hangs in every court in the UK, reminding everyone there of the divine source of the supreme power of law held, a little ambiguously these days, by the king or queen.

The authority of law derives from its position at the apex of a social hierarchy (Figure 19.2). But what has law got to do with leadership and management? Is it not just a question of following the rules, obeying the law, or operating within the code of the Health Professions Council (2008) or the Nursing and Midwifery Council (2008)? This aspect of legal power clearly reflects one of Wong's four-part typology of power – 'power-over' (see Chapter 1).

However, it is an image that frequently obscures the active presence of the other three dynamics of power in relation to law – 'power-with', 'power-to' and 'power-from-within'.

Laws operate at a high level of abstraction but, in some ways, they are intrinsically linked to ideas about leadership – they provide a framework of rules, codes and conceptual structures that guide social, personal and institutional action. In an organisation, while it might be the 'head' or official 'leader' who is ultimately held accountable, the person who is most likely to be called upon to make initial judgements about these frameworks, and to be mindful of their local or agency-specific implications, is the front-line manager. Therefore, they will need the confidence to enact such decisions (power-from-within), working in conjunction with other people (power-with).

How a leader or a manager operates in relation to legal frameworks and the values of law thus communicates much about an organisation, and themselves as a person. These frameworks and values condition the dynamics of practice and the provision of services to clients and users. By exploring some of the relationships between law, management and leadership in health and social care, this chapter will build your understanding about personal conduct, professional responsibilities, and the legal frameworks that structure practice, organisations and institutions.

Try to identify three ways in which law works through you if you are, or have been, a manager.

Please note: you should *not* read this chapter as a detailed guide to specific legislation or refer to it as such a guide. There are more detailed, specific and appropriate forms of legal guidance available to managers in health and social care. Managers should identify these sources and be prepared to familiarise themselves with primary legislation and the accompanying specific guidance documents relevant to their occupational context. These can vary according to the devolved (and evolving) multinational character of the UK. Both Scotland and Northern Ireland and, to a lesser but still significant extent, Wales, have independent legislatures that can amend or originate laws and legal procedures.

If you are concerned about a legal matter, or about the legal implications of any policy, practice or decision, you should always seek professional legal advice. Your organisation or employer should be able to assist you in this respect.

19.3 Frameworks of the law

If you work in health or social care, you will be aware of the presence of law shaping your working environment. For example, if you work in children's social care, you will be aware of the significance of the Children Act 1989, the Acts that preceded it and remain relevant, and those that came after it to amend, refine or rescind its provisions. Table 19.1 lists just a few examples of specific legislation and the kind of frameworks they establish for practice.

Table 19.1 Examples of the variety of laws

Example of legislation	Area of law
Chronically Sick and Disabled Persons Act 1970	Gives authorities duties or powers to provide services and makes people eligible to receive services
Local Authority Social Services Act (LASSA) 1970	Gives authorities powers to intervene in people's private lives
Health and Safety at Work, etc. Act 1974	Sets conditions and terms of reference for employment and working conditions
Local Government Act 1993	Establishes the terms for setting up contracts for services and procedures for tendering
Data Protection Act 1998	Confidentiality and data protection
Freedom of Information Act 2005	Access to data and the sharing of information
Human Rights Act 1998	A person's civil and human rights
Care Standards Act 2000	Establishes minimum standards and inspection regimes for care providers
Equality Act 2010	Anti-discriminatory practice and prejudice
Public Financial Management Act 1999	Public financial management
Charities Act 2011	Charities or companies delivering services
Health and Social Care Act 2012	Establishes a novel financial basis for sustaining the National Health Service

As these examples show, laws establish a dense framework for health and social care practice, covering almost every aspect of human experience, and according to your area of practice, a range of further legal frameworks will also apply. For example, if you work in probation services or youth offending teams, some aspects of management will fall directly under the jurisdiction of the criminal courts and be determined by various features of the criminal law as it relates to sentencing and other features of criminal procedure. In certain specified circumstances, work with young children and some vulnerable adults who are deemed to be not legally competent will be determined by the Court of Protection in England and Wales, the Office of the Public Guardian in Scotland, or the Office of Care and Protection in Northern Ireland.

Managers may also need to be familiar with aspects of civil law concerning slander or defamation, for example, and they must remain mindful of the need to express themselves more carefully in their professional capacities than they might on a strictly personal basis. However, managers are not legal experts, and they are not expected to fulfil such a role. Managers should understand some of the general characteristics of law and how it operates in health and social care. These general characteristics are summarised in Table 19.2.

Table 19.2 Components of law

Component	Example
Statute law – legislation passed by parliament	Children Act 1989
Case law refers to rulings made by higher courts that are binding on lower courts. It is sometimes referred to as 'common law'.	*R.* v. *Avon County Council parte 'M'* [1994] 2 FLR 1006 – this case involved the recognition of the residential needs and entitlements of a young man, 'M', with learning difficulties (see below).
Regulations are made by the Secretary of State for the enforcement of a particular area of policy and carry the full force of law. In Scotland, they are made by the appropriate minister in the Scottish Parliament.	Management of Health and Safety at Work Regulations 1999 (the Management Regulations) make more explicit what employers are required to do to manage health and safety under the Health and Safety at Work, etc. Act 1994. Like the Act, they apply to every work activity.

Guidance sets out expectations about the way the legislation should be implemented to bring about the intended purpose of the law.	'Working together to safeguard children: a guide to inter-agency working to safeguard and promote the welfare of children' (HM Government, 2010) provides definitions of child abuse and neglect and guidance on what action agencies must take to protect children. It includes information about roles and responsibilities, local safeguarding children boards and Serious Case Reviews (conducted after the death or serious injury of a child). Some chapters form statutory guidance while other chapters form 'non-statutory practice guidance'.
Directions can be issued by a Secretary of State in order to place further duties on local authorities.	Section 7 of the LASSA 1970 (see Table 19.1) provides for the Secretary of State to produce directions for the exercise of social services functions.
Policies and Procedures are developed by individual agencies and reflect their particular ethos and practices; they must fall within what has been laid down by law.	Often included in Guidance to cover aspects of practice, e.g. complaints procedures and child protection or safeguarding procedures.
Codes of Practice are advisory and interpret specific legislation to make it more intelligible to practitioners and actual areas of practice.	The Nursing and Midwifery Council (NMC) Code of Conduct 2011 is a set of standards for practice that apply to registered nurses and midwives.
Occupational Standards are similar to Codes of Practice.	The National Occupational Standards for Social Work are organised around areas of competence, or key roles of social workers. For each of the key roles, there is a requirement to 'understand, critically analyse, evaluate, and apply … knowledge' of the legal, social, economic and ecological context of social work practice, country, UK, EU legislation, statutory codes, standards, frameworks and guidance relevant to social work practice and related fields, including multidisciplinary and multiorganisational practice, data protection and confidentiality of information.

Operating in a framework

The words of a statute commonly include a variety of terms that qualify the actions of the law along the lines of various interpretations that have to be resolved in action. For example, a statute may say 'so far as is reasonably possible', 'if it is in the best interest of …' or 'as may be appropriate'. In doing so, the statute defers, to some extent, to the authority of circumstance and the need for judgement to be exercised 'on the ground' and close to specific contexts and realities. This element of discretion is vital, literally, in that it gives life to the law; it is how law works through people rather than simply telling them what to do. But it also makes it complicated. For example, a local authority will have a measure of discretion in defining who, according to various locally determined characteristics, is deemed to be 'a child in need' under the statutory provisions of the Children Act 1989, the Children (Scotland) Act 1995, or the Children (Northern Ireland) Order 1995. Equally, the definition of 'aftercare services' provided by statute in the Mental Health Act 1983 are not specified in the Act and have evolved through practice and precedent. For example, questions of mental capacity in Northern Ireland are not prescribed by law as they are in Scotland (the Adults with Incapacity (Scotland) Act 2000) and England and Wales (the Mental Capacity Act 2005).

Managers may determine who is entitled to a service, and how such access and such services can be delivered, according to national, regional and local frameworks which will vary considerably. The challenges that then arise, and are successfully or unsuccessfully met, provide for the evolution of services and the recognition of leadership. But this process of justifying and accounting for decisions occurs within clearly established frameworks that specify the parameters for discretion. Managers must appreciate these parameters to operate within the law. The following terms used in legislation set some of these parameters.

Professionals have a duty of care and can be deemed negligent if there is a dereliction of that duty.

- *Duty* – something an agency must do under law.
- *Powers* – those things an agency may do, but with a discretionary element that allows for choice, depending on circumstances.
- *Responsibility* – workers' responsibility to carry out their work in accordance with agency policy and professional values.
- *Remedies* – used to enforce rights or ensure powers are properly used.

The procedures for deciding how services are provided, who is entitled to them and how they are delivered often involve extensive consultation. Skills for Health (the Skills Council for the Health Sector in the UK) canvassed widely for the views and experiences of health workers to produce more appropriate guidance and training materials for the manual handling of patients. It obliges employers to ensure staff are appropriately trained for lifting, to comply with Health and Safety at Work legislation, and delivers better care for patients, to comply with Care Standards legislation.

Procedures for consultation are sometimes spelled out as a 'duty' – the highest level of obligation – but all consultations provide for a process that should be as important as the decisions that emerge from them. Poor consultations lead to poor decisions and are commonly grounds for subsequent challenge.

What makes some consultations better than others? Consider how you have been consulted in decisions and/or how you have consulted others in arriving at decisions. How does consultation intersect with leadership?

Increasingly, legislation in health and social care is accompanied by specific, and sometimes quite voluminous, guidance. Managers are usually expected to be familiar with the guidance that applies to their area of practice or service. Guidance documents interpret how the intentions of legislation are expected to be translated into practice and service delivery. They are issued as laws emerge from the parliamentary process but do not stop with their implementation. As practice and procedures develop, they generate new knowledge, encounter obstacles, and meet resistance and other kinds of practical difficulty. Guidance may be revised or updated and some legislation will include the power of substantial modification without recourse to parliament. This is an iterative process involving cycles of 'doing', 'undoing' and learning.

The guidance around child protection is an example of this process in which combinations of research, case law, policy crisis and institutional response generate the basis for the revision of guidance. The pendulum-swings between the terminology of 'protection' and 'safeguarding' demonstrate how language is implicated in this process. Managers need to remain alert to the sometimes subtle evolutions of this terminology in law, and its accompanying guidance, because of its significance for leadership as well as practice (see Featherstone et al., 2012).

As a leader, it is not just your actions that matter; it is also the language you use. The language of leadership can be as important as your actions as a leader.

Negotiating frameworks – balancing the law, agency policy and personal practice

Clearly, the laws that govern the provision of health and social care services form part of a complex framework. The manager's role is to negotiate this framework by recognising how the components interact to shape services and practice. Managers are not (usually) trained lawyers and will not have spent years in legal practice. They are more likely to be conversant with national guidance and, more specifically, how this is expressed in the agency's policy and procedure manuals. These manuals select and distil the most significant elements of legislation and its corresponding guidance as they are understood to apply to the agency's role or service. They may have been contested through the courts and modified according to various findings because the courts are the ultimate decision-making body when interpreting the boundaries of practice and the reach of policy.

The following case study examines how law, policy guidance and judicial procedure interact in setting the parameters for management practice. The scenario involves responsibilities for providing accommodation but corresponding procedures are likely to apply in many areas of health and social care.

Case study 19.1: The cost of living

Mr Bogdan has been assessed as needing residential care. For a variety of reasons he prefers to reside at Gladevale, a privately run home, rather than the local authority's residential care home at Phoenix Park. The National Assistance Act 1948 and the guidance issued by the Department of Health (Choice of Accommodation) Directions 1992 combine to provide for an individual to seek a placement in what is called 'preferred accommodation'. This specifies that a service user's choice is limited only in that the accommodation has to be available on the local authority's usual terms and conditions. As long as Gladevale meets those criteria, Mr Bogdan is entitled to expect that he can live there.

If the local authority or anyone acting on its behalf insisted that Mr Bogdan takes a place at its own Phoenix Park, it would be in breach of its duty not just to provide accommodation but also to allow a choice of accommodation.

Before 1992, Mr Bogdan might have been compelled to accept the local authority placement because his preferences had no force in law. Now they do. The commitment by the post-war national government to provide for people who are unable to provide for themselves has moved through several iterations, most notably for this scenario, the National Health Service and Community Care Act 1990. This law gave effect to the vocabulary of 'choice' and the principles of markets in social care. The endorsement in law of 'user choice' in the provision of health and social care presents managers with a further set of dynamics that must be incorporated into their practice. Even though the cost of accommodation must not be more than the authority would usually expect to pay, this is subject to the *overriding* requirement that the provision should meet the user's individually assessed needs. Significantly, in such a case as Mr Bogdan's, the local authority has a duty to provide suitable accommodation and this *legal duty* overrides any question of resources.

(Based on McDonald and Henderson, 2003)

Today, the priority given to the consideration of specific personal circumstances, and the tensions it can generate, present managers with decisions that may be more open to challenge through the courts. One such influential case in establishing this priority was R. v. *Avon County Council parte 'M'* [1994] 2 FLR 1006. The local authority's preference was for M, the applicant, to be accommodated in one of their own residential homes. M, a young man with learning difficulties, was able to establish that only a placement in his preferred, and more expensive, accommodation with the Home Farm Trust would meet his psychological needs. The claim proceeded through the authority's complaints procedure and subsequently a full judicial review which affirmed that his needs were consistent with his preferences and thus took precedence over the authority's (McDonald and Henderson, 2003).

'Choice would be a fine thing!' Giving people choices sounds great but it can be deceptively complex. Which choices? Whose choices? How often can choices be made or changed? These are all questions that a manager may have to answer.

In many areas of health and social care, the assessment of needs is recognised as an independent service in its own right. Reconciling the satisfaction of these revealed needs with the resources available is subject to several procedures designed to ensure that, at each stage, critical decisions can be both identified and justified. In a significant ruling on balancing the availability of resources with meeting needs, the House of Lords ruled in 1997 on a dispute involving Gloucestershire Council (R. v. *Gloucestershire County Council, ex parte Barry* [1997] 2 All ER 1). They ruled that, while local authorities can take resources into account, they cannot assume they take precedence. The ruling established that rigid criteria on eligibility cannot 'trump' revealed needs. Decision-making procedures must demonstrate their capacity to be flexible enough to accommodate extraordinary circumstances. This places a responsibility on those involved in making decisions to justify their decisions. This justification may be challenged and end up in court where the ultimate ruling will be made.

Recruiting law for fair opportunities

Although the law and its corresponding guidelines provide a framework for management practice, this framework requires constant negotiation. It is tempting to assume that, because it is written in law, it is set in stone, but that is not quite how law works. The ambiguities and contingencies of social life remain an equally determining feature of actual practice. It is managers, though, who are frequently called upon to act decisively to clarify the fuzzy borders and intersecting logics of law and health or social care practice. Strong leadership is often required to do this effectively.

Tables 19.1 and 19.2 set out the basic characteristics of the framework and individual managers will identify the more prominent features of law that apply to their role. By looking at one relatively common area of management practice – the selection and recruitment of staff – you can see how leadership and management operate in, and give life to, these legal frameworks.

Staff recruitment has become a heavily regulated area of practice because research has revealed the extent and impact of discriminatory practice and unfair outcomes that disadvantage, for example, women, people with disabilities, and people in minority ethnic groups. Legislation and guidance in this area has thus become quite comprehensive. Most organisations will ensure that people who take part in short-listing and interviewing applicants have attended fair selection training to give them some familiarity with the law, its associated guidance, their responsibilities and their agency's procedures. Even so, effective leadership may involve taking further action and developing practice. For example, the mental health charity Mind has issued detailed briefings on how disability discrimination is addressed in the Equality Act 2010. They include advice on how managers can lead changes in recruitment practice (see the website at www.mind.org.uk).

Research published in October 2009 by the Department for Work and Pensions showed that substantial discrimination in recruitment still exists towards minority ethnic people, despite efforts to remove some of the most blatant forms of discrimination (Wood et al., 2009). The study showed that, for those job applicants with a name suggesting they were from a minority ethnic group, rather than a name associated with the majority white heritage, there was clear evidence of unwarranted discrimination. For every nine applications sent by an 'apparently white' applicant, an equally good applicant with a minority ethnic name had to send 16 to obtain a positive response. For example, someone named Ofra Diouf was much less likely to be short-listed for interview than someone named Helen Smith, despite having an otherwise identical CV.

Research on the psychological characteristics of prejudice indicates that some significant discriminatory behaviour operates below the level of routine consciousness – that is, people are unaware of the way it influences their behaviour. Some organisations have been forced to confront this issue of 'implicit bias' because of the persistence of unfair outcomes, despite extensive policies and training in addressing them (Taylor, 2012). The law (the Equality Act 2010) obliges them to do so but how it is done is down to the managers. It is often a sensitive issue because no one (almost without exception) likes to think of themselves as racist, or acting on the basis of prejudice. Managers can provide models of behaviour and practice that give staff better ways of dealing with prejudice, as indicated in the next case study.

Case study 19.2: Mahzarin Banaji and ordinary prejudice

Earlier this year, Mahzarin Banaji was in a shop when she saw a young woman dressed in what she describes as a Goth outfit. The young woman was covered in tattoos and had a number of facial piercings. Banaji turned away in distaste. Then she checked herself. She remembered her resolution to engage with people she might otherwise have avoided. She turned back. She made eye contact. She smiled, and initiated a conversation.

> The reason Mahzarin Banaji talks to strangers is because in 1995, while working at Harvard University, she developed a test to measure unconscious racism (Banaji et al., 2003). Except she doesn't call it unconscious racism. Others use that term about her work, but she doesn't. She calls it 'ordinary prejudice', and it is that ordinary prejudice that she has resolved to overcome in her everyday life – anyway she can – sometimes by smiling and talking to complete strangers. Because having created the test, she took the test herself; and she didn't like what she found. In fact she couldn't believe it. She found she had unconscious bias – what others might call racism. Banaji says, 'Being in a minority myself, I didn't feel I would have any biases ... I was shocked and humbled ... and I was deeply embarrassed'.
>
> (Wotton, 2012, p. 15)

Mahzarin Banaji's actions demonstrate her commitment to leading by example.

Equality laws establish a variety of expectations about how people should behave, but understanding why people do or don't behave in certain ways is also important. Do you think it provides opportunities for leadership or problems for management?

19.4 Understanding statutory responsibilities

The law establishes that various agencies and organisations have statutory responsibilities that they must fulfil to comply with the law. For example, the Children Act 1989 establishes a statutory responsibility for local authorities to investigate whether a child is suffering or likely to come to significant harm. The Mental Health Act 1983 (England and Wales) requires an assessment of whether a patient has a mental disorder of sufficient magnitude to warrant their detention in the interests of their own health or welfare, or to protect other people.

Voluntary sector organisations are also vested with statutory responsibilities and must ensure staff are equipped to fulfil them. For example, the manager of a crisis telephone service has a duty to ensure that staff understand how their agency expects them to respond to suspicions or allegations of child abuse. They must also be aware of how these duties intersect with both partner and external agencies. They need to know that, once social services or the police are notified, these agencies will have a duty to investigate which will override any organisational policy on caller confidentiality, for example.

The idea of statutory responsibility is helpful in setting out for managers the boundaries of their field of action. It will determine where their agency's legal strategic responsibilities begin and end. The idea is so important it has become a distinctive area of administrative law defined by the concept of 'ultra vires', which you encountered in Section 19.2. If an action falls outside the statutory responsibility threshold, it may not be legal. Deciding what actions may or may not fall within the statutory responsibilities set out within any particular piece of legislation has become a much more active area of law than when it was invoked by Lord Denning in his landmark ruling of 1977. Administrative discretion in the interpretation of statutory decision-making powers is guided by, and tested on, the assumption that a decision can be shown to be rational. This means that no reasonable person, or properly constituted official body, properly advised and informed, would be expected to reach another conclusion.

Culture and rights: the Human Rights Act 1998

The Human Rights Act (HRA) 1998 adopts into UK law most of the rights contained in the European Convention on Human Rights (1953). It means the relevant protocols of the Convention are directly enforceable in UK domestic courts. As a result, claimants no longer have to go all the way to the European Court of Human Rights (ECHR) in Strasbourg to obtain legal redress for a breach of the rights established by a Convention to which the UK is a signatory. One of the most significant effects of the HRA was to take the protection of these rights beyond the principles of 'negative freedom' (that is, 'freedom from oppression') to a wider conception of liberty based on 'positive rights' (that is, 'freedom to live in certain ways that must be respected and protected'). This shift in emphasis means that the HRA is widely recognised as a statute of major constitutional significance (Klug, 2006), but one that remains poorly understood and underappreciated.

The HRA may be regarded by some people as a rather remote technical intervention: a matter for lawyers and judges rather than managers. However, nothing could be further from its intentions. The success, perhaps even survival, of the HRA rests on an, as yet unrealised, cultural shift that depends on the establishment of a 'human rights culture' (Gies, 2011, p. 169). This involves recognising that 'individual men and women should understand that they enjoy certain rights as a matter of right, as an affirmation of their equal worth, and not as a contingent gift of the state' (Joint Committee on Human Rights, 2003, p. 5). This sense of absolute, universal entitlement, and the protections and possibilities it provides, has been slow to emerge or manifest itself in public life (Klug, 2007; Ministry of Justice, 2008; Kaur-Ballagan et al., 2009). Instead it has animated in some parts of the media, for example, a regressive concern about an interfering 'nanny' state, or undeserving 'victims' sheltering under its protection, and even that it operates as 'a villains' charter' (Gies, 2011).

Leaders and managers in health and social care may encounter a degree of scepticism towards the HRA, general ignorance about its intentions, or even hostility to the wider arena of equality and human rights. Understanding the dangers of the cultures of resentment and suspicion (see Gilroy, 2004) that frequently accompany such sentiments can help managers resist their socially corrosive effects. A robust and coherent advocacy of human rights is likely to be central to a manager's capacity to offer effective leadership around principles of equality and entitlement.

How would you recognise evidence of a human rights culture developing in your workplace? How could you encourage one?

Privacy and transparency: conflicts and tensions

The Data Protection Act 1998 was introduced in the UK in compliance with the European Convention's requirement to establish a clear right to privacy in domestic law. The Act establishes explicit rights in terms of access to files and provides a statutory basis for the protection of confidentiality. Because of these provisions, records have to be kept and maintained according to certain protocols. Under Section 14 of the Act, an individual can apply for the rectification or destruction of erroneous data. But establishing what is erroneous or inaccurate may be far from straightforward. Consider the example of an application for a care order that has been unsuccessful but still exists on a local authority's records. Can an individual ask for it to be destroyed because it constitutes inaccurate information about them? The application may have been dismissed but does that mean the information behind it was false, or simply that it failed to meet the threshold for such an intervention? Such are the tensions and dilemmas between providing rights and fulfilling responsibilities.

The boundaries between a duty of care that may intrude on certain rights to privacy are rarely clear cut or simple to negotiate (see Edwards, 2004). In England and Wales, the legal process attempts to strike a balance through involving legal advisers and guidance specific to certain professions or occupational settings. Managers should become familiar with their local arrangements for legal advice on matters pertaining to the Data Protection Act 1998, the Freedom of Information Act 2005 and the Environmental Information Regulations 2004 They will be regularly amended and updated according to practice and precedence. As in all areas of practice, the law speaks more than once and managers are expected to remain conversant with the amendments and revisions that occur.

Given the intricate web of statutory requirements, regulations, guidance, standards and codes of practice that are in place, you might assume that the resulting legal context provides a foolproof system for ensuring good practice in the health and social care sector. Unfortunately, this is not always the case, as the next section on whistleblowing reveals.

19.5 Facing challenges, blowing whistles

On 31 May 2011, the BBC broadcast the *Panorama* film 'Undercover Care: The Abuse Exposed'. The widespread public outrage that greeted the revelations of the abuse of vulnerable adults in care was matched only by the disbelief that it was apparently conducted under the noses of management and regulators. An earlier undercover investigation by *Panorama* on the medical ward of a failing hospital, aired by the BBC in 2005, led to the whistleblowing nurse Margaret Haywood being struck off the NMC's register of nurses. The programme exposed the neglect of elderly and terminally ill patients. The nurse was eventually reinstated with a caution, after considerable pressure by the Royal College of Nursing and the public.

Public Concern at Work (2011) launched a report on the care sector, detailing its concerns about the non-exposure of abusive practice. The research included the following headlines.

- Over 15% of all whistleblowing concerns to Public Concern at Work's helpline came from the care sector.
- Half are concerns about abuse in care.
- In 40% of cases whistleblowers' concerns were either ignored or denied by management.
- In half of all cases where other staff knew about a risk they were either too scared or felt unable to speak up.
- Over 80% of the whistleblowers had already raised their concern before calling for advice. The majority said they wish they had sought advice from Public Concern at Work before taking action.
- Few care workers knew of or used their whistleblowing policy.

(James, 2011)

In a statement released after the programme in 2011, Cathy James, Chief Executive of Public Concern at Work, asked:

> How much more of a wake-up call do our regulatory bodies, and particularly local authorities and the Care Quality Commission, need before they understand that they can learn more about the culture of a care home from information they receive from a concerned member of staff than they will ever receive from a planned inspection.
>
> (James, 2011)

Both Lord Nolan in 2001 (CTS, 2001) and Cathy James in 2011 identified that the role of an occupational or organisational culture in sustaining or exposing malpractice is profound. The effects of organisational cultures are explored more fully in Chapter 12, but they will be painfully familiar to anyone who followed the revelations of the Leveson Inquiry in 2012 into the *News of the World* phone-hacking scandal. And it is not a problem confined to the cultures of the public sector. For example, organisational culture has been implicated in the collapse of Enron in 2001, WorldCom in 2002 and Lehmans Bank in 2008. It cost the CEO of Barclays Bank, Bob Diamond, his job in 2012. The slack standards that so rightly exercised Lord Nolan are writ large across corporate culture but it is the responsibility of managers in health and social care to demonstrate leadership by offering an alternative that fosters more transparent, accountable and ethical practice (see Chapter 16).

The Public Interest Disclosure Act 1999 sets out a simple framework to promote responsible whistleblowing by:

- reassuring workers that silence is not the only safe option
- providing strong protection for workers who raise concerns internally
- reinforcing and protecting the right to report concerns to the regulator
- protecting more public disclosures, provided there is a valid reason for going wider and that the particular disclosure is reasonable
- helping to ensure that organisations respond by addressing the message rather than the messenger and resisting the temptation to cover up serious malpractice.

Managers can facilitate a culture that tolerates whistleblowing by acknowledging legitimate conflicts and providing mechanisms for venting tensions and difficulties. Sometimes this may involve appraisal procedures, reviewing staff training needs, and seeking independent legal advice. It may involve encouraging regular surveys of service users and their families to establish their views. Managers are as likely – perhaps more likely – to have to wrestle with the competing pressures for disclosure, loyalty and discretion. They can be expected, by law, to both support staff and expose them, and will not be excluded from, or immune to, such procedures themselves. Coping with the intense and conflicting pressures that exposure and external inquiries generate is one of the most daunting tasks of the management role.

19.6 Conclusion

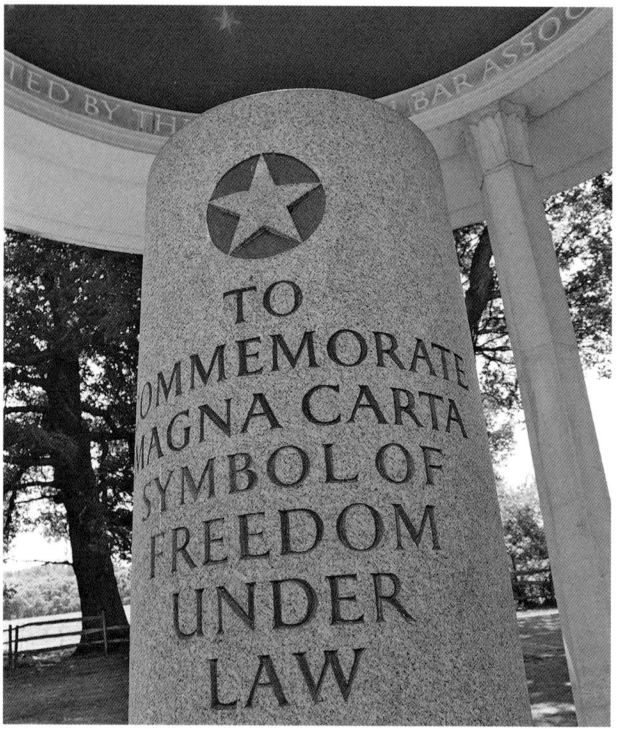

Figure 19.3 Monument to the signing of the Magna Carta in 1215 at Runnymede, Surrey

The Magna Carta established the principle that no one, not even the monarch, is above the law. It reminds us that nothing is beyond criticism – not even the law.

This chapter began with the words of an 18th-century legal scholar: 'Be you never so high, the law is above you.' This sentiment can be both reassuring and worrying. Reflecting on this helps us to understand something of the egalitarian promise and the fearful power of law. It helps us appreciate law's ambivalences and paradoxes. However, as also suggested in the Introduction, the law does not simply sit above us looking down; it works through us. Our actions give it life.

This chapter aimed to convey an image of law that 'lives' through the practice of managers in health and social care. This organic image of law invokes its involvement with living people rather than its abstract presence and symbolic power. In England, 15 June 2015 is the 800th anniversary of the signing of the Magna Carta, demonstrating the longevity of this complex and continuing relationship (Figure 19.3). Questions remain however, and they are: Can law operate without the weight of authoritarian influence? What does it achieve with the power vested in it? Similar questions apply to management and leadership. Reflecting on these questions leads the law out of books and statutes and into practice, management life, the actions of leaders, and the whole future of health and social care.

Key points

- The provision of health and social care services is governed by complex legal frameworks that are subject to change and review.
- Laws applicable to health and social care are very often written to protect vulnerable people.
- It is essential for leaders and managers to have some understanding of both the principles of law and the specific legislation relevant to health and social care.
- Understanding the authority of law and demonstrating an appreciation of legal procedures provides resources and opportunities for leadership.
- Managers and leaders must use their organisation's and profession's guidance on policies and procedures to implement legislation and guide practice.
- Managers must have a thorough knowledge of their organisation's statutory responsibilities and procedures.
- Law is as much about the individuals and cultures which enact it as it is about what is written down in Acts, guidance and codes of practice.

References

Banaji, M., Bazerman, M. and Chugh, D. (2003) 'How (un)ethical are you?', *Harvard Business Review*, vol. 81, pp. 56–64.

Catholic Truth Society (CTS) (2001) *Safeguarding with Confidence – Keeping Children and Vulnerable Adults Safe in the Catholic Church*, The Cumberlege Commission Report, London. CTS.

Edwards, L. (2004) *Taking the 'Personal' out of Personal Data: Durant v FSA and its impact on the regulation of CCTV* [Online], www.law.ed.ac.uk/ahrc/script-ed/issue2/durant.doc (Accessed 9 July 2012).

Featherstone, B., Broadhurst, K. and Holt, K. (2012) 'Thinking systemically – thinking politically: building strong partnerships with children and families in the context of rising inequality', *British Journal of Social Work*, vol. 42, no. 4, pp. 618–33.

Gies, L. (2011) 'A villains' charter? The press and the Human Rights Act', *Crime, Media, Culture*, vol. 7, no. 2, pp. 167–83.

Gilroy, P. (2004) *After Empire: Melancholia or convivial culture?*, Abingdon, Routledge.

Health Professions Council (2008) *Standards of Conduct Performance and Ethics* [Online], www.hpc-uk.org/assets/documents/10002367FINALcopyofSCPEJuly2008.pdf (Accessed 11 October 2012).

HM Government (2010) *Working together to safeguard children: a guide to inter-agency working to safeguard and promote the welfare of children*, London, The Stationery Office.

James, C. (2011) 'Turning a blind eye in the Care Sector', Press release, 2 June, London, Public Concern at Work. Available online at www.pcaw.org.uk/files/press-release-winterbournepanorama.pdf (Accessed 15 June 2013).

Joint Committee on Human Rights (2003) *The Case for a Human Rights Commission, 2002–2003 Session*, 6th Report, Norwich, HMSO.

Kaur-Ballagan, K., Castell, S., Bough, K. and Friemert, H. (2009) *Public Perceptions of Human Rights*, Manchester, Equality and Human Rights Commission.

Klug, F. (2006) 'The long road to compliance', *Northern Ireland Legal Quarterly*, vol. 57, no. 11, pp. 186–204.

Klug, F. (2007) 'A Bill of Rights: do we need one or do we already have one?', *Public Law*, Winter, pp. 701–19.

McDonald, A. and Henderson, J. (2003) 'Managers and the law', in Henderson, J. and Atkinson, D. (eds) *Managing Care in Context*, London, Routledge/The Open University, Chapter 4 (K303 Set Book).

Ministry of Justice, Constitution and Strategy Directorates (2008) *Human Rights Insights Project*, London, Ministry of Justice.

Nursing and Midwifery Council (2008) *The Code: Standards of conduct, performance and ethics for nurses and midwives* [Online], www.nmc-uk.org/Documents/Standards/The-code-A4-20100406.pdf (Accessed 11 October 2012).

Public Concern at Work (2011) 'Speaking up for vulnerable adults – what the whistleblowers say' [Online], www.pcaw.co.uk/news_attachments/Speaking_up_for_vulnerable_adults_what_the_whistleblowers_say_PCAWApril2011.pdf (Accessed 24 September 2012).

Taylor, D. (2012) 'Structured communication in prison – a project to achieve more consistent performance and fairer outcomes for staff and prisoners', *Prison Service Journal*, no. 191, London, CCJS.

Wajcman, J. (1998) *Managing Like a Man – women and men in corporate management*, Cambridge, Polity Press.

Wood, M., Hales, J., Purdon, S., Sejersen, T. and Hayllar, O. (2009) 'A test for racial discrimination in recruitment practice in British cities', Norwich, DWP/HMSO. Available online at http://research.dwp.gov.uk/asd/asd5/rports2009-2010/rrep607.pdf (Accessed 27 September 2012).

Wotton, M. (2010) 'No-one left to blame?', *Prison Service Journal*, no. 191, pp. 15–17, London, CCJS.

Chapter 20 Leading, managing, caring for the future

Sara MacKian

20.1 Introduction

Figure 20.1 People power works!

> Never doubt that a small group of thoughtful, committed citizens can change the world. Indeed, it is the only thing that ever has.
>
> (Margaret Mead, anthropologist, 1901–1978)

When I first heard this quotation, I was in Aberystwyth, in Mid Wales, at a time when the town's hospital, Bronglais, was facing the loss of essential services through restructuring and centralisation. I was meeting Anita Rogers, former Chair of Ceredigion and Mid Wales NHS Trust, but now an informal member of aBer, a campaign group set up to protect services at Bronglais. The group took a petition signed by more than 8000 local people to the Welsh National Assembly in Cardiff to protest against the proposed changes (Figure 20.1). In response to this, the Welsh Assembly Government approved two cross-party motions to ensure that local health boards worked in partnership across boundaries to safeguard essential services. Reflecting on the process, Anita said:

> My previous formal role didn't necessarily give me an immense amount of power, whereas in this informal role as part of a community action group I feel a lot more of a sense of power. But leadership outcomes can take a long, long time!'
>
> (Rogers, 2012)

Anita is right; it can take a long time to see concrete changes. This small victory for the aBer group was the result of many months of hard work canvassing local Welsh Assembly Members, gathering information and putting together clear aims and objectives to achieve their vision; demonstrating how leadership can be exercised by anyone who cares passionately about their vision and is prepared to take steps to see it through. Their vision was to save essential local services. As a team of authors, we also share a vision that, through this book, we can help the leaders and managers of the future to secure the best health and social care services for tomorrow. So this final chapter reflects on the core messages from previous chapters and looks at the context within which a manager might plan for the future, to fulfil not only their own potential but also the potential of those they manage, the organisations they work in and the services they provide.

The chapter begins by looking at the individual but, returning to the four building blocks introduced in Chapter 1 and threaded throughout the book, you will see how that individual must always be seen within the context they find themselves. Given the inherent instability and changing nature of the health and social care context, the chapter moves on to explore what the key challenges are for managers and leaders, and how a sustainable approach can be developed to secure the continuity of effective services for those who need them. Through this, the following core questions are addressed.

- What are the key future challenges facing managers and leaders in health and social care?
- What strategies can help a manager or leader develop a sustainable approach to an uncertain future?
- How can you personally draw on the key themes in this book to become a more effective leader and manager?

20.2 Leading by example

Small adjustments can make a big difference

Not every 'manager' is a 'leader', and important distinctions were drawn between the two in Chapter 1. However, it was also suggested that the underlying basis to each is the same – the four basic building blocks of a **fully rounded caring manager**. This section suggests that thinking of yourself as a leader is a useful starting point to developing a personally sustainable and effective identity as a manager, because it helps to maintain a focus on what you want to achieve and how you can realise it.

'We've come to expect a lot of our leaders' (Ancona et al., 2007, p. 92).

Within the context of health and social care, as the diverse chapters in this book show, we expect a lot from the people in charge. Not only are they expected to be highly trained and competent in their particular practice field, but also they are expected to understand the constantly changing organisational context they work within, and the legal and statutory frameworks of which those organisations are a part. They are expected to be able to involve a diverse range of people, from those who use services to those who deliver them, in complex decisions which can have life-changing impacts. And they are expected to do all this while being aware of the needs of each individual they manage and work with, as well as their own professional and personal development needs.

Managers also routinely have to deal with controversial situations, unhappy workers, disappointed service users, and uncertain futures. It is important, therefore, that they have a clear vision of what they are trying to achieve and why. Keeping that vision alive is often what triggers an individual into becoming the passionate, motivated leader behind a cause they feel strongly about. It can also rekindle a positive relationship with colleagues and service users, like Trisha in the following case study.

Case study 20.1: Trisha

Trisha was the head chef of a care home which had 82 residents. She was responsible for running the kitchen, managing her staff and budgets, but she didn't feel she had a particularly strong relationship with the residents, and felt excluded from any activities which didn't involve the kitchen directly. She had read an article on the therapeutic value of gardening and wanted to establish a kitchen garden project to develop a closer relationship with the residents and enhance their wellbeing. She felt really passionate about showing senior management that she could play more of a role in the daily activities of residents, so she secured a space in the grounds and planted some herbs and lettuces. But she had limited success in generating interest among the residents and couldn't keep on top of it herself as she wasn't much of a gardener. She ended up feeling incompetent! Most of the plants died and her kitchen garden dream failed to take off.

Then Trisha heard that one of the residents, Bill, used to run an allotment and she was surprised as he hadn't been involved in her project. When she talked to Bill about it, he said he thought she was the 'leader' and that he couldn't get involved. Trisha realised that perhaps her enthusiasm had actually excluded people, so she suggested that he take the lead in trying to resurrect the garden.

With Bill's experience, he had a much better idea of what would grow and how to make adjustments to help encourage participation, such as building raised beds. His involvement inspired other residents and staff to join in and soon the garden became the therapeutic space Trisha had originally envisaged. As she stepped back and watched other people take the lead, Trisha felt a real sense of pride and achievement for what they had achieved collectively. She realised her vision had been achieved by letting others shine.

What level of expectation do you place on yourself? Are you always realistic? How do you feel if you fail to meet your expectations?

Trisha had a very positive vision to create a therapeutic garden, but she lost sight of this when her own insecurities about how other people perceived her took over and she became controlling as a result. Taking on the leadership role in a particular situation can be one way to rekindle a positive vision but leadership is also partly about recognising your own limitations and trying to find solutions to those, rather than trying to *do* and *be* everything yourself, however passionate you may feel about it! Trisha achieved her vision, but it needed the expertise and experience of other people to help her realise it; she had to acknowledge that she was not an *incompetent* leader, but an *incomplete* leader (Ancona et al., 2007).

The incomplete leader

> No one person could possibly stay on top of everything. But the myth of the complete leader (and the attendant fear of appearing incompetent) makes many executives try to do just that, exhausting themselves and damaging their organizations in the process.
>
> (Ancona et al., 2007, p. 94)

'[I]ncomplete leaders differ from incompetent leaders in that they understand what they're good at and what they're not and have good judgment about how they can work with others to build on their strengths and offset their limitations' (Ancona et al., 2007, p. 95).

Ancona and her colleagues (2007) suggest that the idea of an all-round complete leader is a myth, and that it is important instead to acknowledge that any leader will have their strengths and weaknesses. They suggest that the 'incomplete leader', having recognised their own strengths and weaknesses, knows when to let go, and will find other people to 'fill the gaps' (this reflects the ideas around distributed and situational leadership in Chapter 3).

To help identify where any individual leader might need support, Ancona et al. identify four 'capabilities' which everyone has different levels of ability in: *sensemaking*, *relating*, *visioning* and *inventing*. Returning to the four building blocks of the **fully rounded caring manager** introduced in Chapter 1, it is easy to see that these capabilities map very effectively across them, to provide a comprehensive way of thinking about the requirements of effective management and leadership (Figure 20.2). A developing manager could use the framework of Ancona et al., together with the four building blocks, to consider their own strengths and any areas which might need development or support.

In what ways are you an incomplete leader? Where do you think your strengths lie?

'It's the leader's responsibility to create an environment that lets people complement one another's strengths and offset one another's weaknesses' (Ancona et al., 2007, p. 100). That sounds like a pretty good recipe for successful management too!

This is not just about the individual feeling comfortable that they are working to their strengths, however; there are wider implications. If someone presses ahead in a role without the necessary skills and capabilities, there is a danger that they become an *incompetent* leader, with consequences for the service provided. In the case of Trisha, far from producing a therapeutic space for residents, she initially caused stress and upset for staff and service users alike by failing to acknowledge her own limitations and the strengths of other people. A manager or leader must never lose sight, therefore, of the context they operate in. This means they must understand their own position and abilities, the people they work with, the organisation they work in, and the wider environment they are all situated within.

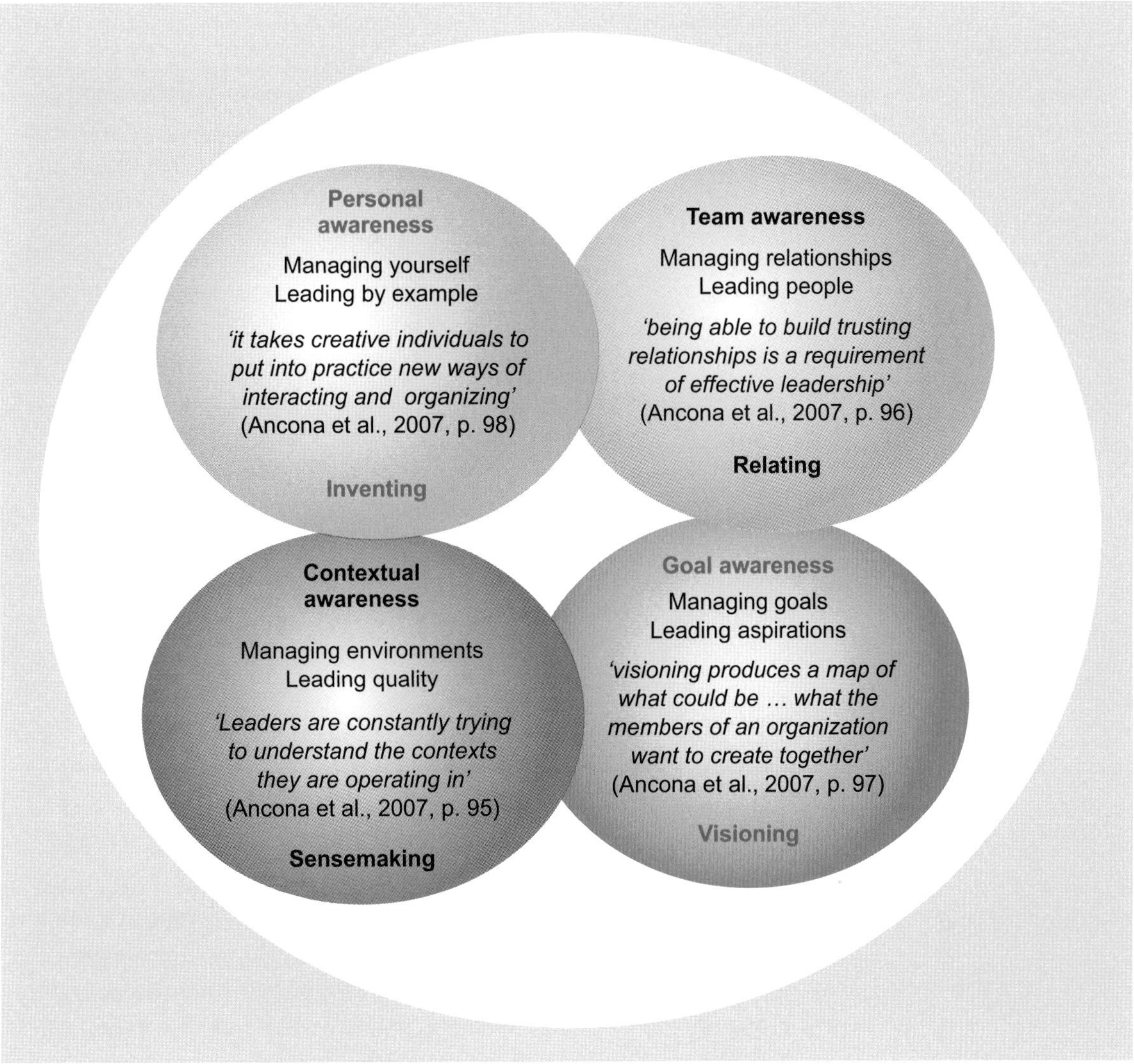

Figure 20.2 The incomplete but caring leader (Ancona et al., 2007)

'Sensemaking, relating, visioning, and inventing are interdependent … No one leader, however, will excel at all four capabilities in equal measure' (Ancona et al., 2007, p. 99).

The situated leader

Figure 20.3 An overreliance on the individual often undermines our collective capacity to get things done

> Although it is individuals who spot and raise challenges, and individuals who make heroic efforts to resolve them, few big challenges are met by one person acting alone.
>
> (Pedler et al., 2004, p. 6)

It is easy sometimes, like Trisha in the case study, to forget that, as a leader or manager, you are never on your own. The real challenge of any management or leadership role is to ensure you bring others with you. However lonely it may sometimes feel as a manager – especially when making challenging and controversial decisions – you are never on your own. The idea of the incomplete leader draws attention to the fact that someone 'in charge' invariably exists in relation to other people. It is useful to think about Wong's web of power here (see Chapter 1). An individual leader may have a high level of self-confidence and consequently a good degree of 'power-from-within'; however, their vision will be realised much more effectively if there is also cooperation to foster 'power-with' as a collective force across the team (see also Chapter 7). So, even when a clear persuasive leader has emerged, the effect will be much more powerful if they can develop shared commitment and a vision that everyone feels a part of. A group of people working towards a particular goal can make achievements that an individual alone simply could not (Figure 20.3).

Recall the four building blocks of the fully rounded caring manager. How do you see each one being useful when trying to lead other people?

Fostering an environment in which people feel understood and appreciated can go a long way (Fry and Slocum, Jr, 2008), and leadership which focuses on caring and understanding the wider context can be particularly effective at meeting service users' needs (Burdett Trust for Nursing, 2006). So, being aware of other people's needs is good for business. If staff and service users feel uncertain about the future and threatened by the changes being made, they are less likely to want to engage in that process of change. Yet, as Chapter 4 shows, change – although unsettling – can be managed effectively to lead to better quality services and improved outcomes for service users and staff. The caring manager-as-leader must therefore acknowledge the wider context they work within and help people to see themselves as part of the future – however uncertain that future may feel. The context in which each individual works is obviously unique to them. However, as we look to the challenges facing the health and social care sector as a whole over the next few decades, there are several common factors which the proactive manager should be aware of. The next section explores some of them and their implications for leadership and management in the sector.

20.3 Future challenges

> The challenge for managers at local level will be to inspire and motivate staff at a time when personal futures are challenged by the inevitable uncertainty that accompanies organisational and service delivery changes, and there are few prospects of increasing financial reward.
>
> (Harvey et al., 2009, p. 45)

Health and social care systems seem to be 'in a perpetual state of reform and upheaval, creating a sense of uncertainty and even crisis' (Sector Futures, 2003, p. 1). The biggest and most pressing challenge at the time of writing has been the financial crisis, and with further cuts in public spending planned, this particular challenge looks set to remain on the horizon for some time. It will leave a lasting legacy on the way health and social care services are designed, managed and delivered in the UK. If the system is to continue to meet the needs of its users, those tasked with managing and leading the changes will need stamina, courage and confidence.

'[I]t seems increasingly likely that the principle of universal access, which has traditionally underpinned the provision of health and social services in Europe, will be further undermined as time goes by' (Sector Futures, 2003, p. 9). How do you feel about the potential loss of universal access?

Traditionally in the UK, the health and social care system has been underpinned by principles of social solidarity, universality and equality, but an increasing emphasis on competition and private provision (see Chapter 14) is likely to mean a shift in priorities. Turner and colleagues (2011) suggest that, in the private sector, there has to be a greater focus on the patient experience but there is evidence to suggest that the sense of moral responsibility to the service user – so core to public provision – is lacking. While an increasing emphasis on efficiency and cost saving is putting greater pressure on managers to develop sound budgeting skills and an understanding of public and private market mechanisms, there is a danger of this marketisation leading to a socially regressive two-tiered system (Cuhls et al., 2002). This is something that managers will have to negotiate, but do marketisation and commodification *have* to undermine public service values? Is this the inevitable consequence of a consumer-driven world facing financially testing times, or is there room for an alternative? (See Box 20.1.)

Box 20.1: Wales, Scotland and Northern Ireland: realising an alternative vision?

> Even if people wanted to shop around for hospitals (which surveys show they neither want nor feel qualified to do), all they want is a good hospital, and their real concern is keeping services local.
>
> (Griffith, 2012)

The Welsh Assembly Government has attempted to tackle deep-seated problems in a more radical and socially just way, placing an emphasis on 'equality of outcome, not just equality of opportunity' (Griffith, 2012). This is a subtle yet profound difference and has led to some very simple, yet powerful changes in the way health and social care services are conceptualised and delivered in Wales. For example, universally free prescriptions since 2007 have been particularly significant in helping people with long-term conditions and high medication costs get back into work. The introduction of free car parking at hospitals was also lauded as a commitment to the principle of an NHS which is free at the point of access (Griffith, 2012). This appears to have been increasingly undermined and lost in recent developments in England, where charging for hospital parking has been described as a 'tax on the sick' by campaign groups and the British Medical Association. Scotland is making similar moves, having introduced free prescriptions and hospital parking, and Northern Ireland offers free parking for priority groups such as cancer patients or those having renal dialysis treatment (Health Estates, 2008). Such moves demonstrate that where there is leadership with a strong moral commitment, it is possible to challenge dominant trends and realise an alternative vision.

However, it is not just the financial and political context which poses challenges for health and social care. The changing demographic profile of our modern society means we have an ageing population, with people living for longer with more complex and expensive needs (Melzer et al., 2012). Healthcare costs for those over 75 years old are estimated to be 4.5 times greater than for those under 65 (Sector Futures, 2003). Increasing pressure is put on social care services as well, as more older people are living alone without familial support, meaning formal care services are having to respond where previously informal care may have played a greater role. At the other end of the age spectrum, the number of applications for children to be taken into care is growing substantially, up 10.8 per cent from April 2011 to March 2012 compared with the previous year (CAFCASS, 2012). This changing social landscape puts greater demands on dwindling resources.

The changing demographic profile means the workforce is also ageing. As the population ages, the pool of potential workers shrinks and, across Europe, there have been reports of acute shortages of qualified staff in health and social care (Sector Futures, 2003). This opens up possibilities for migrant labour and, consequently, the workforce in health and social care is likely to both age and diversify culturally over the next few decades.

'Periods of economic downturn can be times of innovation for service delivery and dynamic changes in roles and skill mix' (Hewison, 2010, p. 524).

Also, thanks to advances in medical treatments, procedures and care, there are more people living with complex health and social care needs which require careful coordination between agencies. These challenges are, therefore, a further incentive for effective partnerships between health and social care services, from policy design to front-line delivery, emphasising the need for managers to work across boundaries in developing fair, adequate and sustainable long-term care solutions (Hirsch, 2006; see also Chapter 8).

In addition, as a result of the growth of information and communications technology (ICT), there is a more demanding customer base of 'expert patients' with a greater awareness of available treatments and services. As Chapter 13 shows, increased participation among service users presents very real opportunities to reduce oppression, strengthen relationships and improve the quality of service provision. However, phenomenal advances in ICT have also brought the growth of shared databases, pooling of information and instant access to a wide range of materials, making the involvement of service users and patients ever-more complex. Self-care applications on smartphones allow individuals to monitor and chart their own wellbeing and health issues, changing the dynamics between 'professional' and 'lay' people. Meanwhile, electronic archiving is changing the way different professional groups access and manage patient information (Murray et al., 2011).

ICT advances are therefore opening up new possibilities for managing care more efficiently (Gibson et al., 2007) and changing the way in which we conceptualise service management and delivery. However, incorporating this into the way services are managed is not always straightforward. For example, Murray and colleagues (2011) found that staff who may not be used to working with ICT might find it challenging, and potentially threatening, to have to integrate it at work. They suggest that implementation is most successful where there is a clear fit with staff skill sets and organisational goals, and when staff can see a positive impact on their relationship with service users and other professional groups.

In what ways might the four building blocks of the fully rounded caring manager help to support the integration of ICT developments at work?

The developments in ICT are clearly shifting the dynamics between service providers and users, as well as influencing working relationships; this demands **contextual awareness** and **team awareness** as well as an understanding of the impact on individuals. People now often spend more time researching their care needs online (Figure 20.4) than actually consulting a professional (Hackworth and Kunz, 2010), and, even after consultation, they might then go on to self-care supported by interactive technologies at home (Gibson et al., 2007). This can be challenging for service providers; however, it also represents a potential new space opening up for constructive dialogue and this is a space that needs careful management (see Box 20.2).

Figure 20.4 Developments in ICT impact on people's care needs

Box 20.2: Negotiating the web?

> [P]roviders must change the way they operate, and go directly to the patient. Social media networks are the most accessible tool to use in today's environment.
>
> (Hackworth and Kunz, 2010, p. 67)

Some service providers use social media networks, such as Facebook, to deliver a fast response service to customer queries. Meanwhile, patients in the Netherlands can consult primary care doctors on Twitter (@tweetspreekuur). Other web forums, such as YouTube and Instagram, are used to promote information about procedures and services, and can be empowering for both patients and staff (Abrams, 2012). These are the sorts of relationships future managers and leaders may need to be considering, particularly when trying to encourage engagement among young people (Gibson et al., 2007) or supporting people living with long-term conditions (Nolte and McKee, 2008).

While the ease and speed of access to information afforded by our increasing web presence can be a beneficial resource for service providers and users alike, it also poses potential problems and challenges. The case in 2011 of a nurse wrongly accused of killing patients at Stockport's Stepping Hill Hospital appeared partly to be fuelled by her online profile on social media websites. The speed with which images and quotes from her personal pages were spread demonstrated how quickly an individual can be demonised and the difficulty of managing this sort of environment.

With the continuing push for 'choice' and 'efficiency' at the heart of service delivery, the use of online social media could revolutionise how service users and providers interact, while ICT developments will increasingly be applied to help improve the way teams work to deliver care. This has the potential to revolutionise service design, delivery and experience, placing unique demands on future managers and leaders. The future is therefore full of challenges. Whether we face fiscal catastrophe and a breakdown of the health and social care system as we know it, or technological advances resulting in a healthier elderly population, cheaper home-based care, and new opportunities for creative management, any manager facing this future needs to develop a sustainable approach to their role.

The changes influencing contemporary health and social care services create both challenges and opportunities. What leadership skills are needed to meet them?

20.4 Sustainable management: leading with vision and compassion

'I was elected by the women of Ireland, who instead of rocking the cradle, rocked the system' (Mary Robinson, quoted in *The Guardian*, 2010; Figure 20.5).

Figure 20.5 Mary Robinson, the first woman to be President of the Republic of Ireland (1990–1997), is a transformative leader with a strong positive vision for equality, justice and dignity

> Sometimes in order to live in line with our values and beliefs, we ... need to make tough choices, choices which are based on something that goes deeper than financial security and fitting in with the establishment.
>
> (Long, 2012, p. 80)

Katherine Long suggests the unrelenting pace of change, coupled with stress, uncertainty and insecurity around global economic crisis, has precipitated an opportunity to explore the values we seek to live by, and a chance to redefine our relationship with work, the meaning we derive from it, and the contribution we make through it. She suggests the current approach is unsustainable.

Management and leadership have a clear role to play here because they are underpinned by particular values about how we see the world, our place within it, and our relationship with other people. Barsh et al.

(2008) promote the idea of 'centred leadership' which acknowledges the importance of physical, intellectual, emotional and spiritual strength in contemporary leadership. Front-line managers are well placed to promote this and to help think through what is personally, psychologically, morally and practically sustainable for them and their staff. Some argue that a whole paradigm shift is taking place, with contemporary management and leadership being shaped by a higher ethical purpose and a more humble approach than was previously considered necessary (Daft, 2008).

'Who ... is likely to be more emotionally robust and mature, more capable and more in tune with his or her fellow workers – the clean-shaven MBAer who has risen meteorically through the ranks without any trace of a stumble and no experience of real hardship, or the battle-scarred, succession plan outsider who has had their ups and downs and has learnt from them?' (Casserley and Megginson, 2009, p. xvi).

However, despite such developments, the increasing stress almost everyone appears to feel under – to deliver more and more for less and less – means sometimes it is easier to make work and the organisation's goals central and be less conscious of our own needs. Casserley and Megginson (2009, p. xvi) suggest there has been a tendency to 'lionize success and denigrate stumbling', preventing people from engaging in the sort of reflexive process championed by Long. This, they say, has resulted in leaders who lack humanity because they fail to acknowledge their weaknesses and lack the self-awareness which might come from admitting to being somewhat 'incomplete'. It may also limit their sense of vision for what they could achieve if they were not so worried about potentially getting it 'wrong'.

This is why it was suggested earlier in this chapter that, to see yourself 'as a leader' is a good starting point for successful and sustainable management – regardless of which particular projects or teams you may or may not be leading at the time. This is because it forces you to reflect on which qualities, values and vision you bring to that role.

What vision do you hold which might make you a sustainable leader?

Good management and leadership are often about motivating other people to act (Schaeffer, 2002); and, once an individual begins to see themselves as a leader with a vision and a purpose, they are more likely to be able to empower others to follow suit, even down a challenging path. As shown in Chapter 3, vision is a powerful force, especially if it is a positive vision. Many organisations attempt to thrive on a negative vision – such as anti-abortion or anti-smoking pressure groups – but, according to Senge (2006), such negative visions are limited because they direct energy towards 'preventing' something we *do not* want to happen rather than building what *is* wanted. Senge argues that negative visions are generally more difficult for people to engage with and commit to, and are invariably short term because they tend to focus on single-issue threats.

Developing a positive vision for an organisation or a particular team is therefore a core part of a manager's role, to ensure a sustainable strategy for the future; such 'positive framing' can make a crucial difference to management outcomes (Barsh et al., 2008). However, remember that building vision is not always down to the individual 'in charge'; everyone has a role to play. As Shirley Findlay, regional service manager for SACRO, Scotland said:

> It's about sometimes having a brainstorm and having that opportunity to say well what are we about, where are we going, how does this fit with what we've been doing and where do we see this and our services developing?
>
> (Findlay, 2012)

'When you take the time to cultivate a productive working relationship – by understanding your boss's strengths and weaknesses, priorities, and work style – everyone wins' (Gabarro and Kotter, 2005, p. 92).

If, as a manager, you can provide opportunities to build vision, you are more likely to create a sustainable work environment which allows people to do what they are there to do – to care. However, even when it is possible to facilitate such opportunities for working more effectively across the team, sometimes managing relationships and expectations upwards may require a different approach. As a manager, you can create space to learn from your team about their needs and vision, but you also need to reconcile this with the needs and vision of those in charge of you. Therefore, it is worth thinking about how you manage your relationship with *your* manager to ensure this is sustainable as well. Tensions can sometimes occur between levels of management as a result of different daily pressures and a distance between the front-line delivery of services and higher level planning processes. Taking time to manage these relationships proactively is therefore worthwhile (Dufour, 2011), and a self-aware front-line manager may have to take the lead by managing 'up' as well as 'down'.

Clearly then, developing a sustainable strategy for management involves an ongoing process of actively understanding not only your own strengths, weaknesses, passion and vision, but also these elements for other people you work with – both those you manage and those who manage you.

In the face of the complex challenges facing the health and social care sector, it is easy to assume nothing can be done to prevent decisions being pushed through that you may not agree with. However, people most commonly give up their power by thinking they do not have any in the first place. As the case of Bronglais hospital at the start of this chapter shows, people can stand up and make a difference, even without a formal leadership position. There is always a way to empower yourself, to seize power, and to make a difference – however small – and sometimes as a leader or manager, you just have to take action even if it feels uncomfortable. Members of the aBer group included hospital staff who were putting themselves in a difficult position professionally, but their underlying values made it imperative for them to take action. Sometimes you just have to stubbornly defy convention to make the world a better place (Schaeffer, 2002).

20.5 Leadership in action: a never-ending journey?

'[L]eadership is not a state, it's a journey' (Schaeffer, 2002, p. 4).

Figure 20.6 The leadership journey is always unfolding. With the right approach, you can help it run smoothly

Reading any book on leadership, it is easy to get the impression that if an individual can acquire all the requisite 'skills' then leadership can be obtained as an 'end-state'. However, as Schaeffer (2002) argues, leadership is not only something that is worked towards purposefully, as part of career progression, it is also something that emerges as the product of life experiences and the decisions an individual makes. It also has to match the requirements and circumstances leaders find themselves in (see Chapter 3 on situational leadership).

As a result, the style you bring to your leadership and management is likely to change over time. Your identity as a manager or leader is likely to be an emergent phenomenon which will shift and grow with each new role and experience. If it *does not*, this might suggest an unawareness and insensitivity to the changing requirements around you. The type and style of leadership you adopt is likely to have to change over time to adjust to new external pressures, emerging relationships and your own learning journey, but there has to be an underlying strategy you feel happy with which makes it sustainable for all concerned.

There is a difference therefore between leadership *in theory* and leadership *in action*; and the latter requires stamina. It is all very well to acquire the tools and skills associated with leadership, to develop your personal vision and to orientate this to the organisation. However, if you do not put this into action – and make adjustments as your journey unfolds – nothing will be achieved.

This book set out to show that decisions and changes in the management of health and social care services do not just happen reactively and unreflectively. They are the consequence of a set of circumstances and a set of decisions, made by particular individuals and groups, and not always those with the most formal power or expertise. The authors have challenged stereotypes about what makes a good manager, how a leader should behave, and where power might be seen to lie. As a result, you should be confident that you, too, are an individual who can take action to influence decisions that are made, whatever your position inside or outside an organisation. By being **personally aware**, **team aware**, **goal aware** and **contextually aware**, your current decisions and actions will create your future power and influence.

Seeing your own development as a journey which unfolds over time and influences your future is a powerful metaphor. Alongside the four 'capabilities of leadership' proposed by Ancona et al. (2007), it reminds us that sometimes individuals will need to take a detour in their journey to develop their ability in a particular area. At other times, they might need to turn back, or enter new, uncharted territory to find someone who can compensate for their weakness or to make the most of an opportunity to develop their strengths. Like the image on the book cover (Figure 20.6), there may be stones in the path of your leadership journey which must be negotiated along the way. The ability to recognise these challenging obstacles as potential opportunities, and to negotiate the path around them smoothly, depends largely on a good level of **personal** and **contextual awareness** – two of the basic building blocks of the **fully rounded caring manager**. On any leadership journey, there will be detours, wrong turns and dead ends, and keeping on track can be the hardest, but most rewarding, part. Remember to keep an eye on the end-point you are trying to reach (**goal awareness**) and to lead others with compassion (**team awareness**); then take it one step at a time:

> [W]hether you're planning a novel or a corporate reorganization, you have to know where you're going to end up. Mountain climbers don't start climbing from the bottom of the mountain. They look at where they want to go, and work backward to where they're starting from. Like a mountain climber, once you have the summit in view, you figure out all the ways you might get there.
>
> (Bennis, 2003, p. 128)

20.6 Conclusion

'There is no "one best way" to lead, or one ideal set of competencies for a leader' (Hewison, 2010, p. 522).

At the time of writing, the shifting political and economic climate is putting an increasing strain on an already complex situation, and the health and social care system is encountering the biggest shake-up since its inception, designed to deal with the toughest challenges it has ever faced. This promises to have long-term impacts for the management and delivery of services across the UK. As the UK turns increasingly towards the US model of privatised care provision, the relationship between government, the private sector and the individual is being redrawn. As Moreira (2012) says, ideology has therefore returned to the forefront of the debate about how we plan for, and provide, health and social care services, and this will have a profound impact on the role of management and leadership in the sector. It will also be morally and ethically challenging for staff at all levels.

Whatever the eventual outcome, it is guaranteed that change will continue as an inevitable part of working in health and social care. It was therefore our intention in this book to provide some insight and inspiration to help future leaders and managers to feel better equipped to deal with this change proactively in their management roles, and to think of themselves always as actual or potential leaders:

> not because they are personally exceptional, senior or inspirational to others, but because they can see what needs doing and can work with others to do it.
>
> (Turnbull James, quoted in The King's Fund, 2011, p. 20)

It may seem hard to confront the challenges facing health and social care in the future. However, those who can weather the storm will be stronger leaders as a result; for the more leadership is realised and *practised*, the more effective any leader is likely to be. The various chapters in this book have shown how leadership is an unfolding journey which must be steered by a personal vision as much as the everyday demands of the job. Yet, as this chapter has shown, at the heart of that it is important to remember that nobody can be the perfect all-rounder. Through the topics and tools covered – framed by the idea of the four building blocks of the **fully rounded caring manager** – you should now be able to see what needs doing and how you can contribute towards achieving it. You may not always get it right, but you can learn from your wrong turns and do it better next time (Larkin, 2008). The authors have also stressed the importance of considering a whole range of techniques and ideas as a possible toolkit, rather than remaining wedded to a single, narrow and possibly outdated view of what leadership might be (Hewison, 2010).

To realise a new vision, or make a significant change in the way something is done, people cannot usually keep doing the same things they have always done (Ancona et al., 2007). Inspiring others to come along in a new direction is a key part of both leadership and management, and often a little creativity is required to see what that new direction might be and to negotiate the unfolding journey.

There is a saying that there are no paths; paths are made by walking. So start walking, and make sure you take enough people with you to create a new path for others, in time, to follow.

> Two roads diverged in a wood, and I –
>
> I took the one less traveled by,
>
> And that has made all the difference.
>
> (Robert Frost, poet, 1920)

Key points

- Several key challenges face the health and social care system, including an ageing population, rising service user expectations, and the opportunities and costs associated with new technological developments. These have huge potential implications for managers.
- For any manager or leader to develop a sustainable approach to their role, it is important to remain mindful of the four building blocks of caring management: **personal awareness**, **team awareness**, **goal awareness** and **contextual awareness**.

- Good management and effective leadership are not about 'getting the right person in charge'; they are about everyone taking responsibility. Good practice can be undermined by one person failing to act because they think someone else is in charge.
- No manager or leader is perfect, but self-awareness and an empathetic approach to staff at all levels in the management hierarchy will help to lead others through necessary, and often uncomfortable, changes.
- Having grown in knowledge and understanding through this book, and equipped with a toolkit to help in problem solving and decision making, you are now well prepared to deal with any challenges you may face. You can also start to positively map out your leadership journey in the direction you want it to go from now on.

References

Abrams, L. (2012) 'Instagram in the OR: hearing restoration surgery live – tweeted', *The Atlantic*, 2 October [Online], www.theatlantic.com/health/archive/2012/10/instagram-in-the-or-hearing-restoration-surgery-live-tweeted/263145/ (Accessed 26 November 2012).

Ancona, D., Malone, T.W., Orlikowski, W.J. and Senge, P. (2007) 'In praise of the incomplete leader', *Harvard Business Review*, vol. 85, no. 2, pp. 92–100.

Barsh, J., Craske, R. and Cranston, S. (2008) 'Centered leadership: how talented women thrive', *McKinsey Quarterly* [Online], www.mckinseyquarterly.com/Centered_leadership_How_talented_women_thrive_2193 (Accessed 2 November 2012).

Bennis, W. (2003) *On Becoming a Leader*, Cambridge, Mass., Perseus Publishing.

Brainy Quotes (n.d.) 'Margaret Mead Quotes' [Online]. Available at http://www.brainyquote.com/quotes/authors/m/margaret_mead.html (Accessed 2 November 2012).

Burdett Trust for Nursing (2006) *Who Cares, Wins: leadership and the business of caring*, London, Office for Public Management/Burdett Trust for Nursing.

CAFCASS (2012) *Care Demand Statistics March 2012*, Children and Family Court Advisory and Support Service [Online], www.cafcass.gov.uk/news/2012/march_care_statistics.aspx (Accessed 2 November 2012).

Casserley, T. and Megginson, D. (2009) *Learning from Burnout*, Oxford, Butterworth-Heinemann.

Cuhls, K., Blind, K. and Grupp, H. (2002) *Innovations for Our Future. Delphi 98: New Foresight on Science and Technology*, Technology, Innovation and Policy Series of the Fraunhofer Institute for Systems and Innovation Research, no. 13, Physica Heidelberg.

Daft, R.L. (2008) *The Leadership Experience* (4th edition), Mason, OH, Thompson South-Western.

Dufour, G. (2011) *Managing Your Manager: How to get ahead with any type of boss*, Maidenhead, McGraw-Hill.

Findlay, S. (2012) Interview for K313 module video, Milton Keynes, The Open University.

Frost, R. (1920) 'The Road Not Taken', in *Mountain Interval*, New York, Henry Holt and Company.

Fry, L.W. and Slocum Jr, J.W. (2008) 'Maximizing the triple bottom line through spiritual leadership', *Organizational Dynamics*, vol. 37, no. 1, pp. 86–96.

Gabarro, J.J. and Kotter, J.P. (2005) 'Managing your boss', *Harvard Business Review*, January, pp. 92–9.

Gibson, F., Miller, M. and Kearney, N. (2007) 'Technology into practice: young people's, parents' and nurses' perceptions of WISECARE+', *Paediatric Nursing*, vol. 19, no. 10, pp. 31–4.

Griffith, N. (2012) 'What can England learn from Wales?', *Chartist*, May/June [Online], www.chartist.org.uk/articles/britpol/may12griffith.htm (Accessed 22 January 2013).

Guardian (2010) 'Mary Robinson: "I feel a terrible sense of urgency"', *The Guardian*, 13 March [Online], www.guardian.co.uk/theguardian/2010/mar/13/mary-robinson (Accessed 27 February 2013).

Hackworth, B.A. and Kunz, M.B. (2010) 'Health care and social media: building relationships via social networks', *Academy of Health Care Management Journal*, vol. 6, no. 1, pp. 55–68.

Harvey, S., Liddell, A. and McMahon, L. (2009) *Windmill 2009: NHS response to the financial storm*, London, The King's Fund.

Health Estates (2008) *Guidance HSC Hospital Car Parking Provision and Management*, Northern Ireland, Health Estates.

Hewison, A. (2010) 'Feeling the cold: implications for nurse managers arising from the financial pressures in health care in England', *Journal of Nursing Management*, vol. 18, pp. 520–5.

Hirsch, D. (2006) *Five Costed Reforms to Long-term Care Funding*, York, Joseph Rowntree Foundation.

Larkin, E. (2008) *Ready to Lead? Prepare to think and act like a successful leader*, Harlow, Pearson Education Limited.

Long, K. (2012) 'The "S" factor: exploring the spiritual dimension to our work as coaches', *The International Journal of Mentoring and Coaching*, vol. X, no. 1, pp. 77–86.

Melzer, D., Tavakoly, B., Winder, R., Richards, S., Gericke, C. and Lang, I. (2012) *Health Care Quality for an Active Later Life: Improving quality of prevention and treatment through information – England 2005 to 2012*, Exeter, PCMD/University of Exeter.

Moreira, J.P.K. (2010) 'Improving health and healthcare: old aims, new issues?', *Journal of Management and Marketing in Healthcare*, vol. 3, no. 2, pp. 112–13.

Murray, E., Burns, J., May, C., Finch, T., O'Donnell, C., Wallace, P. and Mair, F. (2011) 'Why is it difficult to implement e-health initiatives? A qualitative study', *Implementation Science* [Online], vol. 6, no. 6. Available online at www.implementationscience.com/content/6/1/6 (Accessed 27 March 2013).

Nolte, E. and McKee, M. (eds) (2008) *Caring for People with Chronic Conditions*, Maidenhead, Open University Press.

Pedler, M., Burgoyne, J. and Boydell, T. (2004) *A Manager's Guide to Leadership*, Maidenhead, McGraw-Hill Professional.

Rogers, A. (2012) Interview for K313 module video, Milton Keynes, The Open University.

Schaeffer, L.D. (2002) 'The leadership journey', *Harvard Business Review*, vol. 80, no. 10, pp. 3–7.

Sector Futures (2003) *The Future of Health and Social Services in Europe*, Dublin, European Foundation for the Improvement of Living and Working Conditions. Available online at www.eurofound.europa.eu/emcc/publications/2003/sf_hss_1.pdf (Accessed 22 January 2013).

Senge, P.M. (2006) *The Fifth Discipline: The art and practice of the learning organisation* (revised edition), London, Random House.

The King's Fund (2011) *Report from The King's Fund Commission on Leadership and Management in the NHS*, London, The King's Fund.

Turner, S., Allen, P., Bartlett, W. and Pérotin, V. (2011) 'Innovation and the English National Health Service: a qualitative study of the independent sector treatment centre programme', *Social Science and Medicine*, vol. 73, pp. 522–9.

Toolkit

for leadership and management in health and social care

Toolkit for leadership and management in health and social care

Introduction

There are hundreds, maybe thousands, of tools that can be said to be useful to a manager or leader. In this book you will encounter ten carefully chosen tools, which are included for their value in supporting a caring approach to leadership and management in health and social care. These tools have a broad applicability and were selected to equip your development as a leader or manager in relation to the four building blocks of the **fully rounded caring manager**: **personal awareness**, **goal awareness**, **team awareness** and **contextual awareness**.

Some, like the personal awareness or the time management tool, are particularly relevant to the **personal awareness** building block. Others are particularly helpful in developing your **goal awareness** (goal setting, GROW, PDSA), **team awareness** (delegation, managing your manager) or **contextual awareness** (stakeholder mapping, SWOT analysis, force field analysis). However, as you will see as you work with the tools, most of them in fact support development in several of the basic building blocks of leadership and management.

Table T1 gives an overview of the toolkit, including where each tool is mentioned in the book. The two blank columns are for you to record the situations in which you find the tool helpful, and any limitations you feel it has.

As we explore in this book, change is a constant feature of working in health and social care, and all of these tools will help you to manage and lead through change. They will help you work with your team by being inclusive, evaluating your own strengths and weaknesses, and identifying how to capitalise on your opportunities to facilitate change successfully.

Table T1 A toolkit for leadership and management in health and social care

No.	Tool	In Chapters	Particularly useful	Limitations
1	Goal setting	1, 9, 10, 17		
2	Personal awareness	2, 5, 6		
3	Time management	5		
4	Force field analysis	4		
5	Stakeholder mapping	4, 6, 8, 14		
6	SWOT analysis	4, 8, 12		
7	Ten-step delegation	7		
8	GROW	10, 17		
9	Plan–Do–Study–Act	11, 13, 18		
10	Managing your manager	20		

Tip As a manager or leader you will probably come across other useful tools which you may want to add to your toolkit, so there is some extra space in Table T1 for you to do this.

Goal setting

Introduction: Are you SMART, WISE or DIM?

Everybody in health and social care has goals to achieve. There are many ways in which you might go about achieving a particular goal, but there seems to be general agreement that writing it down and careful planning will contribute towards success. Accordingly, a wide range of frameworks have been developed to help, most notably 'SMART' goals (Doran, 1981). Setting SMART goals helps you define a clear, realistic and achievable plan. This idea was extended to 'SMARTER' goals (Hendrick, 2006), to help build in sustainability by making the goal engaging and rewarding, as follows.

Be SMART …		
S	Specific	Significant but simple
M	Measurable	Meaningful, manageable
A	Achievable	Appropriate, action-focused
R	Relevant	Realistic, resourced
T	Time-bound	Timed, timetabled
E	Enthusiasm	Enjoyable, engaging
R	Reward	Recordable, rewarding

The 'SMART(ER)' framework is incredibly useful and widely applied, but Jay (2011) suggests there might be a more powerful way to set goals. She believes SMART goals can limit rather than inspire and proposes setting goals which are 'WISE' as well:

Be WISE …		
W	Written	Instils commitment
I	Integrated	Balanced with other life commitments
S	Synergistic	Contributes to one vision
E	Expansive	Think big for inspiration!

SMART goals are useful for managing change realistically and WISE goals help to inspire and excite, but you should also be open to flexibility, challenges and the unknown. To accommodate this, Hester (2009) proposes that goals should also incorporate the 'DIM' criteria:

Be DIM ...		
D	Demanding	Be aspirational, don't go for something too easy.
I	Innovative	What outcome haven't you thought of before?
M	Moveable	Be flexible and responsive to change.

Each framework differs slightly in approach, but one aspect remains constant – you must *write down your goal*! The tool below includes a space for writing down your goal and then answering a series of questions to assess how SMART, WISE and DIM it is *before* you set out to achieve it. Some of the questions overlap a little, but that helps to ensure you really think carefully about your goal and how you set about achieving it.

The tool

My goal is:

Target	Question	Answer
S	Have you been **specific** and clear?	
M	How will you **measure** success?	
A	Is it **attainable**?	
R	Is it **relevant** to your context?	
T	What is your **timetable**?	
E	How will you ensure **engagement**?	
R	How will you **reward** success?	
W	Don't forget to **write** down your goal!	
I	Does it **integrate** with your other commitments?	
S	Does it **synergise** with your wider vision?	
E	Does this goal inspire and **expand** you?	
D	How is it **demanding**?	
I	How is it **innovative**?	
M	Is it **moveable** if needs be?	

Tip Goal setting is valuable in any context, from your personal life to achieving a work–life balance, right up to managing complex challenges at work.

Personal awareness

Introduction

Personal awareness is a key skill for both new and experienced managers in health and social care and it is one of the four basic building blocks of the **fully rounded caring manager**. This is because a reflective understanding of self can enhance your effectiveness as both a manager and a leader of other people.

Developing your **personal awareness** means examining aspects of yourself such as your level of self-confidence, emotional intelligence, resilience and self-esteem. It also means taking a broader, proactive approach to changes in your professional and personal life, to maintain an appropriate balance and remain effective in both.

This tool comprises four sets of questions which are designed to help you reflect on your current self-perception, your ideas about management and leadership, and your personal and professional goals (based on Chambers et al., 2006). You should answer these questions honestly to get the most from the tool. The final part of it gives you an opportunity to challenge any personal barriers to effectiveness – such as self-defeating beliefs – by creating a self-affirming statement based on your newly acquired **personal awareness**.

The tool

1 Assessing who you are and where you are now

How does your personality affect the choices you make?
What fears do you have that might hold you back?

To what extent do you feel your values are reflected in the work you do?
How do these values enhance your effectiveness as a manager and leader of other people?

What personal qualities do you have that could be usefully harnessed and developed to enhance your leadership and management potential?

2 Assessing your professional life

What aspects of work do you consider to be most important?

Which features of your job fit best with your personal style and who you are?

How do you set yourself new targets within your job to keep your interest alive and provide new challenges?

How do you nurture your relationships with colleagues?

3 Assessing your work–life balance

How does your current work impact on your family and friends and other aspects of your non-working life?

How satisfied are you with your lifestyle and time spent outside work, e.g. sport, relaxation, hobbies, travel?

Do you spend enough quality time with your friends and family?

Are you happy with the balance between your work and other aspects of your life?

4 Making changes

What interests and motivates you to work effectively?

What has limited you from making changes in the past?
Have you overcome those constraints or barriers now? If so, how?

What do you most want to achieve in your role?
What are your career goals?

Do your goals and ambitions fit with your ethics and values?
Do your career goals conflict with your personal goals or ambitions?

Now, reflect on what you have written and, in the box below, highlight any self-defeating beliefs you have uncovered. Then make a statement of positive intent of how you might use your personal strengths to counter these.

Next step: Moving forwards

Self-defeating belief:

Positive statement of intent for change, i.e. what you are going to do differently

Tip Use this tool to develop your **personal awareness** as part of the foundation to adopting a proactive approach to management and emotionally intelligent leadership.

Time management

Introduction

> You can't actually manage time. Time just is. All you can hope to do is manage yourself and what you do with your time …
>
> (Evans, 2008, p. 1)

Time management is an essential skill that helps you keep your work under control, increase productivity and reduce stress. Poor time management can lead to frustration, lack of motivation and poor self-esteem, and it can even undermine health and wellbeing. Therefore, for people working in health and social care – who often care for highly vulnerable people – good time management is crucial, to help ensure safety for you, those you manage and the service users.

Personal awareness and **goal awareness** are both key to effective time management. You need to know both what your important work tasks are *and* what personal goals you hold. You then need to be able to recognise your strengths and weaknesses and to find a way to manage yourself and your time better with this knowledge.

For many people, the first step in time management is to write a 'To Do' list; however, opinion varies about how effective this actually is (Rowan, 2011). It doesn't help you see what the important tasks are, or how you go about tackling your list, or help you to manage yourself better. A simple 'To Do' list doesn't give any indication of how long each task will take and, crucially, it doesn't get over the stumbling blocks you may put in your own path – such as procrastination! And if you fail to complete everything on your 'To Do' list, might that just demotivate you further?

Some people therefore suggest it is also useful to have a 'Don't Do' list (McCrostie, 2010). You may want to include things like 'Don't check email every hour', 'Don't skip a lunch break' or 'Don't schedule an important meeting last thing on Friday'. You may also like to keep a 'Did Do' list at the end of the day, to celebrate what you have achieved!

Clearly, time management is about more than writing a list of tasks, so we have put together the tool below to help you develop your **goal awareness** and **personal awareness** and to manage your approach to time better. You might want to complete the tool once for a general overview of how you approach your work and personal goals, and then again for each week or day you want to get more organised.

The tool

Building block	Task	Hints	Your plan
Goal awareness	Write a list	List your work and personal goals. You need to know what needs to be done, how and when. You could call this your 'To Do' list.	
	Prioritise	Give each item a score from 1 to 5, where 1 is 'extremely important; and 5 is 'not important'.	
	Schedule	When you know what your goals are, you need to plan how to achieve them. If tasks are big, break them down into smaller 'journey goals'. Time your tasks, plan your day, and put in breaks.	
	Minimise interruptions	Clear time and space for big tasks, switch off email, and turn on voicemail.	
Personal awareness	Don't procrastinate	Find out why you put things off and find a way of rewarding yourself for getting things done.	
	Let go and say no!	Do you need to delegate more? Are you taking on too much? You might find it helpful to write a 'Don't Do' list as well, e.g. 'Don't always say yes', 'Don't forget to delegate', 'Don't check email every hour'.	
	Take breaks	Schedule breaks into your day and you will work more effectively. Do you need to add 'Don't skip lunch' to your 'Don't Do' list?	

Tip Good time management also has a positive long-term impact. For example, you may want to start a fresh project, begin a training course, or take up a new hobby, but you never have the time. Start by managing your time more effectively on a daily basis and you will carve out time you thought you never had.

Force field analysis

Introduction

Force field analysis is a management technique for diagnosing situations and supporting sound decision making. It is based on ideas developed by Kurt Lewin, a pioneer in the field of social psychology, in the 1940s (Lewin, 1951; Burnes, 2004). The tool is frequently used today in a range of health and social care environments, particularly when identifying strategies for change and exploring the wider environment affecting a situation (see, for example, Bulcomb, 2003).

The tool will help you to consider two sets of forces: those that are driving the change and those that are against it. 'Driving forces' help you to achieve the change and 'restraining forces' work against the change. Therefore, it is a powerful tool for developing **contextual awareness** and can be used to help develop an action plan to assess the value of making a change or to actually implement that change.

To carry out a force field analysis you need to:

- Identify and list the forces motivating the change ('driving forces').
- Identify and list the forces preventing or blocking the change ('restraining forces').
- Decide how significant each force is.

The next stage is to consider how you can reduce or eliminate the restraining forces and strengthen the driving forces, the aim being to understand how to reach your desired end-state.

Figure T1 shows an example. The size of the arrows indicates how strong each force is perceived to be. If all the arrows on one side are much bigger than on the other side, that might give you an indication of how easy or hard it will be to implement your change!

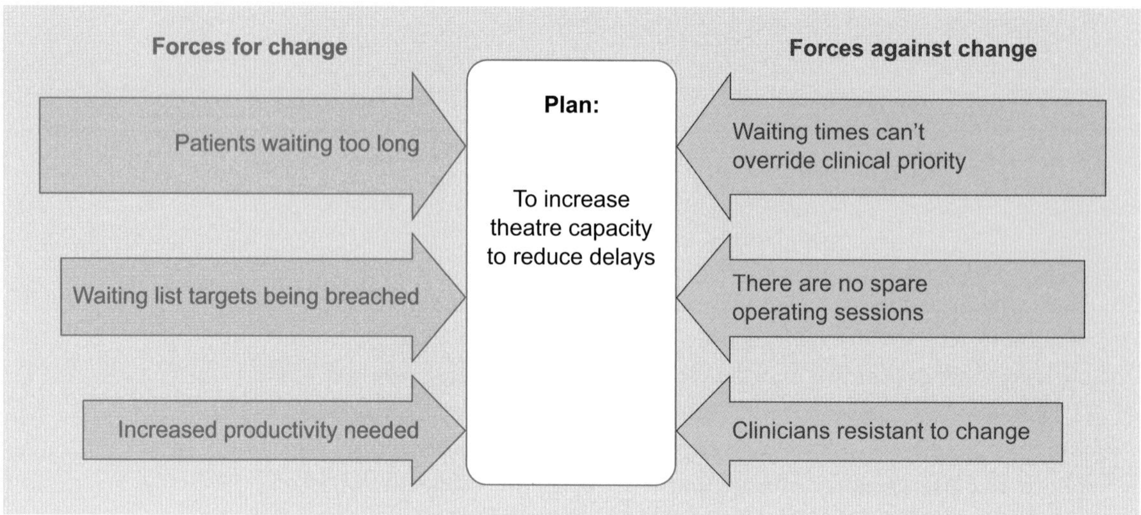

Figure T1 Force field analysis for a hospital operating theatre (based on NHS Institute for Innovation and Improvement, 2008)

Force field analysis is often just the beginning of planning a change. Once you have worked out which forces are helping or hindering your desired change, you need to look at what you are going to do about them and develop an action plan. You can use a range of other techniques to help you here, such as brainstorming or holding an Open Space meeting (see Chapter 7). You may also want to use other tools to explore particular aspects of the situation, such as goal setting, SWOT analysis or PDSA.

The tool

The blank template below will help you get started. You may want to add more arrows and customise the template to fit your needs.

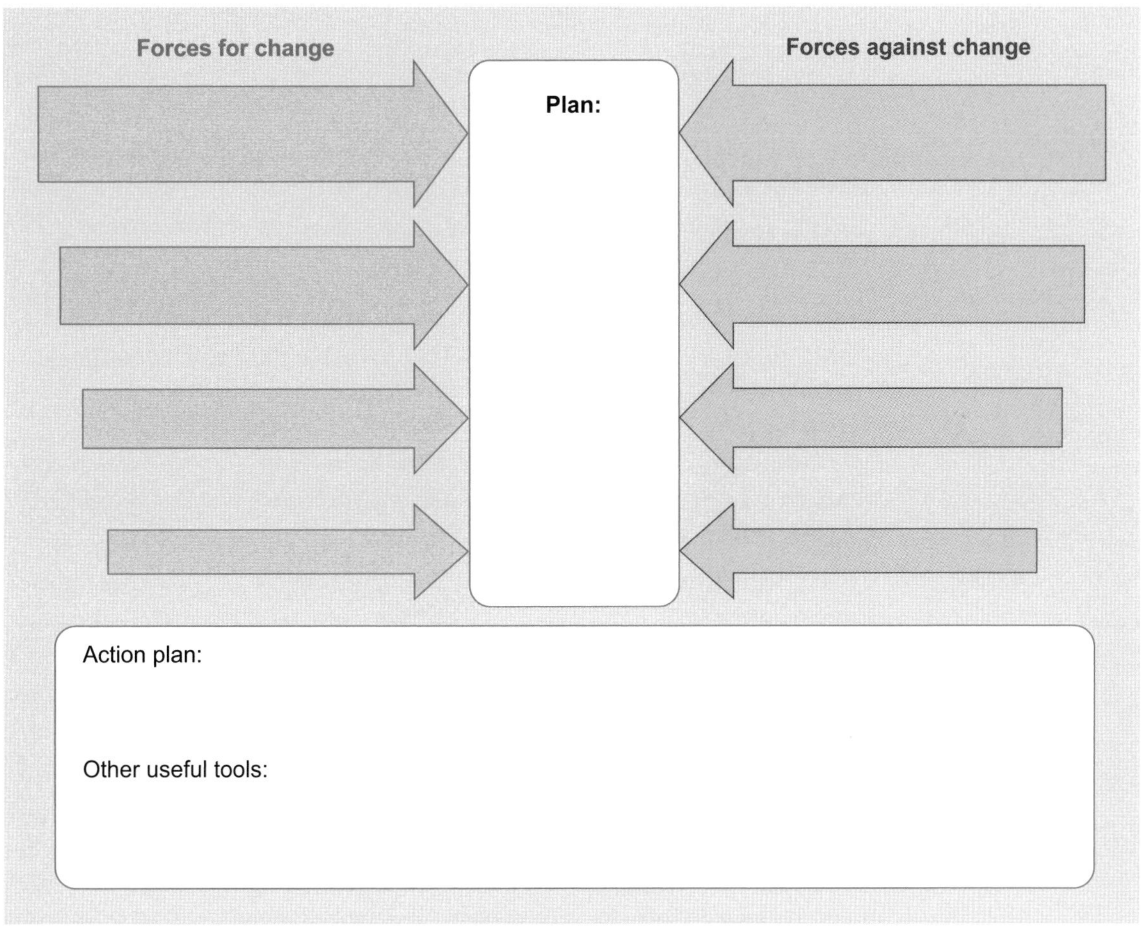

Tip How you introduce change will influence your team members' perception of its impact and can determine whether they act as a negative or a positive force for change. Careful planning which focuses on the benefits of the proposed change should be clearly communicated, to increase your chance of success and diminish the impact of negative forces.

Stakeholder mapping

Introduction

Knowing who your stakeholders are and how you might maximise their involvement is a key tool for any manager. It is particularly important if you are contemplating some kind of time-limited project or change process.

Stakeholder mapping has been around for some time and there are many forms, but the basic idea is to construct a rectangular matrix to map the position of stakeholders according to their interest and influence (see, for example, mindtools.com). This can help you identify who you need to spend more time with, or develop a good relationship with, to increase your chance of achieving your goal successfully. The process involves the following three steps.

Step 1: Identify your stakeholders

List all the people, organisations or groups who are affected by your project, might have an influence over it, or have an interest in it.

Step 2: Map your stakeholders

Some stakeholders will have a particular interest in what you are doing; others may not really care. Some will have the power to block what you are trying to do; some will have the power to advance your project. So the next step is to map your stakeholders accordingly.

For example, if you were trying to implement the Red Water Jug Scheme described in Chapter 17 in a hospital ward, the ward manager is likely to have a high level of power in helping to achieve your goal but may need some persuasion as they may have more pressing interests to attend to. Patients on the ward may have a high level of interest in seeing the scheme implemented, but little power themselves. Nurses and healthcare assistants working on the ward are likely to have a high level of power over whether the scheme runs successfully and a high level of interest in getting it set up. The matrix for this scenario is shown in Figure T2.

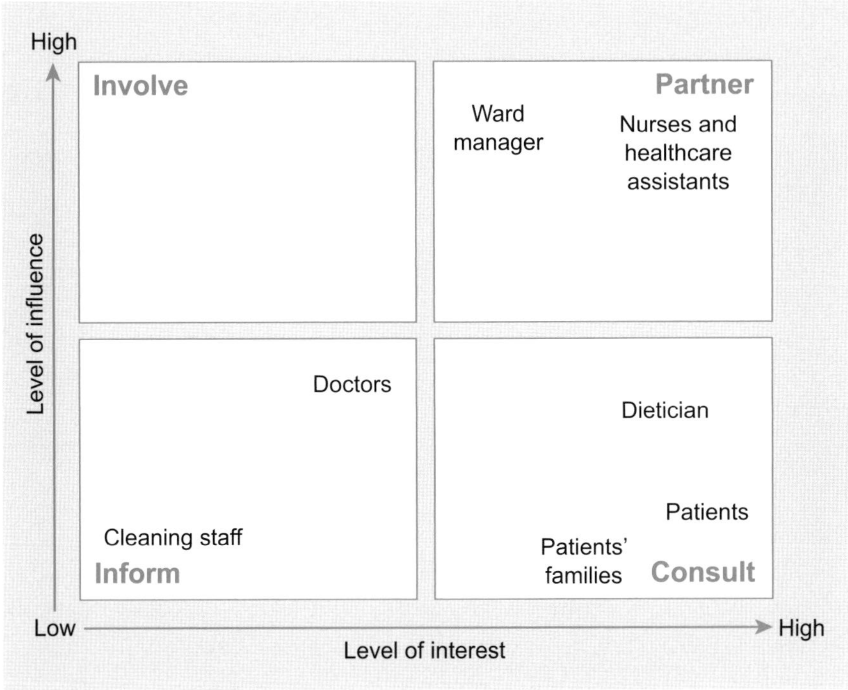

Figure T2 Stakeholder map for the Red Water Jug Scheme

A person's position on your stakeholder map then gives you an indication of how you have to work with them, as follows.

- High power, highly interested people must be fully engaged. These are the people to collaborate with and work in partnership with.
- High power, less interested people need to be closely involved and consulted, to ensure you take into account their needs and concerns.
- Low power people with a high interest need to be kept well informed and should be able to give you feedback and ideas.
- People with low levels of power and less interest in the project should be kept informed about what is going on but don't expect them to become heavily involved.

Step 3: Approaching your stakeholders

Stakeholder mapping is about identifying and starting to understand your most important stakeholders. You should then use the knowledge gained to plan how to engage with each stakeholder in the best way as you advance with your project. The task is then to communicate with the right stakeholders in the right way at the right time.

The tool

Use the blank matrix below for mapping the stakeholders in your organisation or project.

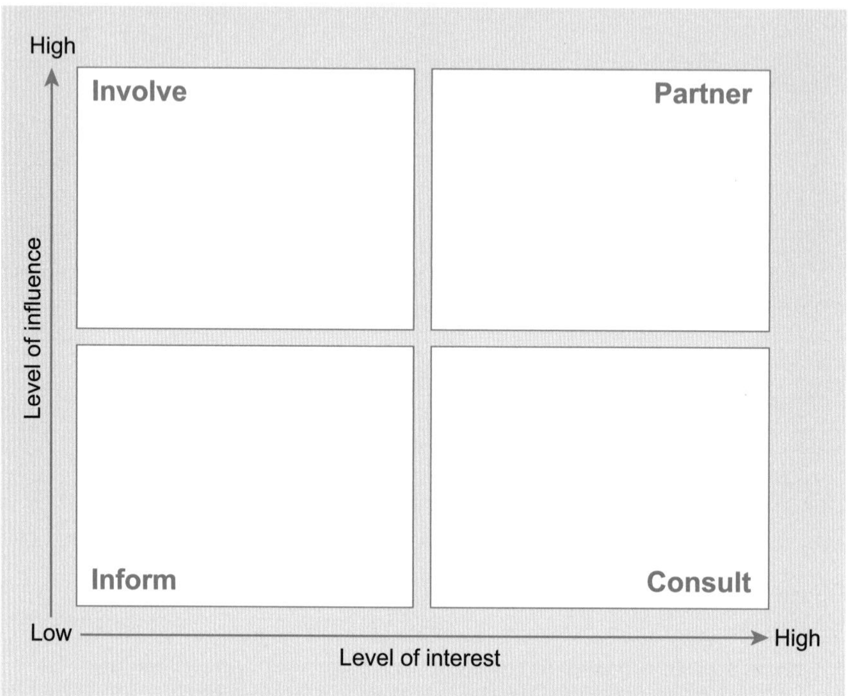

Tip The stakeholder matrix acts as a useful visual summary to boost your **contextual awareness**. Its value can be enhanced by colour coding the stakeholders: for example, use green to show those who are advocates or supporters; red to highlight those who are likely to block your project or be active critics; and orange to indicate those who are likely to be neutral (Mindtools, 2013).

SWOT analysis

Introduction

SWOT stands for Strengths, Weaknesses, Opportunities and Threats. Although SWOT analysis originated in the business sector (see, for example, Hill and Westbrook, 1997), it is a flexible tool that is used widely across health and social care to aid decision making and problem solving, and to help steer organisations through periods of change.

The purpose of a SWOT analysis is ultimately to assess, on balance, whether an objective is achievable. It can be used to support strategic planning as well as the management of smaller-scale local issues. Crucially, it helps to develop your **contextual awareness** by encouraging you to think about the strengths and weaknesses of your situation, while attending to any opportunities and threats that may exist.

At the simplest level, the results of SWOT analyses are presented in a basic grid system, comprising four sections, one for each of the headings:

Strengths	**Weaknesses**
Opportunities	**Threats**

This basic grid can be developed to differentiate internal and external factors: distinguishing between internal strengths and weaknesses and external opportunities and threats. Whether you use the most basic grid or explore the distinctions between internal and external factors, for the most effective use of SWOT you should involve your team fully in identifying what they feel should be in each quadrant. For example, you could use Open Space Technology to organise a meeting where ideas can flow freely (see Chapter 7). Involving people fully in exploring the opportunities and threats around a particular issue in this way can also be a powerful method for addressing resistance to change (see Chapter 4).

While the popularity and widespread use of SWOT is linked to its simplicity, there is a danger that it leads managers to adopt a somewhat simplistic, list-making approach, which fails to get to the heart of complex issues. SWOT analysis is therefore a key tool for developing **goal awareness** and **contextual awareness** – understanding what factors may support or undermine you reaching a particular goal – but you must also *engage critically with what you discover*. Valerie Iles (2006), an expert in healthcare management, suggests that SWOT can be more effective when followed up with critical questions about the issues that have been identified.

So, once you have completed your grid, you need to address the information gathered to help you take a more nuanced and strategic approach when dealing with the issues that have been identified. This is the approach we adopted in designing this tool. By addressing the key critical questions we have identified, you will arrive at an action plan to improve your chances of success.

The tool

You can use the blank grid below for your SWOT analyses.

	Positive	Negative
Internal	**Strengths** What strategies are in place to maintain our strengths?	**Weaknesses** What are the underlying causes of these weaknesses?
External	**Opportunities** How can we capitalise on these opportunities?	**Threats** What do we need to do about these threats?

Tip It is often helpful to do a PESTLE analysis alongside SWOT (see Chapter 4), to help ensure you have a detailed and nuanced understanding of the external environment, thus developing your **contextual awareness** of the issue further.

Ten-step delegation

Introduction

Working in health or social care can be challenging and being a manager adds to that challenge. This is why effective delegation is so important. Managers are not the only ones who can take on the challenging tasks that need to be done to ensure the smooth running of a department or unit, and this is where delegation comes in. Successful delegation promotes distributed leadership and a feeling of greater responsibility within a team.

There is an art to delegation. It requires a focus on the four building blocks of the **fully rounded caring manager**, as well as a good level of emotional intelligence. You need to be able to identify the right person to delegate a task to, which means relying on other people, having confidence in them, and showing that you trust them.

When delegation goes wrong, or is poorly executed, the person being delegated to can feel used, overwhelmed or out of their depth, potentially undermining the quality and safety of the care delivered. Using a checklist-based tool, such as the one outlined below, ensures safeguards are in place to make sure the *right* person is delegated an *appropriate* task and *supported* to complete it successfully.

The tool

		Step	Action	Completed
Personal awareness	1	**Identify the task or activity to be delegated**	Ensure the task is something someone else can do effectively. It may be something that you want a team member to become confident in doing.	
	2	**Identify the individual**	Why this person? What will you as a manager gain from delegating? What will this person gain from taking on the task?	
	3	**Evaluate ability and support needs**	Are you confident that the identified individual has the ability and capacity to take on the task? Do you need to put support in place?	
	4	**What are your reasons for delegation?**	Explain why this task is being delegated and your reasons for choosing this person. Explain the value of the task and its place in the work of the unit.	
Goal awareness	5	**Communicate required results**	State clearly what has to be done, the stages involved and what a successful outcome will be. Provide written information if necessary. Check the requirements are understood.	
	6	**Clarify what is required**	Outline what is required to complete the task. This may involve getting support from others, or finding information from other units.	
	7	**Set a time frame**	Clearly state the expected deadline for completion of the task or, if it is an ongoing responsibility, when it will be reviewed. Agree a review date.	
Team awareness	8	**Ensure wider recognition**	If the task being taken on involves the whole unit, ensure others know of this new level of responsibility and the need for support and/or cooperation.	

		Step	Action	Completed
Contextual awareness	9	**Monitor progress and evaluate success**	Once the task has been taken on, ensure follow-up meetings are scheduled to monitor progress. Review the stages completed by the individual and get feedback on their progress. Identify any obstacles and provide support in overcoming them.	
	10	**Reward success**	On successful completion of the task, or becoming confident in a new responsibility, ensure the individual is given positive feedback. Identify what has been gained and future opportunities for delegation.	

(Adapted from Business Balls, 2012)

Tip A caring manager is aware of individual development needs when delegating. Support the people you delegate to by using other tools when appropriate, such as the goal-setting tool or the time management tool.

GROW

Introduction

There are various models that may be used in coaching; GROW is one that provides a clear structure and many novice coaches are attracted to it because of its simplicity. The GROW model – which stands for Goal, Reality, Options and Way forward – was developed by Sir John Whitmore (2002) and is possibly the best known model for coaching. The particular value of GROW is that it provides a simple, structured approach which helps set goals effectively as well as serving as a problem-solving process. Using the GROW tool will really help to improve your **goal awareness** and **personal awareness**, as you work through a series of questions which explore precisely what your goal is and how it can be effectively achieved.

The simplicity of GROW means this is a very useful tool for beginners at coaching; however, this straightforward nature belies the complexity involved in coaching in a skilful way. Starr (2008) suggests there are four key skills to being an effective coach:

- The ability to build rapport
- Listening skills
- Asking focused questions
- Providing supportive feedback.

It is important to keep a focus on these four skills as you work with the GROW tool. If you are using it when coaching someone, make sure you always build rapport, listen carefully and provide supportive feedback.

The tool

You can use the table below as the basis for your own GROW tool.

Stage	Rationale	Questions	
Goal	To focus on a positive outcome to work towards.	1 Think of your goal. How challenging or exciting is achieving the goal? 2 How will you know you have achieved the goal? 3 Where do you have control or influence with regard to this goal?	Goal awareness
Reality	To check the goal can be achieved.	1 What have you done so far to improve things? What results have you achieved so far? 2 What obstacles are in your way to prevent you moving forward? 3 What resources do you already have to help you achieve your outcome?	Personal awareness
Options	To focus on what actions can be engaged in to move towards the goal.	1 What could you do to move yourself forward just one step now? 2 What else could you do? 3 If you could devote all your time to this one thing, what would you do?	
What will you do next?	To gain commitment for the actions discussed, and make decisions about when and how they will be carried out.	1 List the actions you must go through to complete the task you have chosen. How will these actions meet your main goal? 2 When are you going to take these actions? 3 Should anyone else be involved? Who else should know? When will you tell them? 4 Looking at your first step, can you think of any barriers that might stop you? How will you overcome these obstacles ?	Goal awareness

Tip Effective coaching requires motivation on behalf of those being coached as well as commitment from the coach. If these two essentials are not in place, attempts at coaching can be frustrating, complicated and, ultimately, a pointless waste of time. If both parties are motivated and committed to achieving the stated goal, coaching can provide the support necessary for success.

Plan–Do–Study–Act

Introduction

Sometimes it is hard to know whether a change designed to improve quality will have the desired effect; the Plan–Do–Study–Act (PDSA) tool is useful here. PDSA allows you to make small-scale focused changes, assess their impact and then decide what to do next. In this way, managers can test a new initiative to see if it works and whether it creates unintended problems. The cycle can be rerun several times to improve understanding, so you can think of it as moving in an upwards spiral of learning.

The precise origins of the PDSA cycle used today are vague, but it developed from the ideas of American physicist and engineer Walter A. Shewhart and statistician William Edwards Deming (Moen and Norman, 2010). Based on the idea that continual minor adjustments, properly assessed, will lead to improved performance, the model can be used for implementing ongoing quality improvement in any context. It is widely used in health and social care where it allows the testing of ideas before introducing large-scale change.

The four stages of each PDSA cycle are as follows.

1 Plan

Be clear about your objective, specify what needs to be done and who will be involved. Make predictions for the likely impact of the change, decide what data needs to be collected, and plan how to measure the outcomes.

2 Do

Carry out the plan, and document your observations about what happens. Record the expected and the unexpected, the positive and the negative outcomes.

3 Study

Assess the impact, looking carefully at what worked, what didn't, and why. Consider this against your initial predictions. Evaluate your findings to confirm or adjust your plan and identify ideas for improvement.

4 Act

Based on what you have learned, what should you do? Implement the full plan? Make more minor revisions and begin the PDSA cycle again?

Because PDSA forces you to analyse and reflect on plans, processes and procedures, it also encourages active engagement with the four building blocks of the **fully rounded caring manager**. Using PDSA particularly helps to improve **goal awareness** and **contextual awareness** and can therefore support a wider quality improvement culture. You need to be very clear about your goals and understand the variables you are working with. It also helps to highlight unintended consequences which may impact on other goals and contexts. All too often in health and social care, we hear about the 'unintended consequences' of change. There is little point in implementing a change if it inadvertently causes major problems for another part of the service.

PDSA is about testing small-scale ideas initially. Often there are numerous major changes that are required to improve quality in a service and this may feel like a slow process. To accommodate this, you can run several different PDSA cycles simultaneously, but you then need to be particularly attentive to how different initiatives interact, and to be careful about assumptions around cause and effect.

The tool

You can use the template below for your PDSA cycle.

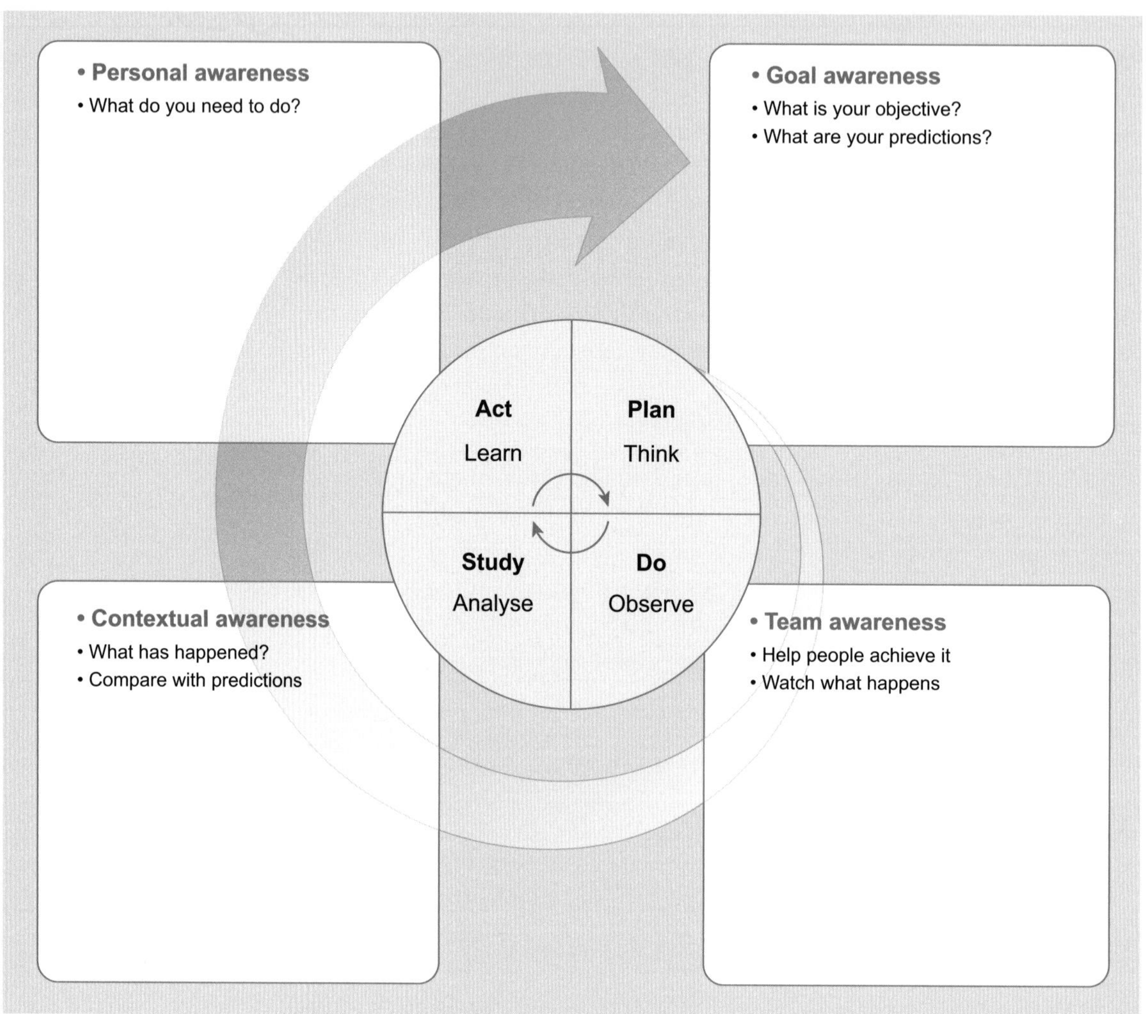

Tip Start small – think one patient, one team, one provider; think hours and days, rather than months or years.

Managing your manager

Introduction

> At a minimum, you need to appreciate your boss's goals and pressures. Without this information, you are flying blind, and problems are inevitable.
>
> (Gabarro and Kotter, 2005, p. 94)

Have you ever stopped to think about why your manager behaves as they do? Or how understanding your manager better can help both of you work more effectively? In 1980, John Gabarro and John Kotter introduced the idea that managers also have to manage their boss, and this idea is now taught across management training programmes worldwide. They suggested that consciously managing this relationship is an essential, but often overlooked, part of management. Their article remains highly influential and was reprinted in 2005 (see References).

Here is Gabarro and Kotter's checklist for managing your boss.

Understand your boss and their context:

- Goals
- Pressures
- Strengths and weaknesses
- Preferred work style

Understand yourself and how this influences the relationship:

- Strengths and weaknesses
- Personal style
- Expectations from authority figures

Develop a relationship that:

- Fits both your needs and styles
- Is based on mutual expectations
- Is based on dependability and honesty

The information you gain from this process is incredibly powerful. Horstman and Auzenne (2012) recommend focusing on the following five key areas.

- Boss goals – Your manager will have other commitments, so they may not spend a lot of time on your particular unit. Be sensitive to this.
- Boss communications – How does your manager communicate? Do they like email, telephone, or face-to-face contact? What language do they use and why?
- Boss schedule – Be sensitive to your manager's time. Pay attention to their schedule and how it affects your working relationship.
- Boss work style – How do they like to work?
- Boss relationships – What are their working networks and where do you fit in?

The tool we have developed draws together these ideas under the framework of the four building blocks of the **fully rounded caring manager**.

Managing your relationship with your manager is a legitimate part of your role within health and social care which can avoid unnecessary problems arising, ensuring a safe and efficient service with positive outcomes for service users. This isn't about being the boss's 'pet', but about you choosing to be consciously aware that developing a greater understanding of your manager as a person can help everyone to do their job better. Even if you get on very well with the person who manages you, it is still a worthwhile exercise and, in the spirit of transformational leadership, you might find it useful to share the tool with the team *you* manage, so they can think about *their* working relationship with *you*!

The tool

For each building block in the template below some key questions are highlighted and there is space for you to reflect and make notes.

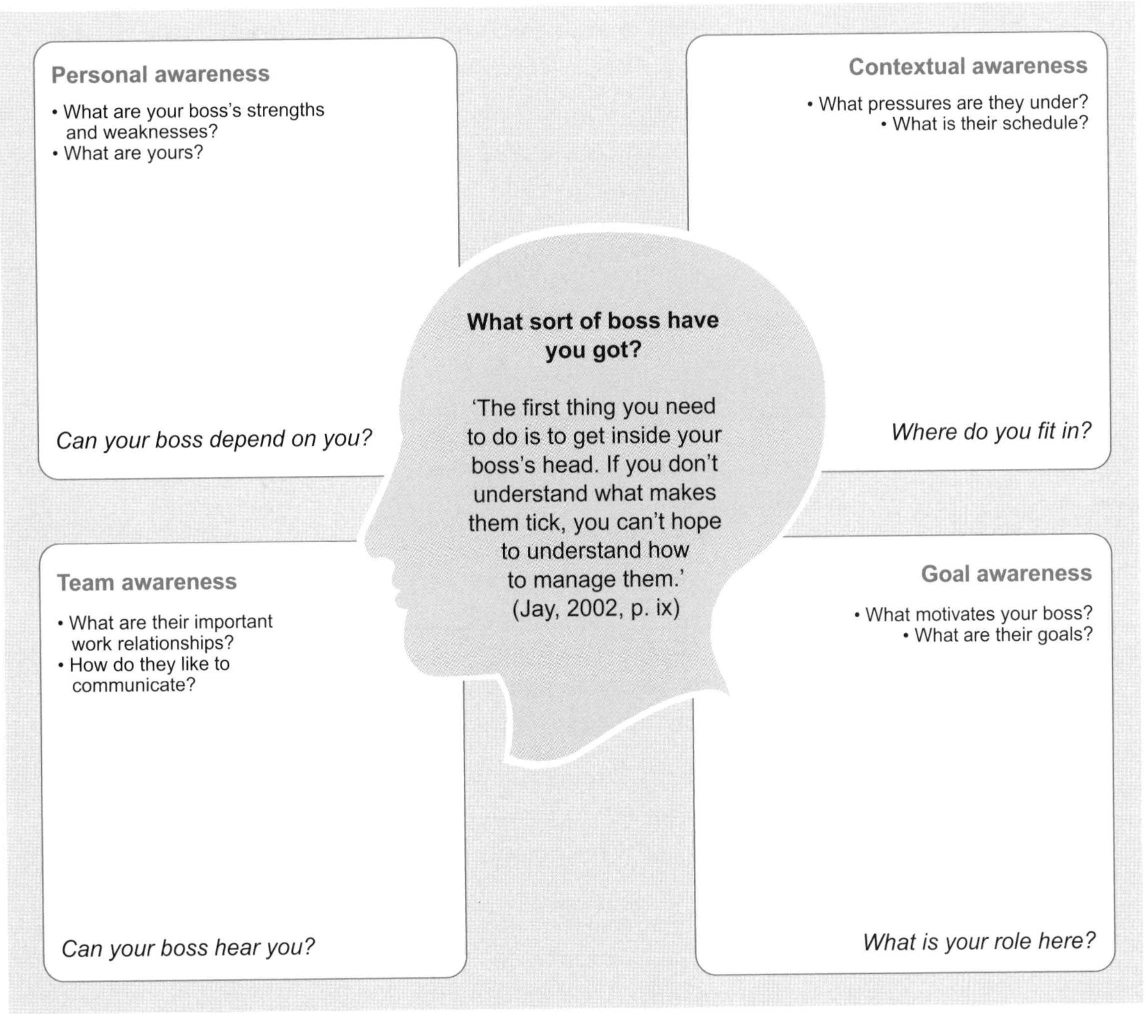

Personal awareness
• What are your boss's strengths and weaknesses?
• What are yours?
Can your boss depend on you?
Contextual awareness
• What pressures are they under?
• What is their schedule?
Where do you fit in?
What sort of boss have you got?
'The first thing you need to do is to get inside your boss's head. If you don't understand what makes them tick, you can't hope to understand how to manage them.' (Jay, 2002, p. ix)
Team awareness
• What are their important work relationships?
• How do they like to communicate?
Can your boss hear you?
Goal awareness
• What motivates your boss?
• What are their goals?
What is your role here?

Tip Developing the 'perfect working relationship' is also about recognising what motivates your manager and what causes them stress (Jay, 2002).

References

Bulcomb, J.S. (2003) 'Management of change through force field analysis', *Journal of Nursing Management*, vol. 11, pp. 275–80.

Burnes, B. (2004) 'Kurt Lewin and complexity theories: back to the future', *Journal of Change Management*, vol. 4, no. 4, pp. 309–25.

Business Balls (2012) 'Delegating authority skills, tasks and the process of effective delegation' [Online], www.businessballs.com/delegation.htm (Accessed 24 January 2013).

Chambers, R., Mohanna, K., Thornett, A. and Field, S. (2006) *Guiding Doctors in Managing Their Careers: A toolkit for tutors, trainers, mentors and appraisers*, Abingdon, Radcliffe Publishing Ltd, pp. 53–57.

Doran, G.T. (1981) 'There's a S.M.A.R.T. way to write management's goals and objectives', *Management Review*, vol. 70, no. 11, pp. 35–36.

Evans, C. (2008) *Time Management for Dummies*, Chichester, John Wiley and Sons Ltd.

Gabarro, J.J. and Kotter, J.P. (2005) 'Managing your boss', *Best of Harvard Business Review*, January, pp. 92–99.

Hendrick, L. (2006) 'Smarter goals … spread it around', *Motivation on the Run*, 27 March. Available online at www.larryhendrick.com/motivate/2006/03/27/smarter-goals-spread-it-around (Accessed 23 April 2012).

Hester, R. (2009) Learning Guide 17 'Target setting', K116 *Working with children and young people in trouble*, Milton Keynes, The Open University.

Hill, T. and Westbrook, R (1997) 'SWOT analysis: it's time for a product recall', *Long Range Planning*, vol. 30, no. 1, pp. 46–52.

Horstman, M. and Auzenne, M. (2012) *Manager's Tools* [Online], www.manager-tools.com (Accessed 3 March 2013).

Iles, V. (2006) *Really Managing Healthcare* (2nd edition), Maidenhead, Open University Press.

Jay, J. (2011) 'Make your smart goals wise goals', *Supervision*, vol. 72, no. 11, pp. 12–13.

Jay, R. (2002) *How to Manage Your Boss*, London, Prentice Hall.

Lewin, K. (1951) *Field Theory in Social Science*, London, Harper & Row.

McCrostie, B. (2010) *Two Alternatives to the To-Do List* [Online], http://bevmccrostie.wordpress.com/2010/03/22/two-alternatives-to-the-to-do-list (Accessed 17 September 2012).

Mindtools (2013) *Stakeholder Analysis: Winning support for your projects* [Online], www.mindtools.com/pages/article/newPPM_07.htm (Accessed 8 January 2013).

Moen, R.D. and Norman, C.L. (2010) 'Circling back: clearing up myths about the Deming cycle', *Quality Progress*, November, pp. 23–28. Available online at www.apiweb.org/circling-back.pdf (Accessed 18 January 2013).

NHS Institute for Innovation and Improvement (2008) *Force Field Analysis* [Online], www.institute.nhs.uk/quality_and_service_improvement_tools/quality_and_service_improvement_tools/force_field_analysis.html (Accessed 24 January 2013).

Rowan, A. (2011) *Kill Your To-Do List* [Online], http://freelancefolder.com/kill-your-to-do-list (Accessed 17 September 2012).

Starr, J. (2008) *The Coaching Manual*, London, Pearson Prentice Hall.

Whitmore, J. (2002) *Coaching for Performance* (3rd edition), London, Nicholas Brealey Publishing.

Whitmore, J. (2009) *Coaching for Performance* (4th edition), London, Nicholas Brealey Publishing.

Acknowledgements

Grateful acknowledgement is made to the following sources.

Every effort has been made to contact copyright holders. If any have been inadvertently overlooked the publishers will be pleased to make the necessary arrangements at the first opportunity.

Cover Image © Yagi Studio/Getty Images

Figures

Figure 1.1 © Matthew Jones/iStockphoto.com; **Figure 1.4** (a) ©Mary Evans/Peter Higginbotham Collection; **Figure 1.4** (b) © tomazl/iStockphoto.com; **Figure 1.5** (a) Taken from Picture Stockton Archive, http://picturestocktonarchive.wordpress.com/2003/02/27/dr-mgonigle-1889-1939; **Figure 1.5** (b) By Library of the London School of Economics and Political Science (William Beveridge, c1910 Uploaded by Fæ) Public domain, via Wikimedia Commons, http://flickr.com/commons/usage; **Figure 1.6** © Alan Wilson; **Figure 2.1** Taken from The Library of Congress, www.loc.gov/pictures/item/2004672782/; **Figure 2.2** © jlmcloughlin/iStockphoto.com; **Figure 2.3** Travers, A. (2011) 'Graph of doom', *The One Barnet Transformation Programme Presentation*, London Borough of Barnet, www.barnet.gov.uk; **Figure 2.5** Taken from Hellenic College Holy Cross, http://www.hchc.edu/studentlife/sfcs/visit; **Figure 3.1** © alexsl/iStockphoto.com; **Figure 3.3** © PictureLake/iStockphoto.com; **Figure 3.5** © Aleksiejwhite/Dreamstime.com; **Figure 3.7** Kenneth Blanchard and Paul Hersey's Situational Leadership Model, taken from www.business-development-1st.co.uk; **Figure 3.8** © ispyfriend/iStockphoto.com; **Figure 3.9** NHS Leadership Academy (2011), 'The framework overview', *The Leadership Framework*, NHS Leadership Academy, www.leadershipacademy.nhs.uk; **Figure 4.1** © BradCalkins/iStockphoto.com; **Figure 4.2** Photo provided by Rusty's Photography; **Figure 4.3** © annedde/iStockphoto.com; **Figure 4.4** © Emotional Intelligence 4 Change, www.ei4change.com; **Figure 5.1** © kupicoo/iStockphoto.com; **Figure 5.2** © Domer48. This file is licensed under the Creative Commons 3.0 License http://creativecommons.org/licenses/by-sa/3.0/; **Figure 5.5** © laflor/iStockphoto.com; **Figure 5.6** © Tom Fishburne/Marketoonist.com; **Figure 6.4** © LV=; **Figure 6.5** © Martin Godwin; **Figure 6.7** © BBC; **Figure 7.1** © Logorilla/iStockphoto.com; **Figure 7.2** © danleap/iStockphoto.com; **Figure 7.3** © Clerkenwell_Images/iStockphoto.com;

Illustration p. 183 © alashi/iStockphoto.com; **Figure 8.1** © alexsl/iStockphoto.com; **Figure 8.2** © Yuri_Arcurs/iStockphoto.com; **Figure 8.5** © fergregory/iStockphoto.com; **Figure 8.6** © nicolesy/iStockphoto.com; **Figure 9.1** © mkaminski/iStockphoto.com; **Figure 9.3** (tea break) © OJO Images Ltd/Alamy; **Figure 9.3** (meeting) © bowdenimages/iStockphoto.com; **Figure 9.3** (watching) © Wavebreakmedia Ltd UC1/Alamy; **Figure 9.5** Driscoll, J. (2000) 'Three functions of Proctor's interactive model', *Practical clinical supervision: a reflective approach for healthcare professionals*, Elsevier Ltd; **Figure 9.7** Driscoll, J. (2000), 'Supervisory dimensions already happening in healthcare', *Practical clinical supervision: a reflective approach for healthcare professionals*, Elsevier Ltd; **Figure 10.1** © zorani/iStockphoto.com; **Figure 10.3** © Microsoft; **Figure 10.4** © Microsoft; **Figure 11.1** © Gabe Palmer/Getty Images; **Figure 11.2** © Martine Hamilton Knight; **Figure 11.3** (birthing room) ©IAN HOOTON/Getty Images; **Figure 11.3** (delivery room) © Trout55/iStockphoto; **Figure 11.4** © Peter Townsend; **Figure 11.5** Courtesy of Julia Johnson; **Figure 12.1** Portrait of Lao Tzu, Artist unknown. Reproduced under the Project Gutenberg licence, http://www.gutenberg.org; **Figure 12.2** © Everett Collection Historical/Alamy; **Figure 12.3** © BBC/www.bbc.co.uk/news; **Figure 12.5** © digitalskillet/iStockphoto.com; **Figure 12.7** © Dag Sjöstrand/iStockphoto.com; **Figure 13.1** © Andrew Toos/www.CartoonStock.com; **Figure 13.2** © Inspired Services, www.inspiredservices.org.uk; **Figure 13.4** © Pen Llyn a'r Sarnau, www.penllynarsarnau.co.uk; **Figure 13.5** © Blend Images/Alamy; **Figure 14.1** © Fran/www.CartoonStock.com; **Figure 14.3** DILBERT © 2007 Scott Adams. Used by permission of UNIVERSAL UCLICK. All rights reserved; **Illustration Box 14.3** © kevinruss/iStockphoto.com; **Figure 15.1** © BBC; **Figure 15.3** © CREATISTA/iStockphoto.com; **Figure 15.4** Taken from http://thinkingspaceconsultancy.com; **Figure 16.1** © vaeenma/iStockphoto.com; **Figure 16.2** © AF archive/Alamy; **Figure 16.4** © Demotix/Press Association; **Figure 16.5** © Mike Baldwin/www.CartoonStock.com; **Illustration p. 411** © James Knopf/Dreamstime.com; **Figure 17.1** © Microsoft; **Figure 17.2** © Microsoft; **Figure 17.3** Adapted from Reason, J. (1998); **Figure 17.1** © Klenova/Dreamstime.com; **Figure 17.5** © Lev Dolgatshjov/iStockphoto.com; **Figure 17.6** © Microsoft; **Figure 18.1** © Paul Carter; **Figure 18.2** © Linda Bailey. This file is licensed under the Creative Commons Attribution-Share Alike Licence http://creativecommons.org/licenses/by-sa/2.0/deed.en; **Figure 18.3** © Fotosearch; **Figure 18.4** © SpotX/iStockphoto.com; **Figure 18.5** © VisualField/iStockphoto.com;

Illustration p. 463 © RuthBlack/iStockphoto.com; **Figure 19.1** © majaiva /iStockphoto.com; **Figure 19.2** © nicoolay/iStockphoto.com; **Figure Case study 19.1** Courtesy of the Communications Team, Hampshire County Council; **Figure 19.3** © Julia Gavin/Alamy; **Figure 20.3** © Tournament Images; **Figure 20.4** © RoosterHD/iStockphoto.com; **Figure 20.5** © Gallo images/Alamy; **Figure 20.6** © Yagi Studio/Getty Images; **Illustration p. 505** © rookman/iStockphoto.com; **Figure T9.1** Adapted from Lewin, K. (2008), *Force Field Analysis*, NHS Institute for Innovation and Improvement.

Tables

Table 5.1 Kübler-Ross, E. (1969), *On Death and Dying: what the dying have to teach doctors, nurses, clergy and their own families*, Simon and Schuster Inc.

Text

Box 17.1 Healthcare Commission, (2006), *Investigation into outbreaks of Clostridium difficile at Stoke Mandeville Hospital*, Buckinghamshire Hospitals, NHS Trust, Commission for Healthcare Audit and Inspection; **Page 5** Adapted from Hendrick, L. (2006), 'Goal setting tool: are you SMART, WISE or DIM?', *SMARTER GOALS... Spread it Around*, www.larryhendrick.com; **Page 27** Whitmore, J. (2009) 'The sequence of questioning', *Coaching for Performance*, Fourth Edition, Nicholas Brealey Publishing. Copyright © 2009 John Whitmore; **Page 33** Adapted from Gabarro, J. J. and Kotter, J. P. (1980), 'Managing Your Boss', *Harvard Business Review.*

Index

A

B

C

D

E

F

G

H

I

J

M

N

O

P

Q

R

S

T

W

Y

BMA LIBRARY
BRITISH MEDICAL ASSOCIATION